Third Edition

# Building *Real Life* English Skills

Carolyn Morton Starkey
Norgina Wright Penn

**National Textbook Company**
*a division of* NTC/CONTEMPORARY PUBLISHING GROUP
Lincolnwood, Illinois USA

# About the Authors

**Carolyn Morton Starkey** is currently head of the English, Social Studies, and Computer Department at Detroit City High School. She has also been a life skills specialist and reading specialist for the Detroit Public Schools, as well as serving as learning consultant to several private and nonprofit organizations.

**Norgina Wright Penn** taught English and drama at the secondary level, along with freshman composition. She also was an instructor for New York Telephone and the New York Business School. Most recently she was Director of the Writing Lab at Bluefield State College. In 1991 she was named Outstanding Educator of the Year in West Virginia.

*Dedicated to our daughters—*
*Suntosha, Samara, and Charlie Allegra . . .*
*and to friendships that transcend time,*
*space, and worldly definitions.*
*I'll see you when I get there.*

C.M.S.

ISBN: 0-8442-5167-4

Published by National Textbook Company,
a division of NTC/Contemporary Publishing Group, Inc.,
4255 West Touhy Avenue,
Lincolnwood (Chicago), Illinois 60646-1975 U.S.A
©1994, 1989, 1984 by NTC/Contemporary Publishing Group, Inc.
Manufactured in the United States of America.
Library of Congress Catalog Card Number: 93-78492

890 VL 987654

# Acknowledgments

Grateful acknowledgment is made to the following instructors for their reviews and helpful suggestions for this new edition of *Building Real Life English Skills:* Prof. Judith Hanley, Wilbur Wright City College, Chicago; Pamela Melendy, Hillcrest High School, Country Club Hills, Illinois; and Janice Bell Ollarvia, Chicago City Schools.

We extend grateful acknowledgment to the following for permission to reprint copyrighted material:

Alberto-Culver Co., Bold Hold coupon.

Ameritech, area code map.

Bantam Books, SWEET DREAMS ad. SWEET DREAMS and its associated logo are trademarks of Bantam Books, Inc.

*Beckley Post-Herald*, Beckley Newspaper Corp.: "Interstate Tunnel Detours Important."

Book-of-the-Month Club, Inc. offer.

Bristol-Myers Squibb Co., Arthritis Strength Bufferin label.

Buick Motor Division, General Motors, owner's manual.

Campbell Soup Co., Home Style Beans label.

Chicago Public Library, Harold Washington Library Center floorplan.

*Chicago Tribune*, "Girls Don't Lag in Math, Study Finds," copyright © 1982, *Chicago Tribune*. "Pupils Go to Mat in Academic Olympics." Copyright © 1982, *Chicago Tribune*. All rights reserved.

Columbia House Company, Columbia House CD club membership ad.

CONSUMER REPORTS, "Table of Contents," copyright © 1992 by Consumers Union of U.S., Inc., Yonkers, NY 10703 1957. Reprinted by permission from CONSUMER REPORTS, July 1992.

Deluxe Check Printers, checks and deposit slips.

*Detroit News*, classified ads and index.

General Drafting Co., Inc., Detroit map. Copyright © General Drafting Co., Inc. All rights reserved. Reprinted with permission.

General Foods Corp., JELL-O and Sugar-Free JELL-O labels. JELL-O and Sugar-Free JELL-O are registered trademarks of General Foods Corp.

General Mills, Inc., Cheerios coupon; Betty Crocker coupon. Used with permission of General Mills, Inc.

Globe Book Co., table of contents. From Henry I. Christ, *Modern Short Biographies*, copyright © 1979, Globe Book Co., Inc.

Johnson Publishing Co., *Jet* subscription form.

Keys Group Burger King, coupon.

The Kroger Co., Mixed Vegetables and Golden Corn labels.

Lustrasilk Corp., Lustrasilk ad.

McDonald's, job application form.

Michigan Bell Telephone, excerpts from yellow pages.

*Minneapolis Star Tribune*, classified ads.

Montgomery Ward & Co., credit application.

MURA Corp., MURA Hi-Stepper care instructions.

Newberry Library, Chicago, call slips

JC Penney Co., credit application form.

Psychological Testing Corp., sample tests.

*Raleigh Register*, Beckley Newspaper Corp., "The Roar of Motorcycles."

Richardson–Vicks, Inc., Vicks DayCare label.

Sam's Drugs, prescription labels.

Scott, Foresman & Co. Excerpts from *Thorndike-Barnhart Advanced Dictionary*, copyright © 1974 by Scott, Foresman & Co. Reprinted by permission.

Sharp Electronics Corp., Sharp CB Warranty.

3M Company, Buf–Oxal ad.

TOPS Business Forms, job application and telephone message form.

The H. W. Wilson Co. *Readers' Guide to Periodical Literature* entries, copyright © 1980, 1981 by the H. W. Wilson Co.

Wisconsin Department of Transportation, state maps.

# Contents

# To the reader

We have designed this Third Edition of *Building Real Life English Skills* to give you both the knowledge and the skills you will need to function successfully in today's complex world. You may be studying the reading, writing, and reference skills covered in this text as part of a school English class. Or, you could be using this text for study on your own. Perhaps you are preparing for a state competency test or taking special reading instruction. You could simply be taking an elective course in life skills. This worktext serves many needs. Whatever the learning situation, *Building Real Life English Skills* can help you acquire the skills you need to cope successfully with everyday situations.

You will have an opportunity to study maps, schedules, advertisements, special offers, agreements, contracts, and warranties. You will learn to identify various street and highway signs. You will write checks, and you will write both business and personal letters. You will also complete a variety of forms and applications. This text even shows you how to complete an income tax return. Throughout this book you will find the real forms and documents you will encounter outside the classroom.

*Building Real Life English Skills* emphasizes effective reading, writing, and communicating. Everyday reference skills are also taught. You will use many of the language skills you have already acquired. These English skills are applied to a variety of real life survival tasks.

There are twelve chapters in this text. Each chapter provides you with instruction and practice in a specific life skills area. For example, Chapter Seven is devoted entirely to getting a job. It teaches you how to compile a fact sheet, write resumes and letters of application, and complete job application forms. The chapter also gives you a chance to practice your job interview skills. Like all the chapters, Chapter Seven features vocabulary study and skills check-ups, as well as opportunities to "Show What You Know."

The final chapter, "Writer's Workshop," covers basic writing skills and strategies. This chapter gives you practice in the mechanics of writing and provides you with a grammar review. Also, it highlights the essentials of a good paragraph or essay: topic sentences, support and closing sentences, organization, and coherence. There are also everyday writing activities and a Writer's Checklist.

The activities in this text are designed to help you develop your skills, as well as give you the opportunity to work cooperatively with others. This book will help you function better in our increasingly complex world.

# 1

# Reading labels

Do you ever read the labels on the products you buy? Government rules require manufacturers to include certain information on their labels. This information is put there to inform and protect you. As a consumer, you can make better buying decisions simply by reading a label.

A *food label* should tell you how much of a product a container holds. Perhaps you have noticed "Net Wt." (net weight) on a food label. A *medicine label* must warn you of the side effects of taking a medicine. For example, will a medicine make you dizzy or drowsy or weak? A *clothing label* should tell you how to care for a product. By reading a care label, you will learn whether to wash, bleach, or dry clean an item of clothing. *Household product labels* list various CAUTIONS and WARNINGS. Misuse of these products can be dangerous to your health.

The examples given above are examples of information *required* by law. In addition to this information, some manufacturers will tell you about a product's use and content. As a result, the amount you learn from a label will vary from product to product.

## Medicine labels

### WORDS TO KNOW

**caution** a warning

**dose** the amount of medicine to be taken at any one time

**hazardous** dangerous

**over-the-counter medicine** medicine you can buy without a doctor's prescription

**pharmacist** a person who is trained and licensed to dispense medicines

**physician** doctor

**prescription** a doctor's order for medicine

**side effect** an effect of a drug, such as an upset stomach, that is not the effect that was intended

**symptom** evidence of an illness, such as a fever or sore throat

Medicine labels contain the information you need to use medicines correctly. Medicines, of course, can be very helpful. They relieve symptoms and can reduce pain. They also stop aches. But remember that most medicines are drugs. They can be harmful, too. Therefore, it is very important to read medicine labels carefully. The label should be read *before* you use the medicine.

## Labels on over-the-counter medicines

You can buy over-the-counter medicines without a doctor's prescription. Labels on these medicines contain a great deal of information.

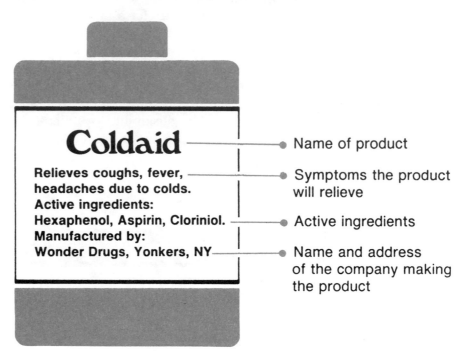

**Coldaid** — Name of product

**Relieves coughs, fever, headaches due to colds.** — Symptoms the product will relieve

**Active ingredients: Hexaphenol, Aspirin, Cloriniol.** — Active ingredients

**Manufactured by: Wonder Drugs, Yonkers, NY** — Name and address of the company making the product

The label gives the name of the product: COLDAID. It also gives information about symptoms the medicine should relieve, its ingredients, and the manufacturer. You learn that COLDAID can be taken for colds, fevers, and headaches. You learn that it contains the drugs hex-a-phe-nol, clor-i-ni-ol, and aspirin. You learn that Wonder Drugs of Yonkers, New York, makes the product.

Over-the-counter medicine labels also give very specific directions for the use of a medicine.

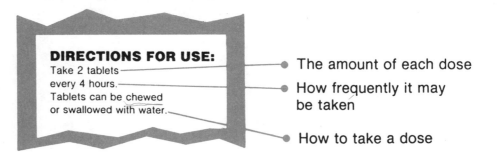

**DIRECTIONS FOR USE:**
Take 2 tablets — The amount of each dose
every 4 hours. — How frequently it may be taken
Tablets can be chewed or swallowed with water. — How to take a dose

The label will also give various warnings or cautions:

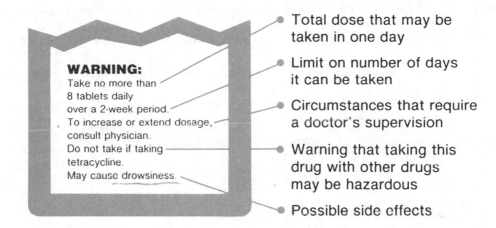

WARNING:
Take no more than
8 tablets daily
over a 2-week period.
To increase or extend dosage,
consult physician.
Do not take if taking
tetracycline.
May cause drowsiness.

• Total dose that may be taken in one day

• Limit on number of days it can be taken

• Circumstances that require a doctor's supervision

• Warning that taking this drug with other drugs may be hazardous

• Possible side effects

## ACTIVITY 1

Interpreting labels on over-the-counter medicines

Study each of the following labels carefully. Answer the questions about each label.

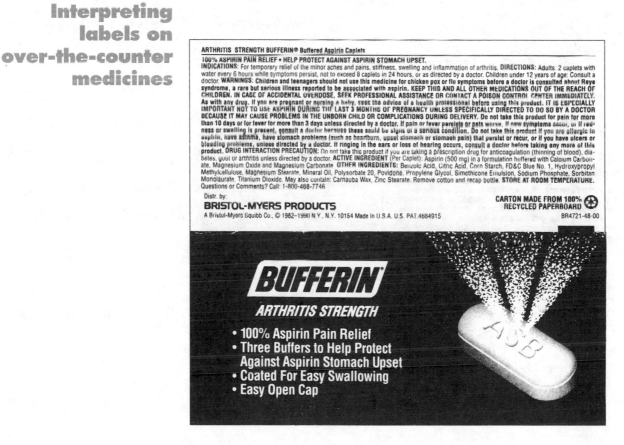

ARTHRITIS STRENGTH BUFFERIN® Buffered Aspirin Caplets

100% ASPIRIN PAIN RELIEF • HELP PROTECT AGAINST ASPIRIN STOMACH UPSET.
INDICATIONS: For temporary relief of the minor aches and pains, stiffness, swelling and inflammation of arthritis. DIRECTIONS: Adults: 2 caplets with water every 6 hours while symptoms persist, not to exceed 8 caplets in 24 hours, or as directed by a doctor. Children under 12 years of age: Consult a doctor. WARNINGS: Children and teenagers should not use this medicine for chicken pox or flu symptoms before a doctor is consulted about Reye syndrome, a rare but serious illness reported to be associated with aspirin. KEEP THIS AND ALL OTHER MEDICATIONS OUT OF THE REACH OF CHILDREN. IN CASE OF ACCIDENTAL OVERDOSE, SEEK PROFESSIONAL ASSISTANCE OR CONTACT A POISON CONTROL CENTER IMMEDIATELY. As with any drug, if you are pregnant or nursing a baby, seek the advice of a health professional before using this product. IT IS ESPECIALLY IMPORTANT NOT TO USE ASPIRIN DURING THE LAST 3 MONTHS OF PREGNANCY UNLESS SPECIFICALLY DIRECTED TO DO SO BY A DOCTOR BECAUSE IT MAY CAUSE PROBLEMS IN THE UNBORN CHILD OR COMPLICATIONS DURING DELIVERY. Do not take this product for pain for more than 10 days or for fever for more than 3 days unless directed by a doctor. If pain or fever persists or gets worse, if new symptoms occur, or if redness or swelling is present, consult a doctor because these could be signs of a serious condition. Do not take this product if you are allergic to aspirin, have asthma, have stomach problems (such as heartburn, upset stomach or stomach pain) that persist or recur, or if you have ulcers or bleeding problems, unless directed by a doctor. If ringing in the ears or loss of hearing occurs, consult a doctor before taking any more of this product. DRUG INTERACTION PRECAUTION: Do not take this product if you are taking a prescription drug for anticoagulation (thinning of blood), diabetes, gout or arthritis unless directed by a doctor. ACTIVE INGREDIENT (Per Caplet): Aspirin (500 mg) in a formulation buffered with Calcium Carbonate, Magnesium Oxide and Magnesium Carbonate. OTHER INGREDIENTS: Benzoic Acid, Citric Acid, Corn Starch, FD&C Blue No. 1, Hydroxypropyl Methylcellulose, Magnesium Stearate, Mineral Oil, Polysorbate 20, Povidone, Propylene Glycol, Simethicone Emulsion, Sodium Phosphate, Sorbitan Monolaurate, Titanium Dioxide. May also contain: Carnauba Wax, Zinc Stearate. Remove cotton and recap bottle. STORE AT ROOM TEMPERATURE. Questions or Comments? Call: 1-800-468-7746

Distr. by:
BRISTOL-MYERS PRODUCTS
A Bristol-Myers Squibb Co., © 1982–1990 N.Y., N.Y. 10154 Made In U.S.A. U.S. PAT.4664915

CARTON MADE FROM 100% ♻ RECYCLED PAPERBOARD

BR4721-48-00

**BUFFERIN**
*ARTHRITIS STRENGTH*

• 100% Aspirin Pain Relief
• Three Buffers to Help Protect Against Aspirin Stomach Upset
• Coated For Easy Swallowing
• Easy Open Cap

1. What is the name of this product?_____

2. What symptoms is this product supposed to relieve?_____

_____

3. How much of this product is to be taken for each dose? _____

4. How often should a dose be taken? _____

   What is the maximum number of tablets that can be taken in a 24-hour period? _____

5. Under what conditions should this product not be used? _____

6. What other cautions should the buyer observe? _____

---

## CONSUMER INFORMATION

# Vicks DayCare

## DAYTIME COLDS MEDICINE

**PURPOSE OF PRODUCT:**
To provide hours of relief from the nasal congestion, coughing, aches and pains, and cough irritated throat of a cold or flu without drowsy side effects.

**BENEFITS FROM PRODUCT:**
• helps clear stuffy nose, congested sinus openings
• calms, quiets coughing
• eases headache pain and the ache-all-over feeling
• soothes cough irritated throat
• No drowsy side effects. Non-narcotic
Relieves these cold symptoms to let you get your day off to a good start.

**DIRECTIONS FOR USE:**
ADULTS: 12 and over—one fluid ounce in medicine cup provided (2 tablespoonfuls)
CHILDREN: 6-12—one-half fluid ounce in medicine cup provided (1 tablespoonful)
May be repeated every four (4) hours as needed. Maximum 4 doses per day.

**WARNING:**
**Do not administer to children under 6 years of age unless directed by physician. Persistent cough may indicate the presence of a serious condition. Persons with a high fever or persistent cough or with high blood pressure, diabetes, heart or thyroid disease should not use this preparation unless directed by physician. Do not use more than ten days unless directed by physician.**

**Do not exceed recommended dosage unless directed by physician. KEEP OUT OF REACH OF CHILDREN.**

**ACTIVE INGREDIENTS:**
Each fluid ounce contains Acetaminophen 600 mg., Dextromethorphan Hydrobromide 20 mg., Phenylpropanolamine Hydrochloride 25 mg.        Alcohol 7.5%

---

1. What is the name of this product? _____

   _____

2. List the symptoms this product is supposed to relieve. _____

   _____

3. How much of this product is to be taken for each dose? _____

4. How often may a dose be taken? _____

   _____

   What is the maximum amount of this product that can be taken in a 24-hour period? _____

5. What signals mean that you should stop using this product? _____

   _____

6. What other cautions should the buyer observe?

   _____

## Labels on prescription medicines

Only a doctor can order prescription drugs. Your doctor tells your pharmacist how you are to use a medicine. When the prescription is filled, the pharmacist types the doctor's instructions on the label. These instructions tell you how much medicine to take at one time. They also tell how often to take the medicine. Unlike over-the-counter labels, prescription labels may not tell what a medicine is for. They may not list side effects. They may not give special cautions. Sometimes even the name of the medicine is not on the label. You may have to ask your doctor for this additional information.

Remember, labels are on medicines for a reason. They tell you how to use a medicine correctly. The law requires that labels carry important information. But the information is useless unless you read and follow it.

## ACTIVITY 2

### Interpreting labels on prescription medicines

Complete the statements about each of the following prescription labels.

```
            SAM'S DRUGS
        14200 FENKELL AVE.    DETROIT, MICH.
        PHONES VE 7-2838 and 7-1575
    Reg. No. 8765          ℞ No 2345
  Patient  Geri Purshing
  Address  43 North

    Take 2 twice daily.

  Dr. Pillston              Reg. No. 2121
  Address 34 South          Date 5/3
    This Prescription cannot be refilled nor a copy given.
```

1. _____ is the only person who should take this medicine.

2. _____ pill(s) should be taken for each dose.

3. The person who prescribed this medicine is _____ .

4. A total of _____ pills should be taken in a day.

5. The patient can have this prescription refilled _____ times.

5

**SAM'S DRUGS**

14200 FENKELL AVE    DETROIT, MICH

PHONES VE 7-2838 and 7-1573

Reg. No. 8765                B No. 2346

Patient Vicki Urkan

Address 543 East

Take 1 every 4 hours.

Dr. Jaons                Reg. No. 2323

Address 23 Bend        Date 4/5

This Prescription cannot be refilled nor a copy given.

1. _____ is the only person who should

   take this medicine.

2. _____ pill(s) should be taken for each dose.

3. The person who prescribed this medicine is _____ .

4. A total of _____ pills should be taken in a day.

5. The patient can have this prescription refilled _____ times.

## CHECK YOUR UNDERSTANDING OF MEDICINE LABELS

Here are some words to know when reading a medicine label. Use these words to fill in the blanks in the following sentences.

| | | |
|---|---|---|
| prescription | symptom | caution |
| side effect | dose | physician |

1. The _____ from some medicines may be an upset stomach.

2. One _____ of a cold is a stuffy nose.

3. A label may _____ you not to take more than 4 pills in 24 hours.

4. The _____ of a medicine is the amount that can be taken at one time.

5. The doctor, or _____ , gave me a _____ for penicillin when I had a sore throat.

# SHOW WHAT YOU KNOW . . .

## About Medicine Labels

Create a medicine label of your own. It may be for a cold, flu, or any other symptoms usually relieved by over-the-counter medicines. Make up:

1. A product name

2. What the medicine can be used for

3. The active ingredients (make up chemical names)

4. The name and address of the company making the product

5. Warnings

Create at least five (5) questions that would check the understanding of your label.

Option: Exchange your label and questions with a classmate. Answer each other's questions.

## Household products labels

Always read the labels on household products. Many of these products, like medicines, can harm you. Air fresheners, insect sprays, detergents, and many other products you use every day must be used with care. Give close attention to the labels on these products. These labels give cautions and warnings. They tell you how to use a product safely. In case you have an accident with a product, the label will tell you exactly what to do.

## ACTIVITY 3
### Reading labels on household products

Read the following labels. Decide whether the statements about them are TRUE (T) or FALSE (F).

# ROXO BLEACH

**CAUTION:**   Roxo bleach may be harmful if swallowed or may cause severe eye irritation if splashed in eyes. If swallowed, give milk. If splashed in eyes, flood with water. Call physician. Skin irritant; if contact with skin, wash off with water. Do not use bleach with ammonia or products containing acids, such as toilet-bowl cleaners, rust removers, or vinegar. To do so will release hazardous gases. Prolonged contact with metal may cause pitting or discoloration. Do not use this bottle to store any liquid other than bleach.

_____ **1.**   This product is not harmful to the skin.

_____ **2.**   Used with ammonia, this product becomes harmless.

_____ **3.**   This product can cause severe eye irritation.

_____ **4.**   This product is harmful if swallowed.

_____ **5.**   The bottle may be safely used for storing other liquids.

# FLYING INSECT KILLER

**FLAMMABLE**—Contents under pressure.  Do not use near fire, spark, or flame.  Never puncture or throw container into fire.  Never set container on stove, radiator, or places where temperature may exceed 120º F., which may cause it to burst.  Foods should be removed or covered during treatment.  All food processing surfaces should be covered during treatment or thoroughly cleaned before using.  When using the product in these areas, apply only when the facility is not in operation.  Do not remain in treated areas.  Ventilate the areas after treatment is completed.  Keep out of reach of children.  Remove pets and cover fish aquariums before spraying.

_____ 1. It is not necessary to ventilate the room where this product is used.

_____ 2. It is safe to remain in the area after using this product.

_____ 3. Foods should be removed or covered when using this product.

_____ 4. This product will not harm pets.

_____ 5. This product should be stored in areas where the temperature is at least 120°F.

_____ 6. It is all right to spray this product near a fire.

_____ 7. The can will burst if it becomes very hot.

_____ 8. Dishes should be covered when this product is used.

_____ 9. The contents of the can are not under pressure.

_____ 10. This product should be kept away from children.

## ACTIVITY 4

### Reading labels on household products

Read the following labels. Complete the statements about each product.

---

# AMMONIA

**FIRST AID**

**External:** Flood with water, then wash with vinegar.

**Internal:** Give large quantities of diluted vinegar or juice of lemon, grapefruit, or orange. Call physician.

**Eyes:** Rinse thoroughly with water, preferably warm, for 15 minutes. Get prompt medical attention.

---

**If this happens**

1. Product in the eyes
2. Product accidentally swallowed
3. Product on hands
4. Product on arms

**You should**

1. _____
2. _____
3. _____
4. _____

---

# RED DEMON LYE

**FIRST AID**

**Skin:** Flush with water for 15 minutes.

**Eyes:** Immediately hold face under running water for 20 minutes with eyes open, by force if necessary.

**In mouth or if swallowed:** Clear mouth. Do not induce vomiting. Give [drink] large quantities of water or milk. Give at least 2 ounces to maximum of one pint equal parts of vinegar and water, followed by olive oil or cooking oil (by teaspoon). **Transport victim to nearest medical facility or call physician immediately.**

---

**If this happens**

1. Product in the eyes
2. Product accidentally swallowed
3. Product on hands
4. Product on arms

**You should**

1. _____
2. _____
3. _____
4. _____

Read the following label and answer the questions about it.

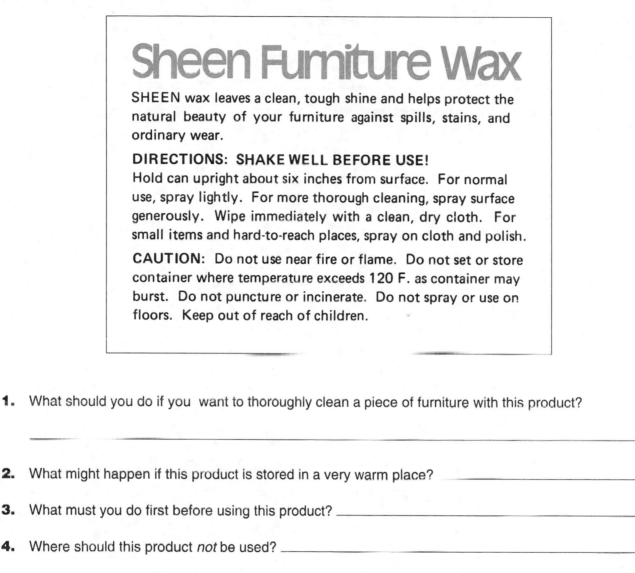

# Sheen Furniture Wax

SHEEN wax leaves a clean, tough shine and helps protect the natural beauty of your furniture against spills, stains, and ordinary wear.

**DIRECTIONS: SHAKE WELL BEFORE USE!**
Hold can upright about six inches from surface. For normal use, spray lightly. For more thorough cleaning, spray surface generously. Wipe immediately with a clean, dry cloth. For small items and hard-to-reach places, spray on cloth and polish.

**CAUTION:** Do not use near fire or flame. Do not set or store container where temperature exceeds 120 F. as container may burst. Do not puncture or incinerate. Do not spray or use on floors. Keep out of reach of children.

**1.** What should you do if you want to thoroughly clean a piece of furniture with this product?

_____

**2.** What might happen if this product is stored in a very warm place? _____

**3.** What must you do first before using this product? _____

**4.** Where should this product *not* be used? _____

**5.** What would happen if you threw the empty can into an apartment building incinerator?

_____

**6.** When using this product, how far away from the surface of furniture should you hold the can?

_____

**7.** Is it OK to spray furniture with this product, then wait for 30 minutes before wiping the furniture?

_____

# SHOW WHAT YOU KNOW . . .

## About Labels on Household Products

Complete the chart below using five (5) labels on products in your home.

| Name of Product | Directions | Cautions |
|---|---|---|
| 1. | | |
| 2. | | |
| 3. | | |
| 4. | | |
| 5. | | |

## Clothing labels

The law says that clothing you buy must carry certain labels. Clothing tags and labels come in many shapes and sizes. These labels tell you what brand name you're buying. They tell you what various items of clothing are made of. And they tell you how to care for these items. Following the instructions on care labels helps you get the most wear and satisfaction from the clothes you buy. Labels that tell you how to care for an item of clothing must be *permanent*. They are usually woven or printed labels. They will be found inside clothing. They are often sewn into seams.

## ACTIVITY 5
### Reading clothing labels

Harriet Foster bought a very expensive dress made of special fabric. The label shown here came inside the dress. Are the statements about the care label TRUE (T) or FALSE (F)?

> DO NOT BLEACH. MACHINE WASH AND TUMBLE DRY AT PERMANENT-PRESS CYCLE. REMOVE FROM DRYER AS SOON AS CYCLE STOPS.

———  **1.**  Harriet can wash this dress, but only by hand.

———  **2.**  Harriet cannot use bleach when washing this dress.

———  **3.**  Harriet's dress must be dried on a clothesline.

———  **4.**  Harriet's dress can go in her dryer, but she must use a permanent-press cycle.

———  **5.**  For the best results, Harriet should remove her dress from the dryer as soon as the dryer stops.

## ACTIVITY 6
### Reading clothing labels

Read the instructions on the labels below. Answer the questions about the labels. Use the letter with each label to answer the questions.

**A**

DO NOT DRY-CLEAN

HAND WASH ONLY
— DRIP DRY

IRON ON
REVERSE SIDE
WITH COOL IRON

**B**

DRY-CLEAN

TOUCH-UP WITH
WARM IRON

**C**

MACHINE WASH
AND DRY

STEAM IRON AT
MEDIUM SETTING

**D**

HAND WASH—
LINE-DRY

STEAM IRON AT
WARM SETTING

**E**

MACHINE WASH
AT COLD SETTING
— GENTLE CYCLE

DRIP-DRY

IRON ON
REVERSE SIDE
WITH COOL IRON

**F**

MACHINE WASH
AND DRY AT
WARM SETTINGS

IRON WHILE
DAMP WITH
WARM IRON

**G**

MACHINE WASH
WARM

LINE-DRY ONLY

IRON ON
REVERSE SIDE
WITH COOL IRON

**H**

HAND WASH—
DRIP-DRY

STEAM IRON AT
WARM SETTING

1. Which item of clothing must be dry-cleaned? _____

2. Which items should be hand washed only? _____

3. Which items require steam ironing? _____

4. Which item must not be dry-cleaned? _____

5. Which items must not be dried in a dryer? _____

6. Which items should be machine washed in warm water? _____

7. Which items should be ironed on the wrong side? _____

8. Which item should be ironed while damp? _____

Read the following label. Then answer the questions about it.

> Permanent Press 60% Polyester 40% Cotton
> Machine wash in warm water with like colors.
> No bleach. Tumble dry at medium setting.

1. The words "permanent press" on a garment mean _____

   _____

2. To wash with "like colors" means to _____

   _____

3. Can this garment be bleached? _____

4. Can this garment be dried in a clothes dryer? _____

5. Should this garment be washed in hot water? _____

# SHOW WHAT YOU KNOW . . .

## About Clothing Labels

Read labels of at least ten (10) articles of your own clothing. Answer the questions below about them.

1. How many labels read "Dry-Clean Only"? _____

2. How many read "Do Not Dry-Clean"? _____

3. How many items can be machine washed? _____

4. How many labels recommend ironing? _____

5. How many items must be hand washed? _____

## Food labels

You will find a lot of information on the labels of the foods you buy. Food labels should give you at least *three* important pieces of information.

- the name of a product (BRAND NAME)

- how much of a product you're getting (NET WEIGHT)

- who makes the product (NAME AND ADDRESS OF THE

  MANUFACTURER OR DISTRIBUTOR)

Many labels list ingredients and give nutrition information. Ingredients are listed in order of their amounts in the product, beginning with the most plentiful ingredient. Nutrition information is usually found on the back of a label. If you read this information, you will find the number of calories and the grams of protein, carbohydrate, and fat in a single serving. The serving size is also given. Food labels also list certain vitamins and minerals. These nutrients are listed with the percent one serving provides of a person's daily needs.

brand name

Campbell's

HOME STYLE Beans

We've added the homey touches you'd add yourself

NET WT. 16 OZ. (1 LB.) 454 GRAMS

net weight

**NUTRITION INFORMATION PER SERVING**
SERVING SIZE . . . . . . . . . . . . . . 8 OZ. (227 g)
SERVINGS PER CONTAINER . . . . . . . . . . . . . 2
CALORIES . . . . . . . . . . . . . . . . . . . . . . . . 270
PROTEIN (GRAMS) . . . . . . . . . . . . . . . . . . . 11
CARBOHYDRATE (GRAMS) . . . . . . . . . . . . . 48
FAT (GRAMS) . . . . . . . . . . . . . . . . . . . . . . . 4

**PERCENTAGE OF U.S. RECOMMENDED DAILY ALLOWANCES (U.S. RDA)**

| PROTEIN | 15 | RIBOFLAVIN | 2 |
| VITAMIN A | 4 | NIACIN | 4 |
| VITAMIN C | 4 | CALCIUM | 10 |
| THIAMINE | 4 | IRON | 20 |

nutrition information

vitamins & minerals in one serving

**INGREDIENTS:** PREPARED PEA BEANS, WATER, TOMATO PASTE, BROWN SUGAR, MOLASSES, BACON (CURED WITH WATER, SALT, SUGAR, SODIUM PHOSPHATE, SODIUM ERYTHORBATE, SODIUM NITRITE), CORN SYRUP, SUGAR, SALT, MODIFIED FOOD STARCH, DISTILLED VINEGAR, DEHYDRATED ONIONS, CITRIC ACID, NATURAL FLAVORING AND SMOKE FLAVORING.

ingredients in order by amount

CAMPBELL SOUP COMPANY
CAMDEN, N.J., U.S.A. 08101
Additional nutritive composition of this and other Campbell products is available on request.

manufacturer's name and address

0    51000 02945

## ACTIVITY 7
### Reading food labels

Read the nutrition information on the following labels. Answer the questions below each label.

**INGREDIENTS:** CORN, WATER, SUGAR, FOOD STARCH—MODIFIED (ADDED TO INSURE SMOOTHNESS), AND SALT.

**NUTRITION INFORMATION**

| | |
|---|---|
| SERVING SIZE . . . . . . . . . . 1 CUP | SERVINGS PER CONTAINER . APPROX. 2 |
| CALORIES . . . . . . . . . . . . . . 210 | CARBOHYDRATE . . . . . . 51 GRAMS |
| PROTEIN . . . . . . . . . . . 4 GRAMS | FAT . . . . . . . . . . . . . . . 1 GRAM |

**PERCENTAGE OF U.S. RECOMMENDED DAILY ALLOWANCES (U.S. RDA)**

| | |
|---|---|
| PROTEIN . . . . . . . . . . . . . . . 6 | RIBOFLAVIN . . . . . . . . . . . . . . 6 |
| VITAMIN A . . . . . . . . . . . . . . 6 | NIACIN . . . . . . . . . . . . . . . . 10 |
| VITAMIN C . . . . . . . . . . . . . 10 | CALCIUM . . . . . . . . . . . . . . . 0 |
| THIAMINE . . . . . . . . . . . . . . 2 | IRON . . . . . . . . . . . . . . . . . . 4 |

DISTRIBUTED BY THE KROGER CO., CINCINNATI, OHIO 45201

SIZE OF CAN: NO. 303

**SATISFACTION GUARANTEED.** If dissatisfied, return unused portion and code numbered can lid and label to store where purchased. If unable to return to store, send reason for dissatisfaction, name, address, label and number from the coded can lid to: The Kroger Co., Consumer Affairs Department, Cincinnati, Ohio 45201.

**CREAM STYLE SWEET GOLDEN CORN**

NET WT 16½ OZ (1 LB ½ OZ) 468 GRAMS

1. One serving of Cost Cutter Corn is equal to ———————— .

2. One can of corn gives you ————— one-cup servings.

3. There are ————————————————— calories in a serving.

4. Cost Cutter Corn has vitamin ——— and vitamin ——— .

5. A serving of corn will give you ——— percent of the amount of protein you need daily.

6. There is 0 percent ————— in Cost Cutter Corn.

**Kroger**

MIXED
**VEGETABLES**

241
GRAMS

NET WT
8½ OZ

INGREDIENTS: CARROTS, POTATOES, CELERY, SWEET PEAS, GREEN BEANS, CORN, LIMA BEANS, WATER, SALT AND GROUND ONION.

**NUTRITION INFORMATION PER SERVING**

| | | | |
|---|---|---|---|
| SERVING SIZE: | 1 CUP | SERVINGS PER CONTAINER: | APPROX. 1 |
| CALORIES | 70 | CARBOHYDRATE | 14 g |
| PROTEIN | 2 g | FAT | 0 g |

PERCENTAGE OF RECOMMENDED DAILY ALLOWANCES (U.S. RDA)

| | |
|---|---|
| PROTEIN | 4 |
| VITAMIN A | 250 |
| VITAMIN C | 10 |
| THIAMINE | 2 |
| RIBOFLAVIN | 6 |
| NIACIN | 4 |
| CALCIUM | 4 |
| IRON | 8 |

DISTRIBUTED BY THE KROGER CO.,
CINCINNATI, OHIO 45201

UNCONDITIONALLY GUARANTEED

*Kroger's First Quality*

1. One serving of mixed vegetables is equal to _____ .

2. This can contains _____ serving(s).

3. There are only _____ calories in a serving.

4. There are _____ grams of protein and _____ grams of carbohydrate in a serving.

5. There is no _____ in this food.

6. This food contains vitamins _____ and _____ .

7. The protein in a serving of mixed vegetables is only _____ percent of the total amount of protein you need daily.

8. List the ingredients in this product. _____
   _____

9. What is the net weight of this product? _____

10. One serving of mixed vegetables will give you _____ percent of the iron you need daily according to the U.S. RDA.

19

## ACTIVITY 8
### Reading and comparing food labels

Read and compare the nutrition information on the following labels. Answer the questions about these labels.

**Regular JELL-O**

NUTRITION INFORMATION • SERVING SIZE: 1/2 CUP • SERVINGS PER PACKAGE: 4
CALORIES..........80   PROTEIN...2 g   -NOT A SIGNIFICANT SOURCE OF PROTEIN
CARBOHYDRATE...19 g  FAT........0   CHOLESTEROL...0   SODIUM.....50 mg
CONTAINS LESS THAN 2% OF THE U.S. RECOMMENDED DAILY ALLOWANCES OF
VITAMIN A, VITAMIN C, THIAMINE, RIBOFLAVIN, NIACIN, CALCIUM AND IRON.
INGREDIENTS: SUGAR, GELATIN, ADIPIC ACID (FOR TARTNESS), DISODIUM
PHOSPHATE (CONTROLS ACIDITY), FUMARIC ACID (FOR TARTNESS), YELLOW 6,
NATURAL FLAVOR, ARTIFICIAL FLAVOR, RED 40, BHA (PRESERVATIVE).     85g
GENERAL FOODS CORPORATION, WHITE PLAINS, NY 10625, U.S.A.

JIGGLERS™   RECIPE ON BACK

orange
ARTIFICIAL FLAVOR

JELL-O®
gelatin dessert   BRAND

FOUR 1/2-CUP SERVINGS   K   NET WT. 3 OZ.

**Sugar Free JELL-O**

NUTRITION INFORMATION PER SERVING • SERVING SIZE: 1/2 CUP • SERVINGS PER PACKAGE: 4
CALORIES...8  PROTEIN...1g  CARBOHYDRATE...0  FAT...0  SODIUM...50mg
NOT A SIGNIFICANT SOURCE OF PROTEIN. CONTAINS LESS THAN 2% OF THE U.S.
RECOMMENDED DAILY ALLOWANCES (U.S. RDA) OF VITAMIN A, VITAMIN C, THIA-
MINE, RIBOFLAVIN, NIACIN, CALCIUM AND IRON.
INGREDIENTS: GELATIN, ADIPIC ACID (FOR TARTNESS), DISODIUM PHOSPHATE
(CONTROLS ACIDITY), MALTODEXTRIN (FROM CORN), ASPARTAME** (SWEETENER),
FUMARIC ACID (FOR TARTNESS), ARTIFICIAL FLAVOR, ARTIFICIAL COLOR.   8.5g
                                          GENERAL FOODS CORP.,
**PHENYLKETONURICS: CONTAINS PHENYLALANINE      WHITE PLAINS, NY 10625, U.S.A.   K

triple berry
ARTIFICIAL FLAVOR
DELICIOUS STRAWBERRY-RASPBERRY-
BLACK RASPBERRY FLAVOR COMBINATION

Sugar Free

JELL-O®
gelatin dessert   BRAND

FOUR 1/2-CUP SERVINGS

NUTRASWEET®
BRAND SWEETENER

only 8 CALORIES
per serving        NET WT. 0.3 OZ.

1. How many calories are in one serving of Sugar Free Jell-O? _____

2. How many calories are in one serving of regular Jell-O? _____

3. How many grams of carbohydrate are in a serving of regular Jell-O? _____

4. What kind of sweetener is used in Sugar Free Jell-O? _____

5. Are these products significant sources of protein? _____

6. List the ingredients found in each of these products. _____


**Sugar Free Jell-O**

_____

_____

_____

_____

_____


**Regular Jell-O**

_____

_____

_____

_____

_____


7. Give the name and address of the manufacturer of these two products. _____

_____

Read the following food label and answer the questions about it.

Nutrition Information Per Portion

| | |
|---|---|
| Portion size . . 6 oz. | Portions per container . 2 |
| calories . . . . 40 | carbohydrate . . . . . . . 9 grams |
| protein . . . . . 1 gram | fat . . . . . . . . . . . . . . 0 grams |

Percentages of U.S. Recommended Daily Allowances (U.S. RDA)

| | |
|---|---|
| protein . . . . . 2% | niacin . . . . . . . . . . . . 8% |
| vitamin A . . . 25% | calcium . . . . . . . . . . . * |
| vitamin C . . . 15% | iron . . . . . . . . . . . . . 6% |
| thiamin . . . . . 4% | phosphorus . . . . . . . . 4% |
| riboflavin . . . 2% | magnesium . . . . . . . . 4% |

*Contains less than 2% of the U.S. RDA of this nutrient.

Ingredients: tomatoes, salt, dehydrated onions, dehydrated garlic, and natural flavors.

1. There are —————— calories in one portion.

2. The main ingredient in this product is ————————— .

3. This container holds ———— portions.

4. The protein in a serving of this product is ——— percent of the total amount of protein you need daily.

5. This product is fairly high in vitamin ———— .

# SHOW WHAT YOU KNOW . . .

## About Food Labels

Select two different brands of the same food. Make sure each container holds the same amount. Compare the following features of each brand.

|  | Brand A | Brand B |
|---|---|---|
| Serving size |  |  |
| Calories |  |  |
| Protein |  |  |
| Carbohydrates |  |  |

# Following directions

Following directions requires special reading skills. Some directions are general; others are very specific. You must read specific directions *completely* to get the whole picture. *All* information must be read very carefully. If you don't read and follow directions, an item may not operate properly. You may spoil something you are cooking. You may fail a test simply because you did not mark an answer card correctly.

In this section, you will practice reading both general and specific directions. They will be the kind of directions you see most often. For example, you will learn how to fold a letter and set a digital watch. You will also practice reading recipes. Recipes are only one example of the step-by-step directions you will study in this chapter. Finally, you will study different kinds of tests and practice following test directions.

## Reading directions

**WORDS TO KNOW**

**abrasive**   something rough used to smooth or polish

**assemble**   to fit parts together

**detergent**   a soap substitute used for washing and cleaning

**immerse**   to lower (something) into liquid until it is completely covered

**peak performance**   the best possible performance

**sequence**   a regular order, as by number or date

Most directions tell you how to assemble or use something. You may have followed such directions if you've ever put together a kite or folded a box. Often directions tell you to follow a certain order. You must read and understand what should be done first, second, and so on until the job is done.

Some directions stress DO and DON'T, especially DON'T. If you don't pay attention to these warnings, you could ruin a new watch or vacuum cleaner or TV set.

## ACTIVITY 1

### Reading directions

The directions below tell you how to clean a blender. Read the questions that follow the directions. Select the phrase that correctly completes each statement about the blender.

---

# HOW TO CLEAN YOUR BLENDER

Your new blender has been designed to give you years of enjoyment, with a minimum amount of care.

To make sure that your blender always operates at peak performance, you should clean the container after each and every use. Please do not use the container to store foods or beverages.

We recommend that you treat your blender container with the same care that you give to your good glassware.

If you have been blending solid foods, you may want to clean the container first with a long-handled brush and warm water to dislodge any food particles that cling to the inside.

After blending ANYTHING—liquid or solid—you should ALWAYS follow this procedure:

1. Put about one cup of warm water and a dash of detergent into your blender container, cover and blend, at a low speed, for about 30 seconds.

2. Rinse and dry the container. (Here's a quick tip: To make sure it is really dry, put it back on your blender base, cover and run the blender, empty, at a low speed, for about 2 to 5 seconds, so that any remaining water drops may evaporate.)

3. To clean your blender base, unplug and use a soft cloth or sponge, warm water and a mild detergent. Do not immerse blender in water, and do not use any harsh or abrasive cleansers.

---

_____ 1. To make sure your blender operates at peak performance, clean the container
    **a.** every time you use it.
    **b.** as little as possible.
    **c.** as often as possible.

_____ 2. You should not use the container to
    **a.** store foods.
    **b.** store beverages.
    **c.** store foods or beverages.

_____ 3. After blending solid foods,
    **a.** clean the container with a brush and warm water.
    **b.** clean the container with a brush and cold water.
    **c.** clean the container with cold water.

____ **4.** The base of this blender
    **a.** cannot be placed in water.
    **b.** cannot take harsh cleansers.
    **c.** cannot be placed in water and cannot take harsh or abrasive cleansers.

These are the steps involved in cleaning the blender:
1) Rinse and dry the blender container.
2) Put a cup of warm water with detergent into the blender.
3) Put the blender on its base and run the blender at a low speed for 2 to 5 seconds.
4) Unplug the blender base and clean it with a soft cloth, warm water, and detergent.
5) Blend detergent and water at a low speed for about 30 seconds.

____ **5.** The correct order of these steps is
    **a.** 4, 2, 5, 3, 1.
    **b.** 2, 5, 1, 4, 3.
    **c.** 2, 5, 4, 3, 1.

# ACTIVITY 2

### Following step-by-step directions

Do you know the correct way to fold a business letter? Which way do you place the letter in the envelope? What do you do when your envelope is too short? Below are the steps for folding a business letter to fit (1) a standard-size business envelope (about 9 1/2 × 4 1/8 inches) and (2) a short envelope (about 3 1/2 × 6 1/2 inches).

1. Folding a Business Letter for a Standard-Size Envelope

| **Step 1** | **Step 2** | **Step 3** |

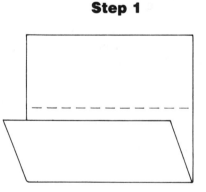
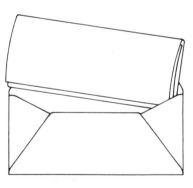

Fold bottom up one-third.

Fold top down, leaving about one-quarter inch of the paper showing below the edge.

Place letter in envelope with open flap facing you, ready to be unfolded.

26

**2.** Folding a Business Letter for a Short Envelope

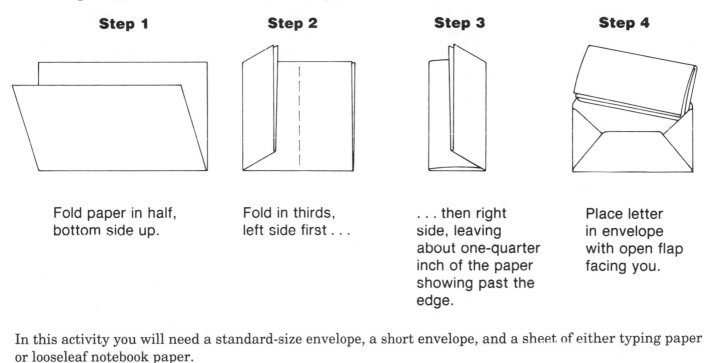

| **Step 1** | **Step 2** | **Step 3** | **Step 4** |
|---|---|---|---|
| Fold paper in half, bottom side up. | Fold in thirds, left side first . . . | . . . then right side, leaving about one-quarter inch of the paper showing past the edge. | Place letter in envelope with open flap facing you. |

In this activity you will need a standard-size envelope, a short envelope, and a sheet of either typing paper or looseleaf notebook paper.

Using the steps shown above,
**a.** fold a letter and correctly place in a business envelope.
**b.** fold a letter and correctly place in a short envelope.

## ACTIVITY 3
### Following directions

Have you ever bought a radio, cassette player, or disc player? If you have, you know that these items come with a set of instructions for the proper use and care of the equipment. Read the following owner's manual. It is for a radio that clips to your belt and has a lightweight headset.

After reading the owner's manual, decide whether the following statements about the instructions for the radio and headset are TRUE (T) or FALSE (F).

# MURA
# hi stepper™

Your new 'hi stepper' portable headphone radio has been designed to provide you with high fidelity FM stereo listening as well as excellent FM monoral reception.

In order to obtain the fullest enjoyment from your 'hi stepper' we suggest that you read the operating instructions carefully before using your new radio.

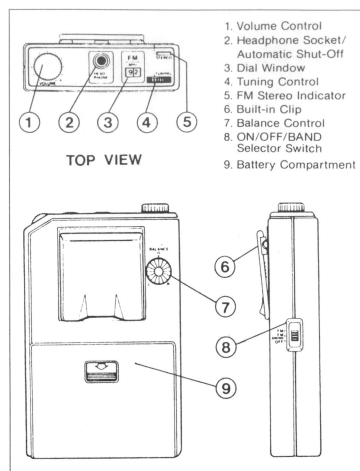

1. Volume Control
2. Headphone Socket/Automatic Shut-Off
3. Dial Window
4. Tuning Control
5. FM Stereo Indicator
6. Built-in Clip
7. Balance Control
8. ON/OFF/BAND Selector Switch
9. Battery Compartment

**TOP VIEW**

**BACK VIEW**          **SIDE VIEW**

## Operation:

1) First insert 4 fresh penlite batteries (size AA or UM3) in the battery compartment (9). Care should be taken to ensure the batteries are inserted in the correct polarity positions as shown on the diagram in the battery compartment.

2) Fully uncoil the headphone cord and insert the headphone plug into the headphone socket (2). Place the headphones on your head while observing that the ear piece with the 'L' mark should be placed over the left ear and the ear piece with the 'R' mark over the right ear. Adjust the head band so that the ear pieces fall comfortably over the center of each ear.

3) Use the ON/OFF/BAND Selector Switch (8) to switch the set on to the FM position. Adjust the Volume Control (1) to a comfortable listening level.

4) Next use the Tuning Control (4) to select your station. The station frequency can be seen in the dial window.

5) If you wish to listen to FM stereo broadcasts, the Band Switch (8) must be in the FM Stereo position. When tuning the radio in this position the Stereo Indicator (5) will light whenever you tune in a station which is broadcasting in stereo. If the stereo indicator flickers and does not stay lighted this indicates that the station you are receiving is too weak and good stereo reception is not possible. If you still wish to listen to this station you must switch from FM Stereo to FM. This will eliminate the hissing and distortion of the weak stereo signal and allow you to listen to this station in monaural FM.

6) After selecting your station and adjusting the volume level it may be necessary to adjust the Balance Control (7) located on the rear of the set. This control will balance the volume level between the left and right headphone receiver so that equal volume is heard in each ear. Once adjusted it should not be necessary to re-adjust this control unless another person is using your set.

7) The built-in Clip (6) at the rear of the set may be used for securing the set to your belt or clipping it in your pocket.

## Recommendations:

HEADPHONES—Inasmuch as the lead wire from the headphones to the set acts as your FM antenna, this wire should always be fully extended. If for safety or comfort reasons it is necessary to bunch up or secure excess wire this should be done on the end nearest the headphones and not near the set.

AUTOMATIC SHUT-OFF—Since your set does not have a loudspeaker to remind you that it is turned on, a specially designed headphone socket has been provided as an alternate means to shut off all power to your set. Even though the switch (8) remains in one of the "ON" positions, all power will shut off whenever the headphone plug is removed from the headphone socket.

BATTERIES—In order to protect your set and obtain maximum battery life we recommend that you use high quality batteries. Additional battery life may be obtained by using alkaline batteries. Since no batteries are completely leak proof we recommend that you remove the batteries from your set during long periods of infrequent use.

CARE AND CLEANING—The cabinet of your set may be cleaned with a damp soft cloth but no solvents or abrasives should be used. Should the ear pads on your headphones become soiled, these may be removed from the headphones, washed in mild soap and water and allowed to air dry.

SERVICE—Should your set become dead, weak, distorted, fail to receive stereo signals, or act improperly in any manner it is most commonly caused by weak batteries. Before returning your set for servicing always test it first with a new set of fresh batteries.

---

### SAFETY PRECAUTIONS

YOUR NEW 'HI STEPPER' PROVIDES YOU WITH PRIVATE RADIO RECEPTION BUT AT THE SAME TIME IT MAY PREVENT YOU FROM HEARING OUTSIDE SOUNDS WHILE YOU ARE WEARING THE HEADPHONES. WHEN WEARING YOUR HEADPHONE RADIO, CARE MUST BE TAKEN WHEN YOU ARE ENGAGED IN ACTIVITIES WHERE YOUR SAFETY MIGHT BE ENDANGERED BY NOT HEARING OUTSIDE WARNINGS FROM HORNS, WHISTLES, SIRENS, ETC. *BE ESPECIALLY CAREFUL WHEN CROSSING STREETS.* PLEASE TAKE THE UTMOST CARE. YOU SHOULD ALSO ENSURE THAT CHILDREN WHO MIGHT BE USING YOUR RADIO ARE ADVISED OF THESE PRECAUTIONS.

_____ 1. This radio requires two size C batteries.

_____ 2. It does not matter how you put the headset on your head.

_____ 3. This radio has two positions: FM and FM Stereo.

_____ 4. This radio picks up AM stations.

_____ 5. The balance control dial adjusts the volume of the headphones for each ear.

_____ 6. This radio will automatically shut off when you remove the headphone plug from the headphone socket.

_____ 7. The lead wire from the headphones acts as an FM antenna.

_____ 8. The main safety problem in the use of the headphones is that they may prevent you from hearing outside sounds, especially horns, whistles, and sirens.

_____ 9. If your set begins to work improperly, the first thing you should do is return it to the dealer for servicing.

_____ 10. The clip at the back of the set is meant to attach the set to a belt or pocket.

# ACTIVITY 4

## Sequential directions—setting a digital watch

The directions in this activity tell you how to operate and set a digital display watch. First read the directions on the OPERATION of a digital watch. Then complete the chart that follows these directions.

## WH-5F-1
### Instructions

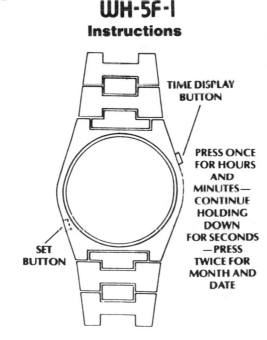

TIME DISPLAY BUTTON

PRESS ONCE FOR HOURS AND MINUTES— CONTINUE HOLDING DOWN FOR SECONDS —PRESS TWICE FOR MONTH AND DATE

SET BUTTON

### Operation

To display the time in hours and minutes, simply touch the TIME display button once. The hours and minutes will remain visible for a short period of time.

If the TIME display button is held down continuously, hours and minutes will disappear and a flashing seconds display will begin, remaining in view as long as the button is depressed.

To display month and date, simply press the TIME display button twice in rapid succession. A continuous display of month-date is available by holding the button down after the second push. Note that the month and date are separated by a dash (—), while hours and minutes are separated by a colon (:).

What will this watch display if you perform the steps in the following chart? Match each step with the correct result.

| IF YOU . . . | YOUR WATCH WILL DISPLAY . . . | | |
|---|---|---|---|
| | TIME HRS: MINUTES | FLASHING SECONDS | MONTH & DATE |
| 1. Press the TIME display button once. | | | |
| 2. Press the TIME display button and hold the button in depressed position. | | | |
| 3. Depress the TIME display button twice. | | | |
| 4. Push the TIME display button twice and hold the button down after the second push. | | | |

Read the instructions for SETTING this watch. Then put the steps for setting the month, date, hour, and minute in the proper sequence.

### Setting instructions

The SET button is used to select specific watch functions for setting. The TIME button is used for the actual setting operation. Pressing the SET button once (with a pointed object, such as a pencil or ball point pen) starts the month number flashing, signifying that the month can be set. Pressing it again enables you to set the date; the third time, the hour; the fourth, minutes and the fifth, normal operation. Note that the SET button operates sequentially. You can always tell which "set mode" your watch is in by observing the position of the flashing digits and noting whether a dash or a colon is displayed. The following table illustrates the SET button cycle.

| ACTION | SET MODE | FLASHING DISPL. |
|---|---|---|
| Press once | Month | 11 — |
| Press twice | Date | — 17 |
| Press 3 times | Hours | 5 : |
| Press 4 times | Minutes | : 46 |
| Press 5 times | Normal | None |

## Setting the month

Press the SET button once and the month number will start flashing. The watch is now in its "month set mode." To change the month, simply hold the TIME button down and the month number will begin to advance. When the desired number flashes into view, release the TIME button. The correct month is now set into your watch.

_____ Press the SET button once.

_____ Release the TIME button when the number of the desired month appears.

_____ Hold the TIME button down.

_____ Look for a flashing month number indicating you are in the "month set mode."

## Setting the date

Press the SET button a second time and the date will begin to flash, indicating that the watch is in its "date set mode." To change the date, press the TIME button and hold it down until the correct number appears. Your watch is programmed to adjust itself automatically for 29, 30 and 31 day months. It is only necessary to advance the date manually on the day following February 28 during non-leap years. To do this, select the "date set mode" and change the date from "29" to "1" (the month will advance automatically).

_____ Press the SET button a second time.

_____ Release the TIME button when the correct date appears.

_____ Hold the TIME button down.

_____ Look for a flashing date indicating you are in the "date set mode."

## Setting hours

Press the SET button a third time. Hours will begin to flash, indicating the "hours set mode." To change hours, press the TIME button until the desired hour is displayed. In doing this, however, it is important to recognize the difference between a.m. hours and p.m. hours. If your watch is set to a.m. hours, the colon will include a dash ($\div$). During p.m. hours, the dash disappears (:). (If you have set your watch correctly during morning hours but the dash is absent, you must advance the hour setting through 12 more hours. By observing this a.m./p.m. difference, your watch will properly change date at midnight rather than at noon. Setting hours does not affect minutes, consequently, you can adjust your watch for time zone or daylight savings time changes without changing minutes.)

_____ Press the SET button a third time.

_____ Release the TIME button when the correct hour is displayed.

_____ Hold the TIME button.

_____ Look for a flashing hour indicating you are in the "hours set mode."

## Setting minutes

Press the SET button a fourth time and minutes will start to flash, indicating the "minutes set mode." If you are not interested in setting your watch to the exact second, simply press the TIME button until the correct minute appears.

_____ Press the SET button a fourth time.

_____ Release the TIME button when the correct minute appears.

_____ Hold the TIME button down.

_____ Look for a flashing minute indicating you are in the "minute set mode."

Here are some words you should know when following directions. Choose the correct word or words for the following sentences.

assemble      abrasive      peak performance
sequence      immerse

**1.** The instructions with my electric coffeemaker say not to _____ the base in water.

**2.** To set my digital watch, I must follow the instructions in exact _____ .

**3.** Some items come with many parts. It is important to follow the instructions exactly to

_____ them properly.

**4.** Some instructions warn against using _____ cleansers on a product.

**5.** I want to get _____ from my new tape deck.

_____ Find the phrase that correctly completes each sentence.

**6.** The most important task you must do when following directions is
     **a.** get someone to work with you.
     **b.** follow the directions in the correct order.
_____      **c.** work as rapidly as you can.

**7.** Some directions warn against using certain kinds of cleansers. Usually the warnings are against using cleansers that
     **a.** are not strong enough to do the job.
     **b.** are liquids.
_____      **c.** will scratch or damage the item.

**8.** Using the wrong sequence when you try to assemble something probably means that
     **a.** the item will be damaged.
     **b.** the instructions don't matter anyway.
_____      **c.** you will lose some of the parts.

**9.** Digital watches must be set to show the correct time. The best way to do this is to
     **a.** ask a friend to show you how to do it.
     **b.** try out various ways of doing it until you get it right.
_____      **c.** read and follow the directions for your particular watch.

**10.** The words "do not immerse in water" are found on many directions and instructions. These words mean
     **a.** do not wash.
     **b.** do not use for cooking.
     **c.** do not cover with water.

# SHOW WHAT YOU KNOW . . .

## About Following Directions

Choose a partner. One person should write the step-by-step directions for tying a shoelace. The other person should write the step-by-step directions for lacing a shoe. After you finish, read your directions to your partner. He or she is to follow your directions *exactly,* in the order they are given.

Are your directions clear and complete enough for your partner to perform the task correctly? If not, rewrite the directions. Then switch. See if you can follow your partner's directions.

## WORDS TO KNOW

**blend**   to combine two or more ingredients

**briskly**   swiftly, with energy

**combine**   mix together

**container**   something to put food in, such as a jar or bowl

**cream**   to mash or beat until smooth

**dash**   a very small amount

**fold**   mix in gently, without stirring

**grate**   to shred with a grater

**ingredients**   anything that goes into a recipe

**preheat**   set oven temperature in advance

**reduce**   lessen, as in turn down heat or allow liquid to boil away

**scald**   to heat to just below the boiling point

**simmer**   to cook in liquid at low heat on top of stove

**yield**   the amount produced

**yolk**   the yellow part of an egg

**c.**   cup

**doz.**   dozen (12)

**gal.**   gallon (128 fluid ounces)

**lb.**   pound (16 ounces)

**lrg.**   large

**min.**   minute

**oz.**   ounce

**pkg.**   package

**pt.**   pint (16 fluid ounces)

**qt.**   quart (32 fluid ounces)

**sm.**   small

**sq.**   square

**tbsp. or T.**   tablespoon

**tsp. or t.**   teaspoon

Recipes have special words of their own. In recipes you will find words and abbreviations you do not use every day. These words and abbreviations tell you how to add ingredients. They tell you what the right measurements are and how long to cook a dish. They list the cooking temperature. The recipe words and abbreviations given above are the ones you will see most often.

Reading a recipe correctly can mean the difference between a good dish and a bad one. In addition to knowing what the words and abbreviations mean, you must be able to follow directions. Most recipes first give you a list of the ingredients you will need. They then tell you step-by-step what you should do to make the dish. Good cooks almost always use recipes.

## ACTIVITY 5

**Understanding recipe vocabulary**

Match the words in column A with the definitions in column B.

| A | B |
|---|---|
| _____ **1.** combine | **a.** yellow part of the egg |
| _____ **2.** briskly | **b.** lessen; turn down |
| _____ **3.** yolk | **c.** mix together |
| _____ **4.** container | **d.** something to put food in |
| _____ **5.** yield | **e.** swiftly |
| _____ **6.** reduce | **f.** the amount produced |

## ACTIVITY 6

**Understanding recipe abbreviations**

Write the correct abbreviation beside each word.

_____ **1.** ounce

_____ **2.** cup

_____ **3.** gallon

_____ **4.** pound

_____ **5.** tablespoon

_____ **6.** quart

_____ **7.** teaspoon

_____ **8.** dozen

_____ **9.** small

_____ **10.** pint

_____ **11.** package

_____ **12.** square

_____ **13.** large

_____ **14.** minute

The illustration below points out the basic parts of a recipe. Study it carefully before doing the activities that follow.

Name of the dish ● ———————————— **BREAD PUDDING**

The ingredients ●
you will need,
and amounts

3 c. milk              2 c. bread, cut in cubes
3 eggs                 ¼ tsp. salt
4 tbsp. sugar          ¾ tsp. vanilla
                       dash nutmeg

Sequence ●
to follow
in putting
ingredients
together

Scald milk and let cool slightly. Beat eggs, add sugar and vanilla. Add the milk and bread cubes to the above ingredients. Put in a buttered baking pan and sprinkle a little nutmeg on top. Bake in preheated oven at 350 degrees for 45 minutes.

● Method,
temperature,
and time of
cooking

Amount you will ●
have when finished

Yield: 6 servings

# ACTIVITY 7

Read the following recipes. Complete the statements about each recipe.

## Reading recipe directions

**POUND CAKE**

½ lb. butter            3 c. sifted flour
⅓ c. shortening        ½ t. baking powder
3 c. sugar             ½ t. salt
5 eggs                 1 c. milk
                       1 t. vanilla

Cream butter, shortening, and sugar. Add eggs one at a time, beating after each addition. Add sifted dry ingredients and milk alternately, beginning and ending with dry ingredients. Add vanilla flavoring. Bake in tube pan at 350 degrees for 1 hour and 30 minutes. Start in cold oven. Yield: 15 servings.

1. _____ butter is needed for this cake.

2. _____ eggs should be added _____ .

3. A _____ pan should be used for this cake.

4. The cake should cook _____ at a temperature of _____ .

5. The cake will serve _____ people.

6. The oven should be _____ at the beginning of cooking.

---

**VEG-A-BURGER**

1 lb. hamburger
½ c. diced onions
1 8-oz. can tomato sauce
¾ c. water
1 c. canned green beans, drained
1 c. uncooked rice
1 c. whole kernel corn, drained
1 c. tomato catsup

    Brown hamburger and onions in pan; add tomato sauce and water. Add green beans, rice, and corn. Heat to simmer; add catsup. Cook until rice is tender, about 30 minutes. Yield: 6 servings.

1. One _____ of tomato sauce is needed for this dish.

2. One _____ of tomato catsup is used.

3. The rice should be _____ when it is added.

4. The whole kernel corn should be _____ .

5. Brown _____ and _____ in a pan.

6. This dish will serve _____ people.

Read the recipes below. Then read the sets of directions below each recipe.
Decide which directions are written in the proper order.

---

**LEMON SPONGE PIE**

4 tbsp. butter or margarine, softened
1 ¼ c. sugar
4 eggs, separated
3 tbsp. flour
dash of salt
1 ¼ c. milk
grated peel of 1 lemon
¼ c. lemon juice
1 unbaked 9-inch pie shell

Use large bowl and spoon or mixer to cream together butter and
sugar until fluffy. Beat in yolks of eggs, flour, salt, milk, lemon peel, and
juice. Use a small bowl with clean beaters to beat egg whites until stiff
but not dry. Fold into milk mixture. Pour into pie shell. Bake in preheated
375° oven 20 minutes; reduce heat to 300° and bake 40 minutes longer
or until top is golden and toothpick inserted in center comes out dry.
Cool on rack. Yields 8 slices.

---

_____ **1.** Beat in egg yolks, flour, salt, milk, lemon peel, and juice.
Cream together butter and sugar until fluffy.
Beat egg whites until stiff.

_____ **2.** Cream together butter and sugar until fluffy.
Beat in egg yolks, flour, salt, milk, lemon peel, and juice.
Beat egg whites until stiff.

_____ **3.** Beat egg whites until stiff.
Cream together butter and sugar until fluffy.
Beat in egg yolks, flour, salt, milk, lemon peel, and juice.

_____ **4.** Pour into pie shell.
Fold into milk mixture.
Bake in preheated oven.

_____ **5.** Bake in preheated oven.
Pour into pie shell.
Fold into milk mixture.

_____ **6.** Fold into milk mixture.
Pour into pie shell.
Bake in preheated oven.

## PIZZA

1 Pizza Dough recipe
cooking oil
1 8-oz. can tomato sauce
1 6-oz. can tomato paste
1 large clove garlic, crushed
2 tsp. sugar
1 tsp. oregano
¾ tsp. basil
½ tsp. crushed red pepper

¼ lb. sweet Italian sausage (skin removed) or
    pork sausage meat, browned and drained.
⅛ lb. pepperoni, sliced thin
¼ c. mushrooms, thinly sliced
¼ c. chopped onion
½ c. chopped green pepper
½ to 1 can (about 2 oz.) anchovy fillets,
    drained.
½ lb. mozzarella cheese, shredded
¼ c. grated Parmesan cheese

Prepare dough as directed. Then gently stretch or roll out dough to fit greased 16-inch pizza pan (or divide dough in half and form two 12-inch circles; place on greased cookie sheets). Crimp edges to form rim. Brush dough with oil. Bake (without toppings) on lowest oven rack in preheated 450° oven 3 to 4 minutes or until crust bottom is slightly golden. Meanwhile, mix tomato sauce and paste, garlic, sugar, oregano, basil, and red pepper. Spread evenly over crust. Top with sausage, pepperoni, mushrooms, onion, green pepper, and anchovies. Bake 15 minutes, then sprinkle with mozzarella and Parmesan. Bake 8 to 10 minutes or until cheese is melted with golden crust. Makes 4 servings.

Which sets of directions are in the proper order?

_____ 1.  Brush dough with oil.
    Crimp edges to form rim.
    Roll out dough to fit pan.

_____ 2.  Crimp edges to form rim.
    Roll out dough to fit pan.
    Brush dough with oil.

_____ 3.  Roll out dough to fit pan.
    Crimp edges to form rim.
    Brush dough with oil.

_____ 4.  Mix tomato sauce and paste, garlic, sugar, oregano, basil, and red pepper.
    Spread evenly over crust.
    Top with sausage, pepperoni, mushrooms, onion, green pepper, and anchovies.

_____ 5.  Top with sausage, pepperoni, mushrooms, onion, green pepper, and anchovies.
    Spread evenly over crust.
    Mix tomato sauce and paste, garlic, sugar, oregano, basil, and red pepper.

_____ 6.  Spread evenly over crust.
    Top with sausage, pepperoni, mushrooms, onion, green pepper, and anchovies.
    Mix tomato sauce and paste, garlic, sugar, oregano, basil, and red pepper.

Here are some of the most important abbreviations a person must know to read a recipe correctly. Write the full word for each abbreviation given below.

**1.** c. _____

**2.** tsp. _____

**3.** qt. _____

**4.** t. _____

**5.** sm. _____

**6.** gal. _____

**7.** doz. _____

**8.** lb. _____

**9.** tbsp. _____

**10.** pt. _____

Here are some of the most important "how to" words used in reading recipes. Write out a definition for each word.

**11.** preheat _____

**12.** cream _____

**13.** grate _____

**14.** scald _____

**15.** simmer _____

# SHOW WHAT YOU KNOW . . .

## About Recipes

Select three (3) recipes from a magazine or newspaper or choose three of your own. Label all the basic parts of each recipe.

Rewrite the list of ingredients and spell out all the abbreviated words.

## Taking tests

**accurate**   correct, without mistake

**ACT**   American College Test; test often required before entering college

**applicant**   person applying for a job

**answer grid**   evenly spaced boxes or lines for marking answers to test questions

**essay question**   a question that requires the writer to explain his or her thoughts

**horizontal line**   a line that runs across a page from side to side

**performance test**   a test that requires a person to perform a task, such as typing or using tools

**SAT**   Scholastic Aptitude Test; test often required before entering college

**tester**   person giving the test

**vertical line**   a line that runs up and down a page

**multiple-choice question**   a question that lists a number of possible answers

Tests are designed to measure both skills and knowledge. They are given in schools and for qualifying for jobs. They require following directions carefully. Tests are also used to determine which colleges you qualify for and, sometimes, the courses you will take. Perhaps you are familiar with the ACT and SAT tests.

Tests can take many different forms. Performance tests ask you to work with tools or objects to demonstrate your skill. You may also have to put something together. Other tests are oral or mechanized. You may be asked to listen to a tape and then respond on a machine or computer. Most tests, however, are "paper and pencil" tests.

Learning to take a paper and pencil test properly is a skill in itself. For example, you may know the answer to the question on a test, but you may not understand where and how to write your answer.

One form of paper and pencil test is the test *booklet*. For this type of test, you record your answer in a booklet or on the separate answer sheet that comes with the test booklet.

## Test booklets

On the first page of a test booklet you are usually asked to identify yourself. There will be very specific questions aimed at you personally. You must answer these questions accurately because they tell the tester *who* you are.

On the following page are two examples of test booklet covers. They are for an employment test. The first example is marked "incorrect." It has not been filled out properly. The second example is marked "correct." The applicant has given all the information requested. The information is clear and complete. Take a moment to study these examples.

The applicant ignored the first request on the form. He wrote in longhand instead of printing.

This line calls for last name first.

The applicant did not indicate if Cherrylawn was a street, avenue, or lane. And where are the city, state, and ZIP Code?

This line is incomplete. The year is omitted.

Miller has *printed* this entry. Perhaps he now realizes the form says "please print."

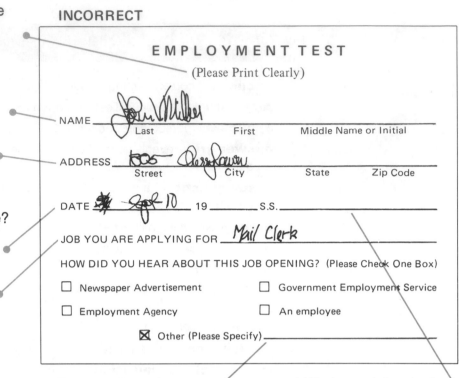

**INCORRECT**

E M P L O Y M E N T   T E S T

(Please Print Clearly)

NAME _____
        Last        First        Middle Name or Initial

ADDRESS _____
        Street   City    State    Zip Code

DATE ____ Sept 10 ____ 19 _____ S.S. _____

JOB YOU ARE APPLYING FOR ___ Mail Clerk ___

HOW DID YOU HEAR ABOUT THIS JOB OPENING? (Please Check One Box)

☐ Newspaper Advertisement          ☐ Government Employment Service

☐ Employment Agency                ☐ An employee

☒ Other (Please Specify) _____

This applicant has not indicated exactly how he learned about this job. The form said "specify."

Miller's social security number should have gone here.

**CORRECT**

Applicant *printed* all information.

Applicant gave his name in the order requested— *last name first.*

The applicant wrote Cherrylawn *Street*. The *city, state,* and *ZIP Code* are given.

The *date is complete*— September 10, 1993.

E M P L O Y M E N T   T E S T

(Please Print Clearly)

NAME    Miller        John        V.
        Last        First        Middle Name or Initial

ADDRESS 1805 Cherrylawn St., Amber, IL        60512
        Street   City    State    Zip Code

DATE September 10 19 **93** S.S. 234-56-8469

JOB YOU ARE APPLYING FOR    Mail Clerk

HOW DID YOU HEAR ABOUT THIS JOB OPENING? (Please Check One Box)

☐ Newspaper Advertisement          ☐ Government Employment Service

☐ Employment Agency                ☐ An employee

☒ Other (Please Specify) School Guidance Counselor

Applicant has *specified how he heard about this job opening.*

The applicant's *social security number is given.*

The personal information requested on test booklets should be *neat* and *complete*. In the first example, John V. Miller's handwriting is careless. If the tester needed to contact John, he or she might not be able to read John's name. Much of the information on this application was left incomplete. One item missing was John's social security number. Perhaps John did not know his social security number. Many people don't. John may not have known what "S.S." means. We know that this applicant *can* print. John's entry on the line "Job you are applying for" is *printed*. Although this entry is not very neat, it is printed. The tester should have no trouble reading it. The last incomplete entry had to do with specifying how John learned about this opening. In the second example we learn that the school guidance counselor told John about the job opening.

## ACTIVITY 9
### Completing test booklet covers

Write out the information requested on the following test booklet cover. Use today's date. This is test form 2-B.

```
┌─────────────────────────────────────────────────────────────┐
│              TROJAN MANUFACTURING COMPANY                     │
│                     Employment Test                          │
│  Print clearly                                               │
│                                                              │
│  Name _____ │
│          Last               First          Middle           │
│                                                              │
│  Address _____ │
│            Street       City        State     Zip           │
│                                                              │
│  Date of Test _____ 19_____        │
│  Form of Test (Check one box):                              │
│    ☐ 1-A            ☐ 2-A            ☐ 3-A                   │
│    ☐ 1-B            ☐ 2-B            ☐ 3-B                   │
│                                                              │
├─────────────────────────────────────────────────────────────┤
│  DO NOT OPEN TEST BOOKLET UNTIL TESTER INSTRUCTS YOU TO      │
└─────────────────────────────────────────────────────────────┘
```

## Following directions on tests

Did you notice in the activity above that the applicant was asked *not* to open the test booklet? When you take tests, especially employment tests, you will be timed. A tester will tell you when to BEGIN a test and when to STOP. There will be directions with your booklet, for example, "DO NOT TURN THE PAGE UNTIL YOU ARE TOLD TO DO SO" or "WAIT FOR FURTHER INSTRUCTIONS." These directions *must* be followed. Many times you will take a test that not only measures *what* you know, but how *quickly* you can use your knowledge. This type of test is called a SPEED AND ACCURACY TEST. You must read and follow directions on a speed and accuracy test exactly. You must begin when the tester tells you to

43

begin. You must stop when the tester tells you to stop. Because you are being timed, you must read and follow these directions quickly. But never begin this type of test without understanding exactly what you are to do.

Read the directions for the speed and accuracy test below. But DO NOT take the test.

## SPEED AND ACCURACY TEST

This is a test of speed and accuracy for a job as a mail room clerk. In this test you will find names and numbers in pairs. If the two names or the two numbers of a pair are exactly the same, put a check ( ✓ ) on the line between them. If the two names or the two numbers are different, do nothing.

EXAMPLE

**(1)** 33155 ——✓—— 33155

**(2)** 45788 ——✓—— 45788

**(3)** Wayne Riley ——✓—— Wayne Riley

**(4)** Janet Martin ———— Janette Martin

Now answer the questions below. This is a SPEED AND ACCURACY TEST. Work as quickly as you can.

**(1)** 5234 ———— 5234

**(2)** 8807 ———— 8807

**(3)** 1243 ———— 1234

**(4)** 10007 ———— 1007

**(5)** Betty Marsh ———— Betty March

**(6)** 8813 ———— 8831

**(7)** 1080307 ———— 1080307

**(8)** Joyce Jackson ———— Joyce Jackson

**(9)** Clarence Saunders ———— Clarence Sanders

**(10)** Emma Whitaker ———— Emma Whitaker

Here are examples of how two applicants responded to this test:

**Applicant 1**

  (1)  5234 \_\_\_\_\_5234
  (2)  8807 \_\_\_\_\_8807
  (3)  1243 \_✓\_1234
  (4)  10007 \_✓\_1007
  (5)  Betty Marsh \_✓\_Betty March
  (6)  8813 \_✓\_8831
  (7)  1080307 \_\_\_\_\_1080307
  (8)  Joyce Jackson \_\_\_\_\_Joyce Jackson
  (9)  Clarence Saunders \_✓\_Clarence Sanders
(10)  Emma Whitaker \_\_\_\_\_Emma Whitaker

**Applicant 2**

  (1)  5234 \_✓\_5234
  (2)  8807 \_✓\_8807
  (3)  1243 \_\_\_\_\_1234
  (4)  10007 \_\_\_\_\_1007
  (5)  Betty Marsh \_\_\_\_\_Betty March
  (6)  8813 \_\_\_\_\_8831
  (7)  1080307 \_✓\_1080307
  (8)  Joyce Jackson \_✓\_Joyce Jackson
  (9)  Clarence Saunders \_\_\_\_\_Clarence Sanders
(10)  Emma Whitaker \_✓\_Emma Whitaker

The second applicant has checked the correct responses. The first applicant has checked all incorrect responses. The first applicant *believes* he has checked all the right responses. Turn back to the original directions. See if you can determine where this applicant went wrong.

The first applicant misread the directions. The directions said "If the two names . . . are *exactly the same*, put a check (✓) on the line. . . . If the two names . . . are *different, do nothing.*" The first applicant read these directions too quickly. He was sure that he would be asked to do nothing when the names or numbers were the same. As a result of this thinking, all of his answers are wrong. If you do not follow the directions on a speed and accuracy test, you could fail the test completely.

# ACTIVITY 10

## Following test directions

Read the test directions for the speed and accuracy test below. Then answer the questions just as you would if you were actually being tested. You will *not* be timed for this practice activity. But you should pretend this is an actual test and work as fast as you can.

## SPEED AND ACCURACY TEST

### Directions

This is a test of speed and accuracy in one type of clerical work. In this test there are pairs of names and pairs of numbers. If the two names or the two numbers of a pair are *exactly the same,* make a check mark on the line. If they are different, make no mark on that line.

Look at the four examples, A, B, C, and D, that have been done correctly. In example A, the two numbers are different, so no check mark was made on the line between them. In example B, the numbers are exactly the same, so a check mark was made on the line between them. Now look at examples C and D.

**A.** 3315 \_\_\_\_\_ 3155      **C.** Jim Battle \_\_\_\_\_ John Battle

**B.** 45782 \_✓\_ 45782      **D.** Bill Evans \_✓\_ Bill Evans

|  | **Numbers** |  |  | **Names** |  |
|---|---|---|---|---|---|
| **1.** | 4721 _____ 4721 | | **6.** | Louis Eldern _____ Louis Eldern | |
| **2.** | 584 _____ 584 | | **7.** | James Meyer _____ James Mayer | |
| **3.** | 80962 _____ 90862 | | **8.** | Arthur Lungren _____ Arthur Lundgren | |
| **4.** | 9325 _____ 9325 | | **9.** | Frank Schaefer _____ Frank Schaefer | |
| **5.** | 0365 _____ 0356 | | **10.** | Allan Kenmore _____ Albert Kenmore | |

# ACTIVITY 11
## Following test directions

In this activity you will take a test. You are to read and follow the directions for the test. *You will not be timed.* This activity will give you practice in following test directions.

## VOCABULARY TEST

### Directions

This is a test of the meanings of words.

Look at the word HURRY, and the four words that follow it.

One of the words—rush—means about the same thing as HURRY, so a check mark has been put on the line next to the word *rush*.

HURRY        move _____    rush _____    shout _____    walk _____

Below are words printed in capital letters. To the right of each word are four more words—like the example shown above. Put a check mark on the line next to the *one* word that means most nearly the same thing as the word printed in capital letters.

Answer each question, but do not spend too much time on any one question.

If you are not sure of the answer, guess.

| | | | | |
|---|---|---|---|---|
| **1.** SAVE | part _____ | keep _____ | spend _____ | sort _____ |
| **2.** STAY | remain _____ | result _____ | leave _____ | press _____ |
| **3.** IDEA | story _____ | value _____ | thought _____ | subject _____ |
| **4.** GATHER | collect _____ | choose _____ | remove _____ | decide _____ |
| **5.** HIRE | raise _____ | locate _____ | divide _____ | employ _____ |
| **6.** NEARLY | every _____ | quickly _____ | almost _____ | never _____ |

## Using tests with separate answer sheets

Many test booklets come with separate answer sheets. Filling in an answer sheet correctly is important. Part of your answer sheet will be for "gridding in" your name. Did Kevin Abraham grid in the answer sheet below correctly?

First name starts here

1. Fill in your name, one letter per box. Notice that the last name is called for first.

2. The rows under each box contain the alphabet. Go down the row and find the letter in the box at the top of the row.

3. Darken that letter and do the same for each box that has a letter in it. This is called "gridding in."

**Note**—If your name has more letters than there are boxes, fill in as much of your name as you can and leave the rest of it off.

**STUDENT'S NAME**
Print last name, one letter per box. Skip a box. Print first name. Darken appropriate circle below each letter. Darken top circles under boxes which do not contain letters.

| A | B | R | A | H | A | M | | K | E | V | I | N | | | |

This section of the answer sheet is for you to fill in additional information about yourself.

1. Mark your I.D. number

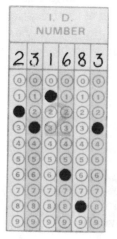

2. Mark the month and year you were born

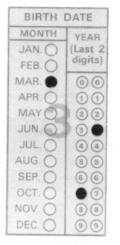

3. Show whether you are male or female

4. Show which test form you are using

47

## Responding on separate answer sheets

When you are asked to answer test questions on a separate sheet, you will usually be given a grid sheet for your answers. Grids may be horizontal. They may also be vertical, or up-and-down, grids.

Beside each question in a test booklet will be a number. The same numbers will appear on the answer sheet. Spaces opposite the number will match the question on the answer sheet. You must always be sure you mark your answer in the space with the same number as the question in the test booklet. You must also mark answers as directed. Study this sample from an answer sheet:

**1.** When is Independence Day?
   A. May 31
   B. June 1
   C. July 4
   D. December 25

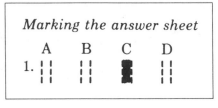

The answer blacked in on the answer sheet is correct—C, July 4.

When marking an answer sheet, remember—
1. Shade in the section you have selected for your response and *only that section.*
2. Stray marks on the answer sheet may be counted as incorrect answers by the scoring machine.
3. If you must erase, erase a mark *completely.*
4. Always be sure the number of the question on the answer sheet corresponds to the number in the test booklet.

## Multiple-choice questions

The questions on the test in Activity 12 are multiple-choice questions. Multiple-choice questions are the most widely used type of test question. Of course, you will not always know the correct answer to a multiple-choice question. Many times, though, you can use the process of elimination to determine the correct response. Although some questions do not lend themselves to guessing, many do. Guess by eliminating wrong answers until you are left with one possible answer.

When answering a multiple-choice question, read the question carefully, especially the first part. Your complete understanding of the question is very important. Try the process of elimination. For example, you may not know who wrote *Gulliver's Travels,* but you may know who didn't.

Who wrote *Gulliver's Travels* ?
A. George Washington
B. Eli Whitney
C. Mark Twain
D. Jonathan Swift

You probably know that D is the correct response even if you never heard of Jonathan Swift. First, you can eliminate George Washington. He is well known for being our first President and for chopping down the cherry tree but not for being a writer. Eli Whitney invented the cotton gin. And you know that when you studied Mark Twain in English class, most of the stories you read were about Tom Sawyer, Huck Finn, and the Mississippi River. So you arrive at Jonathan Swift through the process of elimination.

When you use reason—or plain common sense—to answer a multiple-choice question, look for words and phrases that are clues to the answer—

| | | | |
|---|---|---|---|
| always | the only | except | sometimes |
| never | chief | but | one |
| least | main | or | usually |
| highest | near | not | best |

Always consider how these words and phrases can influence a question. For example, this simple question is difficult to answer.

The reason for the high school drop-out rate is
A. economics
B. outside interests
C. boredom
D. low success in school

Watch how key words and phrases can narrow down the possible responses to this question:

The reason for the high school drop-out rate is *usually* . . .

The *main* reason for the high school drop-out rate is . . .

*One of the least important* reasons for the high school drop-out rate is . . .

What do you feel is the correct (best) response to this multiple-choice question?

A small independent merchant has the best chance to compete with large chain stores by
A. buying in quantity
B. hiring more expert management
C. manufacturing and selling her own items
D. offering more personalized service

Answer A certainly could not be the best way for the merchant to compete with large chains. A small merchant would not have the money or space to buy in large quantities. Although B would improve any business, it is not likely that it would increase business enough for the merchant to be competitive with chain stores. Remember, the question asks for the "best chance." Response C is not even a realistic choice. Most independent merchants do not have the ability to manufacture items. The correct response is D. This is the only area where a small merchant may have an advantage over a large chain. Because a business is small, it has the ability to give customers personal services chain stores cannot provide.

All of the choices were possible to some extent. By using an intelligent process of reasoning and by identifying key phrases, you can answer many multiple-choice questions correctly.

# ACTIVITY 12

## Answering multiple-choice questions

This activity gives you practice in responding to multiple-choice questions. Answer each question on the information test by writing down the letter of the correct answer.

### INFORMATION TEST

_____ 1. What is the capital of the United States?
   A. Washington, D.C.
   B. New York
   C. Philadelphia
   D. Chicago

_____ 2. When is Independence Day?
   A. May 31
   B. December 25
   C. July 4
   D. February 22

_____ 3. Which of these cities has the largest population?
   A. New York
   B. Chicago
   C. San Francisco
   D. Philadelphia

_____ 4. The President of the United States is elected for a term of
   A. four years
   B. two years
   C. ten years
   D. six years

_____ 5. Where does the United States launch spaceflights?
   A. Cape Hatteras
   B. Cape May
   C. Cape Cod
   D. Cape Canaveral

## Test taking tips

Review these TIPS on TEST TAKING. They may help you.

1. Determine a pace for the test you are taking. If you are allowed to look over the entire test before answering any questions, you should. This will give you an idea of how quickly you must work. It's a good idea to wear a watch the day of a test because test sections are often timed.
2. Always work as quickly as you can, but try to answer all questions carefully.

3. You may find it to your advantage to skip a difficult question and go back to it later.

4. On some tests, you can guess at an answer when you are not sure of the correct response. But on other tests, you are penalized for wrong answers. On this type of test, it is better to have *no answer* than a wrong answer. Be sure about these rules before you start the test.

5. The best guess is the one that comes from the process of elimination. Too many wild guesses can hurt your score.

6. Remember to use reasoning on multiple-choice questions. Always look for key words like "always," "most," and "never." These words help narrow down the *best* response.

7. And remember, you must read and follow all directions carefully. If you misread the directions on a test, all your answers could be wrong.

---

## CHECK YOUR UNDERSTANDING OF TAKING TESTS

Here are some words you should know about tests. On your paper write the correct word or phrase for each of the following sentences.

| | | |
|---|---|---|
| multiple-choice | horizontal | SAT |
| applicant | tester | vertical |

1. As a job _____ you may be asked to take an employment test.

2. Be sure to follow the directions given by the _____ when you are taking a test.

3. Test questions with a choice of three or more answers are called _____ questions.

4. Sometimes test answer grids have boxes with lines that run across the page.

   These are called _____ boxes.

5. Many colleges ask for _____ scores to be attached to the college application form.

6. _____ answer grids run up and down the page.

Decide whether each of the following statements is TRUE (T) or FALSE (F).

_____ 7. If you are allowed, you should look over the entire test before answering any questions.

_____ 8. Sometimes it is an advantage to skip a hard question and go back to it later.

_____ 9. Wild guesses can never hurt your score on a test.

_____ 10. Key words like "always," "most," and "never" can help you choose the best multiple-choice answer.

# SHOW WHAT YOU KNOW . . .

## About Taking Tests

Read *all* of the directions below before doing anything. You will have five (5) minutes to complete this test. Write your answers on a separate sheet of paper.

1. Write your name in the upper right-hand corner of your paper.

2. Write the date under your name.

3. At the bottom of your paper, write the name of this course.

4. Draw a small circle at the end of this question.

5. Say your full name aloud.

6. Draw a box around direction number three (3) of this activity.

7. Draw a circle around direction number five (5) of this activity.

8. Write your teacher's name in the center of the paper, at the top.

9. Follow the directions in numbers eight (8) and ten (10) only.

10. Fold your paper in half lengthwise. Write your name on either side of the outside of the folded paper.

# Reading newspapers

One of the best places to learn about events is your newspaper. It gives you the local, national, and world news. It also gives you entertainment, sports, and travel news.

Reading a newspaper is a good way to spend time. A newspaper gives you information on many subjects. In this section, you will study the parts of a newspaper. You will read news stories and editorials. You will read for both facts and opinions. You will also practice using the classified ads. Most emphasis will be on help-wanted ads. The help-wanted ads are a good way to get information about jobs.

## The sections of a newspaper

**WORDS TO KNOW**

**alphabetical**   arranged in the order of the letters of the alphabet

**classified ads**   advertisements for jobs, items for sale, etc., arranged by subject

**editorial**   a written comment on current events that gives the opinion of the newspaper's editor or publisher

**features**   articles about special subjects, such as food or travel

**financial**   having to do with money

**horoscope**   a chart that uses the positions of planets and signs of the Zodiac to predict the future

**index**   a list of items with page numbers, usually arranged alphabetically

**obituary**   notice of a person's death

**real estate**   buildings and land

Newspapers have many sections. By creating different sections, papers make information easy to find. For example, you can quickly turn to the sports section for the score of last night's football game. In the entertainment sections you can find the time of the movie you want to see. Almost all newspapers have these sections:

| | | |
|---|---|---|
| Business | Editorials | News |
| Classified ads | Entertainment | Sports |
| Comics | Fashion | TV guide |
| Death notices | Home | Weather |

## Newspaper indexes

Most newspapers have an index. The index tells you where to find the type of information you want.

Subjects arranged alphabetically →

| | |
|---|---|
| Accent | 1-12F |
| Bridge | 14D |
| Business | 3C |
| Classified | 4-20C |
| Comics | 14, 15D |
| Contact 10 | 16B |
| Crossword | 15D |
| Death notices | 11C |
| Editorial/Opinion | 18, 19A |
| Entertainment | 12, 13D |
| Finance | 3C |
| Horoscope | 14D |
| Kitchen Talk | 1-20E |
| Movie guide | 4C |
| Obituaries | 11C |
| Sports | 1-11D |
| Stock tables | 3C |
| TV | 8, 9E |
| Wonderworld | 15D |

→ Page numbers for this subject

→ Section of the newspaper (each section begins with page 1)

## ACTIVITY 1
### Using the newspaper index

Look at topics 1–10 below. Which index headings will help you find the topics? List the number of each topic beside the correct heading.

1. A restaurant guide
2. Sewing tips
3. Movies in your neighborhood
4. The leader in the baseball pennant race
5. Yesterday's football scores
6. Program on Channel 7 at 8 P.M.
7. Opinions on current issues
8. Nightclub shows
9. Apartments for rent
10. Recipes

**Index Heading**

Sports _____

Editorial _____

Classified ads _____

Entertainment _____

Home section _____

## ACTIVITY 2

### Using the newspaper index

Complete the chart below about this newspaper index.

| | | | |
|---|---|---|---|
| Accent | 1-20 | Editorial/Opinion | 18, 19A |
| Art | 4M | Finance | 1-6E |
| Books | 2M | Hobbies | 5J |
| Bridge | 5J | Homes/Gardens | 1, 2L |
| Business | 1-6E | Horoscope | 19C |
| Camera | 9M | Lively Arts | 1-10M |
| CB Radio | 8M | Movie guide | 6M |
| Classified | 1-8F, 1-8G | Obituaries | 19C |
| Comics | 2-BL | Sports | 1-12D |
| Contact 10 | 1B | Stock tables | 3-6E |
| Crossword | 8K | Travel | 1-6J |
| Death notices | 19C | | |

| Topics | Pages | Section |
|---|---|---|
| How to grow houseplants | | |
| Tours to Las Vegas | | |
| What's in store for a Gemini today | | |
| Stamp collecting | | |
| Job openings | | |
| Your favorite comic strip | | |
| Stock averages | | |

### Getting information from news stories

A news story gives you the facts about current events. After reading a news story, you should be able to answer questions about a news event. Usually a news story will answer who, what, when, and where. Sometimes a story will tell how and why something happened.

## ACTIVITY 3

Read these news stories and answer the questions that follow each story.

### Reading news stories

---

# Girls don't lag in math, study finds

By Jon Van

**GIRLS ARE JUST** as good as boys are at learning difficult mathematics, according to a study by University of Chicago researchers.

The study contradicts a Johns Hopkins University report that concluded that boys are inherently better than girls at mathematical reasoning.

"There just is no difference at all between the ability of boys and girls to learn mathematics," said Zalman Usiskin, associate professor of education at the University of Chicago.

Usiskin and two colleagues, Sharon Senk and Roberta Dees, tested 1,366 high school students in classrooms across the country to measure their ability to write proofs for geometry problems. It was the first large-scale test of geometry proof ability ever undertaken in the United States.

"Writing these proofs involves the highest order of thinking in high school mathematics," Usiskin said. "We found that in some areas the girls did better and in other areas the boys did, but there were no consistent differences that could be explained by sex."

**THE RESULTS** directly contradict a study by J.C. Stanley and C.P. Benbow of Johns Hopkins that was given widespread publicity a few years ago, Usiskin said.

In that study, exceptionally bright children in the 6th and 7th grades were given high school level Scholastic Aptitude Tests, and the boys scored better in mathematics than the girls.

Those tests required a knowledge of high school algebra that neither the boys nor the girls had learned in school, Usiskin said. The fact that boys did better than girls may mean they learned more math outside of class than the girls, but it doesn't prove a genetic difference, he said.

"There was nothing genetic in the Hopkins study, and we felt they were going a little far on the basis of test scores alone to suggest a genetic difference between the sexes," Usiskin said.

**THE UNIVERSITY** of Chicago study tested pupils over material they had been taught in school.

"If boys and girls are in the same class, exposed to the same material, there is no difference in their ability to learn mathematics," Usiskin said.

---

1. What is the main subject of this article? _____

2. What was done? _____

3. Why was it done? _____

4. How was it done? _____

5. Where was it done? _____

6. How many high school students were tested for this study? _____

7. Were the boys and girls in this study tested separately? _____

8. What is the name of the test that was given to 6th- and 7th-grade students in a study done a few years ago? _____

9. What are the names of the three people who did the most recent study? _____

_____

10. Were students in the most recent study tested in algebra or in geometry? _____

_____

# Pupils go to mat in Academic Olympics

By Casey Banas
Education editor

NINE-YEAR-OLD Carl Jones normally kneels at his bedside, says his prayers, climbs into bed and falls fast asleep, but his nightly routine has been different during the last four weeks.

He still recites his prayers without fail, but then reaches under his pillow for a piece of paper and goes to work. "I put my poem under my pillow so I could memorize it," he said.

On Tuesday, his bedtime efforts paid off as Carl became a champion in the District 9 Academic Olympics. He is a 4th grader at Dodge Elementary School, 2651 W. Washington Blvd., and he was the school's representative in the oratory contest, one area of competition among 20 elementary schools in the West Side district.

Standing perhaps two whiskers higher than 3 feet and weighing about 40 pounds, little Carl seemed like a speck on the auditorium stage of Crane High School, 2245 W. Jackson Blvd.

BUT HE WAS dynamite and the jam-packed crowd of 600 children and adults applauded thunderously when Carl finished a spirited recital, complete with extensive gestures, of Lucille Clifton's poem about black pride, "Black B C's."
He began:

*A is for Africa land of sun*
*The king of continents the ancient one*
*B is for books where readers find*
*Treasures for heart and mind*
*C is for cowboys king of the West*
*Black men were some of the best*

And he ended:

*Z is for zenith highest, top*
*The place for us and there we'll stop*

Carl was one of more than 200 youngsters, winners in local school contests, who battled for medals in oratory, math, essay, and quiz competitions as other classmates cheered them on in an atmosphere usually experienced at athletic events.

THE EDUCATORS, seeking to replicate some of the classic rituals of the Olympic games, started the competition with a parade of school banners into the auditorium. Earlean Lindsey, the district council president, carried a torch.

After various events, officials slipped medals around the necks of the champions and runners-up, who stood on pedestals denoting first-, second- and third-place finishes.

The Academic Olympics is not the brainchild of Board of Education members or the superintendent of schools but of inner-city administrators, principals, and teachers who want to elevate the achievements levels of their pupils. They turned to an old-fashioned remedy: Academic competition among schools.

Preston Bryant, superintendent of District 10 on the West Side, started the grass-roots move three years ago with the first districtwide Academic Olympics among elementary schools under his jurisdiction.

"WE SAW a need for encouraging our youngsters to look toward academic instead of sports areas," Bryant said. "It also gave teachers added emphasis and gusto to teach the curriculum."

Now the Academic Olympics idea has spread to seven inner-city districts—Districts 7, 8, 9, 10, 11, 13 and 14 on the West, Near West and South Sides. Each district is having its own competition this month, and on June 1 and 2 there will be a "challenge of champions" for winners from the seven districts at Young High School.

The children and their teachers have worked for weeks to prepare for the competition, putting in scores of hours of their own time in studying math, literature, science, social studies, art and music.

They were kids like Valencia Murray, a 6th grader at Skinner Elementary School, 111 S. Throop St., who admitted she was nervous but said, "I read more science and social studies books at home to prepare for this."

VALENCIA WAS one of five members of her school's "Academic Bowl" and had to be ready to answer in an instant questions on any elementary school subject. The "Academic Bowl" is reminiscent of the old television "College Bowl" show when teams of college students had to answer questions in a flash.

Nine schools competed Tuesday in a semifinal round. The pupils from Gladstone Elementary, 1231 S. Damen Ave., led the way with 225 points as Everette Lowe, an 8th grader, repeatedly came up with instant correct answers to questions such as: "What is conversation between characters called in a short story or novel?" ["Dialogue."] "Who was the first black to sing in the Metropolitan Opera?" ["Marian Anderson."] "What age must a person attain in order to become President of the United States?" [35.] "What are old Egyptian picture writings called?" ["Hieroglyphics."]

Moments after leading his team off the stage, Lowe said:

"I'm relieved and very happy. I was cold all over. My heart was pounding. We came to school early every morning and we were drilled again and again."

He and other Gladstone team members were quick to praise their teacher and coach, Virginia Dow, for her efforts in training them.

Roger Heaps, instructional coordinator for District 9 and quizmaster for the "Academic Bowl," observed:

"See how the kids really get into it? The participants here will go back to their schools and tell others how exciting it is. This will generate more interest next year. But I only wish we would be able to film the competition and show children in schools so they could see the excitement."

1. Who is Carl Jones? _____

2. What did he do? _____

3. Where was the Academic Olympics held? _____

4. Why did educators create the Academic Olympics? _____

5. Where in the city did these educators teach? _____

**Editorials**  The newspaper has an opinion section called the editorial page. On this page the editors write their ideas and opinions on news topics. Sometimes the publisher of a newspaper will comment on a current issue or news event. Some newspapers also ask their readers to write in with their opinions.

Below is a sample editorial. A local newspaper is giving its opinion on an issue that affects its readers.

# Interstate Tunnel Detours Important

Commercial trucking firms hauling hazardous cargoes are likely to look on interstate highway detours as an expensive, time-consuming nuisance.

There are two such detours on Interstate 77 — one at the East River Mountain tunnel on the West Virginia-Virginia state line, and a second at the Big Walker Mountain tunnel in Virginia.

But these two particular detours serve a very important purpose — they route hazardous traffic — such as gasoline and high explosives — around the tunnels, thereby helping to reduce the chance of an accident which could result in fatality-causing explosions and heavy damage or destruction of the tunnels, both of which are about a mile long. Unfortunately, no such restrictions apply to a third tunnel on I-77 — the one on the West Virginia Turnpike section of I-77.

Last week's tanker truck explosion which followed a collision with a bus in an Oakland, Calif. highway tunnel proves just how important detours for hazardous cargoes can be.

The tanker truck, loaded with more than 8,000 gallons of gasoline, blew up in the tunnel, creating a 1,000-degree inferno that melted vehicles in seconds and incinerated their occupants. Six people were known dead.

Spilling gasoline ignited and flashed into a fireball that in seconds roared through about a third of the half-mile-long tunnel, melting brass fittings, popping tipes from the walls, and turning a 2-inch-thick concrete lining into sooty powder.

If such an accident ever occurred in one of the three tunnels on Interstate I-77, the resulting damage could effectively block through traffic for months or years, rendering partially ineffective one of this state's two major north-south highways.

West Virginia and Virginia have too much invested in their high-cost interstates to let this happen. The detour regulation is a good one.

In this editorial the paper lists some of the dangers of driving hazardous cargoes through tunnels. The piece of writing has both facts and opinions. Unlike the news story, the facts are not just reported. They are used to back up the opinion. The whole editorial builds an argument *in favor of* highway detours.

An editorial should not be confused with a news story. News stories are reports. They give the who, what, when, and where of events. They give the facts as they happened. Although an editorial may use facts, it is an *opinion column.*

## ACTIVITY 4

### Editorials and news stories: "facts vs. opinion"

Read each statement below. Decide if the statement belongs in an editorial or in a news story.

1.  Property taxes should not be the way to pay for schools.                                      Editorial    News Story

2.  Thirty-four billion dollars in property taxes are used for schools each year.                 Editorial    News Story

3.  More freeways will bring more business to the downtown area.                                  Editorial    News Story

4.  Two new freeways will be finished in 1993.                                                    Editorial    News Story

5.  If election days were changed to Saturdays instead of Tuesdays, more people would vote.       Editorial    News Story

6.  There was a 65 percent voter turnout at the last election.                                    Editorial    News Story

7.  Our town needs a new park on Main Street.                                                     Editorial    News Story

8.  The city council voted 9–6 in favor of building a park on Main Street.                        Editorial    News Story

9.  The last day of the school year is June 16.                                                   Editorial    News Story

10. The present school calendar is inconvenient for many people.                                  Editorial    News Story

## ACTIVITY 5

Answer the questions about the following editorial.

**Reading editorials**

### The Roar Of Motorcycles

Raleigh County Sheriff Claude England has decided it is a waste of his deputies' time and his department's money to answer calls concerning disturbances by youngsters riding motorcycles.

Even if a deputy can catch a youngster on a motorcycle, he has to release the youngster into the custody of his parents. And more than likely, his parents are the ones who have paid for the motorcycle and given the child permission to ride it.

England is also concerned that a youngster on a motorcycle will be seriously injured if a deputy chases him. An accident can happen during the chase, particularly if the youngster is trying to resist arrest.

Understandably, England doesn't want to get sued over a matter which is mostly a nuisance.

There is something people can do who are sick and tired of juvenile delinquents riding through their flower beds on their motorbikes. They can take out a warrant for the child's parents.

We hope this option will be exercised frequently when youngsters insist on disturbing the peace. The parents are, after all, responsible for their youngster's behavior. They should feel the full weight of the law.

1. This editorial is based on what issue? _____

2. What is the newspaper's opinion? _____

3. Are any facts used to support the paper's opinion? If so, what are these facts? _____

_____

4. Do you agree with the opinion? Explain why or why not. _____

_____

**Using the classified ads**

Many newspaper readers would be lost without the classified ad section. This section tells them about job openings. It tells them where they can buy a doghouse or a used piano. It lists houses for sale. It also lists new and used cars for sale.

Have you ever used the classified section of your newspaper? Ads in this section are in alphabetical order. These listings are grouped under headings. These headings are called "classifications." There may also be classification numbers.

## ACTIVITY 6

### Reading the "classifieds"

Read the classified ads below. They are ads for apartments and used cars. Abbreviations are used in some of these ads. Answer the questions about these ads. Look for clues within the ads to help you figure out what the abbreviations stand for.

---

**UNFURN. APTS.**

4 LARGE RM APT — mod. kitchen & bath, h/hw suppl'd, 2 children accepted. Call 926-0359.

4 ROOM APT — H & HW Supl'd, Avail. Oct. 1st, So. 16th St. Area Sec. Req'd, Call 926-4658

4 ROOMS — H & HW supl'd, $495. Mo. + Sec. 1 child accepted. Call 923-4772

4 ROOMS, H/HW, secure building. See Mark, Apt 8, 830 Clinton Ave. Immed. occup. 372-3919.

517 SO 17th St. 4 rms & bath, HT/Hw incl. $435 + sec. Apply 2nd fl. front. or call 753-6471.

5 NICE RMS. 535 So. 19th St. Rent $365, supply own gas heat. Adults pref. Call eves 992-7199

5 RMS. — 1st flr. 138 Huntington Terr. H/HW supplied. $510 + sec. Call 672-7266 between 6–10PM.

5 1/2 RMS
$580/MO, H/HW
Call aft 6, 374-2836

5 ROOM APT — near downtown. Heat & Hot Water sup'd. $465/Per mo + 1 mo security. Call 624-4399 or 356-4902.

5 ROOMS, 2 BR's, heat furnished, $470., sec required, adults only. Call aft 6pm 672-7786

5 ROOMS. Adult cpl. preferred, Prefer no children, but will accept 1. 137 Seymour Ave.

---

Availabilities

# COLONNADE APARTMENTS

| Studio | $425* |
| 1 Bedrooms | $500* |
| 2 Bedrooms | $575* |
| 2 BRS, Den + 2 Baths | $710* |

*TYPICAL RENTS
SUBJECT TO AVAILABILITY

• 24 HR GUARD SERVICE
• ON SITE PARKING
• BUSES TO N.Y.C.

**Apartment Features Included in Rent**

• GAS
• HEAT & HOT WATER

Call 484-8300

---

1. How much is the rent for the apartment at 517 South 17th Street?

   _____

2. Must the renter pay a security deposit for this apartment? _____

3. What number do you call to inquire about the 5 1/2 -room apartment that rents for $580 a month? _____

4. What four types of apartments can you rent at Colonnade?

   _____

   _____

   _____

5. Which of the Colonnade Apartments is the least expensive? _____

6. Which is the most expensive? _____

7. After reading these ads, what do you think these abbreviations mean?

   rm. _____

   H/HW _____

   sec. _____

   mod. _____

   avail. _____

   immed. occup. _____

   pref. _____

   cpl. _____

| Used Domestic Autos   820<br>For Sale | Used Domestic Autos   820<br>For Sale |
|---|---|
| **FORD '85**—Country Sq. wgn., 9 pass., fully pwr'd. V8, wdgrain, lug. rack, very lo mi., immac. cond., no dents or rust, orig. owner, gar'd. $3350, 555-0915 | **FORD '91**—TAURUS<br>23K mi., V6, loaded, gar. kept. Exc. cond. $8800. 555-0835 |
| **FORD '86**—Escort L Station Wagon, Auto, ps/pb, cruise, a/c, am/fm stereo, delayed wipers, pwr. remote rear view mirrors, very good cond. in/out, good running cond. Must see! Askg. $1,625/? 555-5933 | **FORD '91**—Taurus, 23K mi., V6, loaded, gar. kept, exc. cond., $8800. 555-0835 |
| | **FORD '91** Mustang GT Convt — fully loaded, extend warr., $14,300. 555-9167. eve. |
| **FORD '86**—Escort L Stat. Wgn., auto., ps, pb, a/c, am-fm, delay wipers, low mi., clean $2955-obo. N.W. Chicago. 555-2421 | **LINC. '73**—Mark IV, 71K mi., white orig. paint, exc. cond., no rust, $2900-obo. 555-3014 |
| **FORD '87**—Escort GL, 70K mi., auto., new brks/shcks/tires, fair cond., nd. work, $600/ofr. Mech. special! No radio. 555-5141 | **LINC' 74**—MARK IV. Triple black, slightly damaged, driven daily, $600 555-5461 aft. 5 pm |
| **FORD '87**—TEMPO LX TOP OF THE LINE! EXC. COND.! IMMACULATE! LOW MIS.! health. $2495. 555-6808 | **LINC. '78**—Diam. Jubilee Ed., lo. mi., loaded, mn rf, exc. cond., gar. kept, $1500, 555-0942 |
| | **LINC. '81**—Continental Mark VI, 2 dr., no rust, clean, gar. kept. Must see! $1,995. 555-1485 |
| **FORD '89** Aerostar—38k mi., 5 pass, a/c, tilt, cruise, ster. & 4/def. $6700 obo. 555-5391. | **LINC. '87**—Mark VII, Bill Blass series, all pwr., exc. cond., new brks, hwy. miles, gar'd., must sell! $6,700/obo. 555-3729 |
| **FORD '89**—Taurus GL, 4 dr., V6, a/c, ps., pb., am/fm, tilt, cruise, gar'd. Ready for winter, exc. cond. $5,350. 555-0784 | **LINC '88**—MARK VII CPE. Fully loaded, all opts., gar. kept. Exc. cond. $8,900. 555-5724 |
| **FORD '90**—Taurus Wgn. GL pwr. seats, pl, cruise, tilt, cass, lo. mi., mint. Must sell $7850 555-7385 | **LINC. '89**—TOWN CAR Low mi., like new, $13,200. Call days 555-3232 |
| **FORD'90**—Tempo GL, 4 dr., auto, wht-blue, a/c PW, PL, p-seats, cruise, tilt, cass., 31K mi., exc. cond. $5250. 555-6787 | **LINC. '90**—TOWN CAR SIG. Blk. 26k CM  $17,995  ***WOODFIELD LEXUS*** 555-0200 |

1. After reading these car ads, what do you think these abbreviations mean?

   ps _____

   pb _____

   lo. mi. _____

   gar. kept _____

   exc. cond. _____

   a/c _____

   r/def. _____

2. How many Ford Aerostars are advertised? _____

3. What is the asking price for the '78 Lincoln Diamond Jubilee Edition? _____

4. What is the price of the '91 Ford Mustang?

   _____

5. How many Escorts are advertised? _____

6. List all the features on the 1989 Ford Taurus.

   _____

   _____

   _____

   _____

7. Is the 1990 Lincoln Town Car advertised by an individual or a car dealership? _____

8. When an ad says a car is "loaded," what do you think this means? _____

   _____

9. When an ad says "$5900 firm," what does this mean? _____

   _____

Here are some words you should know when you read and use a newspaper. Choose the correct word or words for the following sentences.

editorial         alphabetical        feature

index              obituary           classified ad

1. I can find the page in the newspaper that lists the movies for today by looking in the _____ .

2. A good way to find a used car is to look in the _____ section.

3. In today's _____ the editor argued against raising telephone rates.

4. Items in an index are usually listed in _____ order.

5. I saw the news of his death listed on the _____ page.

6. I enjoy _____ articles in the travel section.

Decide whether each of the following statements is TRUE (T) or FALSE (F).

_____ 7. An editorial always tells all the facts about an issue.

_____ 8. You can find a list of the restaurants in your neighborhood in the classified section of the newspaper.

_____ 9. "Letters to the editor" in a newspaper are likely to contain the writers' opinions.

_____ 10. Classified ads are grouped by subjects or classifications.

# SHOW WHAT YOU KNOW . . .

## About Reading Newspapers

Use a newspaper to find examples of the following:

1. An index
2. An editorial
3. The horoscopes
4. A news story
5. Classified ads for apartments

## Help-wanted ads

Newspapers charge for classified ads. The longer the ad, the more you pay. People buying ad space usually try to write short ads. To read classified ads, you must know what the abbreviations stand for. Job ads, like all classified ads, may have abbreviations and leave out words.

The name of a job is often shortened. An ad may show a typist job as "TYPST." An opening for a manager could appear as "MGR. WANTED." Look at the job ad abbreviations above. How many of them do you know?

Job ads can be found in the classified section of your newspaper. These ads may have the heading "Help Wanted." They may also appear under headings such as "Employment" or "Employment Opportunity." The help-wanted section is a good source for job leads. There are usually a lot of different job openings listed in this section of the paper. These ads tell you the types of jobs that are open. They also tell you how to apply for a particular job. Many ads tell you how much education you need. Some ads tell you if experience is necessary to get a certain job. Some ads give information about pay, hours, and benefits.

Type of job ● ———————

Experience and/or ● ——————
education needed

> Bus Boys and Girls—Good for H.S. students; afternoon and evening hours; experience preferred but will train; apply in person. Mable's Restaurant, 567 Main St.

——————— ● Hours to work

——————— ● How to apply

## ACTIVITY 7
### Reading want ad abbreviations

For this activity, match the want ad abbreviations in column A with the words in column B.

**A** | **B**

_____ **1.** ass't.     **a.** education

_____ **2.** pref'd.     **b.** department

_____ **3.** educ.     **c.** minimum

_____ **4.** min.     **d.** license

_____ **5.** temp.     **e.** weekly

_____ **6.** dpt.     **f.** preferred

_____ **7.** lic.     **g.** assistant

_____ **8.** trncc.     **h.** veteran

_____ **9.** vet.     **i.** trainee

_____ **10.** wkly.     **j.** temporary

## ACTIVITY 8
### Reading want ad abbreviations

The help-wanted ads below contain abbreviations. Words are left out, too. In this activity, you are to write out each ad in words. If you see an unfamiliar abbreviation, try to use the words you do know as clues to identify it.

Example:

SEC'Y WANTED.
    **F/T**
Work with exec.
in office bldg.
in downtown loc.
Type 45 w.p.m.
Call 999-8383 for appt.
M/F

SECRETARY WANTED
    **Full Time**
Work with executive
in office building
in downtown location.
Type 45 words per minute.
Call 999-8383 for appointment.
Male/Female.

**1.** Apt. Mgr.
Exp. for new high-rise
bldg., salary, apt., and
incentives.

_____

_____

_____

_____

_____

**2.** Sec'y.
Appliance store.
Answer phone, file, no
exp. nec., but must type
60 w.p.m.

_____

_____

_____

_____

**3.** Fitters.
5 yrs. exper. Good wages
and bfts.

_____

_____

_____

_____

**4.** Die Makers
Day wk.  Full bfts.

_____

_____

_____

_____

**5.** Quality Control Asst.
2 yrs. exp. req'd. in
automotive, gd. wages,
bfts.

_____

_____

_____

_____

**6.** Lab Tech.
All-around plate man.
Permanent position,
excel. conditions &
salary.

_____

_____

_____

_____

# SHOW WHAT YOU KNOW . . .

## About Help-Wanted Ads

Write a help-wanted ad for your "ideal" teacher. Use at least five (5) of the abbreviations given in this section.

## ACTIVITY 9

### Reading want ads for information

The want ads below are typical job ads. Notice that these ads are set up in alphabetical order. Words are left out of these ads. Only key words and phrases are used. Read each ad carefully. Then complete the statements below.

DISHWASHER—Exper. only need apply. 151 East Street. Call Larry 555-5035.

EXECUTIVE TRAINEE H.S.G. or some college. No exp. nec. Acme Personnel, 555-1200.

FASHION MODELS Men 5'8" or taller, Women 5'2" or taller needed for commercials, fashion and product advertising, Ms. Modeling Agency, 555-9683.

KITCHEN HELPER Must be dependable. Good bfts. Call at the Money Tree, 222 Lane St. bet. 2:30–5:30 p.m.

LABORERS—General factory work, hard shoes, report ready to work 5:30 a.m. and 2 p.m. 1947 River Rd.

PIZZA MAKER Exp. only. Good wages, full or part time. After 2 p.m. 555-7380.

1. The jobs that require previous experience are _____

_____ .

2. You may apply for the kitchen helper's job at _____ between the hours of _____ .

3. The executive trainee job is being handled by _____ .

4. You would call _____ about the fashion model's job.

5. For the laborer's job you must bring _____ and be ready to work.


## ACTIVITY 10

### Looking for specific jobs in the want ads

1. Look in the want ad section of your local newspaper for job openings for the following types of workers.
   a. Typist—no experience
   b. Secretary—on one year's experience
   c. Laborer—no experience
   d. Waitperson/Server—some experience
   e. Busser/Busperson—six months' experience

2. How would you apply for these positions? List telephone numbers, addresses, person(s) to contact, and any other useful information.

   Typist _____

   _____

Secretary _____

_____

Laborer _____

_____

Server _____

_____

Busser _____

_____

# ACTIVITY 11

## Using the help-wanted section of the newspaper

Have you ever read the help-wanted section of a newspaper for a large city? If you have, you know that there are a variety of jobs advertised. Use these ads from a city paper to answer the questions below.

| 031 HELP WANTED | 031 HELP WANTED |
|---|---|
| ARCADE ATTENDANT 5–10 p.m. 555-6801 | SERVERS—wanted Burger Basement, min. 3 yrs. exper. Apply in person, bet. 7–9 p.m. Mon.–Fri., 33205 Oak, Landview. |
| BEAUTICIANS—Exp. Prefer clientele—555-1410 | STOCK PERSON—No exp. nec. 555-9801 aft. 3 |
| BOOKKEEPER Full charge, exp 10 hrs. wkly. Westwood area. P.O. Box 8170, Westwood | TYPIST—40 wpm, p.t. 3–6 p.m. 555-7870 |
| CAB DRIVER—Exp'd only. 555-4888 aft. 5 | USED CAR BUMP MAN Work on salary, must have tools. Tom or Jim, 555-7272 aft. 10 |
| CAREER MINDED Pay-TV installers. Top wages, need tools. Send resume to Box C–1605, Local Press, Springfield. | WAIT STAFF experienced, good tips, apply in person only. Pine Valley Diner, 16 Elm Street, Pine Valley. |
| CASHIER COUNTER Help Needed Now—Call today, good pay. Call Job Finders, Inc. $60 fee. 555-8400. | |

1. Which number could you call if you were interested in a typist's job? _____

2. How many openings are there for a cab driver? _____

3. If you are a pay-TV installer, where can you send your resume? _____

4. What number would you call if you wanted a job as an arcade attendant? _____

5. Where can a person with no job experience apply? _____

6. Which company charges a fee for locating jobs? _____

Write out the full word for each abbreviation.

1. exp. _____
2. ass't. _____
3. pref'd. _____
4. sal. _____
5. sec'y. _____

6. educ. _____
7. p/t _____
8. wkly. _____
9. trnee. _____
10. dpt. _____

Select the phrase that correctly completes each sentence.

_____ 11. To find the job listings for part-time waitstaff, you must
   a. look through all the job ads.
   b. find the section labeled "Waitstaff" or "Restaurant"
   c. find the sections labeled "Waitstaff" or "Restaurant" and "Part-time."

_____ 12. When an ad says "min. 3 yrs. exp." and you have six months of experience, you should
   a. make an application anyway.
   b. lie about your experience.
   c. keep looking for a job ad that matches your experience and skills.

_____ 13. When a job ad says "apply in person" you should
   a. write a letter and drop it off at the address in the ad.
   b. telephone the place.
   c. go directly to the address in the ad yourself.

_____ 14. When an ad says "must be dependable," the employer will be looking for a person who
   a. arrives regularly and on time.
   b. has a good appearance.
   c. lives nearby.

_____ 15. Ads for secretaries often say "must type 60 w.p.m." or "must type 40 w.p.m."
   This probably means
   a. you can simply say that your typing meets their requirements.
   b. you could be given a typing test.
   c. you simply need to be able to do some typing.

# Reading critically

As a buyer, you see or hear many advertising messages each day. These messages often urge you to buy an item because it is marked down. Sometimes a special offer sounds too good to be true. To spend your money wisely, you must be able to read these ads critically. You must also be able to evaluate special offers.

## Advertisements

### WORDS TO KNOW

**bandwagon appeal**   the suggestion that you should not miss out on something that lots of other people are doing or buying

**consumer**   any person who buys and uses up, or consumes, a product

**endorse**   to give approval, such as the famous football player advertising a well-known soft drink

**imply**   to suggest something that is not said; for example, implying that a beautiful appearance will lead to fame and fortune

**glowing generality**   a statement that says something is wonderful or great without giving proof; no specific information

**guarantee**   a promise of quality or length of use. Often the seller promises to fix or replace a product for a certain length of time

**option**   an extra feature, usually for an additional price

**symbol**   an object that stands for something else, such as beautiful hair for happiness or a car for success

**technique**   a method or way of doing something

**vanity**   inflated pride in yourself or your appearance

Do you read the ads in newspapers and magazines? Have you ever bought something simply because it was on sale? Have you ever bought a product because it was endorsed by a superstar? Advertisements are aimed at consumers. They try to make you spend your money. People do buy products because of ads they have seen.

There are many ways you can learn about a product. A friend could recommend a product to you. You could hear about a product at school or work. Sometimes you see something new and decide to buy it. However, most buyers learn about products through ads.

Makers of products spend millions of dollars a year in advertising. They want you to know what they have for sale. They reach you through television and radio commercials. They advertise in newspapers. They advertise in magazines and on billboards.

As a consumer, there are lots of things you need to know about the products you buy. This makes advertising important. Here are some of the things you can learn from ads:

- What an item costs
- What it looks like
- What features it has
- Where you can get it
- How long it can be gotten
- Who makes it
- How it compares to other brands
- Whether it's guaranteed

This type of information is important to you. Sometimes advertisers forget this. They may be advertising a good product, but they don't tell you much about it. Instead, they try to get your attention in other ways. Some advertisers need to use these techniques to sell their product. They know their product does not have a famous brand name. They know the product may lack quality. And they know it may not have sales appeal.

Many sellers of products hire trained people to write their ads. Ad firms use talented people—artists, photographers, writers—to think up ads that will appeal to you. They create ads that they hope will make you want to buy a product. You may see a movie star holding up a jar of Crunchy Nut Peanut Butter. You may buy this peanut butter just because of the famous person. Children are also targets for ads, especially television ads. TV commercials coax children to ask their parents for Fruity-Froot cereal. They want Fruity-Froot because (1) it comes with a toy whistle, (2) it's chocolate coated, and (3) it's the brand "Super Hero" eats. The point is this: All ads try to make you buy a product. Many of these things you may want, need, and can afford. But there are other products that ads *make* you want. You may not need these things.

As a buyer, you must learn to judge ads. You must watch out for advertising techniques. You must learn to look for the facts about what you are buying.

Here are some things you should know about ads:

1. *Some ads are not truthful.* The seller or maker of a product simply does not tell the truth about the product.
2. *Some ads tell half the truth.* This type of advertising misleads the buyer. The ad will *suggest* that something is true. An ad may say just enough to make you say the rest. Sometimes the ad may tell you only half of what you need to know.
3. *Some ads will appeal to your emotions:*
    - your desire to look and feel younger (or older), sexy, handsome
    - your identification with family, friends, country, a TV star
    - memories of "down home" and "the good ol' days"
    - your need to be part of the crowd
4. *Some ads are filled with glowing generalities.* These ads tell you that a product is WONDERFUL, GREAT, FANTASTIC, SUPER, BETTER THAN EVER!
5. *Some ads appeal to your senses,* especially touch and taste. Cotton Cloud Detergent makes your towels feel soft and fluffy. Lemon-Lime Lemonade tastes lemony, limey, and delicious!

## Truth in advertising

It's hard to know if some ads tell the truth. The claims made sound good. The ads are *believable*. This is why many consumer groups go after advertisers who print misleading ads. There are now laws that make advertisers tell you more about products. It is too bad that most people learn that an ad has misled them only after they have bought and used a product. Jan used Dawn's Magic Beauty Cream for three weeks. But she could not get rid of her freckles. Tommy Madison threw out his Body Tone FLEX-erciser. After two weeks he hadn't lost the eight inches of fat the ad said he'd lose. And Sarah Hart put her trust in M–24 Special Formula Mouth Wash. She may never know it doesn't help fight colds.

It's even harder to point out the half-truths. A mail-order school might say that it helps its graduates find jobs. It doesn't say that it directs graduates to the local newspaper. A record club may promise you FOUR HIT RECORDS FREE. If you read the ad closely, you learn that you have to *buy* four albums to keep the four *free* ones.

## ACTIVITY 1
### Reading ads carefully

Answer the questions about the following ads.

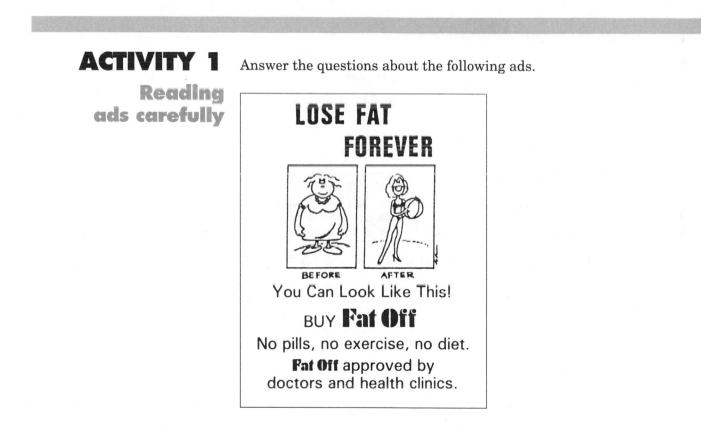

1. List all the information in this ad that you feel may not be true or may be half true.

_____

_____

2. List all the information in this ad that you feel is definitely true (fact).

_____

_____

# GET A CAREER CERTIFICATE

TRAIN AT HOME! ! ! ! ! !

You don't need a high school diploma or an equivalency diploma (GED)—

JUST SIGN UP TODAY

**OUR GRADUATES EARN**

UP TO **$50,000**

Each course is a full semester. You don't have to pay now!
ENROLL NOW FOR THIS SEMESTER! ! !
Just check the home-study course of your choice. Enclose a $10 registration fee.
Begin your training in JUST 2 WEEKS.

- - - - - - - - - - - - - - - - - - - - - - - - - - - - - - - - - - - - - - - - - - - - -

☐ TYPING            ☐ TRUCK DRIVING      ☐ CATERING        ☐ COMPUTER PROGRAMING
☐ AUTO MECHANICS    ☐ HAIR STYLING       ☐ BARBERING       ☐ DRIVER INSTRUCTOR
                                                               TRAINING

GET YOUR CAREER CERTIFICATE TODAY! ! !

I have enclosed $10 for my registration fee. You will bill me later
for tuition. I can choose a convenient payment plan.

I have enclosed a        ☐ Check        ☐ Money Order

Signature _____ Date_____
      (Sign your name in ink)

CAREER CERTIFICATES, Box 80A, Trainingsville, USA

- - - - - - - - - - - - - - - - - - - - - - - - - - - - - - - - - - - - - - - - - - - - -

*********************************************** HURRY ***********************************************

*************** DON'T MISS THIS OPPORTUNITY TO TRAIN AT HOME ***************

**START YOUR NEW CAREER TODAY!**

---

1. Does this ad give you the name of the school? ——————————————

2. Does this ad give you a street address (and a building) or just a box number? ——————

3. List the home study courses being offered.

_____

_____

_____

4. Which of these courses would probably be best taught in a school with an instructor? Explain.

_____

_____

_____

_____

5. Which of these people would probably answer this ad? More than one answer is possible.

_____ a retired person

_____ a college graduate

_____ a high school dropout

_____ a high school graduate with no vocational skills

_____ an adult who never attended high school

6. Which of these things does the ad *imply* (make you think something is true without actually saying it)? More than one answer is possible.

_____ When you finish the course, your "Career Certificate" will help you get a job.

_____ Many people who take a career course earn $50,000 a year.

_____ If you are not happy with the course, you will get your money back.

_____ Your $10 will be refunded if you change your mind in the two weeks before the course begins.

_____ Typing is a better career choice than catering.

_____ You don't have to worry about money now. The important thing is to enroll for the current semester. You can always pay later.

_____ The training is like college. (There are semesters, registration, tuition fees.)

## Emotional appeals

Many ads appeal to your emotions. Some ads may appeal to your vanity. They tell you that you'll look beautiful . . . young . . . sexy . . . handsome. Some ads will touch things dear to you: "Have you talked to your family lately? Call them long distance. It only costs a few pennies." Or "Every American should take stock in America. Buy bonds." Family, friends, country, the flag—all are things that bring out emotions in people. And of course there are strong feelings about things past: homemade goodness, down-home flavor, memories of childhood.

## ACTIVITY 2
### Reading ads with emotional appeal

Each of the ads below appeals to your emotions. Is it your vanity? Your intelligence? Your good looks? Answer the questions about each ad.

INTELLIGENT
  SHOPPERS...

**BUY**

# SUPER SHINE
**FURNITURE POLISH**

They've compared brands-
They know **SUPER SHINE**
**outshines them all!**

What does this ad appeal to?

———

(a) Your need to feel your house is clean?
(b) Your need to feel smart?
(c) Your vanity?

*Feel beautiful. . .*
*    Look beautiful. . .*
*        Be beautiful. . .*

**USE**

*Hair Color Magic*

The shampoo and hair color
for the beautiful you. . .

What does this ad appeal to?

———

(a) Your need to belong
(b) Your intelligence
(c) Your vanity

## ACTIVITY 3
### Reading ads with emotional appeal—"the famous person"

An ad that has a lot of emotional appeal is the famous person ad. Sometimes your favorite television star will endorse a product. You like this person. You are a loyal fan. You transfer your emotions for the person to the product. If "Michael Borden" eats it, wears it, or drinks it, you will too. Maybe if you use Bright White toothpaste, you'll have white, attractive teeth like "Christine Fargate." The next ad is a famous person ad. Answer the questions about this ad.

1. Why do you think this famous person was asked to do this ad? _____

2. This ad is filled with OPINIONS—what a person *thinks* about the product. List all the opinions you

   find in this ad. _____

3. Which of the following statements best summarizes this ad? _____

   (a) Lyle Fetty uses PST in his car, and you should use it in yours.

   (b) Whatever is good for Lyle Fetty's car is good for everybody's car because he's a famous race driver.

   (c) PST will make your car run well enough for the Indiana 600.

## ACTIVITY 4

**Reading ads with emotional appeal—"get on the bandwagon"**

Some ads appeal to your need to follow the crowd. Many people call this the bandwagon ad. The ad makes you feel left out—not in with what everyone else is doing. Read the following ad carefully. Then answer the questions about it.

1. List all the words and phrases that appeal to a person's desire to join the crowd. _____

_____

2. How does this ad use *art* to help convince you that you should "get on the bandwagon"? _____

3. Do you think that buying something because everyone else seems to be is a good reason? Explain why

you feel the way you do. _____

## Glowing generalities

When you read an ad, you should expect to find out more about a product. Has the brand been tested? If so, by whom? What is being said? Are there facts that can be checked out? How does the product compare to other brands? What does it cost? How long does it last? Sometimes, instead of facts, ads contain a lot of general statements. If all the generalities were taken out of the ad, you would find that the ad told you very little, if anything, about the product.

## ACTIVITY 5
### Reading ads— specific information or glowing generality

Read the following ad and the statements from this ad. Do the statements contain specific information or glowing generalities?

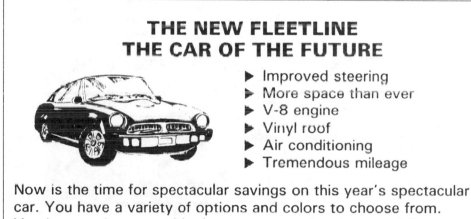

**THE NEW FLEETLINE
THE CAR OF THE FUTURE**

▶ Improved steering
▶ More space than ever
▶ V-8 engine
▶ Vinyl roof
▶ Air conditioning
▶ Tremendous mileage

Now is the time for spectacular savings on this year's spectacular car. You have a variety of options and colors to choose from. You have a chance to ride the most sensational automobile on the road, the Fleetline—Tomorrow's car—today.

|  | Specific information | Glowing generality |
|---|---|---|
| 1. The Fleetline has a V-8 engine. | _____ | _____ |
| 2. The Fleetline gives you tremendous mileage. | _____ | _____ |
| 3. This car has "more space than ever." | _____ | _____ |
| 4. The Fleetline comes with a vinyl roof. | _____ | _____ |
| 5. The Fleetline comes in a variety of colors. | _____ | _____ |
| 6. The Fleetline is this year's spectacular car. | _____ | _____ |

## ACTIVITY 6

**Evaluating popular advertisements: Finding out what types of ads appeal to you**

In this activity you will look at several ads. These ads are for famous products. Many of the ads you may have read before. You will be asked questions about each of these ads. These questions will help you find out (1) if you are able to identify advertising techniques, (2) if you can separate facts from opinions, and (3) what type(s) of ads appeal to you. Be prepared to discuss your answers in class.

Read this ad for Sweet Dreams books. Answer the questions about it.

1. What type of person do you think this ad appeals to? _____

2. Does it appeal to you? Explain why or why not.

_____

3. Give examples of words or phrases in the ad that show these types of emotional appeal.

   (a) a person's need to be popular _____

   (b) a person's desire to be beautiful _____

   (c) a person's identification with dreams and fantasies instead of reality _____

Look at the ad for a hair care product on page 81. Read it carefully. This ad uses pictures of people for much of its appeal. Answer the questions about the ad.

1. What emotion does this ad appeal to? _____

   _____

2. Make a list of the glowing generalities in this ad.

   _____

   _____

   _____

   _____

   _____

   _____

3. Does this ad contain any facts about the product? If so, what are they?

   _____

   _____

   _____

   _____

4. What reasons does the ad give for you to buy this product?

   _____

   _____

   _____

   _____

Read this ad. Separate the facts in it from the opinions.

- "Zits are the Pits."

- Buf-Oxal is a benzoyl peroxide gel.

- Buf-Oxal is gentle.

- You will be surprised at how quickly Buf-Oxal will clean up your pimples, blackheads, and blemishes.

- Buf-Oxal is available in 5% and 10% strengths.

- Buf-Oxal is water-based.


**Facts**

_____

_____

_____

_____

_____

_____


**Opinions**

_____

_____

_____

_____

_____

_____

Here are some words you should know when you are reading ads critically. Find the correct word for each of the statements below.

guarantee              endorse           vanity
bandwagon appeal       optional          glowing generality

1.  My new watch came with a _____ against defects for six months.

2.  The ad for skin cream says that your skin will feel great after using the cream. This statement is a

   _____ .

3.  Ads for certain kinds of sweaters or jackets appeal to a person's _____ .

4.  Ads for certain products say that since so many other people are buying the product, you should

   too. This is called a _____ .

5.  Certain features, like air conditioning, are _____ on a new car.

6.  During baseball season, famous players often _____ certain products.

List the advertising techniques used in each of the following quotations from ads. Refer to p. 72 for a list of the advertising techniques you have been studying.

7.  "Driving is a new sensation . . . America's most popular sports car. Hot stuff." _____

8.  "Don't miss this wonderful product." _____

9.  "Lose 10 pounds in one week without dieting!" _____

10. "Sheets that are soft, smooth, fragrant." _____

# SHOW WHAT YOU KNOW . . .

## About Advertisements

Find at least two (2) examples of each type of ad listed below. Number them 1–8, but do not label them. On a separate sheet of paper, write the numbers 1–8 and identify each ad. This is your answer key.

1. Lies and half-truths

2. Bandwagon appeal

3. Emotional appeal

4. Glowing generalities

During class, exchange ads with a partner. Attempt to identify the ads on a separate sheet of paper. After you are finished, exchange answer keys. Correct your answers.

## Special offers

**WORDS TO KNOW**

**cancel** to call off

**coupon** a printed form that can be used to get money back or obtain a lower price on a product

**discount** a reduction from the regular price

**expiration date** the date after which an offer is no longer available

**obligation** a promise

**redeem** to get back something of value, such as turning in a coupon for cash

**refund** a return of money

**subscriber** person who agrees to buy a certain number of issues of a publication on a regular basis

**subscription** an agreement to buy a certain number of issues of a publication, such as a newspaper or magazine

The consumer's world is filled with sales offers. Many offers are found in newspapers and magazines. Others come to you in the mail. These special offers can mean savings to you. However, you must read these offers very carefully. How much of a savings will you get? What will your responsibilities be?

## Reading magazine subscription offers

With a subscription you can get magazines through the mail at discount prices. Magazine subscriptions are often for one or two years. Sometimes magazines have special offers for short periods. These offers give very low prices. They are for *new* subscribers. A subscriber's rate will be below the newsstand price.

When you read subscription offers, there are three things you want to know: (1) how long your subscription will last (or how many issues you will get), (2) what the subscription will cost, and (3) how much of a savings you will get.

## ACTIVITY 7

**Interpreting magazine subscription offers**

Read the following magazine subscription offer. Decide whether the statements about the offer are TRUE (T) or FALSE (F).

---

**FOR THE 52 WEEKS OF CHRISTMAS**

The one Christmas gift that's
always the right size,
shape, color and price.

**JET**

An Attractive Card Announces Your Gift

First one-year subscription $24.00
Each additional subscription $20.00
Offer Good in United States Only

Your Name_____
*Please Print*

Address_____ Apt. #_____

City_____

State_____ Zip_____

_____My own order          _____Renewal with Gifts

Payment Enclosed $_____ Bill me_____

Mail To: JET Gift Subscriptions, 820 South Michigan Ave., Chicago, Illinois 60605

Name_____
*Please Print*

Address_____ Apt. #_____

City_____

State_____ Zip_____

Gift Card From_____

Name_____
*Please Print*

Address_____ Apt. #_____

City_____

State_____ Zip_____

Gift Card From_____

Name_____
*Please Print*

Address_____ Apt. #_____

City_____

State_____ Zip_____

Gift Card From_____

---

_____ **1.** This is a weekly magazine.

_____ **2.** You may have a gift card sent with gift subscriptions.

_____ **3.** Your first subscription will cost $24.00.

_____ **4.** Each additional subscription will cost $20.00.

_____ **5.** Canadians can take advantage of this offer for a slightly higher cost.

Music club memberships appeal to both teenagers and adults. These offers require specific reading skills. You may be able to save money on recordings. To get the special prices, however, you usually must agree to make more purchases.

When you read these offers, read for specific details. Know how many more purchases you have to make. Read to understand what kind of discount, if any, you will get as a member. Know what kind of musical choices you will have. Will you be able to select classical music? country? dance pop? R & B? hard rock? rap? Read to find out what you must do if you ever want to cancel your membership. All this information should be somewhere in the club membership offer.

## ACTIVITY 8

### Reading a CD offer for details

Read the CD (compact disc) offer on the next page. Then answer the questions below.

1. How much must you send to join the Columbia House CD Club? _____

2. How often will you receive offers of main selections? _____ of special selections? _____

3. If you want the main selection, what do you do? _____

4. If you want an alternate CD, what do you do? _____

5. How many days do you have to make your choice? _____

6. If you receive a CD before this time, can it be returned? _____

7. Will you get full credit? _____

8. Who pays shipping charges? _____

9. What is the regular club price for CDs? _____ the extra bonus offer price? _____

10. When can you cancel your membership? _____

89

Book club membership offers are a lot like record and tape club offers. Best sellers, like hit records, are offered to new members at special low prices. Once you accept a membership offer, you must purchase a certain number of books within a certain amount of time. You may have six months to make these purchases. Sometimes you may have as long as a year. You must read carefully for the specific details of the offer. Know what you're agreeing to do.

## ACTIVITY 9

### Reading a book club offer for details

Read this book club offer. Answer the questions about this offer.

# Choose any 4 for $2.

You simply agree to buy 4 books within the next two years.

Book-of-the-Month Club, Inc., Camp Hill, Pennsylvania 17012          A304-10-1

Please enroll me as a member of Book-of-the-Month Club and send me the 4 books I've listed below, billing me $2, plus shipping and handling charges. I agree to buy 4 more books during the next two years. A shipping and handling charge is added to each shipment.

Indicate by number the four books you want

Mr.
Mrs _____ 2-04
Miss              (Please print plainly)

Address _____ Apt. _____

City _____

State _____ Zip _____

Prices generally higher in Canada

## BOOK-OF-THE-MONTH CLUB
America's Bookstore since 1926.

**Benefits of Membership.** Membership in the Book-of-the-Month Club begins with your choice of 4 of today's best books for $2. Because our prices are generally lower than the publishers' prices, you will save throughout your membership on the finest new titles. In fact, the longer you remain a member, the greater your savings can be. Our Book-Dividend® plan, for which you become eligible after a brief trial enrollment, offers savings from 50% to 75% off the publishers' prices on art books, reference works, classics, books on cooking and crafts, literary sets and other contemporary works of enduring value. Nevertheless, all Book-of-the-Month Club books are equal in quality to the publishers' originals; they are not condensed versions or cheaply made reprints.

As a member you will receive the *Book-of-the-Month Club News*® 15 times a year (about every 3½ weeks). Every issue reviews a Selection and 150 other books that we call Alternates, which are carefully chosen by our editors. If you want the Selection, do nothing. It will be shipped to you automatically. If you want one or more Alternates—or no book at all—indicate your decision on the Reply Form and return it by the specified date. *Return Privilege:* If the *News* is delayed and you receive the Selection without having had 10 days to notify us, you may return it for credit at our expense. *Cancellations:* Membership may be discontinued, either by you or by the Club, at any time after you have bought 4 additional books. Join today. With savings and choices like these, no wonder Book-of-the-Month Club is America's Bookstore.

1. If Book-of-the-Month Club accepts your application, how many books will you receive? _____

2. What will these books cost? _____

3. How many days do you have to decide if you want to keep the main selection? _____

4. If you accept the books, are there any other charges? _____

5. How often will you receive the Book-of-the-Month Club news? _____

6. By accepting this offer, how many books are you agreeing to buy during the next two years? _____

7. If you do not want the Selection of the Month, what do you do? _____

## Coupon savings

Many ads have savings coupons. You can use these discount coupons for savings on a lot of products. First, you clip the coupon. You then redeem it at the time of your purchase. Some coupons will be for refunds. To get a refund you may have to show proof-of-purchase. Proof-of-purchase can be a label, a price code, or a cash register receipt. Shopping with coupons can result in savings. Sometimes there's something free with your purchase. However, coupons are still a form of advertising. Read all coupons carefully. Sometimes a savings may not be on a product you need. Coupons have expiration dates, too. You must use a coupon before it expires.

## ACTIVITY 10
### Reading coupon offers

Answer the questions about the following coupon offers.

1. What two products can you buy with these coupons? _____

_____

2. Do you have to buy a certain size? _____

3. Can you redeem these coupons for cash without making a purchase? _____

4. Do these coupons have expiration dates? _____

## ACTIVITY 11

### Reading refund and free coupon offers

Answer the questions about each of the following offers.

1. How much is this coupon worth? _____

2. Do you have to purchase certain items in order to use this coupon? _____

3. If your purchase comes to 80¢, will you receive change from this coupon? _____

4. How many Key Group Burger Kings are there? _____

---

## GET A $2.00 CASH REFUND

**BUY:** Any 3 <u>different</u> of these brands:
Betty Crocker® SuperMoist® cake mix, Creamy Deluxe® or MiniMorsels Frosting, Gold Medal® or Red Band® Flour (5 lbs or larger), Betty Crocker® Brownie Mix (Frosted, Chocolate Chip, Walnut, Supreme, or German Chocolate), Betty Crocker® Muffin Mix.

**SEND:** 1) The UPC symbols (see sample) from your three purchases
2) This mail-in certificate.

**MAIL TO:** General Mills, Inc.
Box 5237
Minneapolis, MN 55460

**RECEIVE:** Cash Refund of $2.00 by mail.

### MAIL-IN CASH REFUND CERTIFICATE

Name _____

Address _____

City _____

State _____ Zip _____

**OFFER EXPIRES MAY 31, 1988**

Mechanical reproduction, facsimile, purchase or sale or other dissemination of this offer without the written consent of General Mills, Inc. are prohibited. This certificate must accompany your request. Void where taxed, regulated or prohibited. Offer limited to one refund per group, organization or address. Please allow up to 6 weeks per shipment. Qualifiers will not be returned for duplicate requests or requests from outside stated area. Offer good only in VA, WVA, NC, SC, GA, FL, TN.

1. What do you get when you mail in this coupon? _____

2. Do you have to send in proof-of-purchase? If so, what do you send? _____

3. What is the value of this offer? _____

4. Where do you mail this coupon? _____

5. How long do you have to wait for your cash? _____

6. What is the expiration date on this offer? _____

## CHECK YOUR UNDERSTANDING OF SPECIAL OFFERS

Here are some words to know when you are reading a special offer. Find the correct word or phrase for each of the sentences below.

| | | |
|---|---|---|
| redeem | coupon | expiration date |
| discount | refund | obligation |

1. A _____ for 10¢ off on the price of crackers was in the daily newspaper.

2. The _____ of the coupon was March 31, 1993.

3. When I joined a book club, I had a(n) _____ to purchase 4 additional books.

4. The electronic toy I purchased included a coupon for a $5 _____ .

5. I like to buy things at _____ stores because they offer products at lower prices.

6. I decided to buy a certain brand of crackers because I had a coupon to _____ .

Decide whether the following statements are TRUE (T) or FALSE (F).

_____ 7. When a book club offers a number of books for an introductory low price, you can get these books without buying anything else from the club at that time.

_____ 8. Record and tape and book clubs usually automatically send you the selection of the month.

_____ 9. Magazine and newspaper subscriptions cost less than the newsstand price.

_____ 10. Coupons for food products never have expiration dates.

# SHOW WHAT YOU KNOW . . .

## About Special Offers

Design a coupon for a product that you create.
Include all of the important information that a coupon should have.

# Understanding agreements and warranties

Have you ever returned an item for a refund, leased a piece of equipment, or made a credit card purchase? Chapter 5 explores consumer agreements and contracts and the warranties that come with certain purchases. You will study sales and service agreements. You will also study credit agreements. You will interpret the terms used in these agreements. This chapter presents a number of warranties for your review. It includes a cassette player warranty and a new car warranty.

## Agreements and contracts

### WORDS TO KNOW

**annual**   each year

**balance**   the amount you owe after payment; amount left

**collateral**   property promised to a creditor, such as a car or furniture, if a debt is not paid

**co-maker**   second person agreeing to credit terms; also known as co-applicant, co-signer, or co-borrower

**conditions**   terms; special circumstances

**consent**   agree to;  give permission

**consumer**   buyer or borrower

**contract**   legal agreement

**credit**   ability to buy or borrow and pay at a later date

**credit terms**   how you are to pay for a credit purchase or repay a loan

**creditor**   person or business giving you credit; lender; seller

**debts**   bills you owe; obligations

**default**   nonpayment; failure to pay as agreed

**delinquent**   late

**disclosure**   to make known; to state in writing; a written statement of the terms of a loan or credit agreement

**down payment**   money paid in advance on credit purchase

**entitle**   give the right to; permit; allow

**finance charge**   cost of having credit; monthly charge on credit agreement, usually used on charge card agreements

**installment**   monthly payment

(continued)

**interest**   cost of credit, usually used in loan agreements

**landlord**   person who owns and rents out a house, apartment, or building

**lease**   a rent agreement

**liability**   legal responsibility

**lien**   a legal claim on your property for nonpayment of a debt

**option**   choice

**percentage rate**   interest or finance charges stated as a percentage of what you owe

**retailer**   seller or merchant; person or business giving credit

**sue**   take to court; take legal action against

**tenant**   person renting an apartment, a house, or a building

**title**   legal document proving ownership

**violate**   fail to keep an agreement

The special words used for contracts and agreements are very technical. You will see these words in credit agreements. You will see them in rent agreements. You will see them in employment agency contracts, too. You will also see these words in sales and service agreements. For example, retail stores often post rules about returns and refunds. There may be terms on the receipt of your car repair bill. There may be terms on the back of your dry-cleaning ticket. (Dry cleaners take very little responsibility for damaged clothes.) Some of these agreements do not require your signature. But they are still agreements. When you buy goods or pay for services, you are accepting the terms of the seller. Study the *Words to Know* carefully. They are the words you will see and use. Your understanding of them can help you protect your rights.

## ACTIVITY 1
### Using credit terms

The words below are often found in credit agreements. Use these words to complete the statements below.

| | | |
|---|---|---|
| disclosure | percentage rate | debts |
| co-maker | delinquent | default |
| creditor | interest | installment |
| down payment | | |

1. Ira Atkins just got a(n) _____ loan for a new car.

2. Of course, Ira will have to pay _____ on this loan.

3. The annual _____ is stated in the credit agreement.

4. Ira had to read a _____ statement before signing the credit agreement.

5. The _____ must always let you know the terms of credit.

6. There was a _____ required.

7. Ira's wife, Ellen, was _____ of the loan.

8. Ellen will have to repay the loan should Ira _____ .

9. The _____ charges are $5 per month for each late payment.

10. When Ira and Ellen applied for the loan, they had to list all their _____ .

## ACTIVITY 2
### Reading credit agreements

Each of the statements below was taken from a credit agreement. The language is very technical. Which of the statements listed below means the same as the statement from the agreement?

1.
> If an installment is not paid within 10 days after it is due, a delinquent charge of $5 will be paid by the buyer . . .

_____ a. If you are late with your monthly payment, you must pay $5.
_____ b. If you are more than 10 days late with a payment, you must pay a "late charge."
_____ c. If you are more than 10 days late with your monthly payment, you must pay $5 in late charges.

**2.** For the purpose of securing payment of the obligation, creditor holds title to 1993 Buick as collateral and shall have a security interest in said property until said obligation is fully paid . . .

_____ **a.** Your title will be held until you pay your debt.

_____ **b.** You can hold the title to your property, but if you fail to pay this bill, the lender will demand the title to your car.

_____ **c.** To be sure you pay this bill, the lender will hold the registration papers to your car until the bill is paid in full.

**3.** Debtor will not sell or offer to sell or otherwise transfer ownership of the collateral without written consent of creditor . . .

_____ **a.** You can sell the collateral, for example, a car.

_____ **b.** The lender can sell or transfer the collateral (car) if he or she lets you know in writing.

_____ **c.** As the borrower, you can't sell the collateral (car) unless the person holding the collateral or title to the collateral gives you written permission.

**4.** As co-signer of this agreement, I am aware of my liability and I hereby authorize you to obtain credit information relative to me.

_____ **a.** As co-maker of a loan, you are responsible for the loan if it is not paid.

_____ **b.** You have agreed to share the responsibility for a debt.

_____ **c.** You have signed to have your credit checked and to share the responsibility for a debt.

## ACTIVITY 3

### Using agreements and contract words

Match the words on the left with their meanings on the right.

_____ **A.** lease      **1.** failure to pay as agreed

_____ **B.** balance      **2.** amount you owe

_____ **C.** consumer      **3.** rent agreement

_____ **D.** entitle      **4.** terms

_____ **E.** landlord      **5.** buy-now and pay-later plan

_____ **F.** default      **6.** each year

_____ **G.** obligation      **7.** buyer

_____ **H.** annual      **8.** allow

_____ **I.** credit      **9.** apartment owner

_____ **J.** conditions      **10.** responsibility

# ACTIVITY 4

## Reading terms on charge accounts

Many people make purchases by using credit cards or opening charge accounts. The law requires that *all* creditors provide buyers with disclosure information. This means companies offering charge accounts must give you the terms of your agreement in writing. This information will come with your application for credit. Sometimes it is separate from the application. When you put your signature on a credit agreement, you are accepting all of the terms in the agreement. The J. C. Penney revolving credit agreement on the next two pages appears on the *back* of a Penney's Credit Application.

Answer TRUE (T) or FALSE (F) to the following statements about the credit terms.

_____ 1. You will not have to pay finance charges if you make regular monthly installment payments.

_____ 2. Payments must be made within 30 days of the billing date.

_____ 3. If your average daily balance is $28.50, the finance charge is 50¢.

_____ 4. If you make a $10 charge purchase on March 2 and a $150 charge on March 28, your finance charge for the month of March will be based on an average daily balance that does include the $150.

_____ 5. When you pay 1.75% in finance charges each month, you are paying 21% in finance charges each year.

_____ 6. You must pay the minimum payment each month.

_____ 7. You may pay more than the minimum monthly payment, but not less.

_____ 8. If you owe $210, your monthly payment will be $13.

_____ 9. Your signature gives J. C. Penney permission to investigate your credit record.

_____ 10. Unpaid finance or insurance charges are included when an average daily balance is figured.

# YOUR JCPenney RETAIL INSTALLMENT CREDIT AGREEMENT
## (Revolving Credit Agreement)

JCP-9501 (Rev. 1/91)

In this agreement, *you* and *your* mean anyone who has applied for and been accepted for a JCPenney Credit Account. *We, us,* and *our* mean the J.C. Penney Company, Inc., 14841 North Dallas Parkway, Dallas, TX 75240-6760.

**Credit Bureau Reports** — To check the information on your application, we may get a report about you from a credit bureau. When you have an account, we may get a credit report to update our records or to decide whether to give you additional credit. Ask us and we will tell you if we requested a credit report and give you the name and address of the credit bureau.

**Types of Charges** — The purchase of any merchandise or service may be added to your account as a Regular Charge. Certain merchandise (identified in our stores and catalogs) may be added to your account as a Major Purchase Charge.

**Promise to Pay** — You agree to pay for all authorized charges to your account as well as any charges from which you receive a benefit.

**Payment Requirements** — When you have a balance, you agree to pay at least the minimum payment amount due each month. **You can pay your entire balance at any time.** Your required payment may include any past due amounts, late charges, and returned check fees. Your required payment may also include any insurance premiums if your policy is billed with your account.

**Failure to Pay** — If you do not pay on time, we can require that you make immediate payment of your entire balance unless you have rights by state law to correct your non-payment.

We may use an outside attorney to collect your account. If there is a lawsuit and you lose, you agree to pay reasonable attorney's fees, plus court costs, as permitted by the law in your state.

**Annual Fee** — There is no annual fee on your JCPenney Credit Account.

**Grace Period** — You do not pay any finance charge if there is no previous balance or if credits and payments made within 25 days of the current billing date equal the balance at the beginning of the period.

**Finance Charge** — Finance charge not in excess of that permitted by law will be assessed on the outstanding balance(s) from month to month. We figure the finance charge by applying the periodic rate(s) to the Average Daily Balance(s) of your account.

**Balance Calculation Method — Average Daily Balance:** Current purchases are included in the calculation except in the states of ME, MA, MN, MT, NE, and NM.

- To get the Average Daily Balance, we take the beginning balance each day, add new purchases, and subtract payments and credits. In ME, MA, MN, MT, NE, and NM, current purchases are not included during the billing period in which they were made. In AR, CA, HI, LA, MS, ND, and PA, unpaid finance charges from a previous billing period are not included.

- We add all the daily balances for the billing period and divide the total by the number of days in that period. This gives us the Average Daily Balance.

- We figure the Average Daily Balance separately for a Regular Charge balance and a Major Purchase balance. We add these Average Daily Balances to get the account's total Average Daily Balance.

Excluded from finance charge calculation are insurance premiums, returned check fees, and late payment charges.

**Regular Charges** — If you have a Regular Charge balance, you agree to make at least a minimum payment each month as listed below:

| IF YOUR REGULAR CHARGE BALANCE IS: | YOUR MONTHLY PAYMENT IS: |
|---|---|
| $ 20.00 or less | Balance |
| 20.01 — 100 | $ 20 |
| 100.01 — 200 | 30 |
| 200.01 — 250 | 35 |
| 250.01 — 300 | 40 |
| 300.01 — 350 | 45 |
| 350.01 — 400 | 50 |
| 400.01 — 450 | 55 |
| 450.01 — 550 | 60 |
| 550.01 — 600 | 65 |
| Over $600 | 11% of the balance rounded down to the whole dollar. |

**Major Purchase Charges** — If you have a Major Purchase balance, you agree to pay at least a fixed amount each month. This amount is based on your highest Major Purchase balance. Even if you reduce your balance, your monthly payment will remain the same until that balance is paid.

| IF YOUR HIGHEST MAJOR PURCHASE BALANCE IS: | YOUR MONTHLY PAYMENT IS: |
|---|---|
| $200.00 — 240 | $ 15 |
| 240.01 — 270 | 16 |

For balances between $270.01 and $1,000, the monthly payment of $16 is $1 more for each additional $30 or less.

For balances over $1,000, the monthly payment is 4% of the balance rounded down to the whole dollar.

**Our Rights — Warning:** We can change our credit terms at any time. We will notify you in advance of any such changes as required by law. Our new terms may be applied to the existing balance on your account unless prohibited by law. We can limit or cancel your credit privileges. All JCPenney credit cards belong to us, and you must return them at our request.

We give up any lien the law gives us automatically for work performed by us or materials installed by us on real property used or expected to be used as your principal residence. If you live in Florida, we will keep a security interest in any items charged to your account, except for those items that are considered real property under state law.

**If You Move** — You must notify us promptly if you move. If your new residence is in another state, our terms in that state will apply. If you move outside the U.S. (50 states), our standard credit account terms will apply.

**Information About You and Your Account, and Telephone Communications**
We may share information about you with a member of JCPenney's family of companies or in activities conducted by the JCPenney family of companies. We may give information about your account to credit bureaus and where required or permitted by law. Your telephone conversations with employees or agents of JCPenney's family of companies may be monitored for quality assurance purposes, and your use of your account will signify your consent to such monitoring.

**Advertisements and Solicitations** — We send advertisements with billing statements, in separate mailings, and by telephone solicitation, which you agree to receive. However, you can tell us at the credit desk in any JCPenney store or by sending a note to the Credit Service Center address shown on your billing statement, that you do not want to receive these advertisements and telephone solicitations.

**Finance Charge Rates** — The periodic rate for your state is listed below:

| Residence | Periodic Rate | ANNUAL PERCENTAGE RATE | Portion of Average Daily Balance to Which Applied | Minimum Monthly FINANCE CHARGE |
|---|---|---|---|---|
| AL | 1.75%<br>1.5% | 21%<br>18% | $750 or less<br>over $750 | 50¢ |
| AK | 1.5%<br>.79% | 18%<br>9.48% | $1,000 or less<br>over $1,000 | 50¢ |
| CO, DE, GA, ID, IL, KY, LA, MS, MT, NV, NM, OH, OK, SD, UT, WY | 1.75% | 21% | Entire | 50¢ |
| FL | 1.5% | 18% | Entire | 50¢ |
| NE | 1.75%<br>1.5% | 21%<br>18% | $500 or less<br>over $500 | None |
| ND | 1.5% | 18% | Entire | None |
| WV | 1.5%<br>1.0% | 18%<br>12% | $750 or less<br>over $750 | 50¢ |
| Outside U.S. — 50 States | 1.75% | 21% | Entire | 50¢ |

There is no minimum monthly finance charge if you have only a Major Purchase balance.

**Returned Check Fee** — If any check sent to us as payment on your account and/or for insurance premiums is returned unpaid by your bank, we may charge you a reasonable returned check fee.

**Late Payment Charge** — This applies to you if you live in AL, FL, GA, ID, IL, KY, LA, MS, MT, NV, OH, SD, WV, or outside the U.S. If we do not receive your required payment within two consecutive billing periods, we may assess a late payment charge. This charge is 5% of the late payment (excluding any insurance premiums and returned check fees), but not more than $5.00 ($0.00 in Ohio).

**Taxes on Finance Charge** — If you live in MS any finance charge assessed on your account is subject to the MS state sales tax. The current rate of that tax is 6%.

**Transfer of Your Account** — We may transfer your account and our rights under this agreement. The transferee receiving such transfer will be entitled to your account payments and will have all of our rights under this agreement.

**NOTICE: See reverse side for important information regarding your rights to dispute billing errors.**

**To find out if there have been any changes to the credit terms of this agreement, write to the JCPenney Credit Department, P.O. Box 300, Dallas, TX 75221.**

**NOTICE: ANY HOLDER OF THIS CONSUMER CREDIT CONTRACT IS SUBJECT TO ALL CLAIMS AND DEFENSES WHICH THE DEBTOR COULD ASSERT AGAINST THE SELLER OF GOODS OR SERVICES OBTAINED PURSUANT HERETO OR WITH THE PROCEEDS HEREOF. RECOVERY HEREUNDER BY THE DEBTOR SHALL NOT EXCEED AMOUNTS PAID BY THE DEBTOR HEREUNDER.**

**ILLINOIS — Residents of Illinois may contact the Illinois Commissioner of Banks and Trust Companies for comparative information on interest rates, charges, fees, and grace periods (State of Illinois — CIP, P.O. Box 10181, Springfield, IL 62791 or telephone 1-800-634-5452).**

**OHIO — The Ohio laws against discrimination require that all creditors make credit equally available to all creditworthy customers, and that credit reporting agencies maintain separate credit histories on each individual upon request. The Ohio Civil Rights Commission administers compliance with this law.**

**NOTICE TO THE BUYER: Do not sign this credit agreement before you read it or if it contains any blank spaces. You are entitled to a completely filled in copy of the credit agreement when you sign it. Keep it to protect your legal rights. You have the right to pay in advance the full amount due.**

---

**Sign here and keep this Retail Installment Credit Agreement (Revolving Credit Agreement) for your records.**

J.C. Penney Company, Inc.

*Ted L. Spurlock*

Ted L. Spurlock
Senior Vice President
Director of Financial Services

_____  _____
Applicant's Signature        Date

_____  _____
Co-Applicant's Signature     Date

---

## Protect Your JCPenney Account With Credit Insurance

**DISABILITY AND UNEMPLOYMENT BENEFITS** —This insurance protection pays your minimum monthly payment on the covered balance of your JCPenney Credit Account if you the billed accountholder, while insured, become totally disabled or involuntarily unemployed [strike (except Illinois), laid-off, fired] for over 30 days. You're paid benefits from the date your disability or unemployment begins until your covered balance is paid off or you are no longer disabled or involuntarily unemployed. To collect unemployment benefits you must be employed 30 hours per week for four consecutive weeks at the time you become unemployed. "Covered balance" is the outstanding balance on your account, both Regular Charges and Major Purchase Charges, up to $5,000. The covered balance does not include other insurance premiums, nor does it include additional purchases made after the date of loss.

**LIFE BENEFITS** — If you or your spouse die, it pays the covered balance on your JCPenney Credit Account, up to $5,000. Your spouse is only insured for the life insurance coverage and not for disability and unemployment coverage.

**COST** — For the months you have an outstanding balance, THE COST IS 65¢ PER $100 (59¢ PER $100 IN ALABAMA, 73¢ PER $100 IN OKLAHOMA) OF THAT COVERED BALANCE. EXAMPLE: If your cost is 65¢ and your covered balance is $200, an insurance charge of $1.30 will appear on your account statement. You're not charged when you owe no balance. No finance charge will be added to your charged premium. Your insurance premium will be paid for you whenever you're receiving benefits.

**ELIGIBILITY AND TERMS** — The billed accountholder must be under age 66 to enroll (under age 65 for Illinois residents; under age 70 for Oklahoma residents). The insurance effective date is stated on the certificate or policy to be sent to you. Disability and Unemployment coverages stop and the cost of insurance may change at age 66 (all benefits cease at age 66 in DE, FL, NE, NM and WY; life benefits cease at age 70 in Oklahoma). Insurance stops when you're 120 days late paying the minimum payment on your account, the day your account is closed, this group is cancelled or when the accountholder dies. If, after you receive the certificate of insurance, you do not wish to keep the coverage, send the certificate back to us within 30 days from the effective date. We will credit your account for any premium charged for this coverage. ACCEPTING THIS INSURANCE WILL NOT AFFECT WHETHER OR NOT YOU RECEIVE A JCPENNEY CREDIT ACCOUNT. CM200(1/85), CM300(1/85), CI302(8/85) IL, NM. This opportunity is available only to residents of AL, AK, CO, DE, FL, GA, ID, IL, KY, LA, MS, NE, NV, NM, ND, OH, OK, SD, UT, WV, and WY.

Coverage is issued by J.C. Penney Life Insurance Company, and J.C. Penney Casualty Insurance Company, Administrative Offices: 2700 W. Plano Parkway, Plano, TX 75075-8200, each of which is solely responsible for its own financial condition and contractual obligations.

---

JCP-2201 (Rev. 11/91)

┌─PLEASE DETACH HERE — FOLD DOWN TO ARROWS BELOW

## ACTIVITY 5
### Reading agreements

In this activity you will read terms and conditions from various sales and service agreements. They are terms from rental agencies, garages, dry cleaners. Sometimes these terms are posted for customers to read. Sometimes terms or conditions will be on a receipt or sales slip. Your initials or signature may be required. It depends on the type of agreement and the laws in your state. Look at the box below. It contains a list of items that usually come with limits or conditions. Match each of the conditions stated below the box with an item from the box. Use the *letter* that corresponds to the correct item. A letter may be used more than once.

---

**a.** Car Rental Agreement
**b.** Magazine Subscriber's Contract
**c.** Car Repair Bill

**d.** Rent-a-Tool Agreement
**e.** Department Store Refund Policy
**f.** Dry-Cleaning Ticket

---

1. "You or your employees may operate this vehicle for purposes of testing, inspection, or delivery at my risk . . ." _____

2. "In laundering we cannot guarantee colors, shrinkage, or synthetic materials . . ." _____

3. "We cannot assume responsibility for buckles, buttons, suedes, leathers . . ." _____

4. "The renter agrees that the motor vehicle leased to him shall not be operated by any person under the influence of narcotics or intoxicants . . ." _____

5. "A mechanic's lien is acknowledged on this vehicle to secure the amount of repairs . . ." _____

6. "Notify lessor immediately if equipment does not function properly or no refund allowance will be made." _____

7. "Merchandise may be returned within 10 days if in salable condition as new." _____

8. "This policy does not apply to 'as is,' 'final sales,' or 'custom-made' merchandise." _____

9. "Please enter my subscription for the following magazines. I understand that it will take 8 to 12 weeks for normal service for these publications to begin." _____

10. "Vehicle shall NOT be used to tow a trailer or any other vehicle . . ." _____

Choose the best answer to complete the following statements.

_____ 1. The phrase "annual finance charge" means
   a. the weekly charge.
   b. the monthly charge.
   c. the yearly charge.

_____ 2. If you pay your whole bill each month for items you have charged,
   a. you will not have to pay a finance charge.
   b. you still have to pay a finance charge.
   c. you still must make installment payments.

_____ 3. Your monthly payments usually depend on
   a. the fixed amount you have agreed to pay.
   b. the interest rate.
   c. the amount of credit you are allowed.

_____ 4. Installment payments are usually made
   a. monthly.
   b. weekly.
   c. yearly.

_____ 5. A liability is a
   a. type of agreement.
   b. legal responsibility.
   c. rent agreement.

_____ 6. "This policy does not apply to sale merchandise" might be part of a statement in a
   a. dry cleaners.
   b. department store.
   c. car rental agency.

_____ 7. A lease is a
   a. credit agreement.
   b. rent agreement.
   c. type of warranty.

_____ 8. When you leave collateral for a debt, you
   a. agree to repay the loan.
   b. leave the property or the title to property with the lender.
   c. get another person to share the debt.

_____ 9. When you are late with an installment payment, you are
   a. delinquent.
   b. co-maker.
   c. in agreement.

_____ 10. Charge applications ask you
   a. your religion.
   b. your race.
   c. your annual salary.

# SHOW WHAT YOU KNOW . . .

## About Agreements and Contracts

Rewrite the following statements from a credit card agreement in your own words.

1. If I do not make at least the minimum required monthly payment when due, Shears Company may declare my entire balance immediately due and payable.

   _____

   _____

   _____

2. Shears has a security interest under the Uniform Commercial Code in all merchandise charged to the account. If I do not make payments as agreed, the security interest allows Shears to repossess only the merchandise which has not been paid in full.

   _____

   _____

   _____

   _____

3. Upon my default, Shears may charge me reasonable attorney's fees. I am responsible for any loss or damage to the merchandise until the price is fully paid.

   _____

   _____

   _____

# Warranties

**adjustments**   minor changes or repairs

**authorized dealer**   person licensed or trained to sell and service a particular product

**free trial**   an offer to try a product out before you decide to buy it and accept the terms of the warranty

**full warranty**   a guarantee to service, repair, or replace a product for a specified time at no cost to the purchaser. Damage resulting from careless use will not be covered

**guarantee**   same as a warranty; legal promise

**incidental or consequential damages**   any damages resulting from the owner's carelessness

**limited warranty**   a guarantee to service, repair, or replace a product with the purchaser sharing some of the cost. Warranties usually cover defects in materials and workmanship, not careless use.

**maintenance**   everyday care

**manufacturer**   person who makes a product

**prepaid**   paid in advance; describes freight or postage paid by the buyer

**purchaser**   person who buys a product; consumer

**refund**   give back

**repair**   fix; make work

**warranty**   guarantee; legal promise

**workmanship**   how well something is put together

A warranty is the maker's promise that a product is well made. Warranties usually come with such things as cars, tools, appliances, machinery, and electronic equipment.

Every buyer needs to know how to read a warranty. Study the list of words above. It pays to know these words. You will find them in most warranties.

## ACTIVITY 6
### Using warranty words

Match the warranty words below with their meanings:

——— 1. repairs     **A.** to mistreat or misuse

——— 2. guarantee     **B.** maker of a product

——— 3. prepaid     **C.** person licensed to sell or service a product

——— 4. abuse     **D.** how well something is put together

——— 5. authorized dealer     **E.** warranty

——— 6. manufacturer     **F.** paid in advance

——— 7. adjustments     **G.** minor changes

——— 8. workmanship     **H.** fixes

## ACTIVITY 7
### Using warranty words

Use these words to complete the statements below:

| limited warranty | prepaid | manufacturer |
| full warranty | defects | authorized dealer |

1. Marion Martin found the address of the ——————————————— on her warranty.

2. Because Bill Peter's stereo was under ——————————— , the repairs did not cost him anything.

3. John Anderson has a ——————————————— on his stereo and had to pay for some

   of the parts needed to repair it.

4. All freight charges had to be ——————————— when Nancy Ames sent her camera to the nearest

   service center for repairs.

5. Because there were so many ——————————— in Tommy Thomas's new color TV set,

   the merchant, an ——————————————————— , replaced it.

**Reading a warranty**

Smart shoppers read the warranties on the products they buy. The warranties tell them (1) the time period during which the manufacturer will repair, replace, or service a product, (2) whether they will have to pay for repairs or services, (3) who made a product, and (4) how to go about having that product repaired or replaced.

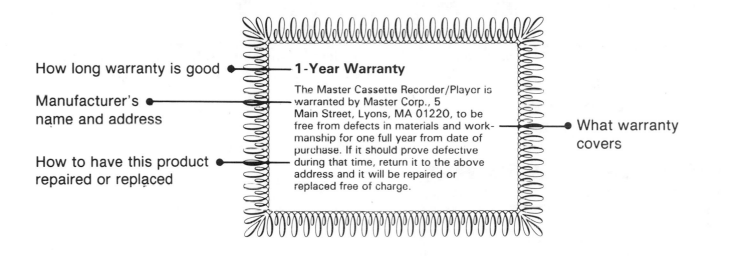

How long warranty is good

Manufacturer's name and address

How to have this product repaired or replaced

**1-Year Warranty**

The Master Cassette Recorder/Player is warranted by Master Corp., 5 Main Street, Lyons, MA 01220, to be free from defects in materials and workmanship for one full year from date of purchase. If it should prove defective during that time, return it to the above address and it will be repaired or replaced free of charge.

What warranty covers

# ACTIVITY 8

**Reading warranties for details**

Answer the questions about the warranty below.

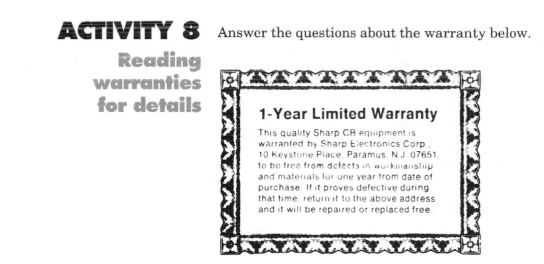

**1-Year Limited Warranty**

This quality Sharp CB equipment is warranted by Sharp Electronics Corp., 10 Keystone Place, Paramus, N.J. 07651, to be free from defects in workmanship and materials for one year from date of purchase. If it proves defective during that time, return it to the above address and it will be repaired or replaced free.

1. What is the name of the product under warranty? _____

_____

2. What are the name and address of the manufacturer?_____

_____

3. What does the warranty cover? _____

_____

**4.** How long is it good? _____

_____

**5.** What do you do if this product doesn't work? _____

_____

## ACTIVITY 9
### Reading warranties for details

Some warranties are more detailed than others. Read the warranty below. Decide whether the statements about it are TRUE (T) or FALSE (F).

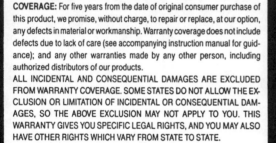

**AMERICAN PRODUCT CO. FULL FIVE-YEAR WARRANTY**

**COVERAGE:** For five years from the date of original consumer purchase of this product, we promise, without charge, to repair or replace, at our option, any defects in material or workmanship. Warranty coverage does not include defects due to lack of care (see accompanying instruction manual for guidance); and any other warranties made by any other person, including authorized distributors of our products.

ALL INCIDENTAL AND CONSEQUENTIAL DAMAGES ARE EXCLUDED FROM WARRANTY COVERAGE. SOME STATES DO NOT ALLOW THE EXCLUSION OR LIMITATION OF INCIDENTAL OR CONSEQUENTIAL DAMAGES, SO THE ABOVE EXCLUSION MAY NOT APPLY TO YOU. THIS WARRANTY GIVES YOU SPECIFIC LEGAL RIGHTS, AND YOU MAY ALSO HAVE OTHER RIGHTS WHICH VARY FROM STATE TO STATE.

**WARRANTY SERVICE PROCEDURE:** When warranty service is needed, deliver or send the product insured and properly packaged, freight prepaid, with a description of the apparent defect and the means to ascertain the date of original consumer purchase (such as a copy of your billing or cancelled check) to one of the factory service centers listed below. If, at any time, you are not satisfied with our warranty service, contact: Vice President, Distribution & Service, American Product Co., 2606 W. Water Street, Minneapolis, Minnesota 55408.

USA:
American Product Co.
General Service Department
2606 W. Water Street
Minneapolis, Minnesota 55408

CANADA:
American Product Co.
General Service Department
138 Tannin Road
Toronto, Ontario M4A 1P4

_____ **1.** This is a limited warranty.

_____ **2.** This warranty is good for five years.

_____ **3.** There will be a small charge if your binoculars have to be replaced.

_____ **4.** There will be no charge if your binoculars have to be repaired.

_____ **5.** If you do not take care of your binoculars as described in your manual, they are still under warranty.

_____ **6.** This warranty covers incidental and consequential damages.

_____ **7.** If you send these binoculars in to be serviced, you must pay the shipping charges in advance.

_____ **8.** You do not have to insure the binoculars when you send them.

_____ **9.** You should include something to show the date of purchase when you send this product in for servicing.

_____ **10.** If you're unhappy with the warranty service you receive, you can write the Vice-President of Distribution and Service.

# ACTIVITY 10

### Reading a car warranty

Every new car owner needs to know how to read a warranty. The warranty explains how to best service and maintain the new car. Car warranties also list what *is* covered and what *is not* covered. Some items will be covered only if a car is properly taken care of. Answer the questions about the following car warranty. The first set of questions deals with what *is* covered. The second set of questions deals with what *is not* covered.

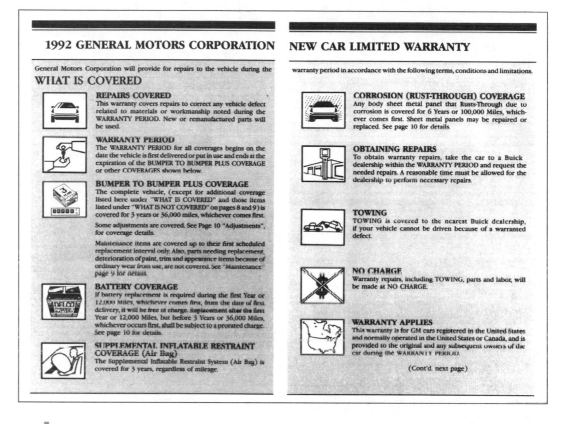

### 1992 GENERAL MOTORS CORPORATION

General Motors Corporation will provide for repairs to the vehicle during the

## WHAT IS COVERED

**REPAIRS COVERED**
This warranty covers repairs to correct any vehicle defect related to materials or workmanship noted during the WARRANTY PERIOD. New or remanufactured parts will be used.

**WARRANTY PERIOD**
The WARRANTY PERIOD for all coverages begins on the date the vehicle is first delivered or put in use and ends at the expiration of the BUMPER TO BUMPER PLUS COVERAGE or other COVERAGES shown below.

**BUMPER TO BUMPER PLUS COVERAGE**
The complete vehicle, (except for additional coverage listed here under "WHAT IS COVERED" and those items listed under "WHAT IS NOT COVERED" on pages 8 and 9) is covered for 3 years or 36,000 miles, whichever comes first.

Some adjustments are covered. See Page 10 "Adjustments", for coverage details.

Maintenance items are covered up to their first scheduled replacement interval only. Also, parts needing replacement, deterioration of paint, trim and appearance items because of ordinary wear from use, are not covered. See "Maintenance" page 9 for details.

**BATTERY COVERAGE**
If battery replacement is required during the first Year or 12,000 Miles, whichever comes first, from the date of first delivery, it will be free of charge. Replacement after the first Year or 12,000 Miles, but before 3 Years or 36,000 Miles, whichever occurs first, shall be subject to a prorated charge. See page 10 for details.

**SUPPLEMENTAL INFLATABLE RESTRAINT COVERAGE (Air Bag)**
The Supplemental Inflatable Restraint System (Air Bag) is covered for 3 years, regardless of mileage.

### NEW CAR LIMITED WARRANTY

warranty period in accordance with the following terms, conditions and limitations.

**CORROSION (RUST-THROUGH) COVERAGE**
Any body sheet metal panel that Rusts-Through due to corrosion is covered for 6 Years or 100,000 Miles, whichever comes first. Sheet metal panels may be repaired or replaced. See page 10 for details.

**OBTAINING REPAIRS**
To obtain warranty repairs, take the car to a Buick dealership within the WARRANTY PERIOD and request the needed repairs. A reasonable time must be allowed for the dealership to perform necessary repairs.

**TOWING**
TOWING is covered to the nearest Buick dealership, if your vehicle cannot be driven because of a warranted defect.

**NO CHARGE**
Warranty repairs, including TOWING, parts and labor, will be made at NO CHARGE.

**WARRANTY APPLIES**
This warranty is for GM cars registered in the United States and normally operated in the United States or Canada, and is provided to the original and any subsequent owners of the car during the WARRANTY PERIOD.

(Cont'd. next page)

## What is covered

Write the letter that best completes these statements about this warranty.

_____ 1. General Motors Corporation will provide for repairs to the vehicle
   a. as long as you own it.
   b. during the warranty period, without limitations.
   c. during the warranty period, with certain terms, conditions, and limitations.
   d. for six (6) years.

_____ 2. Repairs will be made by
   a. the General Motors Corporation.
   b. any mechanic you choose.
   c. the Buick dealer where you bought your car.
   d. any Buick dealer.

_____ 3. The warranty period is for
   a. one year (12 months).
   b. three years or 36,000 miles, whichever comes first
   c. one year or 12,000 miles, whichever you choose.
   d. one year or 12,000 miles, whichever comes first.

_____ 4. This warranty begins
   a. when the car is delivered or put into use.
   b. when you pay your deposit on the car.
   c. the date your car is delivered to the dealer.
   d. the date you decide on the car you want.

**What is not covered**  Answer these questions about this warranty.

1. Give three examples from this warranty of damages due to accidents, misuse, or alterations.

   _____

   _____

2. Give two examples from this warranty of damages from the environment.

   _____

   _____

3. Who pays for routine maintenance services?

   _____

4. How can you determine *when* your new car needs maintenance?

   _____

   _____

Choose the best answer to complete the following statements

_____ 1. "Incidental or consequential" damages describe
   a. defects in workmanship.
   b. defects in the materials.
   c. damage from careless use.

_____ 2. When you send a defective product back to the manufacturer for a repair,
   a. you usually pay the postage.
   b. the manufacturer will pay the postage.
   c. the store where you bought it will pay the postage.

_____ 3. "Damages resulting from workmanship" means
   a. you damaged it when you put it together.
   b. the product was not put together correctly at the factory.
   c. the product was incorrectly packed.

_____ 4. The digital watch you purchased stopped working within one month of purchase. It is covered by a one-year warranty. You should
   a. send or take the watch to the place where you bought it.
   b. take the watch to a local jeweler for repair.
   c. read the warranty and send or take the watch to the place specified.

_____ 5. The warranty on a new car begins
   a. when you order the car.
   b. ten days after you get the car.
   c. when the car is delivered to you.

_____ 6. The tires on new cars are
   a. warranted by the tire maker.
   b. warranted by the automobile company.
   c. not covered by any warranty.

_____ 7. If you buy a new car in New York, and it breaks down In California during the warranty period,
   a. you can take it to an authorized dealer in California.
   b. you must pay for repairs because only the dealer who sold it to you will fix it without charge.
   c. you must pay for repairs and send the bill to the dealer in New York.

_____ 8. If your car windshield is broken by a tree limb during a high wind and the car is under warranty,
   a. the car dealer will replace the windshield without charge.
   b. the car dealer will charge to replace the windshield.
   c. you will pay one-half of the cost of replacing the windshield.

_____ 9. An authorized dealer is
   a. anyone who sells the product.
   b. a seller who is licensed by the manufacturer to sell and service the product.
   c. a repair service.

_____ 10. Warranties usually cover
   a. any damage to a product during the time of the warranty.
   b. defects in workmanship and materials during the time of the warranty.
   c. defects in the product caused by heat or extreme cold.

# SHOW WHAT YOU KNOW . . .

## About Warranties

Write a warranty for a product you create. Include the necessary parts of a warranty. You determine if it will be a full or limited warranty.

CHAPTER

# Writing letters and consumer complaints

Many important communications are in writing. One of the most important everyday writing skills is letter writing. In this section you will practice writing letters. You will write both personal and business letters. A well-written letter may be part of your job search. You may want to write your senator about a new law up for a vote. You may have to write for information to do a term paper. And one day you may have to write a letter of complaint. The products and services we pay for are not always what they should be. Complaints by phone can be effective, too. That is, if you have good telephone skills. What is the best way to handle a complaint? Do you call or write? How do you find out who to see and where to go? The answers to all these questions are found in this chapter.

## Writing letters

### WORDS TO KNOW

**closing**   the ending of a letter, such as "Sincerely yours," or "Cordially,"

**correspondence**   communication by writing or sending letters; the letters themselves

**destination address**   the name and location of the person or organization to whom a letter is addressed

**heading**   the letter writer's address and date placed at the beginning of a letter

**inside address**   the address of the person to whom a letter is written placed before the salutation

**return address**   the letter writer's address placed at the top left corner of the envelope

**salutation**   the greeting, such as "Dear . . .," placed below the inside address

**ZIP Code**   Zone Improvement Plan, a five-digit number used by the U.S. Postal Service to help sort and distribute mail

**Zip + 4**   the old postal ZIP Code plus four new numbers

## The personal letter

Have you ever written a personal letter? If so, did you know the right form? Have you ever written a business letter? There is a special form that business letters should follow. After you wrote your letter, did you address the envelope? Did you use ZIP Codes and state abbreviations correctly? And did your letter reach the person you wanted to reach?

Many Americans do not know how to write letters or address envelopes correctly. Before you start to practice these skills, study the terms under *Words to Know*.

The personal letter is one that you write to friends or relatives. It has five parts: the heading, the salutation, the body, the closing, and the signature.

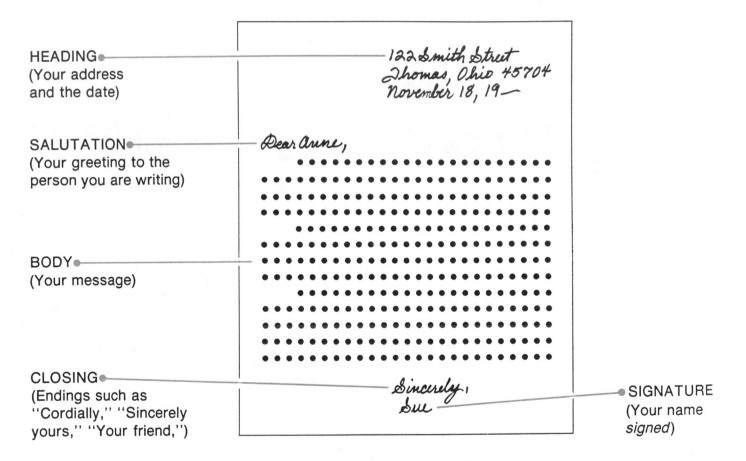

HEADING
(Your address and the date)

SALUTATION
(Your greeting to the person you are writing)

BODY
(Your message)

CLOSING
(Endings such as "Cordially," "Sincerely yours," "Your friend,")

SIGNATURE
(Your name *signed*)

122 Smith Street
Thomas, Ohio 45704
November 18, 19—

Dear Anne,

Sincerely,
Sue

Most personal letters will be written just to keep in touch. They will be written to close friends and relatives. However, sometimes you may write other types of personal letters.

One type of personal letter you may need to write is the letter of thanks. You may wish to thank a relative for a gift. You may want to thank a friend for inviting you to be a weekend guest. There are a number of occasions for writing a letter of thanks.

If you write a letter of thanks, be sure to mention the specific gift or visit. These details help to show that you appreciate what was done for you. If you were given a gift, you may have used it or worn it already. You can mention this in your letter. It should please the person who receives the letter.

## ACTIVITY 1
### Personal letters of thanks

Study the following letter of thanks. Notice that it is short. Also notice that the letter is very specific. Use this letter as a model to write your own letter of thanks. Think of a gift you have received. Or think of something someone has done for you. Then write your letter.

> 1304 Elmwood
> Park Ridge, IL
> March 27, 19—
>
> Dear Aunt Georgia and Uncle Henry,
>     Thank you so much for the portable radio with headphones. It made a great birthday present.
>     I really do like the headphones. Now I can listen to my favorite music when I go jogging. Yesterday, I took the radio with me on a long bike ride. My friends all tell me they want a radio just like mine.
>
>                Love,
>                John

## ACTIVITY 2
### Writing a personal letter

Pretend that your favorite sports star or actor is a good friend of yours. Write a letter to your friend. Tell him or her how much you enjoyed a recent television performance. Look at the sample personal letter on the opposite page. It will give you the correct form.

## ACTIVITY 3
### Writing a letter of invitation

Write a letter of invitation to a friend. Ask your friend to a party at your house. Make up the time and date of the party. Remember to answer the questions who, what, when, where, and why in your letter. Read the finished letter aloud to someone else. Ask that person to repeat the facts of the invitation to you. Have you put in all the necessary details? Have you remembered the five parts of a personal letter?

## The business letter

A business letter has six parts: the heading, the inside address, the salutation, the body, the closing, and the signature. The part included in a business letter that is not in a personal letter is the *inside address*. The inside address gives the name and address of the person you are writing. Including this information gives you a complete record of your correspondence. The inside address is a necessary part of a business letter. It appears just before the salutation.

**HEADING**
(Your address and the date)

122 Smith Street
Thomas, Ohio 45706
November 18, 19___

**INSIDE ADDRESS**
(Address of the person or business you are writing)

Mr. Peter Kells
Personnel Manager
Mill Mart Company
1378 Fulton Drive
Lakeside, Kansas 66043

**SALUTATION**
(Your greeting to the person you are writing)

Dear Sir:

**BODY**
(Your message)

**CLOSING**
(Ending such as "Cordially," "Sincerely," etc.)

Sincerely yours,

*Susan Wright*

**SIGNATURE**
(Your name typed and *signed*)

Susan Wright

Keep these things in mind when writing a business letter:

1. Never forget to put the *date* in your heading. You may need to refer to it at another time. Make a copy of important letters for your records.

2. Again, the *inside address* gives you the name of the person to whom you sent your letter. When you do not have the name of a specific person, use a title or department.

Director of Customer Complaints
Mill Mart Company
1328 Fulton Drive
Lakeside, Kansas 66043

Mill Mart Company
Frozen Foods Division
1328 Fulton Drive
Lakeside, Kansas 66043

3. The *salutation* is followed by a colon (:). Some examples of salutations are:

   Dear Sir:               Dear Ms. Johnson:
   Dear Sirs:              Dear Mr. Ortiz:
   Dear Madam:             Dear Student (Customer, Client, etc.):

4. The *body* of a business letter carries your message. Say what you have to say clearly. Keep your letter as short as possible.

5. Some typical *closings* are:

   Yours truly,            Cordially yours,
   Very truly yours,       Respectfully yours,
   Sincerely,

   Notice that only the *first* letter of these closings is capitalized. A comma comes after the closing.

6. If your letter is handwritten, write your *signature* neatly. If you type or word process a business letter, you still must sign your name. Type the closing and your name. Leave four blank lines between the closing and your name for your signature.

   Sincerely yours,

   *Susan Wright*

   Susan Wright

   The letter you will write to apply for a job is in Chapter 7. It is called the letter of application. It will follow the same form as the business letters you study here.

---

**ACTIVITY 4**
**Writing a business letter**

On your own paper, write a business letter. Use one of the choices below. If you do not know an address, check your telephone directory. You can also check product labels or bills you have received.

a. Write a business letter to the manufacturer of a product you like (or dislike). Explain why you use (or stopped using) the product.

b. Write a letter to a nonprofit organization (religious organization, library volunteers, tutoring services, neighborhood groups, etc.) offering your time and services. Be sure you let them know when and how to contact you.

c. Write a letter to one of the companies listed below. Explain that you wish to cancel your membership:

| The Bookworm Club | CAMCASS Record & Tape Club | Liberty Magazine |
| 888 8th Avenue | 106 S. Martin Street | 1520 Park Avenue |
| Newport, Indiana 47966 | Mainland, Ohio 44057 | Evansville, Maine 04106 |

## Addressing envelopes

Writing the address on the envelope for your personal and business letter is just as important as writing the letter. If the address is written correctly, it means that your letter will get where you want it to go.

The *return address* goes in the upper left-hand corner. Use one line for *your name,* a line for your *street address,* and a line for your *city and state.* The *ZIP Code* is written on the same line as the state.

The *destination address* should be put at about the center of your envelope. Again, use the first line for the *name of the person or business* you are writing to. The next line is for the *street.* Under the street go the *city and state.* The *ZIP Code* follows the state.

Remember to use a comma between city and state.

Notice "Mr." Address the person you're writing as "Mr.", "Mrs.", or "Ms."

Suntosha Starsky
606 Steel St.
Detroit, MI 48125

Mr. Llanos Venegar
2001 Broad St.
Chicago, IL 60609

When addressing an envelope, remember to capitalize all proper nouns. A proper noun names a particular person, place, or thing. Look at the envelope above again. Notice that the sender's name is capitalized—Suntosha Starsky. Notice that the name of the person receiving this letter is capitalized—Mr. Llanos Venegar. And because "Steel" and "Broad" name particular streets, they are capitalized. What about "Detroit, MI" and "Chicago, IL"? Why are they capitalized?

118

## State Abbreviations

If you had to abbreviate *Arkansas,* would you write *Ark.* or *AR*? Both abbreviations are correct. *Ark.* is the traditional abbreviation for *Arkansas.* *AR* is the new two-letter abbreviation. The U.S. Postal Service now suggests we use these two-letter abbreviations. These abbreviations are written with capital letters and no periods.

| | | | | | |
|---|---|---|---|---|---|
| Alabama | AL | Kentucky | KY | Ohio | OH |
| Alaska | AK | Louisiana | LA | Oklahoma | OK |
| Arizona | AZ | Maine | ME | Oregon | OR |
| Arkansas | AR | Maryland | MD | Pennsylvania | PA |
| California | CA | Massachusetts | MA | Puerto Rico | PR |
| Colorado | CO | Michigan | MI | Rhode Island | RI |
| Connecticut | CT | Minnesota | MN | South Carolina | SC |
| Delaware | DE | Mississippi | MS | South Dakota | SD |
| District of Columbia | DC | Missouri | MO | Tennessee | TN |
| Florida | FL | Montana | MT | Texas | TX |
| Georgia | GA | Nebraska | NE | Utah | UT |
| Guam | GU | Nevada | NV | Vermont | VT |
| Hawaii | HI | New Hampshire | NH | Virginia | VA |
| Idaho | ID | New Jersey | NJ | Virgin Islands | VI |
| Illinois | IL | New Mexico | NM | Washington | WA |
| Indiana | IN | New York | NY | West Virginia | WV |
| Iowa | IA | North Carolina | NC | Wisconsin | WI |
| Kansas | KS | North Dakota | ND | Wyoming | WY |

## Common address abbreviations

Here is a list of common address abbreviations. Businesses and organizations often use these abbreviations, with capital letters only and no periods, as recommended when using computer equipment for addressing correspondence for mass mailing.

| | | | | | |
|---|---|---|---|---|---|
| Avenue | AVE | Meadows | MDWS | Shore | SH |
| East | E | North | N | South | S |
| Expressway | EXPY | Palms | PLMS | Square | SQ |
| Heights | HTS | Park | PK | Station | STA |
| Hospital | HOSP | Parkway | PKY | Terrace | TER |
| Institute | INST | Plaza | PLZ | Turnpike | TPKE |
| Junction | JCT | Ridge | RDG | Union | UN |
| Lake | LK | River | RV | View | VW |
| Lakes | LKS | Road | RD | Village | VLG |
| Lane | LN | Rural | R | West | W |

**A word about ZIP Codes**

ZIP stands for Zone Improvement Plan. You should use the ZIP Code on your mail. The ZIP Code helps your letter get where you want it to go. Write your ZIP Code on forms that you fill out, too. It will help your return mail get to you quickly. The ZIP Code is a number that identifies areas in the United States. It helps the Postal Service sort and distribute mail. The correct ZIP Code should be part of the destination address. It should appear on the last line. There should also be a ZIP Code in the return address. Each ZIP Code should follow the name of the state.

You may have experienced ZIP + 4. ZIP + 4 lets the Postal Service make better use of machines to sort certain first-class mail. ZIP + 4 is a voluntary program. If you want your letter to reach the proper address quickly, though, you will always include the proper ZIP Code. ZIP + 4, a nine-digit number, includes your old ZIP Code plus four additional numbers. The extra numbers allow the Postal Service to sort mail by small areas. Mail can be sorted by one side of a city block or both sides of a particular street. Mail can even be sorted by one floor of a building. The U. S. Postal Service does not guarantee delivery of a letter if a ZIP Code is not used. The letter may be returned to the sender.

## ACTIVITY 5

**Addressing envelopes**

Study the samples below. Which sample would reach its destination without any difficulty? The letter is from Elvina Allen, 421 Wonder Lane, Blossom, MI 48106. It is going to Margo Montgomery, 156 Maple Road, Beaverland, IL 60515.

> Elvina Allen
> 421 Wonder Lane
> Blossom, MI 48106
>
>
>         Ms. Margo Montgomery
>         Maple Road
>         Beaverland

> Elvina Allen
> 421 Wonder Lane
> Blossom, MI 48106
>
>
>         Ms. Margo Montgomery
>         156 Maple Road
>         Beaverland, IL 60515

## ACTIVITY 6
### Addressing envelopes

Bring several blank envelopes to class. Address envelopes using the following information.

1.  Stanley Smith lives at 2375 Cherry Lane, Squire, West Virginia 24884. He is writing to Patricia Lee who lives in Lamont, Oklahoma 70215, at 417 West Street.

2.  Michael Dudley, 3245 Euclid Avenue, Detroit, Michigan 48206, is writing to Michael Harper, 201 Northland Drive, Yonkers, New York 10101.

## ACTIVITY 7
### Using state abbreviations

Below is a list of the 50 states in the United States. Next to the name of each state is its traditional abbreviation. Give the two-letter abbreviation for each state. Be sure to capitalize each letter of the abbreviation. And remember not to use periods. The District of Columbia is also included. It brings the total count to 51.

| | | |
|---|---|---|
| _____ Alabama (Ala.) | _____ Kentucky (Ky.) | _____ North Dakota (N. Dak.) |
| _____ Alaska | _____ Louisiana (La.) | _____ Ohio |
| _____ Arizona (Ariz.) | _____ Maine (Me.) | _____ Oklahoma (Okla.) |
| _____ Arkansas (Ark.) | _____ Maryland (Md.) | _____ Oregon (Oreg.) |
| _____ California (Calif.) | _____ Massachusetts (Mass.) | _____ Pennsylvania (Pa.) |
| _____ Colorado (Colo.) | _____ Michigan (Mich.) | _____ Rhode Island (R.I.) |
| _____ Connecticut (Conn.) | _____ Minnesota (Minn.) | _____ South Carolina (S.C.) |
| _____ Delaware (Del.) | _____ Mississippi (Miss.) | _____ South Dakota (S. Dak.) |
| _____ District of Columbia (D.C.) | _____ Missouri (Mo.) | _____ Tennessee (Tenn.) |
| _____ Florida (Fla.) | _____ Montana (Mont.) | _____ Texas (Tex.) |
| _____ Georgia (Ga.) | _____ Nebraska (Nebr.) | _____ Utah |
| _____ Hawaii | _____ Nevada (Nev.) | _____ Vermont (Vt.) |
| _____ Idaho | _____ New Hampshire (N.H.) | _____ Virginia (Va.) |
| _____ Illinois (Ill.) | _____ New Jersey (N.J.) | _____ Washington (Wash.) |
| _____ Indiana (Ind.) | _____ New Mexico (N. Mex.) | _____ West Virginia (W. Va.) |
| _____ Iowa (Ia.) | _____ New York (N.Y.) | _____ Wisconsin (Wis.) |
| _____ Kansas (Kans.) | _____ North Carolina (N.C.) | _____ Wyoming (Wyo.) |

# SHOW WHAT YOU KNOW . . .

## About Writing Letters

Select a local celebrity (TV newsperson, newspaper writer, sports star) or government official (mayor, councilperson, commissioner). Research his or her mailing address by making telephone inquiries or consulting printed literature.

Write the person you select a friendly letter. Say why you selected him or her. You may think that that person is doing a good job. You may want to tell about an idea you have or a suggestion you want to make.

Review the correct form of friendly letters. Address and mail your letter. Who knows? You may receive a reply.

Write a letter to Superintendent of Documents, Government Printing Office, Washington, DC 20402–9325. Ask for a free copy of the *U.S. Government Books Catalog.* This catalog lists nearly one thousand of the most popular books and pamphlets published by the U.S. government. These books and pamphlets cover many subjects. You can learn which parks have the most scenic trails. You can find out how to get more miles per gallon of gas. There are lists of safe boating rules. You can get good material for writing term papers. Many of the booklets are free. Others can be purchased at low prices.

Your letter should include the six parts of a business letter. The envelope should include complete destination and return addresses with ZIP Codes.

Complete this activity by mailing your letter.

## Consumer complaints

### WORDS TO KNOW

**association**   a group of people joined together for a special purpose

**authorized**   given the right or a license to do or sell something

**Better Business Bureau**   a group of store owners and business persons who join to improve local business practices

**complaint**   a statement that says you as a buyer are unhappy about a product or service

**consumer**   buyer, shopper, customer

**consumer protection agencies**   government and volunteer agencies that try to protect the buyer's rights

**corporation**   a business formed by a group of people

**damages**   losses; legal term for money ordered paid by the court for your losses

**dealerships**   stores licensed for sales distribution of the manufacturer's product

**exchange**   return one item for another

**Federal Trade Commission (FTC)**   government agency that enforces consumer laws

**Food and Drug Administration (FDA)**   government agency that enforces consumer laws

**franchises**   chain stores run by private persons but owned in part by a large corporation

**fraud**   deception; a dishonest act

**headquarters**   main office

**local**   in your area

(continued)

You won't always be happy with products you buy or services you pay for. Many things could make you want to complain.

Study the list of consumer words and agencies. This list gives you a *Consumer Complaint Vocabulary*. Knowing the work of these agencies and the meanings of these words will help you when you want to make a complaint.

## ACTIVITY 8

### Defining consumer complaint words

Match the consumer complaint words below with their meanings:

_____ 1. dealership

_____ 2. franchise

_____ 3. retailer

_____ 4. Small Claims Court

_____ 5. State Attorney General

_____ 6. consumer

_____ 7. FTC

_____ 8. FDA

_____ 9. corporation

_____ 10. headquarters

**A.** the store owner

**B.** a court for handling claims of $5,000 or less

**C.** the chief legal officer for your state

**D.** the buyer

**E.** Federal Trade Commission

**F.** Food & Drug Administration

**G.** a chain store

**H.** business licensed to handle a certain product line

**I.** main office

**J.** business formed by a group of people

## ACTIVITY 9

**Using consumer complaint words**

Complete these statements using the words below.

retailer
Food and Drug Administration
franchise

consumer
complaint
Better Business Bureau

1. Jennifer Jackson's mother called Riceland's Department Store with a _____ about her bill.

2. The Moore family has a Pizza World—_____ store.

3. Carlene Cooper had to name the _____ when she took her complaint to Small Claims Court.

4. Melanie Ashton recently learned that the _____ could provide her with information on reading food labels.

5. Students in Milltown High's Cooperative Education program will visit the Milltown _____ _____ on Thursday.

6. Station WXKG in Barbersville has a _____ "Hot Line" for listeners to call in complaints.

---

**Making complaints**

Suppose you buy a pair of running shoes. Then you find that the store has sold you two left shoes. What should you do? There's only one logical thing to do. Take the shoes back to the store. *The first place a consumer should go with a complaint is back to the person who sold the product.* In most cases a merchant will exchange a product or refund your money. But sometimes you run into problems. For example, a merchant refuses to refund your money because you have used a product. You try to explain that when you used the product it did not work. The merchant does not listen. He still will not refund your money. A car repair shop charges you several hundred dollars more than their estimate. You refuse to pay. The repair shop won't let you have your car. A dry cleaner ruins a $200 jacket and refuses to cover damages. The service was so slow at a restaurant that you decide to write someone higher up to tell them about it.

Although most of the things you buy will be fine, sometimes you will have to make a complaint. Who do you write, see, or call? Listed here are at least *five* places you can take your complaint:

1. *Your state or local consumer protection agency can tell you a lot about local business practices.* They can tell you what your rights are for your complaint. You may be able to call them and get the answers to all your questions. If there is no agency in your city, you can always write your nearest agency. Check your phone book for the government agencies. Look under the name of your *state* or the nearest city your phone book serves. These listings will appear under the name of the state or city. For

example, if you want government listings for Los Angeles, you would look under "Los Angeles, City of." If the consumer agency is a *county* agency, you would look under "Los Angeles, County of." A state agency would be under "California, State of." Your phone book will give you the telephone number and sometimes the address of each government agency. It is better to start with a *local* agency. Local agencies know local consumer laws. And they may be near enough for you to explain your problem in person.

2. *The State Attorney General's office* is another place to complain. This office will be in the capital city of your state. If your complaint affects a large number of people, this office might handle your complaint for you.

3. *The FTC and FDA* have regional offices to help consumers with their problems. The main office of the FTC is at Pennsylvania Ave. and 6th St. N.W., Washington, DC 20580. The main office of the FDA is at 5600 Fishers Lane, Rockville, MD 20857. Even if you are able to solve your problem locally, writing these offices is still a good idea. You can send a copy of a letter of complaint you have written. This information can be used to help you and other consumers. These two offices also give you information on consumer rights.

4. *The Office of Consumer Affairs* is located at 1725 I St. N.W., Washington, DC 20006. It is a division of the Department of Health and Human Services. If you get no satisfaction on the local or state level, write this office.

5. *Small Claims Courts* handle consumer complaints and consumer cases involving fraud. People who use this court wish to sue for small amounts of money. Suits in Small Claims Court usually range up to no more than $5,000, depending on the state in which you live. You do not have to have a lawyer to take your case to this court. You can represent yourself.

Always try to use the various agencies set up by city, state, and federal governments. These agencies should be able to solve your problem. However, there are other ways to deal with complaints. Some other places to go and people to see are listed below:

- *The Better Business Bureau.* The Better Business Bureau is a local organization of businesses. The bureau is interested in local consumer problems. It wants good relations with the local buying public. It can give you information about products before you buy. However, it doesn't handle complaints about prices. The Bureau can give specific information about a merchant. It is always interested in local businesses that may be dishonest in their advertising. The Better Business Bureau should be able to tell you how local stores handle complaints.

- *Your local newspaper or television station.* Some local newspapers and TV stations ask you to write or call in with your complaints. If your complaint affects a large number of people, a TV station or a newspaper may investigate this type of complaint for you.

- *The president of a franchise or dealership.* Sometimes a franchise or dealership will not listen to your complaint. If this happens, go right to the top. Get the names and addresses of the people who own large chains and dealerships. These people often act faster than their local representatives.

- *Business associations.* Many businesses often join groups that look out for their general interests. These same groups want to know when one of their members is providing poor service. There is a national hotel and motel association. Its headquarters is in New York City. There is a national tenants organization in Washington, D.C. You can complain about an appliance to the Major Appliance Consumer Action Panel in Chicago, Illinois.

- *A lawyer.* If your complaint involves a large sum of money, you may have to hire a lawyer!

## ACTIVITY 10

### Handling your complaints

Match the names and organizations below with the type of complaint you think they might handle.

A. A hotel complaint

B. Ford automobile complaint

C. GMC automobile complaint

D. Tenant/landlord problems

E. General consumer complaints

F. Dry cleaning complaint

G. Comments about the programs on a radio or TV station

H. Automobile safety

_____ 1. Office of Consumer Affairs

_____ 2. President
The Ford Motor Company

_____ 3. Chairman of the Board
General Motors Corporation

_____ 4. Center for Auto Safety

_____ 5. Federal Communications Commission

_____ 6. President
Neighborhood Cleaners Association

_____ 7. American Hotel and Motel Association

_____ 8. National Tenants Union

## ACTIVITY 11
### Deciding where to go with a complaint

Answer the questions below. They will test your knowledge of where to take your complaint.

1. Who is the first person you should complain to about a product? _____

_____

2. Where do you go if you do not have a *local* consumer protection agency in your area? _____

_____

3. Where is your state attorney general's office located? _____

4. Where is the U.S. Office of Consumer Affairs located? _____

5. If you want to explain your side of a problem in court without a lawyer, what court do you use?

_____

6. If your claim is about a local store that's been running misleading ads, where should you go?

_____

## ACTIVITY 12
### What action would you take?

In each of the situations below, list the action you would take. Would you call the store? Hire a lawyer? Contact the Better Business Bureau? Write the action you feel is best in the space provided. You may feel you should take more than one action. Be prepared to explain why you would take the action you took.

**IF . . .**

**. . .WHAT SHOULD YOU DO?**

1. Your new air conditioner needs repairs. It is covered by a warranty. The authorized dealer wants you to pay for the repairs.

_____

_____

_____

2. A store keeps advertising a "Going Out of Business" sale, but never goes out of business.

_____

3. A furniture delivery included two damaged chairs. The delivery people said they were not responsible.

_____

4. The dry cleaners lost the buttons on your new coat. The owner said, "They must have been loose." She refuses to cover the cost.

_____

5. You feel a local radio station is contributing to racial unrest in your community with their "Let the People Talk" broadcast.

_____

## Calling with a complaint

You may decide to call a business with a complaint. Many complaints can be handled successfully over the telephone. If the newspaper delivery person failed to deliver your newspaper, a simple call should solve the problem. The drugstore delivered the wrong prescription. A call is the most effective way to correct the mistake.

When you decide to call about a problem with a product or service:

- Have at hand all the information you need to explain your problem.
- Be ready to:

    a. give your name, address, and phone number
    b. describe the events that led up to the problem
    c. give any information that will help solve the problem: a date, the name and model number of a product, the name of the person you placed an order with, etc.

Many times, a phone call is the best way to solve a complaint. But your telephone communications skills must be effective.

## ACTIVITY 13

**Handling a complaint by phone**

Read the telephone conversation below. Then answer the questions about how the customer presented this complaint:

KATHY (counter person): Lino's Pizza. Kathy speaking. May I help you?

JOE HUME (customer): Yeah, you can help me all right. Listen, what kind of pizza joint are you people running?

KATHY: What's the problem, sir?

JOE: I ordered a pizza over an hour ago. Some guy *just* delivered it, and the blasted thing is cold. WHAT KINDA' PLACE ARE YOU PEOPLE RUNNING?

KATHY (getting annoyed): I'm sorry that your pizza was cold, sir. But don't take it out on me. We had a lot of orders to fill tonight. We're doing the best we can. Did you try sticking the pizza in the oven?

JOE: No, I didn't try sticking the pizza in the oven. I ordered a hot pizza, and I wanted a HOT PIZZA!

KATHY: I'm sorry your pizza was cold, sir.

JOE: Well, don't let it happen again.

KATHY: I can't promise that, sir. Would you like to order another pizza, sir? Our Deluxe is $14.50. Our medium pizza is . . .

1.  How would you rate this telephone complaint? Was Joe Hume's telephone call effective? Why or why not? _____

_____

2.  What did Joe accomplish? _____

_____

3.  How would you have handled this situation if you were Joe Hume? _____

_____

_____

130

Read the second version of the same telephone complaint. Then answer the questions about how the customer handled this complaint.

KATHY (counter person): Lino's Pizza. Kathy speaking. May I help you?

JOE HUME (customer): Yes, Kathy. This is Joe Hume at 1331 Linwood Drive. I ordered a Deluxe Pizza from Lino's over an hour ago. The pizza was *just* delivered. And it's cold.

KATHY: I'm sorry the pizza was cold, sir. But there's really nothing I can do. We had a lot of orders tonight, and we're really running behind.

JOE: Is the manager in?

KATHY: Yes, he is.

JOE: May I speak with him, please?

DAVID RYAN (manager): Dave Ryan. May I help you?

JOE: Yes, Mr. Ryan. I placed an order over an hour ago for one of your "10-minute" Pizza deliveries. I just paid $14.50 for a Deluxe Pizza that's too cold to eat. This is the second time in two weeks that this has happened.

MANAGER: What's your address, sir?

JOE: 1331 Linwood Drive

MANAGER: Linwood Drive is definitely *within* our 10-minute delivery zone. I'll have someone drop another Deluxe Pizza order by right away. How's that, sir?

JOE: That will be fine.

MANAGER: I'm sorry your order was delayed. We've been training a lot of new people, and we're running behind in our deliveries. Things should be back to normal soon, sir.

JOE: I understand. Thank you very much.

1. How would you rate this telephone complaint? Was Joe Hume's telephone call effective? Explain why or why not. _____

_____

2. What did Joe do differently? _____

_____

_____

**3.** Would you have handled this complaint the same way Joe did? If not, how would you have handled it?

_____

_____

_____

### Handling complaints in writing

Some complaints are _only_ effective in writing. If, for example, there is an error on your bill, you should follow up your phone call with a letter. This letter will give you a record of when and where you wrote. It will also show what you said. It will increase your chances for ACTION. You can always give a company until the next billing period to correct an error. After that, it's time to write a letter stating the problem. You can still call, but writing will protect your legal rights.

Sometimes you need to list the events that led to your complaint. This type of complaint is also handled best in writing. When you choose to complain to the owner or president of a large corporation, write. This person is most likely very busy. The job of following up on your complaint may be given to another person. In a letter you can state your complaint clearly. You can also send copies of any sales receipts or letters. This letter can be looked at again and again until the complaint is resolved.

## ACTIVITY 14

### Writing a letter of complaint

Pretend you are G. W. Anderson. Write Roland's Dinnerware Unlimited. You ordered a set of china. The sugar bowl was chipped when your shipment arrived. You would like a replacement. Your account number is 8611-003-32-4. You can make up addresses. Write the Consumer Sales Department. Use today's date.

_or_

Pretend you are D. R. Harvey. Write Grey's Department Store. The soles on the leather running shoes you bought came apart during the first week you wore them. You want a refund, but the clerk at the store refused. The manager of the shoe department was not available to talk with you. Now you write to the store manager with your complaint. Make up a date for the purchase of the shoes. You paid $75 for them. Make up addresses. Use today's date.

Choose the best meaning for the underlined word in each of the following sentences.

———— **1.** A <u>dealership</u> is
  **a.** a buyer
  **b.** a salesperson
  **c.** a store

———— **2.** <u>Small Claims Courts</u> handle cases involving
  **a.** less than $100
  **b.** $5,000 or less
  **c.** $1,000

———— **3.** A <u>retailer</u> is
  **a.** a buyer
  **b.** a store owner
  **c.** a credit customer

———— **4.** The <u>Better Business Bureau</u> is
  **a.** a local organization
  **b.** a state organization
  **c.** a federal organization

———— **5.** When a consumer suffers <u>damages</u>, he or she
  **a.** has been injured
  **b.** has lost money
  **c.** has been arrested

# SHOW WHAT YOU KNOW . . .

## About Complaints

Write a letter of complaint to a TV network. Complain about a program you recently saw or a change in the schedule of your favorite show.

# Getting a job

Job-hunters need a lot of skills. This chapter outlines skills you need in your job search. Some skills you will need even before you begin your search. Other skills are needed during the search. And other skills are needed during the job interview. *Getting a Job* is divided into four job skill areas:

Fact Sheets, Resumes, and Application Letters
Job Application Forms
Job Interview Techniques
Telephone Communication Skills

First you will learn how to write clear, complete information about yourself. This will be in the form of a fact sheet, resume, and letter of application. Next you will learn to transfer this information to the job application. (A variety of job applications are included here.) How do you handle a job interview? How do you get information about a job over the phone? In this chapter you will learn job interview skills. And you will learn how the telephone can be an effective part of your job search.

## Fact sheets, resumes, and application letters

**WORDS TO KNOW**

**application**   a form used for making a request, such as a job application or an application for credit

**qualifications**   a person's education and skills

**references**   a list of persons who know your work

**resume**   (rez'-ə-mā) a description of education and work experience

## Personal fact sheet

A fact sheet can be useful when you fill out job applications. Carry your personal fact sheet with you to provide names, dates, and numbers asked on application forms. There is no special form for a personal fact sheet. But it can look like the one on the next page. Study the sample. It gives facts about Nicarol Brown.

# PERSONAL FACT SHEET

Name __Nicarol Brown__

Address __101 E. Maple Rd.__     Phone # __555-8848__

__Ronstead, CA 90901__

Social Security # __521-06-9432__

## Education

| Schools Attended | Dates | Graduated | Diploma/Degree |
|---|---|---|---|
| Ronstead Elementary | 1977 - 1983 | yes | |
| Ronstead High School | 1983 - 1988 | yes | Diploma |
| Adams Community College | 1988 -1991 | yes | Certificate |

## Work Experience

| Employer | Address | Dates From | To |
|---|---|---|---|
| Ajax Manufacturing | 10 Main St., Ronstead, CA 90902 | 1991 | Present |
| Adams Community College | 851 North St., Canary, CA 90810 | 1989 | 1991 |
| Win's Pharmacy | 25 West Custer, Ronstead, CA 90901 | 1987 | 1989 |

## Special Interests or Skills

Computers — 2 courses in computer programming

Sports — soccer and softball

Music — member of high school band

## Honors

Computer project award

## References (other than members of the family)

| Name | Address | Phone No. |
|---|---|---|
| Mary Fischer | 19 Willow Pl., Ronstead, CA 90901 | 555-1201 |
| Adam Johnson | 85 West Holiday, Ronstead, CA 90902 | 555-8106 |
| Lenore Bains | 182 Avery Pl., Canary, CA 90812 | 555-1604 |

## ACTIVITY 1
### Making a personal fact sheet

Write your own personal fact sheet. Use the sample to help you.

**Resumes**

Many people apply for jobs by using resumes. A resume is a summary of your education and work experience. Your resume is important. It might be the one thing an employer has that describes *you*. Some job ads will say "send resume." Sometimes people who are looking for certain jobs will send out resumes. They want to know if a business or institution needs someone with their skills.

Resumes may be written in different ways. The type you write depends on what you want. If you are not applying for a specific job, you need to send a detailed resume. You want to know if there are any jobs that match your abilities. If you apply for a specific job, your resume should stress those skills that relate to that job. From time to time, you should update your resume.

**A detailed resume**

A detailed resume includes personal information and special interests. It also lists your educational background and job history. Special skills and references are also sections of a detailed resume. You might not need all of these sections. Employers who see many job requests each day may only want to see education and work background.

Below you will find the sections you *can* include in a detailed resume. Remember, it is always wise to write your resume to fit your own needs.

**Personal Information:** At the top of the resume, put your name, address, and telephone number.

**Special Interests:** Briefly list your special interests and achievements. You can include (1) places you have traveled, studied, or worked. (2) community or school achievement, (3) special hobbies, interests, or projects.

These two sections introduce you in a *personal* way. The rest of the resume should present you in a *professional* way.

**Educational Background:** Give the name and location of each school you have attended. Give your major and minor, and the degree, certificate, or diploma (if any) you received. Give dates attended and your graduation date.

**Employment History:** Starting with your present or most recent job, list the jobs you have held. Briefly describe your duties. If you have a good work record, include how long you worked at each job. If you have changed jobs often, you may want to leave out the dates. Include the name of your employer (e.g., Fine Foods Supermarket). Also include the address.

**Special Skills:** List any special skills that you have obtained during your working career. Include on-the-job training, supervising, or other special skills. Arrange

137

these so that the employer will quickly see what you can do. You can also put the length of time you have used a skill. (We have included just one way of doing this section in the sample resume that follows. You may want to add to it or take away parts.)

References: List the names of at least three people who can comment on your work abilities and personality. If you cannot include employers, list former teachers. You may also want to include community leaders. Give the names, addresses, telephone numbers, and job titles of these people.

---

## RESUME

### PERSONAL INFORMATION

Name:            Clarence E. Smith
Address:         108 Mill Street
                 Bel Air, Maryland 21001
Phone Number:    301-555-0121

### SPECIAL INTERESTS

I attended public schools in Bel Air, Maryland. My career interest since my sophomore year in high school has been in business. I participated in Bel Air High's Distributive Education Program my junior and senior years. The program combined school and work experience through various local businesses.

In high school I served two years as the president of the Minicorp Production Company, a Junior Achievement student business sponsored by the C&P Telephone Company. I was also a member of DECA—Distributive Education Clubs of America. When I graduated from Bel Air High School in 1991, I received an $800 scholarship from the local Chamber of Commerce. I was voted the "outstanding business student of the year." I am presently taking night courses in business at Harford Community College.

### EDUCATIONAL BACKGROUND

Bel Air High School — Graduated 1991
Bel Air, Maryland
Course of Study:  Distributive Education (Business Education)

Harford Community College — Attended Summer 1991–present
Aberdeen, Maryland
Major:  Business Administration

### EMPLOYMENT HISTORY

Employer:   Quick Shop Mini Mart
            Aberdeen, Maryland

Position: Stock person/cashier— I was in charge of pricing and stocking all merchandise for sale. This included creating sales displays and promotions for seasonal and holiday items. I also covered all register tours for employees absent or on vacation. I used the Sharp 3510 electronic cash register.

**Employer:** Baren's Furniture Store
Route 18
Bel Air, Maryland

**Position:** Floor Salesperson — As part of the Distributive Education Program at Bel Air High, I worked part time during school hours at Baren's Furniture. I averaged 20–25 hours per week as a furniture and appliance salesperson. I handled both cash and charge purchases. I operated a Martex 1050 register.

**Employer:** Burger Town
Town Center
Bel Air, Maryland

**Position:** Cashier — In this part-time assignment I gained fast-food experience. At this busy Town Center location, I worked both the "Drive-Thru" service and the regular "eat-in" customer service lines.

## SPECIAL SKILLS

| Type of Skill | Length of Experience | Job or Training Location |
|---|---|---|
| Operating electronic cash registers | 3 years | Quick Shop Mini Mart Baren's Furniture Store Burger Town |
| Stocking | 2 years | Quick Shop Mini Mart |
| Taking inventory | 2 years | Quick Shop Mini Mart Baren's Furniture Store |
| Using office machines: calculators, adding machines, typewriters, etc. | 2 years | Quick Shop Mini Mart Baren's Furniture Store |
| Using Vydec and Wang word processing machines, tele-typewriters, and office computers | 1 semester | Harford Community College: Business Machines and Computer Programming |

## REFERENCES

Mary Wright, Manager
Quick Shop Mini Mart
Aberdeen, Maryland 21001
301-555-4583

Wilson Logan, Owner
Burger Town
Town Center
Bel Air, Maryland 21014
301-555-7983

Laverne Jackson
Supervisor of Distributive Education
Bel Air High School
Bel Air, Maryland 21014
301-555-9786

Regina Holmes, Assistant Manager
Baren's Furniture
Route 18
Bel Air, Maryland 21014
301-555-2933

## ACTIVITY 2
### Writing a detailed job resume

You have just seen a sample of Clarence Smith's detailed resume. Now write *your own* detailed resume. Make sure your resume has these sections:

- Personal Information
  - Name
  - Address
  - Phone No.
- Special Interests

- Educational Background
- Employment History
- Special Skills
- References

### A brief resume

A brief resume should stress your skills for a specific job. It should have at least these four sections: (1) Position Applied For, (2) Experience, (3) Education, and (4) References. Below is a sample of a brief, one-page resume.

---

Thomas A. Lawson
27 Dunbar Street
Townsend, MO 64497
(417) 555-8904

POSITION APPLIED FOR:  Accounting Clerk

EXPERIENCE:
| | |
|---|---|
| June 1991 to present | Accounts receivable clerk<br>Weston's Department Store, Townsend, MO<br>Duties: Posting and balancing accounts, preparing statements<br>Salary: Staring $175  Present $225 |
| August 1989 to June 1991 | Stock clerk (part-time) Thompson's Department Store,<br>Townsend, MO<br>Duties: Organizing and pricing stock |

Education:  High School Graduate, 1989, Townsend High School

| | |
|---|---|
| Major Subjects: | Accounting, Office Machines, Business Mathematics, Business Management |
| Grade Average: | B |
| Extracurricular: | President of Junior Class<br>Treasurer of Senior Class<br>President of Future Business Leaders of America |

---

REFERENCES:

Mr. Frank Marshall, Accounting Supervisor
Weston's Department Store
85 Mason Street
Townsend, MO 64497
(417) 555-7702

Ms. Francine Yamada, Manager
Thompson's Department Store
33 Basin Street
Townsend, MO 64497
(417) 555-9802

Mr. Ira Goldman, Advisor
FBLA Club
Townsend High School
92 Fairlane Drive
Townsend, MO 64497
(417) 555-5400

# ACTIVITY 3
## Writing a brief resume

Write a brief resume. Apply for any job you are qualified to do. See page 140 for the four parts of a brief resume.

## Letters of application

Sometimes you may have to write a letter of application. It may be in response to a help-wanted ad. Or it may simply be part of your own job hunting efforts. Like the resume, the type of application letter you write will depend on the situation. If there are a number of people applying for the same job, you must write an especially effective letter.

The letter of application usually has the resume with it. The letter should contain three parts:

1. A statement of interest in a specific position
2. A brief statement of your abilities for this position (including a comment about your enclosed resume)
3. Information on how and where you can be reached

Remember:

- Try to obtain a *name* of a person. Write your letter of application to that person.

- Your letter should be typewritten and neat.

## ACTIVITY 4

### Understanding letters of application

Answer the questions about this letter of application.

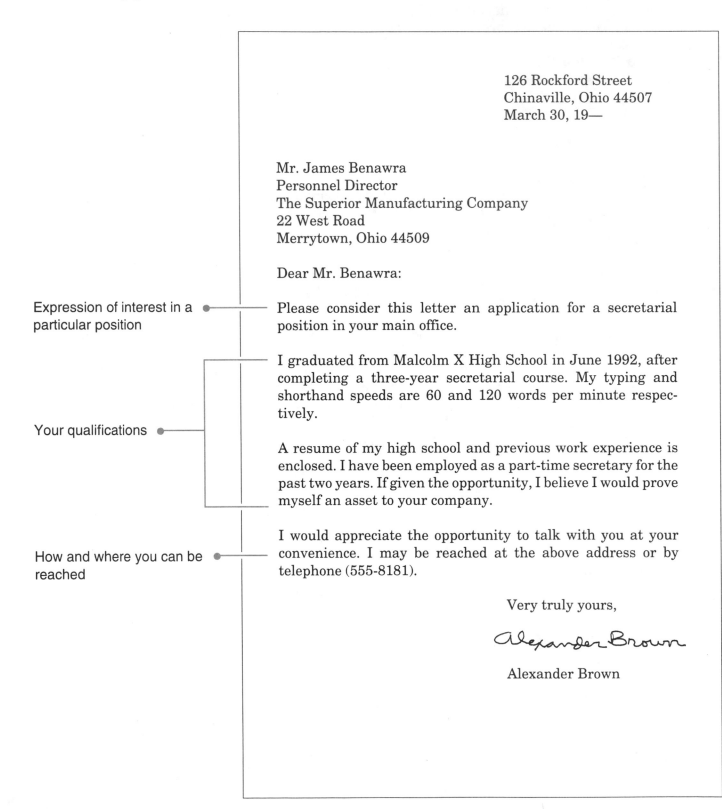

126 Rockford Street
Chinaville, Ohio 44507
March 30, 19—

Mr. James Benawra
Personnel Director
The Superior Manufacturing Company
22 West Road
Merrytown, Ohio 44509

Dear Mr. Benawra:

**Expression of interest in a particular position**

Please consider this letter an application for a secretarial position in your main office.

**Your qualifications**

I graduated from Malcolm X High School in June 1992, after completing a three-year secretarial course. My typing and shorthand speeds are 60 and 120 words per minute respectively.

A resume of my high school and previous work experience is enclosed. I have been employed as a part-time secretary for the past two years. If given the opportunity, I believe I would prove myself an asset to your company.

**How and where you can be reached**

I would appreciate the opportunity to talk with you at your convenience. I may be reached at the above address or by telephone (555-8181).

Very truly yours,

*Alexander Brown*

Alexander Brown

1.  What type of position is Alexander applying for? ——————————————

————————————————————————————————————————————

2.  What is the position of the person Alexander is writing to? ——————

————————————————————————————————————————————

3.  What are Alexander's qualifications? ————————————————————

————————————————————————————————————————————

4.  What is Alexander asking for as a result of his letter? ——————————

————————————————————————————————————————————

5.  How can he be reached? ——————————————————————————

————————————————————————————————————————————

6.  What will Alexander include with his letter of application? ——————————

7.  What previous work experience does he mention? ——————————————

8.  Did Alexander graduate from high school?———— If so, name the school. ——————

9.  What is Alexander's typing speed? ————————————————————

10. What is Alexander's home address? ————————————————————

On your own paper, write a letter of application. Select a job you might be interested in now or in the future.

# SHOW WHAT YOU KNOW . . .

## About Letters of Application

Find four help-wanted ads in your local newspaper. Look for jobs that interest you. After studying the ads carefully, choose two of them to answer. Write a letter of application for each. Be sure that your letters mention the particular position given in the ad.

## Job application forms

Nearly every job requires some form of written application. Most job applications have similar sections: personal information, education, work history, and references. Some applications, however, will have other sections, such as physical record, military service, and special skills. The job application should be completed correctly and neatly. Like the resume, it may be the only thing that tells an employer about you.

## ACTIVITY 5

### Filling out job applications

Study the following completed application and answer the questions about it.

# APPLICATION FOR EMPLOYMENT

**(PRE-EMPLOYMENT QUESTIONNAIRE)     (AN EQUAL OPPORTUNITY EMPLOYER)**

Date _July 17, 19—_

Name [Last Name First] _Johnson, Michael L._          Soc. Sec. No. _621-01-8841_

Address _422 Asbury Dr., Los Angeles, CA 90032_          Telephone _555-6113_

What kind of work are you applying for? _stock worker_

What special qualifications do you have? _strong, reliable_

What office machines can you operate? _typewriter_

Are you 18 years or older?  Yes _X_  No _____

## SPECIAL PURPOSE QUESTIONS

DO NOT ANSWER **ANY** OF THE QUESTIONS IN THIS FRAMED AREA UNLESS THE EMPLOYER HAS **CHECKED A BOX PRECEDING** A QUESTION, THEREBY INDICATING THAT THE INFORMATION IS REQUIRED FOR A BONA FIDE OCCUPATIONAL QUALIFICATION, OR DICTATED BY NATIONAL SECURITY LAWS, OR IS NEEDED FOR OTHER LEGALLY PERMISSIBLE REASONS.

☐ HEIGHT _____ FEET _____ INCHES _____  ☐ WEIGHT _____ LBS.  ☐ CITIZEN OF U.S.  YES _____ NO _____

☐ _____

## MILITARY SERVICE RECORD

Armed Forces Service _____ Yes _____ No _____ From* _____ To* _____

Branch of Service _____ Duties _____

Rank or rating at time of enlistment _____ Rating at time of discharge _____

Do you have any physical limitations that prohibit you from performing any work for which you are being considered?  Yes _____ No _____ . Please describe. _____

## EDUCATION

| SCHOOL | *NO. OF YEARS ATTENDED | NAME OF SCHOOL | CITY | COURSE | *DID YOU GRADUATE? |
|---|---|---|---|---|---|
| GRAMMAR | | | | | |
| HIGH | 4 | L.A. High School | Los Angeles | vocational | yes |
| COLLEGE | | | | | |
| OTHER | | | | | |

*The Age Discrimination in Employment Act of 1967 prohibits discrimination on the basis of age with respect to individuals who are at least 40 but less than 70 years of age.

## EXPERIENCE

| NAME AND ADDRESS OF COMPANY | DATE FROM | DATE TO | LIST YOUR DUTIES | STARTING SALARY | FINAL SALARY | REASON FOR LEAVING |
|---|---|---|---|---|---|---|
| Lynn's Apparel | 1991 | 1993 | preparing stock | $4.35 | $5.60 | need full time |
| | | | | | | |
| | | | | | | |
| | | | | | | |

## BUSINESS REFERENCES

| NAME | ADDRESS | OCCUPATION |
|---|---|---|
| Mr. Ted Anderson | Lynn's Apparel, 14921 Commons Pl. | store manager |
| | | |

This form has been designed to strictly comply with State and Federal fair employment practice laws prohibiting employment discrimination. This Application for Employment Form is sold for general use throughout the United States. TOPS assumes no responsibility for the inclusion in said form of any questions which, when asked by the Employer of the Job Applicant, may violate State and/or Federal Law.

TOPS Form 3286 (Revised)                                    Litho in U.S.A.

1. What position does Michael want? _____

2. Which high school did he attend? _____

3. What was his high school course of study? _____

4. Has Michael attended a college or trade school? _____

5. Can he operate any special machines or equipment? If so, which? _____

6. What kind of job has he had before? _____

7. Does Michael want to work full time or part time? _____

8. Has Michael served in the armed forces? _____

9. Does Michael need to tell this employer how tall he is? _____

10. Did Michael give his weight? _____ Why or why not? _____

# ACTIVITY 6

## Understanding a job application form

The following application is divided into sections. Each section contains step-by-step directions. Read and study these directions before completing this application.

---

# APPLICATION FOR EMPLOYMENT
## (PRE-EMPLOYMENT QUESTIONNAIRE)    (AN EQUAL OPPORTUNITY EMPLOYER)

**PERSONAL INFORMATION**

(1) DATE _____

(2) NAME _____   SOCIAL SECURITY NUMBER _____
    LAST          FIRST          MIDDLE

(3) PRESENT ADDRESS _____
    STREET          CITY          STATE

(4) PERMANENT ADDRESS _____
    STREET          CITY          STATE

(5) PHONE NO. _____   ARE YOU 18 YEARS OR OLDER   Yes ☐   No ☐

---

(1) Print today's date.

(2) Print your last name, then first name, then middle name or initial. Clearly print your social security number.

③ Print your present address. Be sure to include your ZIP Code.

④ If your present address is temporary (such as a summer location), write your regular address here. If your present and permanent address are the same, print "Same" here.

⑤ Clearly print the phone number where you can be reached.

---

**EMPLOYMENT DESIRED**

⑥ POSITION _____ DATE YOU CAN START _____ SALARY DESIRED _____

⑦ ARE YOU EMPLOYED NOW? _____ IF SO MAY WE INQUIRE OF YOUR PRESENT EMPLOYER? _____

⑧ EVER APPLIED TO THIS COMPANY BEFORE? _____ WHERE? _____ WHEN? _____

---

⑥ List the job you are asking for, when you can start, and what pay you expect.

⑦ Print "Yes" if you are working now and "No" if you are not. They are asking your permission to ask your employer about your work ability.

⑧ If you have applied there before, they want to know the location and dates you applied. This is used to locate any records they may have on you.

---

| ⑨ EDUCATION | NAME AND LOCATION OF SCHOOL | *NO. OF YEARS ATTENDED | *DID YOU GRADUATE? | SUBJECTS STUDIED |
|---|---|---|---|---|
| GRAMMAR SCHOOL | | | | |
| HIGH SCHOOL | | | | |
| COLLEGE | | | | |
| TRADE, BUSINESS OR CORRESPONDENCE SCHOOL | | | | |

---

⑨ Name the schools you attended, the years you attended, when you graduated, and the main subjects you studied.

(10) Name any special subject you have studied.

(11) Name, if any, the branch of service you have been in and the rank you obtained. Indicate whether you are presently a member of the National Guard or Reserves.

(12) If you are active in any club, write it here. *Do not* write the name of a club that would indicate your race, beliefs, or national origin.

(13) Starting with your last job, name the company you worked for and give its address. List what you were paid, the position you held, and your reason for leaving.

(14) Name three adults who can say what type of worker you are. Be sure to include full addresses and how long you have known each.

149

**PHYSICAL RECORD:**

(15) DO YOU HAVE ANY PHYSICAL LIMITATIONS THAT PRECLUDE YOU FROM PERFORMING ANY WORK FOR WHICH YOU ARE BEING CONSIDERED? ☐ Yes ☐ No

PLEASE DESCRIBE:

(16) IN CASE OF
EMERGENCY NOTIFY

(17)  NAME                    ADDRESS                    PHONE NO.

"I CERTIFY THAT THE FACTS CONTAINED IN THIS APPLICATION ARE TRUE AND COMPLETE TO THE BEST OF MY KNOWLEDGE AND UNDERSTAND THAT, IF EMPLOYED, FALSIFIED STATEMENTS ON THIS APPLICATION SHALL BE GROUNDS FOR DISMISSAL.

I AUTHORIZE INVESTIGATION OF ALL STATEMENTS CONTAINED HEREIN AND THE REFERENCES LISTED ABOVE TO GIVE YOU ANY AND ALL INFORMATION CONCERNING MY PREVIOUS EMPLOYMENT AND ANY PERTINENT INFORMATION THEY MAY HAVE, PERSONAL OR OTHERWISE, AND RELEASE ALL PARTIES FROM ALL LIABILITY FOR ANY DAMAGE THAT MAY RESULT FROM FURNISHING SAME TO YOU.

I UNDERSTAND AND AGREE THAT, IF HIRED, MY EMPLOYMENT IS FOR NO DEFINITE PERIOD AND MAY, REGARDLESS OF THE DATE OF PAYMENT OF MY WAGES AND SALARY, BE TERMINATED AT ANY TIME WITHOUT ANY PRIOR NOTICE."

(18) DATE                    SIGNATURE

---

(15) Describe any major injuries or handicap that you may have.

(16) Name someone who should be reached if something happens to you on the job. The address and telephone number are very important.

(17) This is a statement written *for you*. It reads as if you wrote it. You are giving the company permission

    (a) to check on any facts you have put on this application.
    (b) to dismiss (fire) you if they find any of your statements false.
    (c) to dismiss you at any time without giving you notice.

(18) Use today's date and sign (write out) your name.

## ACTIVITY 7
### Filling out job applications

Following are two job application forms. Complete each form for practice. Use today's date. Select any position that interests you now or may in the future. The first form is for McDonald's and the second is a general job application.

    The back of the McDonald's application contains a federal Form W-4. For tax purposes, every employer is required by law to obtain the information listed on the Form W-4. If you work, be sure to have a Form W-4 on file with your employer.

# EMPLOYMENT APPLICATION

NAME _____ FIRST NAME _____ MIDDLE INITIAL _____ LAST NAME _____

SOCIAL SECURITY NO. _____

APT. NO. OR BOX _____ CITY _____ STREET ADDRESS _____ STATE _____ ZIP _____

AREA CODE _____ TEL. NO. _____

ARE YOU 18 OR OLDER?  ☐ YES  ☐ NO, IF NOT, AGE _____

EVER WORKED IN A McDONALD'S RESTAURANT BEFORE?  ☐ YES  ☐ NO
IF YES, DATES, LOCATION AND REASON FOR LEAVING. _____

## AVAILABILITY:

TOTAL HOURS AVAILABLE PER WEEK _____

HOURS AVAILABLE:

| | M | T | W | T | F | S | S |
|---|---|---|---|---|---|---|---|
| FROM | | | | | | | |
| TO | | | | | | | |

HOW DID YOU HEAR OF JOB? _____

ARE YOU LEGALLY ABLE TO BE EMPLOYED IN THE U.S.:  ☐ YES  ☐ NO

HOW FAR DO YOU LIVE FROM RESTAURANT? _____

DO YOU HAVE TRANSPORTATION TO WORK? _____

## SCHOOL MOST RECENTLY ATTENDED:

NAME _____ LOCATION _____

TEACHER OR COUNSELOR _____ DEPT. _____ PHONE _____

LAST GRADE COMPLETED _____ GRADE POINT AVERAGE _____

GRADUATED  ☐ YES  ☐ NO    NOW ENROLLED?  ☐ YES  ☐ NO

SPORTS OR ACTIVITIES _____

## TWO MOST RECENT JOBS: (IF NOT APPLICABLE, LIST U.S. MILITARY. WORK PERFORMED ON A VOLUNTARY BASIS OR PERSONAL REFERENCES)

COMPANY _____ LOCATION _____

PHONE _____ JOB _____

SUPERVISOR _____ DATES WORKED: FROM _____ TO _____

SALARY _____ REASON FOR LEAVING _____

MGMT. REFERENCE CHECK DONE BY _____

COMPANY _____ LOCATION _____

PHONE _____ JOB _____

SUPERVISOR _____ DATES WORKED: FROM _____ TO _____

SALARY _____ REASON FOR LEAVING _____

MGMT. REFERENCE CHECK DONE BY _____

**YOUR APPLICATION WILL BE CONSIDERED ACTIVE FOR 30 DAYS - FOR CONSIDERATION AFTER THAT YOU MUST REAPPLY.**

Printed on Recycled Paper

QB PRODUCT NO. 4853125 (REV. 2/93) McCpCo

O'BRIEN BUDD, INC. - 1-800-762-7436

| Form **W-4** | Employee's Withholding Allowance Certificate | OMB No. 1545-0010 |
|---|---|---|
| Department of the Treasury<br>Internal Revenue Service | ▶ **For Privacy Act and Paperwork Reduction Act Notice, see reverse.** | **1993** |

**1** Type or print your first name and middle initial — Last name — **2** Your social security number

Home address (number and street or rural route)

City or town, state, and ZIP code

**3 Marital status**
☐ Single ☐ Married
☐ Married, but withhold at higher Single rate.
**Note:** *If married, but legally separated, or spouse is a nonresident alien, check the Single box.*

**4** Total number of allowances you are claiming (from line G above or from the Worksheets on back if they apply) . . . **4**

**5** Additional amount, if any, you want deducted from each pay . . . . . . . . . . . . . . **5** $

**6** I claim exemption from withholding and I certify that I meet **ALL** of the following conditions for exemption:
- Last year I had a right to a refund of **ALL** Federal income tax withheld because I had **NO** tax liability; **AND**
- This year I expect a refund of **ALL** Federal income tax withheld because I expect to have **NO** tax liability; **AND**
- This year if my income exceeds $500 and includes nonwage income, another person cannot claim me as a dependent.

If you meet all of the above conditions, enter the year effective and "EXEMPT" here . . . . ▶ **6** 19

**7** Are you a full-time student? (**Note:** *Full-time students are not automatically exempt.*) . . **7** ☐ Yes ☐ No

Under penalties of perjury, I certify that I am entitled to the number of withholding allowances claimed on this certificate or entitled to claim exempt status

Employee's signature ▶                                                Date ▶                    , 19

**8** Employer's name and address (**Employer:** Complete 8 and 10 **only if sending to IRS**) | **9** Office code (optional) | **10** Employer identification number

---

**IF YOU WANT THE COMPLETE W4 WITH INSTRUCTIONS, PLEASE ASK THE RESTAURANT MANAGER.**
**W4 IS TO BE FILLED OUT ONLY AFTER HIRE.**

---

**TO MASSACHUSETTS EMPLOYEES:**

An applicant for employment with a sealed record on file with the commissioner of probation may answer "no record" with respect to any inquiry herein relative to prior arrests, criminal court appearances or convictions. An applicant for employment with a sealed record on file with the commissioner of probation may answer "no record" to an inquiry herein relative to prior arrests or criminal court appearances. In addition, any applicant for employment may answer "no record" with respect to any inquiry relative to prior arrests, court appearances and adjudications in all cases of delinquency or as a child in need of services which did **not** result in a complaint transferred to the superior court for criminal prosecution.

It is unlawful in Massachusetts to require or administer a lie detector test as a condition of employment or continued employment. An employer who violates this law shall be subject to criminal penalties and civil liabilities.

# APPLICATION FOR EMPLOYMENT
### (PRE-EMPLOYMENT QUESTIONNAIRE)  (AN EQUAL OPPORTUNITY EMPLOYER)

## PERSONAL INFORMATION

DATE _____

SOCIAL SECURITY
NUMBER _____

NAME _____
LAST _____ FIRST _____ MIDDLE

PRESENT ADDRESS _____
STREET _____ CITY _____ STATE _____ ZIP

PERMANENT ADDRESS _____
STREET _____ CITY _____ STATE _____ ZIP

PHONE NO. _____ ARE YOU 18 YEARS OR OLDER?  Yes ☐  No ☐

ARE YOU EITHER A U.S. CITIZEN OR AN ALIEN AUTHORIZED TO WORK IN THE UNITED STATES?  Yes ☐  No ☐

## EMPLOYMENT DESIRED

POSITION _____ DATE YOU CAN START _____ SALARY DESIRED _____

ARE YOU EMPLOYED NOW? _____ IF SO MAY WE INQUIRE OF YOUR PRESENT EMPLOYER? _____

EVER APPLIED TO THIS COMPANY BEFORE? _____ WHERE? _____ WHEN? _____

REFERRED BY _____

| EDUCATION | NAME AND LOCATION OF SCHOOL | *NO OF YEARS ATTENDED | *DID YOU GRADUATE? | SUBJECTS STUDIED |
|---|---|---|---|---|
| GRAMMAR SCHOOL | | | | |
| HIGH SCHOOL | | | | |
| COLLEGE | | | | |
| TRADE, BUSINESS OR CORRESPONDENCE SCHOOL | | | | |

## GENERAL
SUBJECTS OF SPECIAL STUDY OR RESEARCH WORK _____

SPECIAL SKILLS _____

ACTIVITIES: (CIVIC, ATHLETIC, ETC.) _____
EXCLUDE ORGANIZATIONS, THE NAME OF WHICH INDICATES THE RACE, CREED, SEX, AGE, MARITAL STATUS, COLOR OR NATION OF ORIGIN OF ITS MEMBERS.

U.S. MILITARY OR NAVAL SERVICE _____ RANK _____ PRESENT MEMBERSHIP IN NATIONAL GUARD OR RESERVES _____

*The Age Discrimination in Employment Act of 1987 prohibits discrimination on the basis of age with respect to individuals who are at least 40 years of age.

TOPS ◆ FORM 3285 (89-8)  (CONTINUED ON OTHER SIDE)  LITHO IN U.S.A.

LAST — FIRST — MIDDLE

153

## FORMER EMPLOYERS (LIST BELOW LAST THREE EMPLOYERS, STARTING WITH LAST ONE FIRST).

| DATE MONTH AND YEAR | NAME AND ADDRESS OF EMPLOYER | SALARY | POSITION | REASON FOR LEAVING |
|---|---|---|---|---|
| FROM | | | | |
| TO | | | | |
| FROM | | | | |
| TO | | | | |
| FROM | | | | |
| TO | | | | |
| FROM | | | | |
| TO | | | | |

WHICH OF THESE JOBS DID YOU LIKE BEST? _____

WHAT DID YOU LIKE MOST ABOUT THIS JOB? _____

**REFERENCES:** GIVE THE NAMES OF THREE PERSONS NOT RELATED TO YOU, WHOM YOU HAVE KNOWN AT LEAST ONE YEAR.

| | NAME | ADDRESS | BUSINESS | YEARS ACQUAINTED |
|---|---|---|---|---|
| 1 | | | | |
| 2 | | | | |
| 3 | | | | |

THE FOLLOWING STATEMENT APPLIES IN: MARYLAND & MASSACHUSETTS. (Fill in name of state)
IT IS UNLAWFUL IN THE STATE OF _____ TO REQUIRE OR ADMINISTER A LIE DETECTOR TEST AS A CONDITION OF EMPLOYMENT OR CONTINUED EMPLOYMENT. AN EMPLOYER WHO VIOLATES THIS LAW SHALL BE SUBJECT TO CRIMINAL PENALTIES AND CIVIL LIABILITY.

_____
Signature of Applicant

IN CASE OF
EMERGENCY NOTIFY _____
       NAME          ADDRESS        PHONE NO.

"I CERTIFY THAT THE FACTS CONTAINED IN THIS APPLICATION ARE TRUE AND COMPLETE TO THE BEST OF MY KNOWLEDGE AND UNDERSTAND THAT, IF EMPLOYED, FALSIFIED STATEMENTS ON THIS APPLICATION SHALL BE GROUNDS FOR DISMISSAL.

I AUTHORIZE INVESTIGATION OF ALL STATEMENTS CONTAINED HEREIN AND THE REFERENCES LISTED ABOVE TO GIVE YOU ANY AND ALL INFORMATION CONCERNING MY PREVIOUS EMPLOYMENT AND ANY PERTINENT INFORMATION THEY MAY HAVE, AND RELEASE ALL PARTIES FROM ALL LIABILITY FOR ANY DAMAGE THAT MAY RESULT FROM FURNISHING SAME TO YOU.

I UNDERSTAND AND AGREE THAT, IF HIRED, MY EMPLOYMENT IS FOR NO DEFINITE PERIOD AND MAY, REGARDLESS OF THE DATE OF PAYMENT OF MY WAGES AND SALARY, BE TERMINATED AT ANY TIME WITHOUT PRIOR NOTICE AND WITHOUT CAUSE."

DATE _____ SIGNATURE _____

---

### DO NOT WRITE BELOW THIS LINE

INTERVIEWED BY _____ DATE _____

REMARKS: _____

_____

NEATNESS _____ ABILITY _____

HIRED: ☐ Yes ☐ No     POSITION _____ DEPT. _____

SALARY/WAGE _____ DATE REPORTING TO WORK _____

APPROVED: 1. _____ 2. _____ 3. _____
       EMPLOYMENT MANAGER      DEPT. HEAD      GENERAL MANAGER

154

Answer the following questions about job application forms.

1.  What is your social security number? _____

2.  If you have had three jobs, which one do you list first on a job application form? _____

3.  What is an equal opportunity employer? _____

4.  Which of the following pieces of information should you leave off an application for a job as a mail-room clerk? _____

    **a.** permanent address         **b.** telephone number
    **c.** church membership         **d.** military service

5.  What is the difference between a present address and a permanent address?

    _____

6.  What is a "bona fide occupational qualification"? _____

7.  Some job applications, such as the one shown here, state that "employment . . . may be terminated at any time without prior notice and without cause."

    What does this mean? _____

8.  Many employers use application forms that indicate they are equal opportunity employers. What does this mean? According to the statement on the application shown here, what is one specific factor that a prospective employer cannot legally consider when hiring a new employee?

9.  Suppose you are filling out a job application form at the personnel office of Ace Office Machine Co. You discover that you have written your name in ink on the wrong line of the form. Would you ask the secretary for another form? Why or why not?

    _____

10. Name three major types or sections of information asked on job application forms.

    _____

# SHOW WHAT YOU KNOW . . .

## About Job Application Forms

Obtain at least one job application form from a local employer. Complete the application, using what you have learned in this chapter.

## Job interview techniques

Several people may be right for a job. That is why your interview skills are so important. They may be what gets you the job! There are several points you should think about when getting ready for the job interview.

### Before the Interview:

1. *Go over your school record.* Know what subjects you had in school and which ones relate to the job you want. Be able to list your school activities, honors, hobbies, and your grade average and attendance record.
2. *Understand the job you are applying for.* Learn about the duties of the job.
3. *Pay special attention to your appearance.* Select clothes that are neat, clean, comfortable, and proper. Be sure that you are well rested and well groomed.
4. *Be on time!* Being on time is important on any job. Being late for the interview makes a very poor impression.

### During the Interview:

1. *Be polite.* Listen carefully to what the interviewer has to say. Do not interrupt. Thank the interviewer for time and interest spent.
2. *Use your best speaking manner.* Speak clearly. Answer questions with confidence. Be brief and exact. Avoid long answers, but say enough to answer questions.
3. *Follow the interviewer's lead.* The interviewer will probably tell you about the salary and working hours. Showing too much interest in lunch time, vacation time, sick leave, or short working hours may give the impression that you are more interested in time off than the time on.

## ACTIVITY 8

### Preparing for a job interview

Use the checklist below to rate yourself on how prepared you are for a job interview. This is practice now, but you may save this checklist to use when you prepare for a real job interview.

---

Name _____

| Job Interview Considerations | Yes ✓ | Needs More Work ✓ |
|---|---|---|
| **1.** I am familiar with my qualifications. | | |
| **2.** I understand the job I am applying for. | | |
| **3.** I know proper grooming and dress. | | |
| **4.** I am on time for appointments. | | |
| **5.** I am courteous. | | |
| **6.** I have a good speaking manner. | | |
| **7.** I am able to answer questions directly. | | |
| **8.** I do not smoke or chew gum during the interview. | | |

---

## ACTIVITY 9

### Preparing for a job interview

Below are some usual interview questions and responses. Some of the responses might hurt the applicant's chances of getting a job. Do you think the interviewer will *like* or *dislike* these responses? Code each response as L (like) or D (dislike). Explain each of your choices.

---

| Interviewer's Question | Applicant's Response | L | D | Explain |
|---|---|---|---|---|
| **1.** "Why did you apply to our company?" | "Because I live close to here." | ___ | ___ | _____ |
| **2.** "Why did you leave your last job?" | "I couldn't get along with my boss." | ___ | ___ | _____ |

**3.** "Are you willing to work overtime?"

"It depends on which days. I play softball on Tuesdays and Thursdays."

_____ _____

**4.** "Why are you applying for this job?"

"Because I need a job."

_____ _____

**5.** "When can you start?"

"Not until next week. I want to get a little more tennis practice in before it gets too hot."

_____ _____

## ACTIVITY 10

### Preparing for a job interview

Your ability to communicate well in a job interview is important. Often _how_ you say something can decide an interviewer's reaction. Did you say enough to answer questions completely? Did you say too much? Did you say something that will hurt your chances of getting a job? Did your need for better language skills prevent you from saying what you meant? Select the _best_ response for each of the questions below.

_____ **1.** "When can you start work?"
   **(a)** "Anytime next week."
   **(b)** "Will next week be okay with you?"
   **(c)** "Although I prefer Monday, I can start now, if you would like me to."

_____ **2.** "Can you give me one or two references?"
   **(a)** "One of my teachers, I guess."
   **(b)** "You can talk to the manager at Sun Ray Cleaners or my teachers."
   **(c)** "You can contact Miss Anne Willis, my high school English teacher, and Mr. Randy Campos, the manager at Sun Ray Cleaners, where I worked last summer."

_____ **3.** "Why did you leave your last job?"
   **(a)** "I wasn't learning nothing, and I never was going to get ahead."
   **(b)** "I couldn't get along with those people. They didn't show you how to do the job."
   **(c)** "I wanted to find a company that offered opportunities for advancement and training for its _new_ employees."

_____ **4.** "I noticed on your application that you live all the way across town. Will you have any difficulty getting to work?"
   **(a)** "Yeah. That's why I started not to come here."
   **(b)** "Well, this morning I caught a ride with a friend. It really is difficult to get a ride out this far."
   **(c)** "I've already considered that. And I can make arrangements to get to work every day, on time."

_____ **5.** "On your application you indicate that you have cashier experience. What can you tell me about your experience?"

   **(a)** "Ain't nothing to tell. I just used the register."

   **(b)** "I operated the Accu-Count XL3 register while working at Barclay's Department store as a cashier."

   **(c)** "I worked the register at Barclay's."

_____ **6.** "We were expecting you at 9:00 and you arrived at 9:30. Did you have any trouble finding us?"

   **(a)** "No, I didn't have any trouble."

   **(b)** "Finding you wasn't the problem. Getting up was the problem. My alarm clock didn't go off."

   **(c)** "I hope my being late has not inconvenienced you. The delay was unavoidable."

_____ **7.** "Why did you decide to try our company?"

   **(a)** "I don't know. . . . I'm just trying everybody."

   **(b)** "In today's tough job market, a person has to try every company with an opening that matches his or her qualifications and experience."

   **(c)** "I couldn't leave a stone unturned."

_____ **8.** "Why did you decide to take a job while still in school?"

   **(a)** "There're some things I want to do, and a job will make it a lot easier."

   **(b)** "My mother said find a job . . . so here I am."

   **(c)** "I'm old enough now to work a part-time job after school, and my family could really use the extra income."

Read each of the statements. Decide if each is TRUE (T) or FALSE (F).

_____ **1.** It is OK to chew gum during a job interview.

_____ **2.** It is not a good idea to wear blue jeans to a job interview.

_____ **3.** It is not necessary to prepare for an interview.

_____ **4.** It is all right to interrupt an interviewer.

_____ **5.** You will not be asked your school grade point average at an interview because that is private information.

Rewrite the following statements made during job interviews. Change them to improve the impression the applicant will make on the interviewer. You may want to model your answers after the best responses in Activity 10.

**6.** "I left my last job because I couldn't get along with my boss."

_____

_____

**7.** "I won't have no trouble getting to work because my sister's boyfriend works two miles from here, and he can bring me."

_____

_____

**8.** "I was late for the interview because my alarm didn't go off this morning."

_____

_____

**9.** "I quit my last job because I had a fight with another person who worked there."

_____

_____

**10.** "I came to this company because I need a job."

_____

_____

# SHOW WHAT YOU KNOW . . .

## About Job Interviews

You and a partner may use the situations below to role-play job interviewing. One of you act as the interviewer, and the other one act as the applicant. Select at least two situations for practice.

1. You are applying to be a salesclerk at a local department store.

2. You are applying to work in the stockroom at a local department store.

3. You are applying to be a counter person in a local burger place.

4. You are applying to be a bus person in a local restaurant.

5. You are applying to be an office helper at a local business.

## Telephone communications skills

It is important to know how to inquire about a job by phone. You may get an interview based on how well you handle a telephone call. Often help-wanted ads will tell you to call about the job advertised. You need to know how to take clear, complete phone messages while on the job, too. Good telephone skills can be an important part of getting and keeping a job.

## Job hunting and telephone interview skills

Have you ever used the classified-ad section of the newspaper to find a job? You may know that many help-wanted ads ask you to call about the opening. Sometimes the name and address of the company are in the ad. Sometimes they aren't. Many employers do not have the space or staff to see many applicants. When you call about an ad, these employers screen you. They ask you questions to see if you should come in for an interview. Employers may ask if you have a driver's license. They may ask if you own a car. They will want to know how much experience you have. They may ask how far you live from the job. Your call will also tell you if a job is still open. Many jobs are filled soon after they appear in the paper.

Some ads give you specific job information. They list hours, pay, location, and qualifications. When employers run these ads, they expect *you* to screen yourself. The call you make should only be to find out *how* to apply: whom to see, where to go, and what time. Your phone interview should be brief. Your goal is simply to find out what to do to get this job.

There are times, however, when an ad does not tell enough about a job. This may be on purpose. If you have questions, you must ask them with caution. Some employers receive many calls each day. The only way they will give you information is to have you come in. To ask too many questions can only annoy the employer. Read job ads carefully. Decide *before* you call which questions are proper and which are not. If the employer has given you information in the ad, know that information. Don't ask for the location when it's already given. Plan your questions before the call, especially the *first* question. And follow the flow of the conversation. Sometimes, employers will volunteer information. George Jennings called Bilko Manufacturing about a plant job. The phone conversation appears below:

INTERVIEWER: "Bilko Manufacturing. Personnel Department."

GEORGE: "Do you still have openings for plant workers?"

INTERVIEWER: "Yes, we have several left. The night shift pays $6.35 per hour. The day shift pays $5.20. If you would like to apply, you can come into our personnel office from 9–4, Mondays through Fridays."

GEORGE: "Thank you."

If the person on the phone sounds rushed, you must cooperate. If the person insists that you set up an interview, then set it up.

PERSONNEL INTERVIEWER: "Johnson Book Distributors."

APPLICANT: "Do you still have openings for book packers?"

PERSONNEL INTERVIEWER: "Yes, we do. If you want to apply, you must come in to our personnel office. Interviews are being held tomorrow between 8 A.M. and 2 P.M."

APPLICANT: "What working hours are available?"

PERSONNEL INTERVIEWER: (sounding annoyed) "I'm sorry, I'm unable to discuss work hours or pay rates over the phone. If you're interested, you *must* come in tomorrow between 8 and 2."

APPLICANT: "Where are you located?"

PERSONNEL INTERVIEWER: "We're at 1581 Grand Boulevard East. We're across from Worldwide Manufacturers. The personnel office is on the first floor" (telephone click).

APPLICANT: "Thank you."

Let's hope this applicant got the address and hours. A second call would annoy this interviewer. And the whole experience may have discouraged the job applicant. In this phone interview, a pencil and paper would have come in handy. It's always good to write down information you will need later. You should also circle the job ad you're interested in. You may need to look at the ad when you call about the job.

# ACTIVITY 11

### Telephoning about a job

Below you will find some job ads. There are also questions an applicant might ask. Some of these questions are proper over the phone. Others are not. In this activity you will decide which questions are suitable or proper and which are not.

```
WANTED
HIGH SCHOOL STUDENTS
FOR SUMMER WORK
CALL 555-7013
for information
```

- Which of these questions are suitable on the phone? Which are not? Explain your answers.

| | Suitable (✓) | Unsuitable (X) | Explain |
|---|---|---|---|
| "Do you *have* to be in high school to get this job?" | _____ | _____ | _____ _____ _____ _____ |
| "Can you give me any information about the job over the phone?" | _____ | _____ | _____ _____ _____ _____ |
| "How can I find out more about the job for summer work you advertised in today's paper?" | _____ | _____ | _____ _____ _____ _____ |

```
TUTORS NEEDED

Teenagers and adults.
Area high schools.
Nights. Help adults with
English, basic math, and
reading. Call: 555-6130
Ext. 481
```

• Which of these questions are suitable over the phone? Which are not? Explain your answers.

| | Suitable (✓) | Unsuitable (X) | Explain |
|---|---|---|---|
| (After reaching ext. 481) "To whom may I talk to find out more about the openings for tutors advertised in today's (name of newspaper)?" | | | |
| (After reaching ext. 481) "How much do the tutor positions pay?" | | | |
| (After reaching ext. 481) "Are there any day openings? I don't really want to work nights." | | | |
| (Reaching switchboard) "I'd like to come in and apply for the job of tutor. Can you help me?" | | | |
| (Reaching switchboard) "Will you connect me with extension 481, please?" | | | |

## ACTIVITY 12

### Evaluating telephone interviews

Below are several job ads. The applicant's *goals* are also stated. First, you are to read each ad. Then read the telephone conversation that follows the ad. Decide how the phone interview went. Did the applicant accomplish his or her goal?

---

Counselors Wanted
Summer day camps. Must
be 17 years or older. Some
day camp experience helpful
or experience with children
as day care aide, tutor, YMCA
worker, etc. Call Camping Inc.
555-1703, Ext. 43

---

*Applicant's goals:*

1. To find out if there are still openings.

2. To try to determine if the job pays above the minimum wage before spending money to go across town for the interview.

---

APPLICANT: "Extension 43, please."

BOB MORRISON: "Bob Morrison."

APPLICANT: "I'm calling about your ad in the *Daily News* for day camp counselors."

BOB MORRISON: "Just a minute. I'll connect you with someone who can help you."

INTERVIEWER: "Hello. This is Anne Richardson. May I help you?"

APPLICANT: "Yes. It's about the counseling job . . ."

INTERVIEWER: (silence)

APPLICANT: "I'm interested in the job you advertised in the paper." (long pause . . . no response) "Do you still have positions available?"

INTERVIEWER: "Yes, we do. When can you come in for an interview?"

APPLICANT: "Well, I'd like to know how much the job pays first."

INTERVIEWER: "I'm sorry. We do not discuss salary over the phone."

APPLICANT: "Ohhh . . . I see . . . Does it pay above the minimum wage?"

INTERVIEWER: "Sir, we do not discuss salary over the phone. You will have to come in for an interview."

APPLICANT: "Okay. I just thought . . ."

INTERVIEWER: "When can you come in?"

APPLICANT: "How about Thursday . . . no, no . . . Friday would be better. I have a game Thursday."

INTERVIEWER: (Silence . . .)

APPLICANT: "Must I come at any special time on Friday?"

INTERVIEWER: "No."

**1.** How do you think the applicant handled this phone interview? Explain.

_____

_____

**2.** Did he achieve his goal? Why or why not?

_____

_____

Major department store needs sales-clerks w/experience. H.S. grads only. Some college preferred. Call Anne Hutchinson for interview appointment. 555–1890

*Applicant's goals:*

Joan Pillerman is calling in reference to this job. Joan's qualifications match those outlined. Joan's goal: an interview.

SWITCHBOARD OPERATOR: "Bergman's Department Store."

JOAN: "Anne Hutchinson, please."

SWITCHBOARD OPERATOR: "Is she with personnel?"

JOAN: "Yes, I think so."

SWITCHBOARD OPERATOR: (Rings Personnel)

ANNE HUTCHINSON: "Personnel Department, Miss Hutchinson."

JOAN: "Is this *Anne* Hutchinson?"

ANNE HUTCHINSON: "Yes, it is."

JOAN: "My name is Joan Pillerman. I'm calling about your ad in today's paper. Do you still have openings for salesclerks?"

ANNE HUTCHINSON: "Yes, we do."

JOAN: "I would like to come in for an interview."

ANNE HUTCHINSON: "Are you a high school graduate?"

JOAN: "Yes, and I'm taking evening classes in business management at the Community College."

ANNE HUTCHINSON: "Oh, that's great! How about tomorrow morning at 9:00, Joan?"

JOAN: "Tomorrow morning at nine would be fine."

ANNE HUTCHINSON: "Do you know where Bergman's is located?"

JOAN: "Yes, I do."

ANNE HUTCHINSON: "Come to the personnel office. We're on the eighth floor."

JOAN: "Thank you . I'll see you tomorrow morning at nine."

**1.** How do you think the applicant handled this phone interview? Explain. _____

_____

_____

**2.** Did she achieve her goal? Why or why not? _____

_____

_____

## Taking telephone messages

After you are on the job, the phone will still be important. Almost everyone has had to leave a telephone message. Have you ever taken a telephone message? Did you tell the person who received the call what the other person said? Did you write a memo? Communicating by phone is a skill you need at home and on the job.

Whether the message you take is personal or job related, there are certain skills you must have. First, you must know *what* information a message should have. How do you decide this? Ask yourself what *you* would want to know if you got a telephone message. What do you expect when someone says, "Anne called"? The person taking the message "Anne called" has already told you who called. You might ask, "What did Anne want?" or "What was the message?" Not everyone leaves a message, especially friends and family. Sometimes people just call. But the person who wasn't in may still have questions. He or she may want to know who called and WHEN they called. Sometimes the person calling may leave a telephone number. This person wants you to know HOW TO REACH them. When you take a phone message, find out:

- Who is calling
- When (the time of the call)
- What is the message
- How to reach the caller

Read the call memo below. It is a job memo. Does it answer *WHO CALLED?* *WHEN? WHAT* was said? *HOW TO REACH THE CALLER?*

CALL MEMO

```
┌─────────────────────────────────────────────────┐
│          ( IMPORTANT MESSAGE )                   │
│  FOR    Anne Smith                               │
│  DATE   5-16            TIME  10:15  A.M.         │
│                                      P.M.        │
│  M r. Robert Grimes                              │
│  OF   Best Value Office Supply                   │
│  PHONE              555-0010                      │
│         AREA CODE        NUMBER       EXTENSION   │
│  ┌──────────────────┬───┬───────────────────┐    │
│  │ TELEPHONED       │ ✓ │ PLEASE CALL       │    │
│  ├──────────────────┼───┼───────────────────┤    │
│  │ CAME TO SEE YOU  │   │ WILL CALL AGAIN   │    │
│  ├──────────────────┼───┼───────────────────┤    │
│  │ WANTS TO SEE YOU │   │ RUSH              │    │
│  ├──────────────────┼───┼───────────────────┤    │
│  │ RETURNED YOUR CALL│  │ SPECIAL ATTENTION │    │
│  └──────────────────┴───┴───────────────────┘    │
│  MESSAGE  Your order will                        │
│   be ready Thursday                              │
│                                                  │
│                                                  │
│  SIGNED    Janet Walters                         │
│  LITHO IN U.S.A.                                 │
└─────────────────────────────────────────────────┘
```

TOPS FORM 3002P

On the job, there are likely to be many telephone calls each day. Some of these people may not leave a message. They may simply call back later. But it's a good idea to ask, "Is there a message?" If the person does not tell you a telephone number, you could ask, "Is there a number where you can be reached?" You have to follow the flow of the conversation. For example, the memo above resulted from this phone conversation.

JANET WALTERS: "Janet Walters, Quick Copy Printing."

ROBERT GRIMES: "This is Best Value Office Supply. Is Anne Smith in?"

JANET WALTERS: "No, Ms. Smith is out of the office at the moment."

ROBERT GRIMES: "Well, just tell her that her order will be ready Thursday."

JANET WALTERS: (writing . . .) "Her order will be ready Thursday."

ROBERT GRIMES: "Yeah, that's right."

JANET WALTERS: "And you're with . . . ?"

ROBERT GRIMES: "Best Value Office Supply. I'm Robert Grimes."

JANET WALTERS: "Is there a number where Ms. Smith can reach you?"

ROBERT GRIMES: "Yes. 555–0010."

Janet Walters had to question the caller. She wanted to leave a complete message for Anne Smith. If Ms. Smith has a question about the order, she can call Robert Grimes at 555–0010. If she doesn't remember the salesman, Robert Grimes, she will find the company's name on the memo. And you will recall that the memo had the message, "Your order will be ready Thursday." Janet Walters took a very effective memo. It answered:

- Who called        Robert Grimes, Best Value Office Supply
- When             10:15, May 16
- The message     "Your order will be ready Thursday."
- How to reach
  the caller            555–0010

Janet's message was also brief. She only wrote the important details. You should notice that Janet Walters did not say where Ms. Smith was when Robert Grimes called. It would *not* be proper to say "Ms. Smith is not back from lunch yet, " or "Ms. Smith is late for work this morning."

## ACTIVITY 13

### Taking phone messages

Pretend that you are the receptionist handling the following call. Read the conversation carefully. Then write the information required by the call memo.

Time: 9:40 A.M.

RECEPTIONIST: "This is Baker and Bailey Law Firm. May I help you?"

CLIENT: "This is Robert Whitney. I'd like to speak with Mr. Baker about a case he's handling for me."

RECEPTIONIST: "Mr. Baker is not in."

CLIENT: "When do you expect him?"

RECEPTIONIST: "He'll be in after lunch."

CLIENT: "I'll try again after 2:00. If I don't reach him today, will you have him call me tomorrow at my home? The telephone number is 555–0703. Thank you."

```
┌─────────────────────────────────────────────┐
│         (IMPORTANT MESSAGE)                  │
│                                              │
│  FOR _____ │
│                                        A.M.  │
│  DATE _____ TIME _____ P.M.   │
│                                              │
│  M _____ │
│                                              │
│  OF _____ │
│                                              │
│  PHONE _____  │
│        AREA CODE      NUMBER     EXTENSION   │
│  ┌──────────────────┬──┬───────────────┬──┐  │
│  │ TELEPHONED       │  │ PLEASE CALL   │  │  │
│  ├──────────────────┼──┼───────────────┼──┤  │
│  │ CAME TO SEE YOU  │  │ WILL CALL AGAIN│ │  │
│  ├──────────────────┼──┼───────────────┼──┤  │
│  │ WANTS TO SEE YOU │  │ RUSH          │  │  │
│  ├──────────────────┼──┼───────────────┼──┤  │
│  │ RETURNED YOUR CALL│ │ SPECIAL ATTENTION│ │ │
│  └──────────────────┴──┴───────────────┴──┘  │
│                                              │
│  MESSAGE _____ │
│  _____ │
│  _____ │
│  _____ │
│  _____ │
│  _____ │
│  _____ │
│                                              │
│  SIGNED _____ │
│  LITHO IN U.S.A.                             │
└─────────────────────────────────────────────┘

TOPS ▽ FORM 3002P
```

- In this conversation, you are Tracy E. Johnson, a co-worker of John Penn. Read the talk that follows. Then write the memo just as Tracy would. Be sure to initial the memo.

3:30 P.M.

TRACY JOHNSON: "John Penn's line . . . Tracy Johnson speaking. May I help you?"

ARNOLD JENKINS: "Yes. This is Arnold Jenkins of Whitney Electronics. I'd like to speak with Mr. Penn if that's possible."

TRACY JOHNSON: (Leaves the phone) "I'm sorry, I'm unable to locate Mr. Penn. May I take a message?"

ARNOLD JENKINS: "Tell him that I will have the information he asked for tomorrow morning at 9 o'clock."

TRACY JOHNSON: "Does Mr. Penn have your number?"

ARNOLD JENKINS: "You'd better take it. He may wish to call me today. It's 252–0401, area code 304, extension 21."

TRACY JOHNSON: "Thank you, Mr. Jenkins. I'll see that Mr. Penn gets your message."

```
┌─────────────────────────────────────────────────┐
│            ⟨IMPORTANT MESSAGE⟩                   │
│                                                  │
│  FOR _____ │
│                                          A.M.    │
│  DATE _____ TIME _____ P.M.  │
│                                                  │
│  M _____  │
│                                                  │
│  OF _____  │
│                                                  │
│  PHONE _____   │
│          AREA CODE        NUMBER      EXTENSION  │
│  ┌──────────────────┬──┬──────────────────┬──┐   │
│  │ TELEPHONED       │  │ PLEASE CALL      │  │   │
│  ├──────────────────┼──┼──────────────────┼──┤   │
│  │ CAME TO SEE YOU  │  │ WILL CALL AGAIN  │  │   │
│  ├──────────────────┼──┼──────────────────┼──┤   │
│  │ WANTS TO SEE YOU │  │ RUSH             │  │   │
│  ├──────────────────┼──┼──────────────────┼──┤   │
│  │ RETURNED YOUR CALL│ │ SPECIAL ATTENTION│  │   │
│  └──────────────────┴──┴──────────────────┴──┘   │
│                                                  │
│  MESSAGE _____   │
│  _____   │
│  _____   │
│  _____   │
│  _____   │
│  _____   │
│  _____   │
│                                                  │
│  SIGNED _____   │
│  LITHO IN U.S.A                                  │
└─────────────────────────────────────────────────┘
TOPS ⬢ FORM 3002P
```

If no printed message forms are available, be sure that you provide the following information on a piece of paper:

- Date and exact time of the phone call

- Correct name, company, and phone number of the caller

- Message

- Desire regarding the return call

- Your name or initials

To make certain you have written the correct information, repeat the message, including the phone number, to the caller for confirmation.

Rewrite the following message in a brief, businesslike form. The message is for David Jacobson.

Today when the phone rang it was Jim from the bookstore on the corner called Jim Brown's Bookstore. He said that your order has been held up. He said that you ordered a book called *How to Write a Resume.* The book will probably be in on January 1. He will call you when the book comes in. He kept being interrupted by customers, but he said his telephone number is 555-4582.

Fill in the blank spaces in the following statements. Choose words that are appropriate and businesslike.

**1.** (Your boss has been at lunch for the past two hours. You answer his calls.)

"Mr. Greene is _____ . May I help you?"

**2.** (You are calling Burger Barn about a part-time job that was advertised in the newspaper.)

"Hello. I _____ about _____ ."

**3.** (Your boss, Mr. Greene, wants to make an appointment with Ms. Carolyn Benson of Northwest Industries. She is expecting him to call. He asks you to make the call asking for an appointment either Monday or Tuesday morning.)

"Hello. This is _____ . I am calling for _____ . Mr. Green would like to _____

_____ ."

**4.** (You are calling Ajax Manufacturing about a part-time warehouse job. You want to know if after-school hours are available.)

"Hello. I _____ about _____ . I need to know _____

_____ ."

**5.** (You want to get a part-time job. You would like to work at the department store where your friend works. They have not advertised for workers. But you decide to call and inquire.)

"Hello. I would like _____ . Will you please tell me _____ ."

# SHOW WHAT YOU KNOW . . .

## About Telephone Skills

Select a partner to role-play the telephone situation described below.

PARTNER 1: You are calling about a job as a stock person advertised in the local newspaper. The person you need to speak to is Marci Snead. She is not in at this time. You want to leave her a message and want her to call you back.

PARTNER 2: You are the switchboard operator at Roosevelt Department Store. You receive a call intended for Marci Snead. The person is asking about a job as stock person. You must take the message for Ms. Snead. Be sure to get all of the information she will need to return the call.

# Filling out forms

Have you ever applied for a library card? Did you sign up for the school soccer team? Perhaps you have ordered something from a catalog or applied for a social security card. We fill out forms for lots of reasons. They are a necessary part of our lives.

In filling out any form you need to know two things: (1) what you have been asked, and (2) how and where to write the answers. This chapter will teach you the language of forms. You will learn the vocabulary you need in filling out applications. This will help you understand what you have been asked. You will also learn where and how to write your answers.

First you will study some forms you see every day. Examples are an application for a library card and a voter registration form. You will study an application for a social security number. Then you will study and practice writing checks, filling out deposit slips, and keeping a check register. You will learn about consumer credit applications. You will also practice filling out a catalog order form.

## Everyday forms

### WORDS TO KNOW

**applicant's signature**   your name written out

**apt.**   apartment

**disability**   any physical or medical problem that might affect your ability to drive or work

**in lieu of**   in place of

**maiden name**   the last name of an unmarried woman

**mailing address**   address to which your mail is sent

**mandatory**   required, such as proof of age

**native-born**   born in the country (not state) shown on the form

**naturalized**   not native-born; became a citizen of the country shown on the form

**occupation**   what you do for a living

**restriction**   limitation; something you should not or cannot do

**revoke**   to take back; cancel

**suspend**   to come to a stop, usually for a short time

**valid**   proper; legal

**voluntary answer**   an answer that you may or may not choose to give

**witness**   person who writes his or her name on a form to show that he or she saw someone else sign it

Study the words in the *Words to Know* section. Knowing these words will help you do the activities in this section.

## ACTIVITY 1

### Understanding the vocabulary of everyday forms

Match the words in Column A with their definitions in Column B.

**A**

_____ 1. disability

_____ 2. native-born

_____ 3. mandatory

_____ 4. revoke

_____ 5. in lieu of

_____ 6. restriction

_____ 7. occupation

_____ 8. suspend

_____ 9. witness

_____ 10. valid

**B**

**A.** person who signs a form to show he or she saw someone else sign it

**B.** limitation

**C.** physical or mental problem that might affect your ability to drive or work

**D.** in place of

**E.** proper; legal

**F.** born in the country shown on the form

**G.** required

**H.** what you do for a living

**I.** to take back; cancel

**J.** to come to a stop, usually for a short time

Complete the statements below using words from the *Words to Know* list.

**11.** The examiner asked whether my driver's license had been _____

   or _____ .

**12.** I can drive to the lake because my driver's license is still _____ .

**13.** You may be asked whether your driver's license is being held _____ bail.

**14.** I became a _____ citizen last October.

**15.** Is it _____ to show a birth certificate to get a social

   security card?

Always briefly look over a form before you fill it out. Determine *how* and *where* to write your responses. For example, a form may require that you print or type your answers. It may require that you write in *ink*. There may be sections that don't apply to you. You may be asked to write your last name first. You may have to write smaller than you usually do.

Most people fill in the information on a form as they come to it. Here are examples of what can happen when you do this:

(maiden name)

Name Georgiana (Wright) Power SS# 000-00-000

Address 411 Park Avenue

East Orange, New Jersey

Maiden Name Georgiana Wright

Georgiana Power wanted the person inspecting this form to know her former name. Notice that she included her maiden name on the first line. If she had skimmed the entire application first, she would have seen the space provided for this information.

| Name | | Age | Sex |
|---|---|---|---|
| Lynda Coles | | 18 | F |

Address
118 Woodlawn, Belaire, Maryland

| Home phone | Work phone |
|---|---|
| 555-7210 | 555-1304 |

Occupation
Short Order Cook

Soc. Sec. No. 000-14-1910
DO NOT WRITE BELOW THIS LINE

Lynda Coles ran out of space before answering all of the questions. She still had to give her social security number. All the information requested should have been written *above* the lines, *not below*.

```
Name          Pamela Hughes

Address       1181 Congress Ave., Apt. 8-J,   Columbus
                                              Ohio
                                              43012

City          Columbus              State    Ohio

ZIP Code      43012                  SS #     000-10-6191

Birth Date    2    10    76
              M    D     Yr
```

Some of the information on this form has been crossed out. Pamela Hughes filled in her complete address on the line requesting address. She later realized that the address line was for the street. A different space was provided for city, state, and ZIP Code.

## REGISTRATION FORM

All classes meet at Mountain View Community Center, 55 E. Valley Rd., Mountain View, Colorado. Enrollments are limited and registration is on a first-come, first-served basis. Registration must be accompanied by payment. Classes are $40 each.

```
Name        SANCHEZ      RAFAEL
            LAST         FIRST

Address     414 N. PINE     Apt.   212

City        MOUNTAIN
            VIEW      State   CO   ZIP _____
```

I wish to take the following class(es):

| | | |
|---|---|---|
| _____ | Woodworking | |
| _____ | Cooking | |
| _____ | Spanish | |
| _____ | English | |
| _____ | Sewing | |
| _____ | Accounting | |
| _____ | Auto Repair | |

I enclose the amount of

$ _____

Make checks payable to
Mountain View Community
Center.

Signature:

_____

Date received    AUG. 3, 1994

Payment          _____

No. of classes   _____

Enrollment  _____  WW
            _____  C
            _____  S
            _____  E
            _____  SE
            _____  A

This applicant started to complete his registration without reading over the form. He dropped down to Name and began writing. As he worked *across* the form, he saw Date received. He started to fill out these blanks also. The heading above reads DO NOT WRITE ON THIS SIDE.

Always look over a form before filling it out. Make all answers neat and complete. The information requested may differ from form to form, but there are certain questions you can be ready to answer. Always know who your references are. Know what county you live in. Know your phone number and your social security number. If you are applying for a driver's license, have your driver's education certificate handy. You may be asked about it. If you are applying for a student loan, you may be asked about your income or your parents' income. One day you may be filling out a voter registration form. Know the name of your county or township. An application should always be as *complete* as possible.

## ACTIVITY 2
### Completing forms

Complete the forms below as neatly and accurately as possible.

---

# PUBLIC LIBRARY

APPLICATION FOR LIBRARY CARD

NAME _____

ADDRESS _____

    City       State  ZIP   County

TELEPHONE _____ BIRTH DATE _____
                                     M   D  YR

    I understand that I must abide by all rules and regulations of this library and all city branches.

       Signature _____

---

For your free Kentucky travel packet, call toll-free or write:
Travel, Dept. ML-02, Box 2011, Frankfort, KY 40602.

Name _____

Address _____

City _____ State _____ Zip _____

*The Uncommon Wealth of*
# KENTUCKY
1-800-225-TRIP

## ACTIVITY 3   Study the next form and answer the questions.

### VOTER REGISTRATION FORM
PLEASE PRINT IN INK OR TYPE

**1** Name of the registrant (Please Print):
*Patterson,*          *Lance*          *Adam*
LAST                  FIRST            MIDDLE

**2** Residence of the registrant: *803 Long Lake Road*
STREET ADDRESS                                    APARTMENT NUMBER
*Elizabeth*          *Union*          *07201*
MUNICIPALITY         COUNTY          ZIP

**3** Rural Mailing Address (if any):

R.D. NUMBER          BOX          MUNICIPALITY          ZIP

**4** This form is being used as (Check One):
☑ New Registration   ☐ Change of Address   ☐ Change of Name

**5** Birth Date:
*12* | *19* | *74*
MONTH   DAY   YEAR

**6** From what address did you last register to vote, and under what name?

LAST NAME          FIRST          MIDDLE

STREET ADDRESS                    APARTMENT NUMBER

MUNICIPALITY          COUNTY          STATE          ZIP

**7** I am a ☑ native born   ☐ naturalized citizen (Check One).
I was naturalized:

MONTH          DAY          YEAR          MUNICIPALITY          STATE

**8** By the time of the next general election, I will be at least 18 years of age, I will be a citizen of the United States, and I will have resided in this State at least 30 days and in the county of *Union* at least 30 days. To the best of my knowledge and belief, all the foregoing statements made by me are true and correct. I understand that any false or fraudulent registration or attempted registration may subject me to a fine of up to $1,000.00 or imprisonment of up to 5 years, or both pursuant to R.S. 19:34-1.

*Lance A. Patterson*          | *10-21-93*
SIGNATURE OR MARK OF THE REGISTRANT          DATE OF SIGNATURE

**9** I, being a registered voter in *Union* county in the State of New Jersey, witnessed the making of the above signature or mark.

*Vaughn P. Jonas*          | *10-21-93*
SIGNATURE OF THE WITNESS          DATE OF WITNESSING

*Vaughn P. Jonas*
NAME OF THE WITNESS (Please Print):

*816 Long Lake Road, Elizabeth*          *Union*          *07201*
STREET ADDRESS OF THE WITNESS          MUNICIPALITY          COUNTY          ZIP

1. The registrant is _____ .

2. He is registering to _____ .

3. He lives at _____ in _____ County.

4. This form is being used as _____ .

5. His witness is _____ .

## Application for driver's license

In many states you do not have to fill out an application for a driver's license. Instead, you are asked questions by an employee of a driver's license facility or office. Your answers will then be typed directly into a computer. Your local facility will tell you what you are required to have when you apply for a license. You will probably need identification that will verify your name, your birth date, and your social security number. You may be asked questions like the following. Study these questions as if you were preparing to apply for a license; answer them for yourself.

1.  Is your driver's license or privilege to obtain a license suspended, revoked, canceled, or refused in any state under this or any other name? _____

2.  Do you presently hold a valid driver's license in this or any other state? _____

3.  Is your driver's license being held in court in lieu of bail? _____

4.  Do you have any condition that might cause a temporary loss of consciousness? (If yes, a physician's statement is required.) _____

5.  Do you have any mental or physical condition that might interfere with safe driving?
    _____

## Application for a social security card

One of the most important forms you will ever complete is your application for a social security number. Everyone in the United States who has a job should have a social security card. Your social security card shows your social security number. Tax laws require that taxpayers show social security numbers for their dependents on tax forms. Children now receive social security numbers before they enter school. Should you ever apply for social security benefits, you will need your social security number.

181

If you were born in the United States and have never had a social security number, you must show documents that give your age and citizenship. You will need to show your birth certificate and some form of identification.

If you are a U.S. citizen who was born outside the United States, you will need your consular report of birth, if you have one. You will also need one form of identification. If you do not have your consular report of birth, you will need your foreign birth certificate and one of the following: a U.S. Citizen ID card, U.S. passport, Certificate of Citizenship, or a Certificate of Naturalization.

Here are some examples of the kinds of documents that will show who you are.

- Driver's license

- U.S. government or state employee ID card

- Passport

- School ID card, record, or report card

- Marriage or divorce record

- Health insurance card

- Clinic, doctor, or hospital records

- Military records

- Court order for name change

- Adoption records

- Church membership or confirmation record (if not used as evidence of age)

- Insurance policy

- Any other document that establishes your identity

# ACTIVITY 4

## Filling out an application for a social security card

Study the social security card application on the next page including the instructions at the top. Decide whether the statements below are TRUE (T) or FALSE (F).

_____ 1. You may print on the application form.

_____ 2. You may use a typewriter to complete the form.

_____ 3. You may complete the form in red ink.

_____ 4. You may skip question 5—Race/Ethnic Description.

_____ 5. If you give false information on the form, you may be sent to prison.

# SOCIAL SECURITY ADMINISTRATION
## Application for a Social Security Card

Form Approved
OMB No. 0960-0066

| INSTRUCTIONS | • Please read "How To Complete This Form" on page 2. |
|---|---|
| | • Print or type using black or blue ink. DO NOT USE PENCIL. |
| | • After you complete this form, take or mail it along with the required documents to your nearest Social Security office. |
| | • If you are completing this form for someone else, answer the questions as they apply to that person. Then, sign your name in question 16. |

**1 NAME**
To Be Shown On Card
▶

FIRST         FULL MIDDLE NAME         LAST

FULL NAME AT BIRTH
IF OTHER THAN ABOVE

FIRST         FULL MIDDLE NAME         LAST

OTHER NAMES USED

**2 MAILING ADDRESS**
Do Not Abbreviate
▶

STREET ADDRESS, APT. NO., PO BOX, RURAL ROUTE NO.

CITY         STATE         ZIP CODE

**3 CITIZENSHIP**
(Check One)
☐ U.S. Citizen  ☐ Legal Alien Allowed To Work  ☐ Legal Alien Not Allowed To Work  ☐ Foreign Student Allowed Restricted Employment  ☐ Conditionally Legalized Alien Allowed To Work  ☐ Other (See Instructions On Page 2)

**4 SEX**
☐ Male  ☐ Female

**5 RACE/ETHNIC DESCRIPTION**
(Check One Only—Voluntary)
☐ Asian, Asian-American Or Pacific Islander  ☐ Hispanic  ☐ Black (Not Hispanic)  ☐ North American Indian Or Alaskan Native  ☐ White (Not Hispanic)

**6 DATE OF BIRTH**
MONTH DAY YEAR

**7 PLACE OF BIRTH**
(Do Not Abbreviate)
CITY    STATE OR FOREIGN COUNTRY    FCI

Office Use Only

**8 MOTHER'S MAIDEN NAME**
FIRST         FULL MIDDLE NAME         LAST NAME AT HER BIRTH

**9 FATHER'S NAME**
FIRST         FULL MIDDLE NAME         LAST

**10** Has the person in item 1 ever applied for or received a Social Security number before?

☐ Yes (If "yes", answer questions 11-13.)  ☐ No (If "no", go on to question 14.)  ☐ Don't Know (If "don't know", go on to question 14.)

**11** Enter the Social Security number previously assigned to the person listed in item 1.

☐☐☐ – ☐☐ – ☐☐☐☐

**12** Enter the name shown on the most recent Social Security card issued for the person listed in item 1.

FIRST         MIDDLE         LAST

**13** Enter any different date of birth if used on an earlier application for a card.
MONTH    DAY    YEAR

**14 TODAY'S DATE** ▶ MONTH DAY YEAR    **15 DAYTIME PHONE NUMBER** ▶ ( )
AREA CODE

DELIBERATELY FURNISHING (OR CAUSING TO BE FURNISHED) FALSE INFORMATION ON THIS APPLICATION IS A CRIME PUNISHABLE BY FINE OR IMPRISONMENT, OR BOTH.

**16 YOUR SIGNATURE**
▶

**17 YOUR RELATIONSHIP TO THE PERSON IN ITEM 1 IS:**
☐ Self  ☐ Natural Or Adoptive Parent  ☐ Legal Guardian  ☐ Other (Specify)

| DO NOT WRITE BELOW THIS LINE (FOR SSA USE ONLY) | | | | | |
|---|---|---|---|---|---|
| NPN | | DOC | NTI | CAN | ITV |
| PBC | EVI | EVA | EVC | NWR | DNR | UNIT |
| EVIDENCE SUBMITTED | | | | SIGNATURE AND TITLE OF EMPLOYEE(S) REVIEWING EVIDENCE AND/OR CONDUCTING INTERVIEW | |

DATE

DCL          DATE

Form **SS-5** (5/88)    1/85, 8/85, and 11/86 editions may be used until supply is exhausted

Look at the blank social security application form on page 183. Fill out the application as if *you* are applying for a social security number.

# SHOW WHAT YOU KNOW . . .

## About Forms

Assume that you are in charge of a summer art and craft show in your community. Design an entry form for those who want to display their work.

## Bank forms

Banks offer their customers many money-related services. They loan money for buying cars. They sell savings bonds. They make loans for home improvements. They also provide checking accounts so people need not carry large sums of cash. People put money into a checking account. Then they write checks on the money they have deposited. They use checks just as other people use money. They pay bills. They buy things. They pay the rent. The bank gives each checking customer an account number. Each customer has personalized checks in a checkbook. Personalized checks have the customer's name and address on them. These checks have printed numbers.

Study the sample. It shows you how to fill out a check.

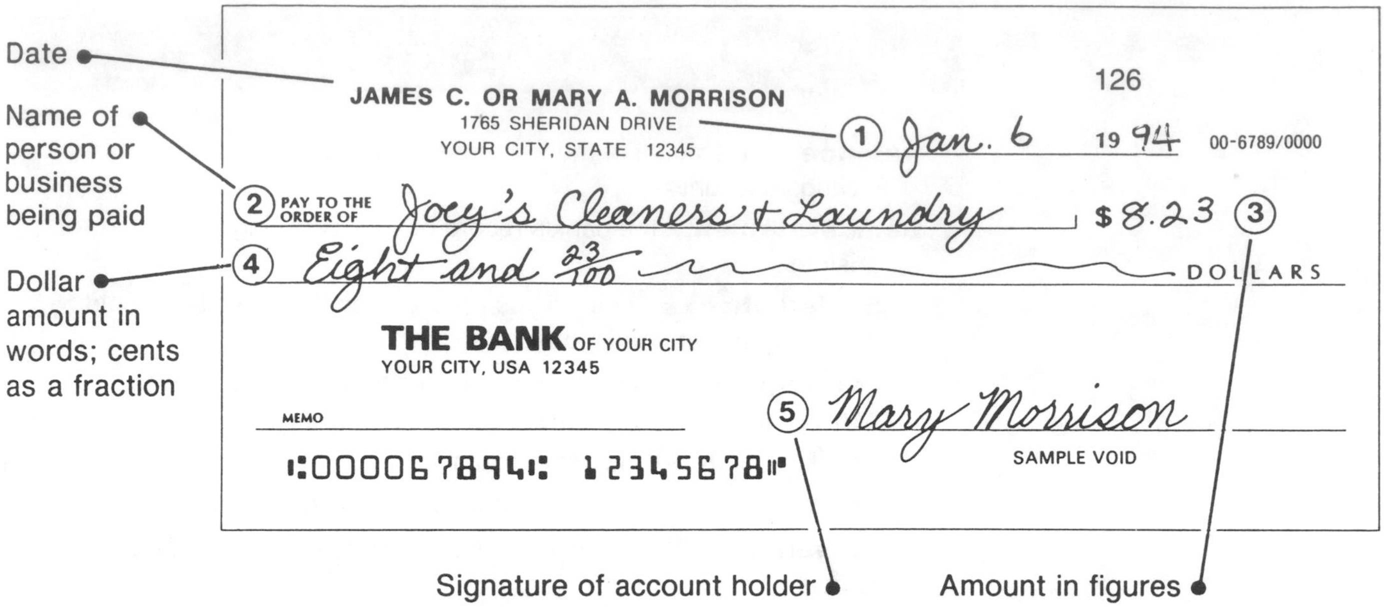

## Check diagram

Date •

Name of person or business being paid •

Dollar amount in words; cents as a fraction •

**JAMES C. OR MARY A. MORRISON**
1765 SHERIDAN DRIVE
YOUR CITY, STATE   12345

126

① *Jan. 6* 19 *94*   00-6789/0000

② PAY TO THE ORDER OF *Joey's Cleaners + Laundry*   $*8.23* ③

④ *Eight and 23/100* ———————————— DOLLARS

**THE BANK** OF YOUR CITY
YOUR CITY, USA 12345

MEMO _____

�5 *Mary Morrison*
SAMPLE VOID

⑁:000067894⑁: 12345678⑁

Signature of account holder •      Amount in figures •

**Checks**   This check was written by Mary A. Morrison. She and her husband, James C. Morrison, have a joint checking account with a bank in the town where they live. Their account number is on the check. It's 12345678. On January 6, 1994, Mary wrote check number 126 to Joey's Cleaners & Laundry. The check was for $8.23. Here are the steps Mary took to write this check:

① She filled in the *date* she wrote the check.

② She wrote the name of the business receiving the check. *Pay to the order of* refers to the name of the person, organization, or business you are paying.

③ She wrote the *amount* of the check in figures.

④ The dollar amount was then written in words. The 23¢ was shown as a fraction of a dollar, or 23/100.

$8.23 =   *Eight and 23/100* ———— DOLLARS
or
*Eight and ———— 23/100* DOLLARS

Mary filled in the entire *dollars line*. Notice that the word *and* divides the dollar amount from the cents. The wavy line fills the entire space. This keeps others from changing the amount of the check.

⑤ Mary wrote her *signature* last. This check is good only if Mary or her husband signs it.

Did you notice the memo space on this check? Some people like to note the purpose of a check here.

## ACTIVITY 5

### Filling in the "dollars" line

Write the following amounts as they should appear on the dollars line. You may use either method. Remember to use "and" to divide the dollars from the cents.

*Example:*

$7.29 ___Seven and $\frac{29}{100}$___ DOLLARS

1. $5.26 _____ DOLLARS

2. $23.01 _____ DOLLARS

3. $15.29 _____ DOLLARS

4. $121.00 _____ DOLLARS

5. $51.82 _____ DOLLARS

6. $342.21 _____ DOLLARS

7. $85.50 _____ DOLLARS

8. $92.28 _____ DOLLARS

9. $247.18 _____ DOLLARS

10. $92.28 _____ DOLLARS

## ACTIVITY 6

### Writing checks

Pretend you are Mary A. Morrison or James C. Morrison. You have a checking account with a bank where you live. Write a check for each of the following situations. Use today's date.

1. You owe Payne's Department Store a payment of $10.30. Today you write them check #127.

| | |
|---|---|
| **JAMES C. OR MARY A. MORRISON** | 127 |
| 1765 SHERIDAN DRIVE | |
| YOUR CITY, STATE  12345 | _____ 19 ___   00-6789/0000 |
| PAY TO THE ORDER OF _____ | $ |
| _____ DOLLARS | |
| **THE BANK** OF YOUR CITY | |
| YOUR CITY, USA  12345 | |
| MEMO _____ | _____ |
| ⑈000067894⑈  123456780⑈ | SAMPLE VOID |

**2.** Next, you write check #128 for $9.17. This check is for Leeds' Variety Store. It is for art supplies. This year you will keep a record of all art expenses. You will list these expenses when you file your tax return at the end of the year. Make a note to yourself in the memo space.

| | |
|---|---|
| **JAMES C. OR MARY A. MORRISON** | **128** |
| 1765 SHERIDAN DRIVE | |
| YOUR CITY, STATE 12345 | _____ 19 ___ 00-6789/0000 |
| PAY TO THE ORDER OF _____ | \| $ |
| | DOLLARS |
| **THE BANK** OF YOUR CITY | |
| YOUR CITY, USA 12345 | |
| MEMO _____ | _____ |
| ⑆000067894⑆ 12345678⑈ | SAMPLE VOID |

**3.** Write check #129 to the Appalachian Power Company. It's for this month's electric bill. Your account number is 853–470. You owe $29.

| | |
|---|---|
| **JAMES C. OR MARY A. MORRISON** | **129** |
| 1765 SHERIDAN DRIVE | |
| YOUR CITY, STATE 12345 | _____ 19 ___ 00-6789/0000 |
| PAY TO THE ORDER OF _____ | \| $ |
| | DOLLARS |
| **THE BANK** OF YOUR CITY | |
| YOUR CITY, USA 12345 | |
| MEMO _____ | _____ |
| ⑆000067894⑆ 12345678⑈ | SAMPLE VOID |

## Deposit slips

Before you write checks, you have to put money into your checking account. Your bank will issue you deposit slips. Like your checks, they will most likely have your name printed on them. You will have to fill out a deposit slip when you put money into your checking account.

Cash amount

CHECKING ACCOUNT DEPOSIT TICKET

Account holder's name

JAMES C. OR MARY A. MORRISON
1765 SHERIDAN DRIVE
YOUR CITY. STATE 12345

DATE Sept. 15 19 94

CHECKS AND OTHER ITEMS ARE RECEIVED FOR DEPOSIT SUBJECT TO THE PROVISIONS OF THE UNIFORM COMMERCIAL CODE OR ANY APPLICABLE COLLECTION AGREEMENT

DEPOSITED IN

THE BANK OF YOUR CITY
YOUR CITY. USA 12345

⑈0000678941⑈ 12345678⑈

CASH ➔ 10 00
LIST CHECKS SINGLY 101 38
10 00

00-6789/0000

TOTAL FROM OTHER SIDE

USE OTHER SIDE FOR ADDITIONAL LISTING
◀ ENTER TOTAL HERE

TOTAL ITEMS

TOTAL 121 38

BE SURE EACH ITEM IS PROPERLY ENDORSED

Checking account number

Total deposit

Amount of checks being deposited

## ACTIVITY 7
### Filling out a deposit slip

Answer these questions about the deposit slip you have just studied.

1. How much cash did James and Mary Morrison deposit? _____

2. What was the date of their deposit? _____

3. Do they have to sign the deposit slip? _____

4. How many checks did they deposit? _____ What was the amount of each check? _____

5. What is the account number? _____

## The checkbook register

There are many reasons people use checks instead of cash. For one thing, checks are safe to mail; you can pay bills and buy things without worrying. There is no chance that your money will be lost or stolen. Checks are good records, too. Many banks return the checks paid out of your account with your monthly statement. Your canceled checks become your receipts.

Sometimes, a bank will not pay your check because you don't have enough money in your account. The check is marked "insufficient funds" and is returned to the person or company to whom you wrote it. If your account is overdrawn, you'll be charged an overdraft or penalty fee. The bank notifies you by mail of the overdraft and the resulting charges.

189

How do you avoid this problem? It is very simple. Use the register that you receive with your checks. Record every check you write in the register. Also list the deposits you make. Some banks charge for each check that you write. Other banks have a monthly service charge. Be sure to record all fees and service charges in your register. Always know how much money you have in your checking account.

Study the sample below. It shows the *single-line* method of entering checks in a register.

### RECORD ALL CHARGES OR CREDITS THAT AFFECT YOUR ACCOUNT

| NUMBER | DATE | DESCRIPTION OF TRANSACTION | PAYMENT/DEBIT (-) | √ T | FEE (IF ANY) (-) | DEPOSIT/CREDIT (+) | BALANCE $ 1687 42 |
|--------|------|----------------------------|-------------------|-----|------------------|--------------------|---------|
| 201 | 3/7 | National Gas Company | $ 55 87 | | $3/7 | $ 625 00 | |
| 202 | | Lance Mortgage Co. | 250 00 | | | | |
| 203 | | General Telephone Co. | 35 68 | | | | |
| 204 | 3/10 | Bob's Meat Store | 26 89 | | 3/10 | 300 00 | 2243 98 |
| 205 | | Leed's Dept Store | 278 19 | | | | |
| 206 | | Cash | 200 00 | | | | |
| 207 | | Gus's Service Station | 32 41 | | | | |
| 208 | 3/11 | Acme Furniture Store | 389 88 | | 3/11 | 200 00 | 1543 50 |
| 209 | | Easy Credit Card | 56 90 | | | | |
| 210 | | Lancaster Hardware | 14 26 | | | | |
| | | | | | | | |

REMEMBER TO RECORD AUTOMATIC PAYMENTS / DEPOSITS ON DATE AUTHORIZED.

This checking customer uses each line of the register. All checks and deposits are recorded. A balance is noted from time to time.

The next sample shows the *double-line* method.

### RECORD ALL CHARGES OR CREDITS THAT AFFECT YOUR ACCOUNT

| NUMBER | DATE | DESCRIPTION OF TRANSACTION | PAYMENT/DEBIT (-) | √ T | FEE (IF ANY) (-) | DEPOSIT/CREDIT (+) | BALANCE $ 1687 42 |
|--------|------|----------------------------|-------------------|-----|------------------|--------------------|---------|
| 201 | 3/7 | National Gas Company | $ 55 87 | | $ | $ | 55 87 |
| | | February Payment | | | | | 1631 55 |
| 202 | | Lance Mortgage Co. | 250 00 | | | | 250 00 |
| | | February House Note | | | | | 1381 55 |
| 203 | | General Telephone Co. | 35 68 | | | | 35 68 |
| | | February Bill | | | | | 1345 87 |
| | | Cash Deposit | | | | 625 00 | 625 00 |
| | | | | | | | 1970 87 |
| 204 | | Bob's Meat Store | 26 89 | | | | 26 89 |
| | | Steaks | | | | | 1943 98 |
| | | | | | | | |

REMEMBER TO RECORD AUTOMATIC PAYMENTS / DEPOSITS ON DATE AUTHORIZED.

In the double-line method, two lines are used for each check written. One line gives the name of the person or business who will get the check. The next line tells what the check is for. The amount of each check is subtracted from the balance. A new balance is shown after each check.

## ACTIVITY 8

**Keeping a checkbook register**

Anne Marie Ramos has a checking account. Below is a page from her register. Study her register. Then answer the questions.

| CHECK NO. | DATE | CHECK ISSUED TO | AMOUNT OF CHECK | | √ | DATE OF DEP. | AMOUNT OF DEPOSIT | | BALANCE | |
|---|---|---|---|---|---|---|---|---|---|---|
| | | BALANCE BROUGHT FORWARD → | | | | | | | 500 | 00 |
| 863 | 7/16 | Montgomery Ward<br>Scarf | 10 | 00 | | | | | 10 | 00 |
| | | | | | | | | | 490 | 00 |
| 864 | 7/16 | Dr. Altchek<br>Office Visit | 50 | 00 | | | | | 50 | 00 |
| | | | | | | | | | 440 | 00 |
| 865 | 7/21 | Prudential Insurance<br>August Premium | 52 | 50 | | | | | 52 | 50 |
| | | | | | | | | | 387 | 50 |
| | | Cash Deposit | | | | 7/22 | 50 | 00 | 50 | 00 |
| | | | | | | | | | 437 | 50 |
| 866 | 7/22 | Peter Simpson<br>Gift | 7 | 50 | | | | | 7 | 50 |
| | | | | | | | | | 430 | 00 |
| 867 | 7/22 | John's Garage<br>Oil Change | 60 | 00 | | | | | 60 | 00 |
| | | | | | | | | | 370 | 00 |
| 868 | 7/23 | Montgomery Ward<br>Drapes | 100 | 00 | | | | | 100 | 00 |
| | | | | | | | | | 270 | 00 |
| | | Cash Deposit | | | | 8/4 | 100 | 00 | 100 | 00 |
| | | | | | | | | | 370 | 00 |

1. What was Anne Marie's balance when she started making entries on this page? _____

2. To whom did she write check #863? _____

3. When did she write this check? _____

4. What did she buy? _____

5. What was the balance after check #864 was written? _____

6. Who received the check? _____

7. What was the balance after check #865 was written? _____

8. What was the last date a deposit was made? _____

9. What was Anne Marie's balance after the deposit was made? _____

10. What was the number of the last check that was written? _____

## ACTIVITY 9

### Keeping a checkbook register

Record the following items in a checkbook register. Use the *single-line method* and today's date. Begin with check #201.

**Checks**

| | |
|---|---|
| Myrtle's Daycare | $35.00 |
| Lum's Drugs | $15.82 |
| Jackson's Dept. Store | $21.00 |
| Consumer's Power | $46.82 |
| Carson's Boutique | $56.94 |
| Ned's Place | $48.52 |

**Deposits**

$400.00 (Cash)

| | | RECORD ALL CHARGES OR CREDITS THAT AFFECT YOUR ACCOUNT | | | | | BALANCE | |
|---|---|---|---|---|---|---|---|---|
| NUMBER | DATE | DESCRIPTION OF TRANSACTION | PAYMENT/DEBIT (-) | √ T | FEE (IFANY) (-) | DEPOSIT/CREDIT (+) | $ 300 | 00 |
| 201 | | | $ | | $ | $ | | |
| | | | | | | | | |
| | | | | | | | | |
| | | | | | | | | |
| | | | | | | | | |
| | | | | | | | | |
| | | | | | | | | |
| | | | | | | | | |
| | | | | | | | | |

REMEMBER TO RECORD AUTOMATIC PAYMENTS / DEPOSITS ON DATE AUTHORIZED.

## Checking account statements

Each month your bank will mail you a statement of account. This statement shows your checks that came into the bank during the month. It also shows the deposits you made. If there are any other charges, they appear on the statement. Following is a sample of a monthly statement.

# Community Trust Bank

STATEMENT OF CHECKING ACCOUNT                    PREVIOUS BALANCE    $500.00

Account Number   10-437-112          From   July 15    to   Aug 14

| CHECKS AND CHARGES | DEPOSITS | DATE | BALANCE |
|---|---|---|---|
| 10.00 | | 7-18 | 490.00 |
| 50.00 | | 7-18 | 440.00 |
| | 50.00 | 7-22 | 490.00 |
| 52.50 | | 7-23 | 437.50 |
| 7.50 | | 7-25 | 430.00 |
| 60.00 | | 7-25 | 370.00 |

IF    Insufficient Funds                              BALANCE   $370.00
DM   Debit Memo
CM   Credit Memo              PERIOD ENDING   Aug 14
SC   Service Charge

---

## ACTIVITY 10   Complete these sentences using the monthly statement above.

### Reading a monthly statement

1. A monthly statement shows the _____ you wrote and the deposits you made.

2. The statement above begins _____ and goes through _____ .

3. The balance on July 15th was $ _____ .

4. The balance at the close of the statement is $ _____ .

5. Five _____ came into the bank during this period.

6. Only one _____ was made.

7. It was for $ _____ .

8. It was made on July _____ .

It is important to compare the bank's records with your records. On page 191 you looked at the checkbook register of Anne Marie Ramos. Then you looked at the statement from Community Trust Bank. Compare these two records. The records do not match exactly. Which check and which deposit do not show on the bank statement?

## CHECK YOUR UNDERSTANDING OF BANK FORMS

Write out the following dollar amounts in words. Remember to show cents as a fraction of a dollar.

**1.** $3.49 _____

**2.** $43.52 _____

**3.** $207.09 _____

**4.** $764.50 _____

**5.** $25.02 _____

Choose the best answer for the following statements. Write the letter of the answer in the blank.

_____ **6.** A canceled check is a check
    **a.** with your name printed on it.
    **b.** the bank has paid and returned to you.
    **c.** that is no good.

_____ **7.** When a check is endorsed, it
    **a.** has been received by the writer.
    **b.** cannot be paid until 30 days after it is written.
    **c.** has been signed by the person or business to whom it is written.

_____ **8.** A check returned because of "insufficient funds" means
    **a.** there is not enough money in the account to pay the check.
    **b.** the bank is in financial trouble and cannot pay the check.
    **c.** the bank's records are not up to date.

_____ **9.** A check register is a list of
    **a.** canceled checks.
    **b.** the checks you have written.
    **c.** the checks that have been written to you.

_____ **10.** A joint account is an account that
    **a.** can be used by more than one person.
    **b.** is good at two different banks.
    **c.** is good in several states.

## Consumer credit applications

When you buy on credit, you buy now and pay later. To get credit you usually have to fill out a credit application. Some people use credit cards. When a credit card is approved, you can buy things and charge them with your card. Sometimes you may make a single, large purchase. It might be for a new car. For some purchases you may need a loan. For large purchases, you will have to fill out a loan application. The money you borrow is paid back in monthly payments that include interest. Before you can get a loan, your credit must be approved.

## Credit cards

Look at the following sample credit card application. Most credit applications ask for information about your *work experience, income,* and *credit history*. The company giving credit wants to know (1) if you have a job, (2) how long you've had the job, (3) how much you earn, (4) who you owe, and (5) how promptly you pay.

What you write on the credit card application will help determine if you are a *good credit risk*. Once you sign a credit application, you give permission to have your credit record checked. Your signature also gives the creditor the right to check other information on the application. Most often your *credit references, employment,* and *income* are checked.

You may not get credit if your application is not filled in properly. You probably won't get a chance to explain your answers. Computers are often a part of the processing so you must do it correctly from the start. Study the blank application on the next page carefully.

## JCPenney **Credit Application**

| Associate Number | | Account Number |
|---|---|---|
| | 1438 | |

**CREDIT INSURANCE ENROLLMENT**

Your signature if you wish to insure your credit purchases

**YES** I wish to protect my JCPenney Account with Credit Insurance for the cost as described above. I understand the insurance is not required.

**APPLICANT (SIGN TO ENROLL)** — Date of Birth

**NO** I waive my right to enroll for Credit Insurance at this time.

**SPOUSE'S NAME** — Date of Birth

In signing this enrollment form, I authorize J.C. Penney Company, Inc. to advance to J.C. Penney Life Insurance Company and J.C. Penney Casualty Insurance Company amounts equal to the premiums becoming due under the policy applied for and bill such amounts with my JCPenney Credit Account. I agree to pay such amounts when billed.

**INFORMATION ABOUT APPLICANT** — **PLEASE PRINT** — An Applicant, if married, may apply for a separate account.

Name of your husband or wife

Your name printed

Your Name (First, Middle Initial, Last) — Social Security Number

Present Street Address — City — State — Zip

Include area code

Home Phone — Business Phone — No. of Dependent Children: None / One / Two / Three / Four or More

How much you pay monthly for where you live

Applicant's Date of Birth — Do You: Own / Rent / Own Mobile Home / Live With Parents / Other (Please Specify) — Monthly Mortgage/Rent

How Long at This Address: 0 - 6 mos. / 7 mos. - 1 yr. 6 mos. / 1 yr. 7 mos. - 2 yrs. 6 mos. / 2 yrs. 7 mos. - 5 yrs. 6 mos. / 5 yrs. 7 mos. - 8 yrs. 6 mos. / 8 yrs. 7 mos. - 15 yrs. 6 mos. / 15 yrs. 7 mos. or More

Where you lived before you moved to your present address

Former Street Address (If at Current Address Less Than Two Years) — City — State — Zip

Employer's Full Name — Employer's Address (Street, City, State)

How Long on Job: 0 - 6 mos. / 7 mos. - 1 yr. / 1 yr. 1 mo. - 2 yrs. / 2 yrs. 1 mo. - 4 yrs. 6 mos. / 4 yrs. 7 mos. - 6 yrs. 6 mos. / 6 yrs. 7 mos. - 10 yrs. 6 mos. / 10 yrs. 7 mos. or More

Your job title

Present Position — Monthly Salary — Source(s) of Other Income* — Monthly Amount

What you make before deductions

**INFORMATION ABOUT (check one)** — Co-Applicant - Also Responsible for Account — Authorized Buyer - Allows Other Person to Purchase on Your Account

Name of person who will share account if you are requesting joint account or name of another person who will use your credit card

Name of Co-Applicant/Authorized Buyer — Relationship to Applicant: Spouse / Other — Social Security Number

Date of Birth — Business Phone — Employer's Full Name — Employer's Address (Street, City, State)

How Long on Job: 0 - 6 mos. / 7 mos. - 1 yr. / 1 yr. 1 mo. - 2 yrs. / 2 yrs. 1 mo. - 4 yrs. 6 mos. / 4 yrs. 7 mos. - 6 yrs. 6 mos. / 6 yrs. 7 mos. - 10 yrs. 6 mos. / 10 yrs. 7 mos. or More

This area for information on co-applicant or authorized buyer only

Present Position — Monthly Salary — Source(s) of Other Income* — Monthly Amount

**INFORMATION ABOUT YOUR CREDIT AND OTHER REFERENCES (Include Co-Applicant's, if Joint Account Requested)**

Bank–Branch — Account in the Name of — Account Number — Checking and Savings/NOW Acct. / Checking / Savings/CD / Loan

Credit Cards: MasterCard/Visa / AMEX/Diners / Department Store / Other Credit References (List Below)

Places where you owe or have owed money, such as banks, stores, and credit unions

List Other Credit References (Include Loan or Finance Company) — Firm Name — Location — Account/Loan Number — Account/Loan in the Name of
1.
2.

Name of Nearest Relative Not Living at Address of Applicant or Co-Applicant — Relationship to Applicant — Present Address (Street, City, State) — Home Phone

### Sign here to complete your JCPenney Credit Application.

Your Signature(s) mean(s) that you have read, understood, and agree to the terms of the above Retail Installment Credit Agreement.

Applicant Signature — Date — Co-Applicant Signature

*You Need Not Furnish Alimony, Child Support or Separate Maintenance Income Information If You Do Not Want Us to Consider It in Evaluating Your Application.    B4 ●

JCP-2201 (Rev. 11/91) Printed 11/91

↑ **AFTER COMPLETING APPLICATION, DETACH AT TOP PERFORATION, FOLD TOP DOWN TO ARROWS, MOISTEN BOTTOM FLAP, FOLD FLAP OVER AND SEAL. POSTAGE PAID BY JCPenney** ↑

196

# ACTIVITY 11

## Filling out an application for a credit card

Study the following credit card application. Answer the questions on page 198.

**JCPenney Credit Application**

| Associate Number | 1438 | Account Number |
|---|---|---|

### CREDIT INSURANCE ENROLLMENT

[ ] **YES** I wish to protect my JCPenney Account with Credit Insurance for the cost as described above. I understand the insurance is not required.

[X] **NO** I waive my right to enroll for Credit Insurance at this time.

APPLICANT (SIGN TO ENROLL) — Date of Birth

SPOUSE'S NAME — Date of Birth

In signing this enrollment form, I authorize J.C. Penney Company, Inc. to advance to J.C. Penney Life Insurance Company and J.C. Penney Casualty Insurance Company amounts equal to the premiums becoming due under the policy applied for and bill such amounts with my JCPenney Credit Account. I agree to pay such amounts when billed.

### INFORMATION ABOUT APPLICANT    PLEASE PRINT    An Applicant, if married, may apply for a separate account.

Your Name (First, Middle Initial, Last): **CHARLES E WRIGHT**
Social Security Number: **000726352**

Present Street Address: **5001 Congress Ave. Apt. 3**
City: **Havre DeGrace** State: **MD** Zip: **21078**

Home Phone: **(301) 555-7082** Business Phone: **(301) 555-7623**
No. of Dependent Children: [X] None [ ] One [ ] Two [ ] Three [ ] Four or More

Applicant's Date of Birth: **10 16 70**
Do You: [ ] Own [X] Rent [ ] Own Mobile Home [ ] Live With Parents [ ] Other (Please Specify)
Monthly Mortgage/Rent: **$500**

How Long at This Address: [ ] 0 - 6 mos. [ ] 7 mos. - 1 yr. 7 mos. [ ] 1 yr. 7 mos. - 2 yrs. 7 mos. [ ] 2 yrs. 7 mos. - 5 yrs. 0 mos. [ ] 5 yrs. 7 mos. - 8 yrs. 6 mos. [ ] 8 yrs. 7 mos. - 15 yrs. 6 mos. [ ] 15 yrs. 7 mos. or More

Former Street Address (If at Current Address Less Than Two Years): — City — State — Zip

Employer's Full Name: **Harford Company**
Employer's Address (Street, City, State): **2401 Harvey Aberdeen, Md.**

How Long on Job: [ ] 0 - 6 mos. [ ] 7 mos. - 1 yr [ ] 1 yr. 1 mo. - 2 yrs. [ ] 2 yrs. 1 mo. - 4 yrs. 6 mos. [X] 4 yrs. 7 mos. - 6 yrs. 6 mos. [ ] 6 yrs. 7 mos. - 10 yrs. 6 mos. [ ] 10 yrs. 7 mos. or More

Present Position: **Office Manager**
Monthly Salary: **$2500**
Source(s) of Other Income*: — Monthly Amount:

### INFORMATION ABOUT (check one) [X] Co-Applicant - Also Responsible for Account   [ ] Authorized Buyer - Allows Other Person to Purchase on Your Account

Name of Co-Applicant/Authorized Buyer: **PATRICIA WRIGHT**
Relationship to Applicant: [X] Spouse [ ] Other
Social Security Number: **000826977**

Date of Birth: **06 04 70** Business Phone: **301 555-8020**
Employer's Full Name: **Harford County Schools**
Employer's Address (Street, City, State): **Bd. of Education Bel Air, MD**

How Long on Job: [ ] 0 - 6 mos. [X] 7 mos. - 1 yr. [ ] 1 yr. 1 mo. - 2 yrs. [ ] 2 yrs. 1 mo. - 4 yrs. 6 mos. [ ] 4 yrs. 7 mos. - 6 yrs. 6 mos. [ ] 6 yrs. 7 mos. - 10 yrs. 6 mos. [ ] 10 yrs. 7 mos. or More

Present Position: **Teacher**
Monthly Salary: **$2000**
Source(s) of Other Income*: — Monthly Amount:

### INFORMATION ABOUT YOUR CREDIT AND OTHER REFERENCES (Include Co-Applicant's, if Joint Account Requested)

Bank–Branch: **Raleigh Co. Bank** Account in the Name of: **Charles Wright** Account Number: **7-9-2438-05**
Checking and Savings/NOW Acct. [X] Checking [X] Savings/CD [ ] Loan

Credit Cards: [X] MasterCard/Visa [ ] AMEX/Diners [X] Department Store [ ] Other Credit References (List Below)

List Other Credit References (Include Loan or Finance Company):

| | Firm Name | Location | Account/Loan Number | Account/Loan in the Name of |
|---|---|---|---|---|
| 1. | SMITH'S CLOTHING | Havre DeGrace | 64-120-378 | CHARLES WRIGHT |
| 2. | SCHOOL EMPLOYEES CREDIT UNION | Bel Air | 79-320-900 | Patricia Wright |

Name of Nearest Relative Not Living at Address of Applicant or Co-Applicant: **FRANCES WRIGHT**
Relationship to Applicant: **Mother**
Present Address (Street, City, State): **122 Grant St., Beckley, WV 25801**
Home Phone: **304 555 5082**

### Sign here to complete your JCPenney Credit Application.

Your Signature(s) mean(s) that you have read, understood, and agree to the terms of the above Retail Installment Credit Agreement.

Applicant Signature: **Charles E. Wright** Date: **12-2-94** Co-Applicant Signature: **Patricia Wright**

B4 ●

*You Need Not Furnish Alimony, Child Support or Separate Maintenance Income Information If You Do Not Want Us to Consider It in Evaluating Your Application.

JCP-2201 (Rev. 11/91) Printed 11/91

**AFTER COMPLETING APPLICATION, DETACH AT TOP PERFORATION, FOLD TOP DOWN TO ARROWS, MOISTEN BOTTOM FLAP, FOLD FLAP OVER AND SEAL. POSTAGE PAID BY JCPenney**

1. Who is applying for a credit card? _____

2. How many persons will use this credit account? _____

3. Has the applicant lived at 5001 Congress Avenue over one year? _____

4. Is the applicant buying a home or renting an apartment? _____

5. Is the applicant employed? If so, where? _____

6. How much does the applicant earn each month? _____

7. How much does the applicant's spouse earn? _____

8. Does the applicant have a checking account? savings account? bank loan? _____

9. Who is the applicant's nearest relative not living at his address? _____

10. What store does the applicant list as a credit reference? _____

_____

11. Who is Patricia Wright? _____

12. What is her occupation? _____

13. Did both applicants sign the application? _____

14. Do you think this applicant will get a credit card? Why or why not? _____

## ACTIVITY 12
### Completing credit card applications

Following is a Montgomery Ward credit application form. Pretend it is five years from now. Complete this application for yourself. List the type of job you might have. List the salary that you expect to be making. Decide what your marital status might be. Make up credit references. When you're finished, you will have a picture of yourself as a future credit applicant.

## ELECTRIC AVENUE   GOLD 'N GEMS   AutoExpress   HOME IDEAS   APPAREL

### Montgomery Ward
# EXPRESS credit

| Source Code | Customer Waiting | Amount of Sale $ | Dept. |
|---|---|---|---|

**For Office Use Only ▼**

| Credit Limit $ | | Sale Appr. $ |
|---|---|---|
| Key # | | |
| Acct. # | | Expir. Date |

Source Code: **966**

**FIRST NAME** / **INITIAL** / **LAST NAME** / **TITLE (JR,SR,ETC.)**

**PRESENT ADDRESS** / **STREET**

**CITY** / **STATE** / **ZIP**

**PREVIOUS ADDRESS** (IF LESS THAN TWO YEARS AT PRESENT ADDRESS) **CITY** / **STATE** / **ZIP**

**DATE OF BIRTH** / **SOC. SEC. NO.** / **HOME PHONE** ( ) / **BUSINESS PHONE** ( )

**EMPLOYER** / **HOW LONG** / **ANNUAL INCOME*** / **OCCUPATION**

**NO. DEPENDENTS**
- ☐ OWN
- ☐ RENT
- ☐ BOARD – LIVE W/RELATIVE(S)

**HOW LONG (YEARS)** / **MORTGAGE/RENT PAYMENT**

**HAVE YOU EVER HAD A MONTGOMERY WARD CHARGE CARD?**
- ☐ NO
- ☐ YES   ACCT. NO.

**CREDIT REFERENCES**
- ☐ CHECKING
- ☐ SAVINGS
- ☐ VISA
- ☐ MASTERCARD
- ☐ SEARS/DISCOVER
- ☐ AMERICAN EXPRESS/OPTIMA
- ☐ DEPT. STORE

## PLEASE COMPLETE FOR CO-APPLICANT OR AUTHORIZED USER

**FIRST NAME** / **INITIAL** / **LAST NAME** / **TITLE (JR,SR,ETC.)**

**PRESENT ADDRESS** (IF DIFFERENT THAN ABOVE) **CITY** / **STATE** / **ZIP**

**ANNUAL INCOME*** / **SOC. SEC. NO.** / **RELATIONSHIP TO APPLICANT**
- ☐ SPOUSE
- ☐ OTHER

Co-Applicant must sign Agreement. If individual listed above is Co-Applicant, check box ☐

*Alimony, Child Support or Separate Maintenance Payments Need Not Be Disclosed Unless Relied Upon for Credit

---

I desire Montgomery Ward Credit Security Plan Insurance on my Montgomery Ward credit accounts as described in the brochure furnished me and in accordance with the terms stated in the Certificates of Insurance to be sent. The cost is 50¢ per $100 (AZ 57¢, CA 48 6¢***, IL 82 9¢/85¢*, MD 51 5¢/50¢*, MT 70¢, NM 75¢**, NV 85.9¢/69¢*, OH 67¢/57¢*, OR 75¢***, VA 48¢**) of my previous balance each month. This insurance is voluntary, it may be obtained through a person of my choosing (in IL, CSP property insurance pays first but may limit recovery from similar coverages) and I may cancel at any time.

  *First rate to age 66: second rate at and after 66.
  **Not available age 70 and older.
***Not available age 65 and older.

**Holder Signature** / **Age**

**Yes,** I accept your invitation to apply for a Montgomery Ward Credit Account and if I do not qualify, please consider this as an application for a Montgomery Ward Starter Account. I authorize you to verify the information concerning me in accordance with your established credit policy. See reverse side for terms of both Accounts and legal disclosures.

X _____
Signature / Date

X _____
Signature / Date

37492-3 AZ, CA, DC, DE, IL, KY, MD, MT, NH, NM, NV, OH, OR, VA   REV. 7/91

# SHOW WHAT YOU KNOW . . .

## About Credit Applications

Obtain two different credit applications from local stores. Bring them to class and fill them out. Make up credit references and bank accounts, but use your own name, address, and phone number. Exchange completed forms with a classmate. Check each other's applications and make suggestions for improvement.

## Installment purchases and loans

Making monthly installment payments is often easier than making one large payment. That is one reason people have credit cards. Sometimes people make expensive purchases. They may buy a refrigerator, a sofa, or new carpeting. They will pay for these things in monthly installments.

In order to pay for a college education, a car, or a house, many people borrow money from a bank, a credit union, or a finance company. When you apply for a loan, you will be asked the same type of information you are asked when you apply for a credit card. You also may be asked for more specific information. A creditor will look closely at these things:

- your *assets* (whether you own stocks or bonds, have a savings account, own a car)

- your *debts* (how much you pay out each month for other loans, credit cards, and so forth)

- your *work and salary history* (how long you have held your job and whether your job pays enough for you to make any new credit payments)

- your *credit references* (credit accounts you have paid up and how well you paid these accounts)

- the size of your *down payment* (On major purchases, such as cars, vans, homes, or campers, most applicants must make a cash payment.)

You need to remember that you will be charged for the privilege of paying monthly installments. A finance charge will be added to the unpaid balance of your credit card account. An interest charge will be added to the amount you repay on a loan.

# ACTIVITY 13
## Applying for a loan

Pretend that you need a student loan. Complete the application below. Make all your answers as realistic as you can.

---

LENDER COPY

GUARANTEED STUDENT LOAN
(GSL) APPLICATION
PROMISSORY NOTE

**SECTION A - TO BE COMPLETED BY BORROWER** *(PRINT IN INK—PRESS FIRMLY—OR TYPE)*

| 1. NAME (NO NICKNAMES) | | | 2. SOCIAL SECURITY NUMBER | 3. WHEN WERE YOU BORN? MO DAY YR |
|---|---|---|---|---|
| LAST | FIRST | M.I. | | |

| 4. PERMANENT ADDRESS | 5. PERMANENT HOME PHONE ( ) |
|---|---|
| CITY | STATE | ZIP |

| 6. U.S. CITIZENSHIP STATUS (CHECK ONE) <br> ☐ U.S. CITIZEN OR NATIONAL   ☐ PERMANENT RESIDENT OR OTHER ELIGIBLE ALIEN | ALIEN ID NUMBER IF APPLICABLE | 7. PERMANENT RESIDENT OF WHICH STATE | 8a. DRIVER LICENSE NUMBER (IF YOU DO NOT HAVE A LICENSE, PRINT "NONE" AND GO TO 9) | 8b. STATE IN WHICH ISSUED |
|---|---|---|---|---|

9. ADDRESS WHILE IN SCHOOL (STREET, CITY, STATE, ZIP)

| 10. PHONE AT SCHOOL ADDRESS ( ) | 11. MAJOR COURSE OF STUDY; SEE INSTRUCTIONS IN APP. BOOKLET | 12. LOAN AMOUNT REQUESTED $ .00 | 13. LOAN PERIOD FROM MO YR TO MO YR |
|---|---|---|---|

**PRIOR LOAN INFORMATION**

| 14. HAVE YOU EVER DEFAULTED ON A GSL, SLS (ALAS), PLUS, CONSOLIDATED, OR INCOME CONTINGENT LOAN? ☐ YES (GIVE DETAILS ON SEPARATE SHEET) ☐ NO | 15a. DO YOU HAVE ANY PRIOR UNPAID GSL LOANS? ☐ YES (GO TO 15b) ☐ NO (GO TO 20a) | 15b. IF YES, TOTAL UNPAID BALANCE OF GSL LOANS $ |
|---|---|---|

| 16. UNPAID PRINCIPAL BALANCE OF MOST RECENT GSL $ | 17. GRADE LEVEL OF MOST RECENT GSL, SEE INSTRUCTIONS IN APP. BOOKLET | 18. LOAN PERIOD START DATE OF MOST RECENT GSL MO DAY YR | 19. INTEREST RATE OF MOST RECENT GSL ☐ 7% ☐ 8% ☐ 9% |
|---|---|---|---|

| 20a. DO YOU HAVE ANY PRIOR UNPAID SLS (ALAS) OR PLUS LOANS? ☐ YES (GO TO 20b) ☐ NO (GO TO 21a) | 20b. IF YES, TOTAL UNPAID PRINCIPAL BALANCE OF PRIOR SLS (ALAS) LOANS RECEIVED DURING ▶ UNDERGRADUATE STUDY $____ GRADUATE STUDY $____ | 21a. DO YOU HAVE ANY UNPAID PLUS LOANS IF YOU BORROWED AS A PARENT UNDER THE PLUS LOAN PROGRAM? ☐ YES (GO TO 21b) ☐ NO (GO TO 22a) | 21b. IF YES, TOTAL UNPAID PRINCIPAL BALANCE OF PLUS LOANS $ |
|---|---|---|---|

**REFERENCES** (YOU MUST PROVIDE THREE DIFFERENT NAMES, WITH DIFFERENT U.S. ADDRESSES AND PHONE NUMBERS)

| PARENT OR GUARDIAN | 22a. NAME____ STREET____ CITY, STATE, ZIP____ PHONE ( ) | RELATIVE | 22b. NAME____ STREET____ CITY, STATE, ZIP____ PHONE ( ) | FRIEND | 22c. NAME____ STREET____ CITY, STATE, ZIP____ PHONE ( ) |
|---|---|---|---|---|---|

**NOTICE TO BORROWER:** *You must read the additional Promissory Note terms and the Borrower's Certification on the reverse side before signing this Promissory Note. PROMISE TO PAY: I promise to pay to the order of my lender the entire Loan Amount Requested shown above, to the extent that it is advanced to me, including the Guarantee Fee and the Origination Fee and interest of the unpaid principal balance, subject to the terms and conditions described on the reverse side of this Promissory Note and to the terms and conditions contained in the Disclosure Statement that will be provided to me no later than the time of the first disbursement of this loan. I have read, I understand, and I agree to the Borrower's Certification on the reverse side of this Promissory Note. I understand that this is a Promissory Note. I will not sign it before reading all of its provisions, even if otherwise advised. I am entitled to a copy of this Promissory Note. By signing this Promissory Note I acknowledge that I have received an exact copy of it.*

| 23a. SIGNATURE OF BORROWER (APPLICATION CANNOT BE PROCESSED WITHOUT SIGNATURE) X | 23b. DATE BORROWER SIGNED MO DAY YR |
|---|---|

**SECTION B - TO BE COMPLETED BY SCHOOL**

| 24. NAME OF SCHOOL | 26. PHONE ( ) | 27. SCHOOL CODE |
|---|---|---|

| 25. ADDRESS (STREET, CITY, STATE, ZIP) | 28. |
|---|---|

| 29. | 30. PERIOD LOAN WILL COVER FROM MO DAY YR TO MO DAY YR | 31. STUDENT'S GRADE LEVEL (CHECK ONE) CORRESP [0] UNDERGRAD [1][2][3][4][5] GRAD [6][7][8][9][10] | 32. ANTICIPATED GRADUATION DATE MO DAY YR | 33. STUDENT STATUS (CHECK ONE) ☐ DEPENDENT ☐ INDEPENDENT |
|---|---|---|---|---|

| 34. ADJUSTED GROSS INCOME (AGI) $ | 35. COST OF ATTENDANCE FOR LOAN PERIOD $ | 36. ESTIMATED FINANCIAL AID FOR LOAN PERIOD $ | 37. EXPECTED FAMILY CONTRIBUTION (EFC) $ | 38. DIFFERENCE (ITEM 35 LESS ITEMS 36 AND 37) OR LEGAL MAXIMUM $ |
|---|---|---|---|---|

| 39. SUGGESTED DISBURSEMENT DATES 1ST DISB. MO DAY YR | 2ND DISB. MO DAY YR | 3RD DISB. MO DAY YR |
|---|---|---|

| 40. DO SUGGESTED DISBURSEMENT DATES CORRESPOND TO SCHOOL TERMS? YES ☐ NO ☐ | 41. WILL THE STUDENT ATTEND A FOREIGN SCHOOL? YES ☐ NO ☐ | 42. SCHOOL USE ONLY |
|---|---|---|

| I HAVE READ, I UNDERSTAND, AND I AGREE TO THE TERMS OF THE SCHOOL CERTIFICATION PRINTED ON THE REVERSE SIDE OF THIS APPLICATION. | 43a. SIGNATURE OF SCHOOL OFFICIAL X | 43b. DATE MO DAY YR | 43c. PRINT NAME AND TITLE |
|---|---|---|---|

**SECTION C - TO BE COMPLETED BY LENDER**

| 44. NAME OF LENDER | 46. LENDER CODE | 50. LOAN DISBURSEMENTS MO DAY YR AMOUNT $ |
|---|---|---|

| 45. ADDRESS (STREET, BUILDING, CITY, STATE, ZIP) | 47. BRANCH CODE | MO DAY YR AMOUNT $ |
|---|---|---|

| 52. IS THIS AN UNSUBSIDIZED LOAN? YES ☐ NO ☐ | 53. LENDER ACCOUNT NUMBER | 54. LENDER USE ONLY | 48. | MO DAY YR AMOUNT $ |
|---|---|---|---|---|

**SECTION D - TO BE COMPLETED BY HEAF**

| | | 55a. SIGNATURE OF LENDING OFFICIAL X | 49. | 51. TOTAL LOAN AMOUNT APPROVED $ .00 |
|---|---|---|---|---|
| 56. HEAF USE ONLY | 57. PROMISSORY NOTE STATUS | PRINT NAME AND TITLE | | 55b. DATE SIGNED MO DAY YR |

## Order forms

When you order from a catalog, you need to know how to fill out an order form. Even if you are telephoning your order, it is helpful to fill out the order form before you make the call. You can refer to the order form as you give your order on the phone.

You will usually find space for the following information on an order form: number of the page showing the item you want, item number, description of item, and quantity. If you are ordering clothing, you will have to fill in color and size. You will also have to show the price of each item and figure shipping costs. In some states, you will have to add sales tax. Then you must total the amount owed.

## ACTIVITY 14
### Completing order forms

Below is a sample catalog page. On page 204 is a sample order form. The first item ordered is filled out for you. Add at least two items from the catalog to the order form. Assume that the sales tax is 6 percent. Total the amount due.

# Summer weight
## 100% cotton
## short-sleeved shirts

*Striped: green/white. blue/white. tan/white*
S1147 Men's **$26.00**
S1148 Women's **$26.00**

*Solid: plum, jade, khaki, gray, teal, white, mustard, chili*
L4132 Men's **$25.00**
L4133 Women's **$25.00**

**16**  Men's neck sizes: S (14–14 $1/_2$), M (15–15 $1/_2$), L (16–16 $1/_2$), XL (17–17 $1/_2$)
Women's sizes: S (6–8), M (10–12), L (14–16), XL (18–20)

# Athletic Shoes

*Practical!*
*Built-in comfort!*
*Provides support*
*where needed!*

A-7231
Women's fabric

A-7462
Women's leather

A-9851
Men's leather

| | |
|---|---|
| A-7231 Sizes 5–12 AA–C | **$40.50** |
| A-7462 Sizes 5–12 A–D | **$49.50** |
| A-9851 Sizes 9–12 B–C | **$52.95** |
| Sizes 11–14 B–EE | **$52.95** |

**42**

# Lightweight nylon jacket

**Sale!**

- *Drawstring hood*
- *Elastic wrists*

*Made in USA*
*Colors: Green or blue only*

Men's and women's sizes:
M (38–40), L (42–44), XL (46–48)

**46**   J614NS   ~~$32.50~~   **Now: $17.95**

FOSTER & HARLEY
4 E. Main St.
Lake Edge, Indiana

Your Name _____

Address

_____

Street               Apt.

_____

City           State          ZIP

Day phone ( ) _____

Evening phone ( ) _____

| Page | Item No. | Description | Color | Size | Qty. | Price | Total |
|------|----------|-------------|-------|------|------|-------|-------|
| 16 | S1147 | Men's Striped Shirt | Green/White | L | 1 | 26.00 | 26.00 |
| | | | | | | | |
| | | | | | | | |
| | | | | | | | |

Shipping, Handling, & Insurance

If merchandise total is

| up to $20 | add $3.95 |
| $20.01 to $40 | add $4.95 |
| $40.01 to $60 | add $5.95 |
| $60.01 to $80 | add $6.95 |

Total Merchandise $ _____

Applicable Sales Tax $ _____

Shipping, Handling, & Insurance $ _____

Total Amt. Due $ _____

Please check your method of payment:

_____ Full payment enclosed—check or money order

_____ American Express _____ VISA _____ MasterCard _____ Discover

Account number _____ Expiration date: _____

# SHOW WHAT YOU KNOW . . .

## About Order Forms

Bring one or two catalogs with order forms to class. Fill out an order form and have another class member check your work and your arithmetic.

# Filing a 1040EZ

## WORDS TO KNOW

**adjusted gross income**   total amount earned before any tax or other  money is withheld

**dependent**   anyone who depends on another for support; a dependent may be a child, wife, husband, parent, or other relative

**exemption**   fixed amount that may be deductible for support of one or more dependents or oneself

**filer**   person who submits (files) a tax return

**refund**   money returned from the Internal Revenue Service or a state or provincial department of revenue because taxes were overpaid

**standard deduction**   fixed amount that may be subtracted from adjusted gross income

**tax table**   table in instruction booklet used to find out how much tax is owed

**W–2 Form**   a yearly statement from an employer showing what was earned and withheld; a wage and tax statement

**withholding**   money deducted or withheld from a paycheck by an employer

If you hold a paying job, you will probably have to report your wages, salary, and tips to the Internal Revenue Service (IRS) of your federal government. You may also have to report the same amounts to the revenue department of the state or province in which you live.

Before the deadline of April 15, taxpayers prepare a tax return reporting all income from the previous calendar year. U.S. federal tax form 1040EZ is a simple form for persons who are single and have no children. If you are filing a return for the first time, you can find tax forms at most post offices, libraries, and banks. If you have paid taxes before, tax forms and instructions will usually be mailed to you. (NOTE: Since tax forms and tax laws almost always change from year to year, you must read the instructions that accompany the form you file.)

## ACTIVITY 15
### Understanding income tax words

Match the tax words below with their meanings.

**A**

_____ 1. exemption

_____ 2. refund

_____ 3. adjusted gross income

_____ 4. dependent

_____ 5. W–2 Form

_____ 6. tax table

_____ 7. standard deduction

_____ 8. interest income

_____ 9. withholding

_____ 10. filer

**B**

**A.** total amount you earned before anything was withheld

**B.** person who submits a tax return

**C.** what your employer provides to show earnings and withholding

**D.** fixed amount you may deduct for support of dependents and self

**E.** fixed amount you may be able to deduct from adjusted gross income

**F.** table showing what your taxes are

**G.** money you earned on a savings account

**H.** money your employer deducted from your paycheck

**I.** money the IRS owes you

**J.** person who depends on you for support

## ACTIVITY 16
### Working with income tax words

Below is a story about Timothy J. Chen, a taxpayer. Fill in each of the missing terms from the list.

| adjusted gross income | interest income | withheld |
| wages | W–2 Form | refund |
| return | dependent | tax table |

Timothy J. Chen, a student who worked in 1992, had to file his first income tax _____ . Tim, who is sixteen, worked at Super Burger during the year. He earned $2,000 in _____ and no tips. The _____ on his savings account was $50. His _____ was $2,050. Since Tim's parents provided most of his support, they will be able to claim him as a _____ on their tax return. Tim's employer _____ a total of $40 in federal taxes from Tim's wages. Tim checked the _____ to see what taxes, if any, were owed. He found out that the IRS was overpaid by $31. Tim will get a small _____ !

206

# ACTIVITY 17
## Using a 1040EZ

Look at the 1040EZ for Timothy J. Chen. Part of the reverse side of the form is shown below. Answer the questions about Tim's return.

1. Tim checked _____ for the Presidential Election Campaign.

2. Tim earned _____ in wages in 1992.

3. Tim had interest income of _____ .

4. Tim checked _____ for line 4.

5. Look at the worksheet below from the reverse side of 1040EZ. Is this worksheet completed correctly?

_____

6. On what line is Tim's refund shown? _____

---

**1992**          **Instructions for Form 1040EZ**

**Use this form if**
- Your filing status is single.
- You do not claim any dependents.
- You were under 65* and not blind at the end of 1992.
- Your taxable income (line 5) is less than $50,000.
- You had **only** wages, salaries, tips, and taxable scholarship or fellowship grants, and your taxable interest income was $400 or less. **Caution:** *If you earned tips, including allocated tips, that are not included in box 13 and box 14 of your W-2, you may not be able to use Form 1040EZ. See page 12 in the booklet. Also, you cannot use this form if you had more than one employer and your total wages were over $55,500.*
- You did not receive any advance earned income credit payments.

\* *If you turned 65 on January 1, 1993, you are considered to be age 65 at the end of 1992.*

If you are not sure about your filing status, see page 6 in the booklet. If you have questions about dependents, see Tele-Tax (topic no. 155) on page 20 in the booklet.

If you can't use this form, see Tele-Tax (topic no. 152) on page 20 in the booklet.

**Filling in your return**

Please print your numbers inside the boxes. Do not type your numbers. Do not use dollar signs.

Most people can fill in the form by following the instructions on the front. But you will have to use the booklet if you received a scholarship or fellowship grant or tax-exempt interest income, such as on municipal bonds. Also, use the booklet if you received a Form 1099-INT showing income tax withheld (backup withholding).

**Remember,** you must report your wages, salaries, and tips even if you don't get a W-2 form from your employer. You must also report all your taxable interest income, including interest from savings accounts at banks, savings and loans, credit unions, etc., even if you don't get a Form 1099-INT.

If you paid someone to prepare your return, that person must also sign it and show other information. See page 15 in the booklet.

Department of the Treasury—Internal Revenue Service

**Income Tax Return for
Single Filers With No Dependents** (L) **1992**

OMB No. 1545-0675

**Name & address**

Use the IRS label (see page 10). If you don't have one, please print.

L A B E L / H E R E

Print your name (first, initial, last)
Timothy J. Chen

Home address (number and street). If you have a P.O. box, see page 10. | Apt. no.
885 Scott Street

City, town or post office, state, and ZIP code. If you have a foreign address, see page 10.
Anytown, MD 01234

Please see instructions on the back. Also, see the
Form 1040EZ booklet.

**Presidential Election Campaign** (See page 10.)
Do you want $1 to go to this fund?

Note: *Checking "Yes" will not change your tax or reduce your refund.* ▶

Please print your numbers like this:

9 8 7 6 5 4 3 2 1 0

Your social security number

000 00 0000

Yes  No
☑

Dollars | Cents

**Report your income**

Attach Copy B of Form(s) W-2 here. Attach tax payment on top of Form(s) W-2.

Note: *You **must** check Yes or No.*

**1** Total wages, salaries, and tips. This should be shown in box 10 of your W-2 form(s). Attach your W-2 form(s). | 1

2,000.00

**2** Taxable interest income of $400 or less. If the total is more than $400, you cannot use Form 1040EZ. | 2

50.00

**3** Add lines 1 and 2. This is your **adjusted gross income.** | 3

2,050.00

**4** Can your parents (or someone else) claim you on their return?
☑ **Yes.** Do worksheet on back; enter amount from line E here.
☐ **No.** Enter 5,900.00. This is the total of your standard deduction and personal exemption. | 4

2,000.00

**5** Subtract line 4 from line 3. If line 4 is larger than line 3, enter 0. This is your **taxable income.** | 5

50.00

**Figure your tax**

**6** Enter your Federal income tax withheld from box 9 of your W-2 form(s). | 6

40.00

**7 Tax.** Look at line 5 above. Use the amount on **line 5** to find your tax in the tax table on pages 22-24 of the booklet. Then, enter the tax from the table on this line. | 7

9.00

**Refund or amount you owe**

**8** If line 6 is larger than line 7, subtract line 7 from line 6. This is your **refund.** | 8

31.00

**9** If line 7 is larger than line 6, subtract line 6 from line 7. This is the **amount you owe.** Attach your payment for full amount payable to the "Internal Revenue Service." Write your name, address, social security number, daytime phone number, and "1992 Form 1040EZ" on it. | 9

.

**Sign your return**

Keep a copy of this form for your records.

I have read this return. Under penalties of perjury, I declare that to the best of my knowledge and belief, the return is true, correct, and complete.

Your signature
X *Timothy J. Chen*

Date
2-14-93

Your occupation
server

For IRS Use Only—Please do not write in boxes below.

## Filing a 1040A

Many taxpayers use Form 1040A. This return is for both married and single persons. On Tim Chen's 1040EZ, he reported income from wages and interest income. On the 1040A, taxpayers also report dividends, IRA distributions, unemployment compensation, and other sources of income. This form allows for certain tax credits, such as credit for child and dependent care expenses. A parent who works may qualify for earned income credit.

The activities that follow deal with the 1040A. Become familiar with the 1040A "Words to Know" before beginning these activities.

## ACTIVITY 18
### Working with income tax words

Complete the statements about John and Lisa Chen's income tax return. The couple is filing a joint return using Form 1040A. Fill in each of the missing terms from the list.

| | |
|---|---|
| dependent | IRA |
| refund | unemployment compensation |
| joint return | dividends |
| exemptions | tax-exempt |
| interest income | withheld |

Because John and Lisa Chen are married, they are filing a _____ using 1040A. They will claim son Timothy as a _____. They can claim themselves as _____ . In addition to the salaries that both Chens earn, they also receive _____ from a savings account and _____ from investments in the stock market. However, some of the interest they receive is _____ , meaning they don't have to pay federal taxes on that interest. Since neither of the Chens was out of work, they will not have to show _____ . Neither John nor Lisa received any payments made from an individual retirement arrangement known as an _____ . Since Lisa and John have already had money_____ from their pay checks, they are hoping to get a _____ this year.

# ACTIVITY 19
## Using 1040A

The Chens used the fifteen steps outlined in their instruction booklet for 1040A to help complete their return. The final return appears on the next two pages. Review the information for both pages before completing the statements below.

1. Do John and Lisa want $1 to go to the Presidential Election Campaign Fund? _____

2. Which filing status is checked on the return? _____

3. Is box 6a checked? _____

4. Who is Timothy J. Chen? _____

5. How many exemptions did the Chens claim? _____

6. What is the total income of both John and Lisa? _____

7. How much taxable interest income did they have? _____

8. Did they have any tax-exempt interest? _____

9. On what line are dividends shown? _____

10. Did the Chens add their total income correctly? _____

11. Did they have any IRA distributions? _____

12. Do the Chens qualify for "Earned income credit"? _____

13. Did the Chens enter the correct standard deduction on line 19? _____

14. What is the amount entered on line 21? _____

15. What is the Chens' taxable income? _____

16. Did the Chens use the tax table? _____

17. The total tax for the Chens is on line _____ .

18. Total federal income tax withheld is on line _____ .

19. Do the Chens owe money? _____

20. Did the Chens prepare their own return? _____

| Form **1040A** | Department of the Treasury—Internal Revenue Service |
|---|---|

**Form 1040A**

Department of the Treasury—Internal Revenue Service

## U.S. Individual Income Tax Return (L)  1992

IRS Use Only—Do not write or staple in this space.

OMB No. 1545-0085

### Label
(See page 14.)

**Use the IRS label.** Otherwise, please print or type.

L A B E L   H E R E

Your first name and initial: John T.     Last name: Chen

If a joint return, spouse's first name and initial: Lisa M.     Last name: Chen

Home address (number and street). If you have a P.O. box, see page 15.   885 Scott Street   Apt. no.

City, town or post office, state, and ZIP code. If you have a foreign address, see page 15.   Anytown, MD 01234

Your social security number: 000 00 0000

Spouse's social security number: 000 00 0000

**For Privacy Act and Paperwork Reduction Act Notice, see page 4.**

**Presidential Election Campaign Fund** (See page 15.)

| | Yes | No |
|---|---|---|
| Do you want $1 to go to this fund? | ✔ | |
| If a joint return, does your spouse want $1 to go to this fund? | ✔ | |

**Note:** *Checking "Yes" will not change your tax or reduce your refund.*

### Check the box for your filing status
(See page 15.)

Check only one box.

1  ☐ Single

2  ☑ Married filing joint return (even if only one had income)

3  ☐ Married filing separate return. Enter spouse's social security number above and full name here. ▶ _____

4  ☐ Head of household (with qualifying person). (See page 16.) If the qualifying person is a child but not your dependent, enter this child's name here. ▶ _____

5  ☐ Qualifying widow(er) with dependent child (year spouse died ▶ 19 ____ ). (See page 17.)

### Figure your exemptions
(See page 18.)

If more than seven dependents, see page 21.

6a ☐ **Yourself.** If your parent (or someone else) can claim you as a dependent on his or her tax return, **do not** check box 6a. But be sure to check the box on line 18b on page 2.

b ☐ **Spouse**

c **Dependents:**

| (1) Name (first, initial, and last name) | (2) Check if under age 1 | (3) If age 1 or older, dependent's social security number | (4) Dependent's relationship to you | (5) No. of months lived in your home in 1992 |
|---|---|---|---|---|
| Timothy S. Chen | ✔ | | Son | 12 |
| | | | | |
| | | | | |
| | | | | |
| | | | | |
| | | | | |
| | | | | |

d If your child didn't live with you but is claimed as your dependent under a pre-1985 agreement, check here . . . . . . . ▶ ☐

e Total number of exemptions claimed.

No. of boxes checked on 6a and 6b: **2**

No. of your children on 6c who:
- lived with you: **1**
- didn't live with you due to divorce or separation (see page 21)

No. of other dependents on 6c:

Add numbers entered on lines above: **3**

### Figure your total income

**Attach Copy B of your Forms W-2 and 1099-R here.**

If you didn't get a W-2, see page 22.

Attach check or money order on top of any Forms W-2 or 1099-R.

| 7 | Wages, salaries, tips, etc. This should be shown in box 10 of your W-2 form(s). Attach Form(s) W-2. | 7 | 48,672 | 00 |
|---|---|---|---|---|
| 8a | **Taxable** interest income (see page 24). If over $400, also complete and attach Schedule 1, Part I. | 8a | 180 | 00 |
| b | **Tax-exempt** interest. DO NOT include on line 8a.   8b  75 | | 47 | 00 |
| 9 | Dividends. If over $400, also complete and attach Schedule 1, Part II. | 9 | | |
| 10a | Total IRA distributions.   10a | **10b** Taxable amount (see page 25).   10b | | |
| 11a | Total pensions and annuities.   11a | **11b** Taxable amount (see page 25).   11b | | |
| 12 | Unemployment compensation (see page 29). | 12 | | |
| 13a | Social security benefits.   13a | **13b** Taxable amount (see page 29).   13b | | |
| 14 | Add lines 7 through 13b (far right column). This is your **total income.** ▶ | 14 | 48,899 | 00 |

### Figure your adjusted gross income

| 15a | Your IRA deduction from applicable worksheet.   15a | | | |
|---|---|---|---|---|
| b | Spouse's IRA deduction from applicable worksheet. **Note:** *Rules for IRAs begin on page 31.*   15b | | | |
| c | Add lines 15a and 15b. These are your **total adjustments.** | 15c | | |
| 16 | Subtract line 15c from line 14. This is your **adjusted gross income.** If less than $22,370, see "Earned income credit" on page 39. ▶ | 16 | 48,899 | 00 |

Cat. No. 12601H

**1992 Form 1040A page 1**

| Name(s) shown on page 1. | Your social security number |
|---|---|
| John T. & Lisa M. Chen | 000 00 0000 |

**Figure your standard deduction, exemption amount, and taxable income**

| | | | |
|---|---|---|---|
| 17 | Enter the amount from line 16. | 17 | 48,899 00 |

18a Check if: ☐ **You** were 65 or older  ☐ Blind  **Enter number of boxes checked ▶** 18a ☐
☐ **Spouse** was 65 or older  ☐ Blind

b If your parent (or someone else) can claim you as a dependent, check here . . . . . . . . . . . . . . . ▶ 18b ☐

c If you are married filing separately and your spouse files Form 1040 and itemizes deductions, see page 35 and check here ▶ 18c ☐

19 Enter the **standard deduction** shown below for your filing status. **But if you checked any box on line 18a or b,** go to page 35 to find your standard deduction. **If you checked box 18c,** enter -0-.
- Single—$3,600  • Head of household—$5,250
- Married filing jointly or Qualifying widow(er)—$6,000
- Married filing separately—$3,000

| | | | |
|---|---|---|---|
| | | 19 | 6,000 00 |
| 20 | Subtract line 19 from line 17. (If line 19 is more than line 17, enter -0-.) | 20 | 42,899 00 |
| 21 | Multiply $2,300 by the total number of exemptions claimed on line 6e. | 21 | 6,900 00 |
| 22 | Subtract line 21 from line 20. (If line 21 is more than line 20, enter -0-.) This is your **taxable income.** ▶ | 22 | 35,999 00 |

**Figure your tax, credits, and payments**

If you want the IRS to figure your tax, see the instructions for line 22 on page 36.

| | | | |
|---|---|---|---|
| 23 | Find the tax on the amount on line 22. Check if from: ☐ Tax Table (pages 48–53) or  ☐ Form 8615 (see page 37). | 23 | 5,419 00 |
| 24a | Credit for child and dependent care expenses. Complete and attach Schedule 2. 24a | | |
| b | Credit for the elderly or the disabled. Complete and attach Schedule 3. 24b | | |
| c | Add lines 24a and 24b. These are your **total credits.** | 24c | |
| 25 | Subtract line 24c from line 23. (If line 24c is more than line 23, enter -0-.) | 25 | |
| 26 | Advance earned income credit payments from Form W-2. | 26 | |
| 27 | Add lines 25 and 26. This is your **total tax.** ▶ | 27 | 5,419 00 |
| 28a | Total Federal income tax withheld. If any tax is from Form(s) 1099, check here. ▶ ☐ 28a 6,841 00 | | |
| b | 1992 estimated tax payments and amount applied from 1991 return. 28b | | |
| c | **Earned income credit.** Complete and attach Schedule EIC. 28c | | |
| d | Add lines 28a, 28b, and 28c. These are your **total payments.** ▶ | 28d | 6,841 00 |

**Figure your refund or amount you owe**

Attach check or money order on top of Form(s) W-2, etc., on page 1.

| | | | |
|---|---|---|---|
| 29 | If line 28d is more than line 27, subtract line 27 from line 28d. This is the amount you **overpaid.** | 29 | |
| 30 | Amount of line 29 you want **refunded to you.** | 30 | 1,422 00 |
| 31 | Amount of line 29 you want **applied to your 1993 estimated tax.** 31 | | |
| 32 | If line 27 is more than line 28d, subtract line 28d from line 27. This is the **amount you owe.** Attach check or money order for full amount payable to the "Internal Revenue Service". Write your name, address, social security number, daytime phone number, and "1992 Form 1040A" on it. | 32 | |
| 33 | Estimated tax penalty (see page 41). 33 | | |

**Sign your return**

Keep a copy of this return for your records.

Under penalties of perjury, I declare that I have examined this return and accompanying schedules and statements, and to the best of my knowledge and belief, they are true, correct, and complete. Declaration of preparer (other than the taxpayer) is based on all information of which the preparer has any knowledge.

| Your signature | Date | Your occupation |
|---|---|---|
| John T. Chen | 2-15-93 | sales assistant |
| Spouse's signature. If joint return, BOTH must sign. | Date | Spouse's occupation |
| Lisa M. Chen | 2-15-93 | Receptionist |

**Paid preparer's use only**

| Preparer's signature ▶ | Date | Check if self-employed ☐ | Preparer's social security no. |
|---|---|---|---|
| Firm's name (or yours if self-employed) and address ▶ | | E.I. No. | |
| | | ZIP code | |

☆ U.S. GOVERNMENT PRINTING OFFICE: 1992 315-035

213

Below you will find profiles of two different taxpayers. Each one has chosen the 1040EZ return. Pretend you are one of these persons. Complete the 1040EZ on the next page for the person you select.

---

PROFILE:  Tracy E. Alexander
SS# - 574-22-2364
Age - 16
Occupation - Student/Part-time Stock Person
Marital Status - Single

Tracy lives at 886 George Street in St. Albans, West Virginia. The ZIP Code is 25314. Tracy's W-2 Form showed $2,350.17 in gross income. Federal taxes paid were $72. Tracy:

1. Has no children and no other dependents
2. Will be claimed on parents' return
3. Earned $36 in interest income

The tax table shows $6 due on Tracy's income.

---

PROFILE:  Jackie Fletcher
SS# - 584-01-1775
Age - 23
Occupation - Secretary
Marital Status - Single .

Jackie lives at 8134 C Street, Apt. E-13, in Raleigh, North Carolina. The ZIP Code is 27609. Jackie lives alone and earns about $200 per week. This year's W-2 Form shows $975 paid in federal taxes and $11,020 in gross income. Jackie:

1. Has no children or other dependents
2. Earned $380 in interest income

The tax table shows $829 due on Jackie's taxable income.

---

Form **1040EZ**

Department of the Treasury—Internal Revenue Service

# Income Tax Return for
# Single Filers With No Dependents (L) **1992**

OMB No. 1545-0675

**Name & address**

Use the **IRS label** (see page 10). If you don't have one, please print.

L A B E L

H E R E

Print your name (first, initial, last)

Home address (number and street). If you have a P.O. box, see page 10. | Apt. no.

City, town or post office, state, and ZIP code. If you have a foreign address, see page 10.

Please print your numbers like this:

9 8 7 6 5 4 3 2 1 0

Your social security number

**Please see instructions on the back. Also, see the Form 1040EZ booklet.**

**Presidential Election Campaign** (See page 10.)
Do you want $1 to go to this fund?

Note: *Checking "Yes" will not change your tax or reduce your refund.* ▶

Yes  No

Dollars    Cents

**Report your income**

**1** Total wages, salaries, and tips. This should be shown in box 10 of your W-2 form(s). Attach your W-2 form(s). **1**

Attach Copy B of Form(s) W-2 here. Attach tax payment on top of Form(s) W-2.

**2** Taxable interest income of $400 or less. If the total is more than $400, you cannot use Form 1040EZ. **2**

Note: *You must check Yes or No.*

**3** Add lines 1 and 2. This is your **adjusted gross income.** **3**

**4** Can your parents (or someone else) claim you on their return?
☐ **Yes.** Do worksheet on back; enter amount from line E here.
☐ **No.** Enter 5,900.00. This is the total of your standard deduction and personal exemption. **4**

**5** Subtract line 4 from line 3. If line 4 is larger than line 3, enter 0. This is your **taxable income.** **5**

**Figure your tax**

**6** Enter your Federal income tax withheld from box 9 of your W-2 form(s). **6**

**7** **Tax.** Look at line 5 above. Use the amount on **line 5** to find your tax in the tax table on pages 22-24 of the booklet. Then, enter the tax from the table on this line. **7**

**Refund or amount you owe**

**8** If line 6 is larger than line 7, subtract line 7 from line 6. This is your **refund.** **8**

**9** If line 7 is larger than line 6, subtract line 6 from line 7. This is the **amount you owe.** Attach your payment for full amount payable to the "Internal Revenue Service." Write your name, address, social security number, daytime phone number, and "1992 Form 1040EZ" on it. **9**

**Sign your return**

I have read this return. Under penalties of perjury, I declare that to the best of my knowledge and belief, the return is true, correct, and complete.

Keep a copy of this form for your records.

Your signature | Date

X

Your occupation

For IRS Use Only—Please do not write in boxes below.

Form **1040EZ** (1992)

215

# Reference strategies

Do you know how to use a computer or a card catalog to find a book in a library? Do you know how useful a dictionary is? Do you use a book's index or table of contents when you need information quickly?

In this chapter you will learn about using the library. You will also practice dictionary skills and learn how to use tables of contents and indexes. All of these are reference skills. The first topic is using the library.

## The library

### WORDS TO KNOW

**alphabetical**   in the same order as the letters of the alphabet

**call number**   set of numbers and letters used by a library to identify a book

**call slip**   a form for writing down the author, title, and call number of a book

**card catalog**   a collection of cards in drawers that lists the books in a library

**circulation desk**   the place in a library where books are checked in and out

**closed shelves**   parts of a library not open to users

**cross reference**   the suggestion of an additional source to examine

**Dewey decimal system**   a system of classifying books by subjects

**encyclopedia**   a book or set of books that has articles on many subjects

**fiction**   writing, such as novels and short stories, that tell about imaginary people and happenings

**general collection**   the materials in a library that can be checked out

**nonfiction**   writing, such as history and biography, that deals with real people or events

**numerical order**   in order by numbers

**periodical**   something published weekly or monthly like a magazine

**reference book**   a book, such as a dictionary or an encyclopedia, used to find facts or information quickly

A library has three kinds of resources. One is the general collection. You may check out books from this group. A card catalog or computer helps you find these books. To search for books you must understand the Dewey decimal system. Another resource is the reference collection. It has dictionaries, encyclopedias, and more. You must use these books at the library. The third kind of resource is periodicals. The periodicals collection has pamphlets and magazines. You must also use these at the library.

## The card catalog

Some libraries have a card catalog. It helps readers find the books they want.

All books in the library are listed in the card catalog. The card catalog helps identify and locate books. It is a series of drawers. The cards in each drawer are arranged alphabetically. The drawers are also arranged alphabetically. Each drawer has cards listing books in the library. You can find a book listed in the catalog by *author, title,* or *subject.*

By AUTHOR

| 635.9 |
| T768C |
|    Truex, Philip E. |
|      The city gardener |

Writer's last name

By TITLE

| 635.9      The city gardener |
| T768C |
|    Truex, Philip E. |
|      The city gardener |

Name of book

By SUBJECT

| 635.9      Gardening |
| T768C |
|    Truex, Philip E. |
|      The city gardener |

Subject

How do you find a book you want? There are several ways. You can look up the author's last name. You can look up the title of the book. Or you can look up the subject you want to read about. Author and title cards are often in one section of the card catalog. Subject cards are in their own section.

When you find the card, you must note the call number from the card.

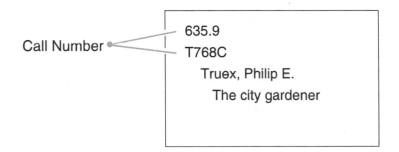

Call Number

| 635.9 |
| T768C |
|    Truex, Philip E. |
|      The city gardener |

The call number on the author, title, and subject cards is the same. It is in the upper left-hand corner. This call number directs you to the book. Call numbers are based on the Dewey decimal system of subject categories. See pages 223–224 for more information about the Dewey decimal system. *The City Gardener* by Philip Truex has call number 635.9 T768C. This tells you that it is in the 600 section of the library. All the books are on the shelves in numerical order. You locate the books in the 600 section of the library. Then you find the books marked 635. The *T* stands for the first letter of the author's last name. Your book should be among these. Works of fiction are put on the shelves alphabetically by the author's last name. They will be in a section of the library labeled "Fiction." Many libraries also have separate sections labeled "Poetry" and "Drama."

Here are things to keep in mind when you are searching for a book in a card catalog.

- Look for authors by their last name. For example, look for Alice Walker under Walker.

- Subject cards show last names first, too. If your subject is Eleanor Roosevelt, look under her last name in the card file.

- Ignore *a, an,* or *the* if it is the first word in a subject or title. The book title *The Scarlet Letter* will be in the card catalog under *S*.

- Remember there are three ways to find a book. The book *Outline of History* by H. G. Wells can be found by searching for

  the title: *Outline of History*
  the author: Wells, H. G.
  the subject: History.

## ACTIVITY 1

### Using the card catalog

You want to look up the following authors, titles, and subjects. Look at the drawing of the fronts of the drawers in a library card catalog. Which drawers will have cards on the information you want?

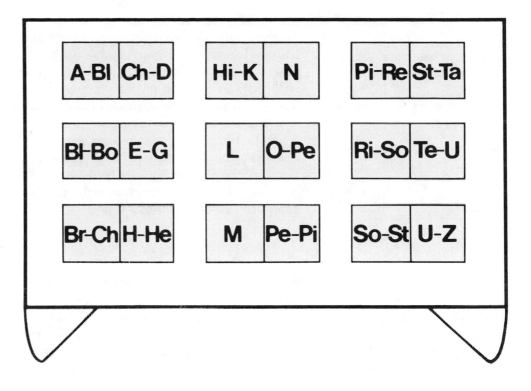

**Drawers**

1. camping _____

2. *The Outsiders* _____

3. wrestling _____

4. Arna Bontemps _____

5. *The Pearl* _____

6. George Bernard Shaw _____

7. Sandra Cisneros _____

8. *Are You in the House Alone?* _____

9. *A Separate Peace* _____

10. photography _____

11. Toronto _____

12. cooking _____

13. Madeleine L'Engle _____

14. genealogy _____

15. Norma Fox Mazer _____

**The computer** Many libraries use computers to store information about their books. Library computer systems are similar, but there are some differences. Each library has detailed instructions on how to use its computer system. In most systems you can find a book by typing in the author, the title, or the subject. You can find out how many books the library has by one author. You can discover the location of the book in the library, and you can tell whether the book is in the library or has been checked out.

Hal's library has a computer system. He wants to find *The City Gardener,* but he can't remember the author. He doesn't know the call number. He won't be able to find the book on the shelves without knowing the call number. Hal will have to look for the book by typing the title into the computer. Here is what he types:

T City Gardener

The *T* stands for *title.* In some systems you must leave a space between *T* and the title. In other systems you must type slash (/) or another symbol after the *T* and before you type the title. After you type the information you want, you must touch a key that starts the search. Sometimes this key is labeled *Enter.* Sometimes it is labeled *Return.*

Here is what Hal sees on the screen after he presses the *Return* key:

NUMBER OF MATCHES: 2

T CITY GARDENER

Choose line number(s) and press return key:

1. CITY GARDENER
2. CITY GARDENERS HANDBOOK FROM BALCONY TO BACKYARD

Hal knows he doesn't want the second title. He wants the first one. He types the number 1 and presses the *Return* key. Here is what he sees next.

Truex, Philip E.
The city gardener

New York, Knopf [distributed by Random]

| | COPIES IN BRANCH: 1 | SYSTEM: 7 | |
|---|---|---|---|
| LOCATION | CALL NUMBER | DUE DATE | STATUS |
| BST OPEN | 635.9T768C | 4-04-94 | CHARGED |

220

Now Hal knows the author and location. In Hal's library, BST stands for "Business, Science, and Technology." Hal will find the book in this section. Hal also knows the call number. Unfortunately, the book is charged out and is not due until April 4. The computer also shows that Hal's branch of the library has 1 copy. There are 7 copies in the whole system.

Rose wants to find a book by Alice Walker, but she can't remember the title. Here is what she types into the computer. (The *A* stands for author.)

A Alice Walker

Rose has made a mistake. She should have typed the last name first. She sees the following message on the computer screen:

No match found. Try again.

When Rose tries again and types in A Walker Alice, here is what she sees on the screen:

---

NUMBER OF CITATIONS: 4
A   WALKER ALICE


Choose a line number and press return key:


1. Walker, Alice, 1944–
   The color purple
2. Walker, Alice, 1944–
   Horses make a landscape look more beautiful: poems
3. Walker, Alice, 1944–
   In love and trouble; stories of black women
4. Walker, Alice, 1944–
   In search of our mother's gardens

---

When Rose sees the first title, *The Color Purple,* she remembers that this is the title she wants. Rose types in the number 1 and presses the *Return* key. The screen then shows this:

---

Walker, Alice, 1944–
The color purple: a novel

New York, Harcourt Brace Jovanovich


| CALL NO. | DUE DATE | STATUS |
|---|---|---|
| Fiction W | | SHELF |

---

Notice that Alice Walker's birth year is shown. This helps to identify her, since there may be other authors named Alice Walker. Notice also that the city where the book was published is shown. The publisher is also shown. Some systems will also show the date the book was published. Rose will find this book in the Fiction section of the library with the Ws.

If Rose wants to find a book on a particular subject, like carpentry or gymnastics, a librarian can show Rose how to narrow her search. To find gymnastics, for example, she may have to type in Sports—gymnastics.

## ACTIVITY 2
### Using a computer

Suppose you want to find the following books on a computer. Write the first word of each title that you would type into a computer. Write the part of the author's name that you would type first into the computer. (Titles are in italic type.)

1. *The Witch of Blackbird Pond* _____

2. *Jane Eyre* _____

3. Emily Brontë _____

4. Jane Austen _____

5. *The Old Man and the Sea* _____

6. Arthur Conan Doyle _____

7. M. E. Kerr _____

8. Neil Simon _____

9. *A Raisin in the Sun* _____

10. *David Copperfield* _____

### Open and closed shelves

In most libraries you may take a book from a shelf yourself. This is called the *open-shelf system*. You get the book and take it to the checkout desk. You then use your library card to check out the book. Sometimes someone who works at the library gets your book from the shelves. This is called the *closed-shelf system*. Many college and reference libraries have closed shelves. If you use this type of library, you will have to fill out a call slip. This call slip will identify the book you want.

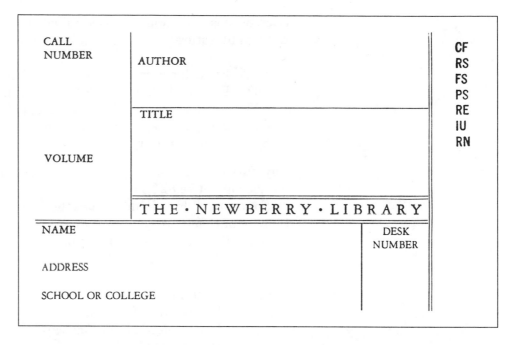

You take your call slip to a call desk. A library employee will get your book using the information you put on the slip. A library with open shelves may have some books that need a call slip. These might be rare or valuable books that need special care and cannot be checked out.

## The Dewey decimal system

Libraries are divided into sections. Books on similar subjects are grouped together. This grouping is called the Dewey decimal system. The call number on a book stands for the subject and helps locate the book. Here are the number categories in the Dewey decimal system:

| | | | |
|---|---|---|---|
| 000–099 | General works | 500–599 | Pure sciences |
| 100–199 | Philosophy | 600–699 | Technology |
| 200–299 | Religion | 700–799 | The Arts |
| 300–399 | Social sciences | 800–899 | Literature |
| 400–499 | Language | 900–999 | Geography & History |

Each section is further divided into *ten* parts. Here are the ten parts of the 800—Literature:

| | |
|---|---|
| 800 | General literature |
| 810 | American literature |
| 820 | English literature |
| 830 | Germanic literature |
| 840 | Romance literature |
| 850 | Italian, Romanian literature |
| 860 | Spanish, Portuguese literature |
| 870 | Latin & Italic literature |
| 880 | Greek literature |
| 890 | Other literatures |

Each of these divisions is further divided. Here are the parts of the 820s—English literature:

| | | | |
|---|---|---|---|
| 821 | English poetry | 826 | English letters |
| 822 | English drama | 827 | English satire |
| 823 | English fiction | 828 | English miscellany |
| 824 | English essays | 829 | Anglo-Saxon |
| 825 | English oratory | | |

Any further divisions are shown with a decimal. For example, a call number might be 821.09.

Some large libraries do not use the Dewey decimal system. They use the Library of Congress system. Both systems have author, title, and subject cards. Both systems use call numbers, but the Library of Congress system divides books into lettered classes:

| | |
|---|---|
| A | General works |
| B | Philosophy—Religion |
| C | History—Auxiliary Sciences |
| D | History and Topography (except America) |
| E-F | America |
| G | Geography—Anthropology |
| H | Social Sciences (Economics and Sociology) |
| J | Political Science |
| K | Law |
| L | Education |
| M | Music |
| N | Fine Arts |
| P | Language and Literature |
| Q | Science |
| R | Medicine |
| S | Agriculture |
| T | Technology |
| U | Military Science |
| V | Naval Science |
| Z | Bibliography and Library Science |

## ACTIVITY 3

### Using the Dewey decimal system

Rose and Hal are browsing through the library. They each have a list of topics they would like to know more about. In which section of the library would each of them go to find books on the topics below? Use the Dewey decimal numbers to show the sections.

| | | | |
|---|---|---|---|
| 000–099 | General works | 500–599 | Pure sciences |
| 100–199 | Philosophy | 600–699 | Technology |
| 200–299 | Religion | 700–799 | The Arts |
| 300–399 | Social sciences | 800–899 | Literature |
| 400–499 | Language | 900–999 | Geography & History |

**Rose's List**

1. American literature _____
2. Oriental philosophy _____
3. English poets _____
4. Women artists _____
5. Botany _____

**Hal's List**

6. Chemistry _____
7. African history _____
8. Building construction _____
9. The Bible _____
10. slang _____

---

## The Readers' Guide to Periodical Literature

Suppose you want to find something in a back issue of a magazine. Magazines are not shown in a card catalog. You will need to use the *Readers' Guide to Periodical Literature*. This reference work has many volumes. It will help you find what you want in a magazine.

In the front of the *Readers' Guide* is a list of the magazines that are in the guide. Here are some of the magazines.

*American Craft*            *Down Beat*
*American Heritage*         *Ebony*
*Better Homes and Gardens* *Motor Trend*
*Black Enterprise*         *National Wildlife*
*Car and Driver*           *Popular Mechanics*
*Consumer Reports*         *Popular Science*
*Cycle*                    *Rolling Stone*
*Dance Magazine*           *Runner's World*

Here are some of the abbreviations used in the entries in the *Readers' Guide*.

| J | January | + | continued on later pages |
| F | February | | of same issue |
| Mr | March | por | portrait |
| Ap | April | int | interviewer |
| My | May | m | monthly |
| Je | June | pt | part |
| Jl | July | v | volume |
| Ag | August | w | weekly |
| S | September | il | illustrated |
| O | October | | |
| N | November | | |
| D | December | | |

Here is a sample entry from the March 1980–February 1981 *Readers' Guide.*

---

**READERS' GUIDE TO PERIODICAL LITERATURE March 1980–February 1981**    **1297**

**ROCK GROUPS**
   *see also*
Beatles (rock group)
Chipmunks (recording group)
Disco groups
Phonograph records—Rock music
Rock musicians

Title of article •————— Abba: ready for the Fortune 500. S. Graham. il Hi Fi 30:95-7 Mr. '80
AC/DC shrugs off a death and rocks on. D. Fricke. il Roll Stone p 17-18 O 30 '80
Accounts of Cincinnati tragedy conflict [Who concert at Riverfront Coliseum] D. Krieger. Roll Stone p 23 Ap 3 '80
After 15 nowhere years: the Whispers make a noise—but is it the wrong kind of hot rock? R. K. Rain. il People 13:42+ Ap 7 '80
Magazine: •————— Ann Wilson puts zip into Heart with her vocals [interview by E. Miller] A. Wilson. il por Seventeen 30:74+ D '80
• volume
• page(s)
• month
• year
Artful Dodger earn a second chance to rock. J. Henke il Roll Stone p 16+ D 11 '80
Aynsley Dunbar sues Journey for $3.25 million. M. Branton Roll Stone p12 Ag 7 '80
B–52's. J. Henke il Roll Stone p9-10+ D 11 '80
B–52's return home. A. DeCurtis. il Roll Stone p84 N 27 '80
Bee Gees sue Stigwood, charge mismanagement. M. Kirkeby. il por Roll Stone p23 N 13 '80
Britain's ska king [Specials] R. Graustark and others. il Newsweek 95:74 Ap 7 '80
Brothers Johnson: a world-class club band. D. Fricke. il Roll Stone p20+ Jl 10 '80
Author •————— Bus Boys are moving in [release of Minimum wage rock & roll] J. Cocks and M. Smilgis. il Time 116:105 D 8 '80
Bus Boys rock for the underdog. C. Morris. il Roll Stone p26-7 N 27 '80
Buzzcocks and Magazine: Different kinds of tension. C. Morris. il por Roll Stone p23+ F 21 '80
The Cars. M. Gilmore. il Roll Stone p10-14 O 30 '80
Cars' Ben Orr. por Teen 23-46 D '80
Caught in the act: the Eagles. il Teen 24:25 N '80
Cheap Trick: marvelous mismatched musicians. il Teen 23:50 F '80
Cher plays it low-key with Black Rose. J. Farber. il por Roll Stone p32 O 16 '80
Chronicling the Sex Pistols' rise and fall. M. Gilmore. il Roll Stone p20-1 My 1 '80
The Clash. J. Henke. il Roll Stone p38-41 Ap 17 '80

---

The subject head is "Rock groups." Subject heads are either topics or authors' names. They are alphabetical. Entries are alphabetical by title. When you find what you are looking for in the *Readers' Guide*, you will need to go to the periodicals section of a library. Here you will find bound back issues of many magazines. If you wanted to read the article on Abba, you would look for the March 1980 issue of *Hi Fi* magazine.

## ACTIVITY 4

### Using the Readers' Guide

Study the sample entries from the *Readers' Guide to Periodical Literature.* Answer the following questions.

1. Cross references are shown under the subject head. A reader looking up rock groups could also look under other subject heads. What are two other subject heads that would have information on rock groups?

   _____

2. What is the title of the first article?

   _____

3. In what magazine did the first article appear? _____

4. Where would you find an article about Cheap Trick? _____

5. "Bus Boys rock for the underdog" is the title of an article in what issue of *Rolling Stone?*

   _____

6. What would you look under to find all the articles on the Chipmunks?

   _____

7. Who wrote about Cher? _____ Is the article illustrated? _____

8. Articles about the B–52's appeared in which two months of *Rolling Stone* in 1980?

   _____

9. Look at the entry for "After 15 nowhere years." What is the volume number of the *People* in which it

   appears? _____

10. Was Ann Wilson a singer in 1980?

   _____

The statements below are about the library. Mark these statements TRUE (T) or FALSE (F).

_____ **1.** To find an author in a card catalog, you must look under the last name.

_____ **2.** To find an author in a computerized catalog, you must look under the last name.

_____ **3.** A library computer will show you the call number of a book.

_____ **4.** A library computer may tell you whether a book is checked out or on the shelf.

_____ **5.** You can find books by subject in the card catalog and on a computer.

_____ **6.** The Dewey decimal system is a reference work in the general collection.

_____ **7.** A call slip is used to obtain a book in a library that has open shelves.

_____ **8.** In some libraries, books are arranged according to the Library of Congress system.

_____ **9.** If a book title begins with *Of,* you must search for the book under the second word in the title.

_____ **10.** The *Readers' Guide to Periodical Literature* will be in the fiction section of the library.

# SHOW WHAT YOU KNOW . . .

## About Reference Works

Find *one* fascinating fact in one of the following reference works and report it to the class: almanac, gazetteer, world atlas.

## Dictionary skills

A dictionary is an important reference work. All the words in a dictionary are in one alphabetical list. This list makes up the main part of a dictionary. Many dictionaries have special sections at the back. These sections may have maps, pictures of state or national flags, listings of state capitals, or other lists of facts. You can find a lot of information if you know how to use a dictionary.

### Types of dictionaries

Dictionaries are not all the same. Some dictionaries are intended for use by young children. Some are intended for high school or college students. There are paperbound dictionaries, which have smaller type and fewer entries than most high school or college dictionaries. Large dictionaries, called *unabridged dictionaries,* are not portable and have many more words than college dictionaries. Many people and all libraries have unabridged dictionaries.

Ways of defining and pronouncing words can be different in various dictionaries. Some dictionaries place an accent mark before a syllable and others place it after. The symbols used to show pronunciation may mean different things in different dictionaries. Some dictionaries have a few drawings to help you understand definitions. Others have many drawings and photos. Sometimes biographical and geographical names are at the back of a dictionary and sometimes they are included in the regular alphabetical listing, as in the following example from a page of *Webster's Ninth New Collegiate Dictionary:*

geo·pol·i·tics \-'päl-ə-,tiks\ *n pl but sing in constr* (1904)  **1** : a study of the influence of such factors as geography, economics, and demography on the politics and esp. the foreign policy of a state  **2** : a governmental policy guided by geopolitics  **3** : a combination of political and geographic factors relating to something (as a state or particular resources) — **geo·po·lit·i·cal** \-pə-'lit-i-kəl\ *adj* — **geo·po·lit·i·cal·ly** \-i-k(ə-)lē\ *adv*
geo·pres·sured \,jē-ō-'presh-ərd\ *adj* (1968) : subjected to great pressure from geologic forces (~ methane)
Geor·die \'jord-ē\ *n* [Sc, dim. of the name *George*] *chiefly Brit* (1866) : an inhabitant of Newcastle-upon-Tyre or its environs; *also* : the dialect of English spoken by Geordies
George \'jo(ə)rj\ *n* [St. *George*] (1506)  **1** : either of two of the insignia of the British Order of the Garter  **2** : a British coin bearing the image of St. George
geor·gette \jor-'jet\ *n* [fr. *Georgette,* a trademark] (1915) : a thin strong clothing crepe of fibers woven from hard-twisted yarns to produce a dull pebbly surface
¹Geor·gian \'jor-jən\ *n* (15c)  **1** : a native or inhabitant of Georgia in the Caucasus  **2** : the language of the Georgian people
²Georgian *adj* (1607) : of, relating to, or constituting Georgia in the Caucasus, the Georgians, or Georgian
³Georgian *n* (1741) : a native or resident of the state of Georgia
⁴Georgian *adj* (1762) : of, relating to, or characteristic of the state of Georgia or its people
⁵Georgian *adj* (1875)  **1** : of, relating to, or characteristic of the reigns of the first four Georges of Great Britain  **2** : of, relating to, or characteristic of the reign of George V of Great Britain
⁶Georgian *n* (1901)  **1** : one belonging to either of the Georgian periods  **2** : Georgian taste or style
Geor·gia pine \'jor-jə-\ *n* (1796) : LONGLEAF PINE
¹geor·gic \'jor-jik\ *n* [the *Georgics,* poem by Vergil, fr. L *georgicus*] (1513) : a poem dealing with agriculture

It is a good idea to own an up-to-date school or college dictionary. You should become thoroughly familiar with your dictionary so that you can use it easily. The more you use one dictionary, the easier it will be to understand all its features.

# ACTIVITY 5
## Locating words in a dictionary

The words below are entries from a dictionary. These words are no longer in alphabetical order. Arrange these words alphabetically.

| Dictionary entries | Alphabetical arrangement | Dictionary entries | Alphabetical arrangement |
|---|---|---|---|
| complex | _____ | possessed | _____ |
| competitive | _____ | possess | _____ |
| complacency | _____ | posse | _____ |
| complacence | _____ | position | _____ |
| compete | _____ | point | _____ |
| competency | _____ | postage | _____ |

230

**short pronunciation key**

**pronunciation**

**entry word divided into syllables**

**inflected form**

**part of speech**

**restrictive label**

**guide words**

**illustrative sentence**

**definition**

**etymology**

| | | | | | |
|---|---|---|---|---|---|
| a hat | i it | oi oil | ch child | | a in about |
| ā age | ī ice | ou out | ng long | | e in taken |
| ä far | o hot | u cup | sh she | ə = | i in pencil |
| e let | ō open | ù put | th thin | | o in lemon |
| ē equal | ô order | ü rule | ᴛʜ then | | u in circus |
| ėr term | | | zh measure | | < = derived from |

**bounce** (bouns), *v.*, **bounced, bounc ing,** *n.* —*v.i.* **1** spring into the air like a rubber ball: *The baby likes to bounce up and down on the bed.* **2** come or go noisily, angrily, etc.; burst or bound: *She bounced out of the room.* **3** leap; spring **4 bounce back,** begin anew, especially with vigor or enthusiasm. **5** INFORMAL. (of a check) be returned uncashed by the bank on which it is drawn because of insufficient funds in the account of the person who signed it. —*v.t.* **1** cause to bounce. **2** (of a communications satellite) relay or reflect (a signal, message, etc.). **3** SLANG. throw out; eject. **4** SLANG. discharge from work or employment.
—*n.* **1** a springing back; bound; rebound. **2** a sudden spring or leap. **3** a boasting; a bragging. **4** INFORMAL. energy; spirit: *I was in the hospital for a week, but now I am as full of bounce as ever.* **5** a heavy blow or thump. **6** SLANG. discharge from work or employment.
[Middle English *bunsen*]

**bounc er** (boun′sər), *n.* **1** one that bounces. **2** anything very large of its kind. **3** INFORMAL. braggart. **4** SLANG. a strong man hired by a nightclub, hotel, etc., to throw out disorderly persons.

**bounc ing** (boun′sing), *adj.* **1** that bounces. **2** big and strong. **3** vigorous; healthy: *a bouncing baby.* —**bounc′ing ly,** *adv.*

**bouncing Bess** (bes), bouncing Bet.

**bouncing Bet** (bet), a species of soapwort with pink or white flowers.

**bound¹** (bound), *adj.* **1** under some obligation; tied down by circumstance, duty, etc.; obliged: *I feel bound by my promise.* **2 bound up in** or **bound up with, a** closely connected with. **b** very devoted to. **3** certain; sure: *It is bound to get dark soon.* **4** INFORMAL. determined; resolved. **5** put in covers: *a bound book.* **6** tied fast; fastened: *bound hands.* **7** held by a chemical bond. —*v.* pt. and pp. of **bind.** *She bound the package with string.* [Middle English *bounden*]

**bound²** (bound), *v.i.* **1** spring back; bounce; rebound: *The rubber ball bounded from the wall.* **2** leap or spring lightly along; jump: *The deer bounds through the woods.* **3** leap or spring upward or onward. —*v.t.* cause to bound or rebound; bounce. —*n.* **1** a springing back; bounce; rebound. **2** a leaping or springing lightly along; jump. **3** a leap or spring upward or onward. [< Middle French *bondir* to leap, originally, resound, ultimately < Latin *bombus.* See BOMB.]

**bound³** (bound), *n.* **1** Usually, **bounds,** *pl.* a limiting line; boundary; limit: *Keep your hopes within bounds.* **2 bounds,** *pl.* **a** land on or near a boundary. **b** area included within boundaries. **3 out of bounds,** outside the area allowed by rules, custom, or law: *This town is out of bounds for soldiers.* —*v.t.* **1** form the boundary of; limit. **2** name the boundaries of: *Bound the state of Maine.* —*v.i.* share a boundary with; have its boundary (on): *Canada bounds on the United States.* [< Old French *bodne, bonde* < Medieval Latin *bodina*]

**bound⁴** (bound), *adj.* intending to go; on the way; going: *I am bound for home.* [< Scandinavian (Old Icelandic) *búinn* prepared]

**bound ar y** (boun′dər ē), *n., pl.* **-ar ies.** a limiting line or thing; limit; border: *the boundary between Canada and the United States.*

**bound en** (boun′dən), *adj.* **1** required; obligatory: *one's bounden duty.* **2** under obligation because of favors received; obliged.

**bound er** (boun′dər), *n.* INFORMAL. a rude, vulgar person; cad.

**bound form,** a linguistic form which does not occur alone or independently but is always part of a word, as *-s, -ly,* and *pre-.*

**bound less** (bound′lis), *adj.* **1** not limited; infinite: *Outer space is boundless.* **2** vast: *the boundless ocean.* —**bound′less ly,** *adv.* —**bound′less ness,** *n.*

**boun te ous** (boun′tē əs), *adj.* **1** given freely; generous. **2** plentiful; abundant. —**boun′te ous ly,** *adv.* —**boun′te ous ness,** *n.*

**boun ti ful** (boun′tə fəl), *adj.* **1** giving freely; generous. **2** plentiful; abundant. —**boun′ti ful ly,** *adv.* —**boun′ti ful ness,** *n.*

**boun ty** (boun′tē), *n., pl.* **-ties. 1** a generous gift. **2** generosity in bestowing gifts; liberality. **3** reward; premium: *The state government gives a bounty for killing predatory animals.* [< Old French *bonté* < Latin *bonitatem* < *bonus* good]

from *Thorndike Barnhart Advanced Dictionary*

## Guide words

Guide words can help you locate a word on a dictionary page. Guide words are usually at the top of a page. If there are two guide words at the top of a page, they show the first and last words on that page. (See the illustration on page 231.) Sometimes there is a guide word at the top of the left-hand page and a guide word at the top of the right-hand page. The left guide word shows the first word at the top of the left page. The right guide word shows the last word at the bottom of the right page. You decide whether the word you want falls alphabetically between the guide words.

## ACTIVITY 6
### Using guide words

Below is a list of words from three different pages of a dictionary. Then there are guide words from those pages. Put each word in the column where it belongs.

| | | |
|---|---|---|
| history | hogwash | hives |
| homework | hoax | hint |
| honey | honest | homage |
| horoscope | hole | horror |
| hostage | hotshot | hospital |

**hilt/hold**

**holder/hooky**

**hooligan/houseboat**

_____     _____     _____

_____     _____     _____

_____     _____     _____

_____     _____     _____

_____     _____     _____

## Entry words

Each word that is explained in a dictionary is called an *entry word*. Entry words are shown divided into syllables.

    o pin ion

    pub lic

Entries that have two or more words are not usually divided into syllables.

    public opinion

    public schools

Some two-word entries are divided into syllables, however.

    Puer to  Ri co

## Pronunciation key

Dictionaries tell you how to pronounce a word. To pronounce a word you need to learn the pronunciation key. The *symbols* in the key tell you how letters are pronounced. Each symbol stands for a particular sound. A short form of a pronunciation key is usually found on every other dictionary page.

The *schwa* (ə) is one of the symbols used to help you pronounce words correctly. The pronunciation key tells you what a letter or letters sound like when the schwa symbol is used. The following key is from *Thorndike Barnhart Advanced Dictionary.*

### Pronunciation Key

| | | | | | |
|---|---|---|---|---|---|
| a | hat, cap | j | jam, enjoy | u | cup, butter |
| ā | age, face | k | kind, seek | ů | full, put |
| ä | father, far | l | land, coal | ü | rule, move |
| | | m | me, am | | |
| b | bad, rob | n | no, in | v | very, save |
| ch | child, much | ng | long, bring | w | will, woman |
| d | did, red | | | y | young, yet |
| | | o | hot, rock | z | zero, breeze |
| e | let, best | ō | open, go | zh | measure, seizure |
| ē | equal, be | ô | order, all | | |
| ėr | term, learn | oi | oil, voice | ə | represents: |
| | | ou | house, out | | a in about |
| | | | | | e in taken |
| f | fat, if | | | | i in pencil |
| g | go, bag | p | paper, cup | | o in lemon |
| h | he, how | r | run, try | | u in circus |
| | | s | say, yes | | |
| i | it, pin | sh | she, rush | | |
| ī | ice, five | t | tell, it | | |
| | | th | thin, both | | |
| | | ŦH | then, smooth | | |

**foreign sounds**

Y as in French *du.*
Pronounce (ē) with the lips rounded as for (ü).

à as in French *ami.*
Pronounce (ä) with the lips spread and held tense.

œ as in French *peu.*
Pronounce (ā) with the lips rounded as for (ō).

N as in French *bon.*
The N is not pronounced, but shows that the vowel before it is nasal.

H as in German *ach.*
Pronounce (k) without closing the breath passage.

### Grammatical Key

| | | | |
|---|---|---|---|
| *adj.* | adjective | *prep.* | preposition |
| *adv.* | adverb | *pron.* | pronoun |
| *conj.* | conjunction | *v.* | verb |
| *interj.* | interjection | *v.i.* | intransitive verb |
| *n.* | noun | *v.t.* | transitive verb |
| *sing.* | singular | *pl.* | plural |
| *pt.* | past tense | *pp.* | past participle |

## ACTIVITY 7
### Using the pronunciation key

Using the short pronunciation key, write a word that has the same sound as the symbol in dark type. The first two are done for you.

| | | | | |
|---|---|---|---|---|
| **a** hat | **i** it | **oi** oil | **ch** child | ( a in about |
| **ā** age | **ī** ice | **ou** out | **ng** long | e in taken |
| **ä** far | **o** hot | **u** cup | **sh** she | ə = { i in pencil |
| **e** let | **ō** open | **ù** put | **th** thin | o in lemon |
| **ē** equal | **ô** order | **ü** rule | **ŦH** then | u in circus |
| **ėr** term | | | **zh** measure | < = derived from |

1. **a** hat _sat_

2. **ā** age _page_

3. **ä** far _____

4. **e** let _____

5. **ē** equal _____

6. **ėr** term _____

7. **i** it _____

8. **ī** ice _____

9. **o** hot _____

10. **ō** open _____

11. **ô** order _____

12. **oi** oil _____

13. **ou** out _____

14. **u** cup _____

15. **ù** put _____

16. **ü** rule _____

17. **ch** child _____

18. **ng** long _____

19. **sh** she _____

20. **th** thin _____

21. **ŦH** then _____

22. **zh** measure _____

**Accent marks**  Pronounce this word with the help of the pronunciation key.

jim nā´ zē əm

Notice that there is an accent mark after the second syllable. This tells you to stress that syllable. This mark is a *primary accent*. Some words have more than one accent. If a word has a *secondary accent*, the accent mark is in lighter type. Here is a word with two accents. Pronounce the word.

kə les´ tə rol´

Some words have two or more pronunciations. In some dictionaries the first pronunciation is the one most commonly used.

## ACTIVITY 8
### Using the pronunciation key and accent marks

Using the pronunciation key, match the pronunciations in Column A with the words in Column B.

| | | | | |
|---|---|---|---|---|
| **a** hat | **i** it | **oi** oil | **ch** child | ⎧ a in about |
| **ā** age | **ī** ice | **ou** out | **ng** long | ⎪ e in taken |
| **ä** far | **o** hot | **u** cup | **sh** she | ə = ⎨ i in pencil |
| **e** let | **ō** open | **ù** put | **th** thin | ⎪ o in lemon |
| **ē** equal | **ô** order | **ü** rule | **ŦH** then | ⎩ u in circus |
| **ėr** term | | | **zh** measure | **<** = derived from |

**A**                                                                          **B**

1. sin´ ə mə  ————————————                    jaw

2. klas´ ə kəl  ————————————                  Florida

3. kom´ plə kā´ shən  ————————————            cinema

4. en sī´ klə pē´ dē ə  ————————————          joy

5. flôr´ ə də  ————————————                   classical

6. hyü´ stən  ————————————                    encyclopedia

7. jô  ————————————                           complication

8. joi  ————————————                          Houston

9. bi ling´ gwəl  ————————————                thyme

10. tīm  ————————————                         bilingual

11. ŦHō  ————————————                         whim

12. hwim  ————————————                        though

---

# SHOW WHAT YOU KNOW . . .

## About the Pronunciation Key and Accent Marks

Write the answer to the question by spelling each word.

A suspected burglar led police on a high-speed chase through a town. The chase lasted twenty minutes, but the police had no trouble following the man. Why?

Bi kôz´ hē pùt ôn his tėrn sig´ nəl ev´ rē tīm hē mād ə tėrn.

**Definitions**

Many people use a dictionary to find meanings of words. When you look for a meaning, you may find only one definition. Sometimes you may have to read several definitions to find the meaning you want. Some definitions may have several parts.

Suppose you read in a story that a student took a *satchel* to school. What is a satchel? Look below at the entry for *satchel*. How many syllables does the word have? Is the accent on the first or second syllable? Read the definition. Could you put a pair of shoes in a satchel?

**sar·cas·tic** (sär kas′tik), *adj.* using sarcasm; sneering; cutting: "*Don't hurry!*" *was his sarcastic comment as I began to dress at my usual slow rate.* —**sar·cas′ti·cal·ly,** *adv.*

**sar·coph·a·gus** (sär kof′ə gəs), *n., pl.* **-gi** (-jī), **-gus·es.** a stone coffin, especially one ornamented with sculpture or inscriptions. [< Greek *sarkophagos,* originally, flesh-eating (stone) < *sarkos* flesh + *phagein* eat]

**sar·don·ic** (sär don′ik), *adj.* bitterly sarcastic, scornful, or mocking: *a sardonic outlook.* [< Greek *sardonios,* alteration of *sardanios,* perhaps influenced by *sardonion,* a supposed Sardinian plant that produced hysterical convulsions] —**sar·don′i·cal·ly,** *adv.*

**sa·ri** (sär′ē), *n.* the principal outer garment of Hindu women, a long piece of cotton or silk wrapped around the body, with one end falling nearly to the feet and the other end thrown over the head or shoulder. [< Hindi *sārī* < Sanskrit *śāṭī*]

**sa·rong** (sə rông′, sə rong′), *n.* a rectangular piece of cloth, usually a brightly colored printed material, worn as a skirt by men and women in the Malay Archipelago and certain other islands of the Pacific. [< Malay *sārung*]

sarong

**sar·sa·pa·ril·la** (sas′pə ril′ə, sär′sə pə ril′ə), *n.* **1** any of various species of tropical American climbing or trailing greenbriers. **2** the dried roots of any of these plants, formerly used in medicine. **3** a soft drink, usually carbonated, flavored with the root of any of these plants. [< Spanish *zarzaparilla*]

**sas·sa·fras** (sas′ə fras), *n.* **1** a slender eastern North American tree of the same family as the laurel, having fragrant, yellow flowers, bluish-black fruit, and soft, light wood. **2** the aromatic dried bark of its root, used in medicine and to flavor candy, soft drinks, etc. [< Spanish *sasafrás*]

**sas·sy** (sas′ē), *adj.,* **-si·er, -si·est.** rude. —**sas′si·ly,** *adv.* —**sas′si·ness,** *n.*

**satch·el** (sach′əl), *n.* a small bag for carrying clothes, books, etc.; handbag. [< Old French *sachel* < Latin *succellus,* diminutive of *saccus* sack¹]

**Parts of speech and plurals**

Dictionary entries show the part of speech. The abbreviations for parts of speech are shown on page 233. Look at the entry for *sari.* What part of speech is *sari*?

An entry may also show how to spell the plural form of a noun. If a plural is formed by adding -*s* or -*es,* it is usually not shown. If a plural is formed in a different way, the spelling is shown. There is no plural shown for *sari.* This means that the plural is formed by adding -*s.*

Now look at the first part of the entry for *sarcophagus.* The plural can be formed with -*gi* or -*guses.*

The explorer found several *sarcophagi.*

*or*

The explorer found several *sarcophaguses.*

**Other forms of a word**  Sometimes other forms of a word are shown. Look at the entry for *sassy* on page 236. What part of speech is *sassy*? Notice that two more adjective endings are shown: *-sier* and *-siest*. What form of *sassy* would you use in this sentence?

My sister is the ——————————————— person I know.

What is the noun form of *sassy*? ———————————————

## ACTIVITY 9
**Understanding dictionary entries**

Answer the following questions by looking at the dictionary entry on page 236.

1. What is the adverbial form of *sardonic*? _____

2. What part of speech is *sarsaparilla*? _____

3. Can you drink *sarsaparilla*? _____

4. Is *sarcastic* an adjective? _____

5. What is the plural of *sarong*? _____

6. How many pronunciations are shown for *sarong*? _____

7. Would you wear a sarong around your head? _____

8. Which meaning of *sassafras* would describe what you might have in your yard?

(Give the number of the definition.)

———————————————

> **sar casm** (sär′kaz′əm), *n.*  **1** a sneering or cutting remark; ironical taunt. **2** act of making fun of a person to hurt his or her feelings; harsh or bitter irony: *"How unselfish you are!" said the girl in sarcasm as her brother took the biggest piece of cake.* [< Greek *sarkasmos* < *sarkazein* to sneer, strip off flesh < *sarkos* flesh]
> ➔ **Sarcasm, irony, satire** are often confused, although they are not synonyms. *Sarcasm* is the use of language to hurt, wound, or ridicule: *Why don't you give us your advice since you know everything?* That is also an example of irony, although not all sarcasm is irony nor is all irony sarcasm. *Irony* is the deliberate use of language in a sense opposite to that which the words ordinarily have: *This cloudburst makes a fine day for a picnic.* *Satire* uses irony and sarcasm to expose and attack vices or follies: *In "Gulliver's Travels" Jonathan Swift makes notable use of satire.*
> **sar dine** (sär dēn′), *n., pl.* **-dines** or **-dine. 1** a young pilchard preserved in oil for food. **2** any of certain similar small fish prepared in the same way. **3 packed like sardines,** very much crowded. [< Latin *sardina* < Greek *sardēnē*, probably originally, Sardinian fish] —**sar dine′like′,** *adj.*
> **Sar din i a** (sär din′ē ə), *n.* **1** large Italian island in the Mediterranean Sea, west of the Italian peninsula. 1,582,000 pop.; 9300 sq. mi. (24,100 sq. km.) **2** former kingdom (1720-1860) that included this island, Savoy, Piedmont, and eventually most of the Italian mainland. —**Sar din′i an,** *adj., n.*
> **sar to ri al** (sär tôr′ē əl, sär tōr′ē əl), *adj.* of tailors or their work: *His clothes were a sartorial triumph.* [< Latin *sartor* tailor, ultimately < *sarcire* to patch] —**sar to′ri al ly,** *adv.*
> **sa shay** (sa shā′), *v.i.* INFORMAL. glide, move, or go about. [alteration of *chassé* a gliding dance step < French]
> **sa shi mi** (sä shē′mē), *n.* a Japanese dish consisting of thin slices of raw fish, usually dipped in a sauce and eaten as an appetizer. [< Japanese]
> **Sas quatch** (sas′kwach), *n.* Bigfoot. [< its American Indian name]
> **sass** (sas), INFORMAL. —*n.* rudeness; back talk; impudence. —*v.t.* be rude or disrespectful to. —*v.i.* talk rudely or impudently. [variant of *sauce*]

**Etymologies**

A dictionary entry may contain an etymology. An etymology tells the history of a word. Look at the entry for *sardine* on page 237. The etymology appears in brackets at the end of the definition. The etymology tells you that the word is from ( < ) the Latin word *sardina*. This word is from the Greek word *sardēnē*. The word probably meant "Sardinian fish." (Note that the entry following *sardine* tells you about Sardinia.)

**Illustrative sentences and usage notes**

Dictionaries usually include sentences that show how a word is used. The second meaning of *sarcasm* shows a sentence in italic type. It is called an illustrative sentence because it illustrates, or shows, how a word is used.

At the end of the entry for *sarcasm* there is a usage note. This explains the similarities and differences among *sarcasm*, *irony*, and *satire*.

**Restrictive labels and idioms**

Now look at the entry for *sass*. There you see the label INFORMAL. This is called a restrictive label. The label INFORMAL means that the word is common in everyday speech or writing. It is not normally used in formal writing or speech. If you were writing a business letter, you would not use the word *sass*. You could use the word in a friendly letter.

Some entries show idioms. Look again at the entry for *sardine*. The idiom with the entry for sardine is "packed like sardines." Native speakers of a language usually understand idioms. Non-native speakers are sometimes puzzled by idioms. Idioms cannot be understood simply by knowing the meanings of the words in the idiom. Some other examples of English idioms are: *stand a chance, play off, rough it.*

# ACTIVITY 10
## Understanding dictionary entries

Answer the following questions by looking at the dictionary entries on page 237.

1.  What language does *sashimi* come from? _____

2.  What is the illustrative sentence for *sartorial*? (Copy it.) _____

3.  What is the restrictive label for *sashay*? _____

4.  Where is the accent in *sashay*? _____

5.  What language does *Sasquatch* come from? _____

6.  What is another name for *Sasquatch*? _____

7.  Is the sentence below an example of *sarcasm*? _____

    Having a flat tire is a wonderful way to start our vacation.

**Homographs**

Look at the entries for *sash*. Notice the small numbers [1] and [2]. Although these words are pronounced and spelled the same, they have different etymologies. These words are homographs. Which word, sash[1] or sash[2], could you tie around your waist?

> **sash[1]** (sash), *n.* a long, broad strip of cloth or ribbon, worn round the waist or over one shoulder. [< Arabic *shāsh* muslin]
> **sash[2]** (sash), *n.* 1 frame for the glass of a window or door. 2 part or parts of a window that can be moved to open or close a window. [alteration of *chassis*, taken as plural]

**People and places**

Entries for people and places give you a few basic facts. Birth and death dates are shown for people. Entries will also tell you why the people are well known. Entries for places tell their location and their size.

# ACTIVITY 11

## Understanding dictionary entries

Answer the following questions about the entries for people and places.

1. When was John Singer Sargent born? _____

2. What was Saroyan's first name? _____

3. Which ocean is the Sargasso Sea part of? _____

4. When did Sargon II die? _____

5. What is the capital of the province of Saskatchewan? _____

> **Sar gas so Sea** (sär gas′ō), part of the Atlantic extending from the West Indies northeast to the Azores.
> **Sar gent** (sär′jənt), *n.* John Singer, 1856-1925, American portrait painter.
> **Sar gon II** (sär′gon), died 705 B.C., king of Assyria from 722 to 705 B.C.
>
> ‒ ‒ ‒ ‒ ‒ ‒ ‒ ‒ ‒ ‒ ‒
>
> **Sa roy an** (sə roi′ən), *n.* **William,** 1908-1981, American playwright and short-story writer.
>
> ‒ ‒ ‒ ‒ ‒ ‒ ‒ ‒ ‒ ‒ ‒
>
> **Sa skatch e wan** (sa skach′ə won), *n.* 1 province in S central Canada. 947,000 pop.; 251,700 sq. mi. (651,900 sq. km.) *Capital:* Regina. *Abbrev.:* Sask. 2 river flowing from SW Canada into Lake Winnipeg. 1205 mi. (1939 km.)

Look at the entry for *correct*. At the end of the definition is the abbreviation **Syn.** What follows is a synonym study. Words that mean about the same thing are called synonyms. *Correct, accurate,* and *exact* all mean about the same thing. The synonym study explains small differences among the three words. Synonym studies can be helpful in your writing.

**cor rect** (kə rekt′), *adj.* **1** free from mistakes or faults; right: *the correct answer.* See synonym study below. **2** agreeing with a recognized standard, especially of good taste; proper: *correct manners.* —*v.t.* **1** change to what is right; remove mistakes or faults from: *Correct any misspellings that you find.* **2** alter or adjust to agree with some standard: *correct the reading of a barometer.* **3** point out or mark the errors of; check: *correct test papers.* **4** set right by punishing; find fault with to improve; punish: *correct a child for misbehaving.* **5** counteract or neutralize (something hurtful); cure; overcome; remedy: *Medicine can sometimes correct stomach trouble.* [< Latin *correctum* made straight < *com-* + *regere* to guide] —**cor rect′a ble,** *adj.* —**cor rect′ly,** *adv.* —**cor rect′ness,** *n.* —**cor rec′tor,** *n.*
**Syn.** *adj.* **1 Correct, accurate, exact** mean without error or mistake. **Correct** adds nothing to that basic meaning: *I gave correct answers to the questions.* **Accurate** emphasizes the careful effort to make something agree exactly with the facts or with a model: *I gave an accurate account of the accident.* **Exact** emphasizes the complete agreement in every detail with the facts or with a model: *The painting is an exact copy of the original.*

# ACTIVITY 12
## Using a dictionary to check spelling

Many people use a dictionary to find the correct spelling of a word. Use your dictionary to check the spelling of the words below. One word in each pair is spelled correctly. Write out the correct spelling.

1. recommend, reccommend  _____

2. accomodate, accommodate  _____

3. accumulate, accummulate  _____

4. occassion, occasion  _____

5. personell, personnel  _____

6. benefit, benifit  _____

7. nineth, ninth  _____

8. vaccuum, vacuum  _____

9. omitted, omited  _____

10. occurred, occured  _____

11. committee, comittee  _____

12. valueable, valuable  _____

13. seperate, separate  _____

14. arrangment, arrangement  _____

Use the dictionary entries to answer these questions.

**1.** Does the first syllable in *bower* rhyme with "cow" or "low"? _____

**2.** What part of speech is *bower*? _____

**3.** Which definitions for *bow*[1] have illustrative sentences? _____

**4.** What does the idiom *bow and scrape* mean? _____

**5.** After which syllable is the accent in *bouzouki*? _____

**6.** For whom was the bowie knife named? _____

**7.** Where is Corregidor? _____

**8.** Who was Correggio? _____

**9.** Is Corpus Christi a city in Arizona? _____

**10.** How do you spell the plural of *bowman*? _____

---

**bou zou ki** (bü zü′kē), *n.* a stringed instrument that is somewhat like a mandolin and has a very brilliant tone. [< New Greek *mpouzouki*]

**bow**[1] (bou), *v.i.* **1** bend the head or body in greeting, respect, worship, or submission. **2** give in; submit; yield. —*v.t.* **1** bend (the head or body) in greeting, respect, worship, or submission. **2** express by a bow: *He bowed his approval.* **3** usher with a bow or bows. **4** cause to stoop; bend: *The old man was bowed by age.*
**bow and scrape,** be too polite or slavish.
**bow down, a** weigh down: *bowed down with care.* **b** worship.
**bow out, a** withdraw: *She sprained her wrist and had to bow out of the tennis tournament.* **b** usher out.
—*n.* **1** a bending of the head or body in greeting, respect, worship, or submission. **2 take a bow,** accept praise, applause, etc., for something done.
[Old English *būgan*] —**bow′er,** *n.*

**bow ie knife** (bō′ē, bü′ē), a heavy hunting knife with a long, single-edged blade, curved near the point, and carried in a sheath. [< Colonel James *Bowie*, 1799-1836, American pioneer who made it popular]

**bow er** (bou′ər), *n.* **1** shelter of leafy branches. **2** summerhouse or arbor. [Old English *būr* dwelling]

**bow man** (bō′mən), *n., pl.* **-men.** archer.

---

**Cor pus Chris ti** (kôr′pəs kris′tē), **1** feast of the Roman Catholic Church in honor of the Eucharist, celebrated on the first Thursday after Trinity Sunday. **2** city in S Texas. 232,000. [< Latin *corpus Christi* body of Christ]

**Cor reg gio** (kô rej′ō), *n.* **An to nio Al le gri da** (än tō′nyō ä lā′grē dä), 1494-1534, Italian painter.

**Cor reg i dor** (kə reg′ə dôr), *n.* fortified island at the entrance to Manila Bay, Philippines.

# SHOW WHAT YOU KNOW . . .

## About Dictionaries

Make up a word and write a dictionary entry for it. (1) Show the word divided into syllables; (2) show the pronunciation; (3) write one definition for the word; (4) write an illustrative sentence; and (5) make up an etymology.

## Tables of contents

A table of contents lists the chapter names or article titles with page numbers on which they begin in the publication. Unlike an index, this arrangement is not alphabetical. The contents page usually lists items in order of appearance. In this section, you will study several tables of contents. A table of contents gives a preview of all the things in a book or magazine. It also helps you find a specific chapter or article quickly.

**Books**  A book's table of contents is usually arranged in chapters. Each chapter is numbered in order. Study the following partial contents page of a book. It shows chapters with subsections.

# Contents

Textbook contents may be divided into units or parts. And these may have sections and chapters. A textbook contents page might look like this.

# CONTENTS

## ACTIVITY 13
### Using the table of contents of a book

This table of contents is divided into units. It also has sections. Use it to answer the questions below.

# Table of Contents

*v*

1. How many units are there on this page? _____

2. What is the title of Unit One? _____

   Unit Two? _____

3. How many pages in this book are about Ralph J. Bunche? _____ Anne Sullivan Macy? _____

4. To which page would you turn to read about Martin Luther King, Jr.? _____ Leonard Bernstein? _____

5. Who was Countee Cullen? _____

6. What science fiction writer is included here? _____

_____

## Magazines

Information in tables of contents pages may be grouped by subject. Groupings such as "gardening," "decorating," or "crafts" might contain all the articles on those subjects, regardless of where they appear in the magazine. Often the contents of a magazine are shown in the order in which they appear.

Many magazines have sections such as "letters" that appear in every issue. Sometimes these sections are listed under the word *Departments* in the table of contents. Frequently there is a preview of what's coming up in the next issue.

Contents pages can help you decide whether you want to buy a magazine. Subscribers and purchasers of magazines can skim the contents pages to decide what they want to read.

## ACTIVITY 14

### Using the table of contents of a magazine

Look at the table of contents from the magazine *Consumer Reports* on the facing page. Use the contents page to answer the questions that follow.

1. Is this table of contents arranged by subject groupings or by the order in which the articles appear? _____

2. Indicate whether the following features are in *Consumer Reports* every month or are included in this month only by putting a check in the correct column.

| | Every Month | This Month |
|---|---|---|
| a. Pocket Guide to Money | _____ | _____ |
| b. Movies | _____ | _____ |
| c. Electric fans | _____ | _____ |
| d. Wasted health-care dollars | _____ | _____ |
| e. Which tea is best? | _____ | _____ |

3. On what page does the article on hand vacuums start? _____

4. How many teas did the tea tasters sample? _____

5. How many kinds of autos will be featured in future issues? _____

# IN THIS ISSUE

July 1992          Volume 57, No. 7

**415** **Electric fans**

Their breeze may be enough to keep you cool this summer. We tested window fans, box fans, pedestal fans, floor fans, and table fans.

**420** **Air-conditioners**
For the days when just a breeze isn't enough. We tested 15 models with enough capacity to cool and dehumidify a medium-sized bedroom.

**425** **Road test: Four sporty coupes**
Nissan NX 2000, Saturn SC, Mazda MX-3, Toyota Paseo.

**432** **Remember the ape and the camcorder?**

That was one TV ad used to promote a credit card's "purchase protection" insurance. The memory lingers; the protection has been fading away.

**435** **Wasted health-care dollars**

The money we now spend could be used to deliver high-quality medical care for every American. But instead, we're squandering our resources—and wasting at least $200-billion a year. **Part 1 of a 3-part series.**

**451** **Hand vacuums**

We tested cordless, corded, and car vacs. Some were powerful, some convenient. A few were powerful and convenient.

**456** **Refrigerators**
Our comprehensive guide—with Ratings of 22 models—can help you choose the right size and the right style at the right price.

**468** **Which tea is best?**
Loose tea or bagged? How do herbal teas stack up? Our expert tasters sampled 78 teas, with and without caffeine.

# IN FUTURE ISSUES

**Auto insurance** Next month, Ratings of the best and worst auto insurers, plus ways to save money on your insurance.

**Autos** Acura Legend, Audi 100, Mazda 929, Volvo 960 **Home** Household insect control ■ Washing machines ■ Food processors ■ Vinyl floor coverings **Personal Business** suits ■ Blow dryers ■ Mouthwashes ■ Electric toothbrushes ■ Toothpastes **Health and fitness** Ratings of HMOs ■ A look at Canada's health-care system ■ Tennis racquets **Food** Low-fat ice cream ■ Seltzer

247

Study the following textbook contents page. Notice that it has a number of divisions. Then answer the questions on page 249.

# Contents

1. The contents page on page 248 shows two main divisions. What are these two divisions?

   _____

2. Chapter 1 is divided into four subsections. What are they?

   _____

3. On what page does the subsection called "Run-on Sentences" begin? _____

4. What is the title of Section 2? _____

5. How many pages are there in the subsection on "Making a Journal Entry"? _____

6. What can be found on page 51? _____

7. If you wanted to learn how to write a personal letter, what chapter would you read? _____

8. What is the title of Part 1? _____

9. How many divisions or subsections are there in Chapter 3? _____

10. How many chapters are there in Section 1? _____

## Indexes

### WORDS TO KNOW

**classification number**   the number of a section of classified ads, not a page number

**index**   an alphabetical list of the subjects in a book

**subject**   the name of an item in an index; a topic

**subtopic or subentry**   an entry in an index that is secondary to the main topic, such as elementary schools under the main topic of schools

**topic**   the name of an item in an index; a subject

**Book indexes**   A book index is in the back of a book. It lists people, titles, or topics alphabetically. It gives page numbers where you will find these entries. This makes finding information easier. Most textbooks have an index. Look at the following book index.

Alphabetical arrangement
of the entries

Book title

Author

Page on which this
item can be found

Topic found in this book

Subtopics

Notice the alphabetical arrangement of people, topics, and subtopics. An index should list every page on which a topic appears. Of course, not every word in a book appears in the index. Most often you find key words, key people or places, special terms, and general topics discussed in that book.

## ACTIVITY 15

**Using a book index**

Study the following book index and answer the questions about it.

# Index

1. On what pages do you find complex sentences? _____

2. On what page will you find the word "couplet"? _____

3. How many pages does Chief Joseph appear on? _____

4. What pages deal with Jimmy Carter? _____

5. What page(s) should you turn to if you want to read about American Indian dances? _____

   popular dances? _____

   ballet? _____

**Catalog indexes**     Catalogs have indexes, too. A catalog index lists the items you can order. It also lists the pages where you can find these items.

Like all indexes, the catalog index is alphabetical. Most people use a catalog index when they want a certain item. For example, Bobby Goldstein wants to order a new basketball. He just got the mail-order catalog. Bobby turns to the index on page 253. He looks under the Bs for "Basketball." He finds "Basketballs . . . . 233."

## ACTIVITY 16

### Using a catalog index

Use the catalog index on page 253 to answer these questions:

• First, use the "Find-It-Fast Index" to complete the chart below:

| Type of Product | Pages | |
| | From | To |
| Appliances | _____ | _____ |
| Giftware | _____ | _____ |
| Watches | _____ | _____ |
| Tools | _____ | _____ |
| Jewelry | _____ | _____ |
| Home Entertainment | _____ | _____ |

# Index

253

- Use the main index on the previous page to find the specific items below:

| Item | Page(s) | Item | Page(s) |
|---|---|---|---|
| Fondue Pots | _____ | Frying Pans | _____ |
| Drip Coffee Makers | _____ | Salad Bowls | _____ |
| Cookie Jars | _____ | Blenders | _____ |
| Humidifiers | _____ | Calculators | _____ |
| Electric Brooms | _____ | Movie Cameras | _____ |
| Clothes Hampers | _____ | Barbells | _____ |
| Fire Extinguishers | _____ | Ironing Boards | _____ |

## CHECK YOUR UNDERSTANDING OF INDEXES

Following is the first page of a yellow pages index from a telephone book. Study it carefully. Then answer the questions about it.

On which page would you look if . . .

1. you needed a dentist? _____

2. you were trying to locate a non-denominational church? _____

3. you wanted to find a dealer to buy your coin collection? _____

4. you wanted to find a chiropractor? _____

5. you were trying to find a place to buy a part for your car? _____

6. you wanted to find all the bicycle stores in the area? _____

7. you wanted to find the number to call for a bus schedule? _____

8. you wanted a listing of the campgrounds in the area? _____

9. you wanted to get your hair styled? _____

10. you wanted to rent a boat? _____

# This is your YELLOW PAGES

# INDEX

(ALPHABETICALLY ARRANGED)

# Using Directories and Floor Plans

When you look up numbers in a telephone book, you use a directory. When you read a list of departments in a store, you use a directory. A shopping mall or library may display floor plans with directories. These help you find locations or information fast. Directories can save you time.

In this section, you will practice using directories and floor plans.

## Directories and floor plans

**WORDS TO KNOW**

**annex**   an addition to a building

**directory**   a listing of names and addresses

**floor plan**   a drawing showing the size and arrangement of rooms on each floor of a building

**mezzanine**   a low story between two main stories in a building, usually above the ground floor, sometimes in the form of a balcony

Directories are alphabetical listings. Sometimes they are in book form, like the telephone book. Sometimes they are in display form, like those in department stores. They help you find an address or a phone number. They help you find which floor an office is on. They help you locate what you want in a big store. Directories are arranged in several different ways.

Some directories are simply alphabetical lists. The white pages of the telephone book is one such alphabetical list. In the white pages you can find telephone numbers listed by a person's last name. You can also find business listings under the name of the business.

Another way to arrange a directory is to list the floors of a store or office building in order, then to list items by their floor location. Another way is to use section headings, such as the sections of a shopping mall.

A floor plan is both a map and a directory. With a floor plan you get both a list of items *and* a drawing. Floor plans can be very helpful for buildings with a number of stores, offices, or departments.

# ACTIVITY 1

## Using store directories

Department store directories are usually arranged like the directory below. Use this directory of Morton's Bargain City to locate the items listed below. On which floor would you find each of these items?

**Morton's Bargain City**

| | Floor | | Floor |
|---|---|---|---|
| Appliances | 1 | Infants' Wear | 3 |
| Books | 2 | Lingerie | 2 |
| Cafeteria | 2 | Luggage | 1 |
| Children's Wear | 3 | Men's Wear | 2 |
| Cosmetics | 2 | Office Supplies | 1 |
| Kitchen and Bath | 3 | Shoes | 2 |
| Handbags | 2 | Toys | 1 |
| Infants' Furniture | 3 | Women's Wear | 2 |

1. Baby Crib _____

2. Baby Doll _____

3. Makeup _____

4. Woman's Dress _____

5. Man's Shirt _____

6. Boots _____

7. Dishwasher _____

8. Index Cards _____

9. Purse _____

10. Baby Blanket _____

11. Lunch _____

12. Cookware _____

13. Novel _____

14. Hosiery _____

15. Bicycle _____

16. Clothes Dryer _____

17. Typewriter _____

18. Woman's Blouse _____

19. Place mats _____

20. Stroller _____

21. Refrigerator _____

22. Bath Towels _____

23. Nightgown _____

24. File Folders _____

25. Coffee Maker _____

26. Sneakers _____

27. Briefcase _____

28. Hair Dryer _____

29. Man's Tie _____

30. Baseball Bat _____

## ACTIVITY 2
### Using a floor directory for a department store

This is a floor directory. A floor directory is often found on or near the elevators of large department stores. It lists each floor. It also lists what may be found on each floor. Use the sample floor directory to answer the questions below.

**MAIN FLOOR**
Girl's Wear
Women's Wear

**SECOND FLOOR**
Accessories
Boy's Wear
Budget Dresses
Ladies' Lounge

**THIRD FLOOR**
Alterations
Coats
Men's Wear
Men's Lounge

**FOURTH FLOOR**
Furniture
Carpeting

**FIFTH FLOOR**
Housewares
Silverware

**SIXTH FLOOR**
Beauty Salon
Pillows, Linen, Bedding

**SEVENTH FLOOR**
Personnel Office/Credit
Restaurants
    On Top
    Ice Cream Parlor

On which floor would you get off the elevator if . . .

1. you wanted to pay on your charge account? _____

2. you wanted to price a microwave oven? _____

3. you were on the fifth floor and you wanted to go to the nearest rest room? _____

4. you were Jennifer Mallory and you wanted to pick up your husband's suit? _____

5. you were Tom Mallory and you promised to meet Jennifer on the carpet floor? _____

6. you were looking for a small appliance to give as a wedding gift? _____

7. you had an appointment at the store's "Sophisticated Scissors" beauty salon? _____

8. you were looking for furniture for your new apartment? _____

9. you wanted to apply for a job as a salesperson? _____

10. you wanted a chocolate sundae? _____

# ACTIVITY 3
## Using building directories

This is the building directory for The Enterprise Tower. It lists all offices in the building. Use this directory to answer the questions below:

### Building Directory

| | Floor | | Floor |
|---|---|---|---|
| Acme Enterprises | 10 | Kilpatrick Construction | 8 |
| Armstrong Gallery | 10 | Kroop Advertising | 2 |
| Barclay Consultants | 10 | LeGrand, J. S., M.D. | 6 |
| Bartlett & Bartlett Law Offices | 10 | Lerner, Gwen, M.D. | 6 |
| Bear & Bear Job Consultants | 8 | Longman Employment | 3 |
| Boston, Harry E., D.D.S. | 7 | Martin, W. E., M.D. | 6 |
| Brown, Boveri, & Barton Corp. | 10 | Martin Wholesalers | 8 |
| C&H Associates | 2 | Marvel Photos | 4 |
| Carteret Bank | 3 | Mondi Exports | 8 |
| Christens, Nancy, M.D. | 6 | Morrison, Patricia, D.D.S. | 7 |
| Claytor, Harold, M.D. | 6 | Neal & Neal Consultants | 2 |
| Cutler, Stanley, Attorney | 5 | Neptune Unlimited | 3 |
| Cyrus, Lynette, Attorney | 5 | Nile Products | 10 |
| D'Angelo, Kenneth, M.D. | 6 | O'Shea, Matthew, M.D. | 6 |
| Daniels Realty | 2 | Rosenberg Studios | 2 |
| Daniels, Sandra, M.D. | 6 | Sanchez, Dorothy, D.D.S. | 7 |
| Designer Fur Headquarters | 3 | Sanchez, Louis, D.D.S. | 7 |
| Family Health Center | 6 | Santiago, Louis, M.D. | 6 |
| Ferrell Employment Agency | 4 | Sibeski Brothers | 5 |
| Flynn & Flynn Accounting | 4 | Tami Studios | 5 |
| Goldman, Ronald, M.D. | 6 | Technical Labs | 2 |
| Green, Terry Phillip, M.D. | 6 | Tutor Computers | 2 |
| Green, Thomas, M.D. | 7 | Tutor Electronics | 2 |
| Higgins, Higgins, & Higgins | 8 | Tyler Textiles | 8 |
| Ingram Consultants | 9 | Wong's Distributors | 10 |
| International Banking Inc. | 10 | World Enterprises | 10 |
| International Publishing | 10 | World Health Inc. | 6 |
| J&E Imports | 10 | World Publishers | 8 |
| J&W Exports | 10 | Young Galleries | 2 |
| Jones & Jones Enterprises | 9 | Zee, Pauline, M.D. | 6 |

1. On which floor will you find J&E Imports? _____

   J&W Exports? _____

2. On which floor will you find the legal offices of Bartlett & Bartlett? _____

259

3. Does Dr. Harold Green have an office in this building? _____

4. Does Dr. Ronald Goldman have an office in this building? _____

5. On which floor is Wong's Distributors? _____

6. Is Kroop Advertising located in this building? _____

7. What listing comes *before* Dr. W. E. Martin's name? _____

8. What listing comes *after* Dr. Martin's name? _____

9. If this directory is on the first floor, how many floors will you have to walk up in order to visit the Young Galleries? _____

10. If you were on the 5th floor and used the elevator to go to Dr. Terry Green's office, how many floors up would you travel? _____

11. On what floor is Dr. Lerner? _____

12. The first number of the office numbers in the Tower tells you what floor the office is on. Complete the *room numbers* of these offices:

   a.  Dr. Harry Boston         _____ 08

   b.  Sibeski Brothers         _____ 02

   c.  Dr. Harold Claytor       _____ 11

   d.  Dr. Sandra Daniels       _____ 13

   e.  Dr. Patricia Morrison    _____ 07

   f.  Dr. Pauline Zee          _____ 05

   g.  World Enterprises        _____ 13

   h.  Tami Studios             _____ 10

---

**Floor plans**   Using a floor plan is like using a map. Floor plans help you find your way. They help you in malls, shopping plazas, and office buildings. The key to reading a floor plan is knowing where you are.

You must find your location on the floor plan. Then you can locate other places. Decide if your destination is in front or in back of you. Decide if it is to your left or right. See if it has a name or number. See if there is a pattern to the floor plan. Is it an L-shape? Is it a circle? Is it in sections? Are there section numbers?

## ACTIVITY 4
### Using floor plans

Study the floor plan of the third floor of the Harold Washington Library Center, the Chicago Public Library, and answer the questions below.

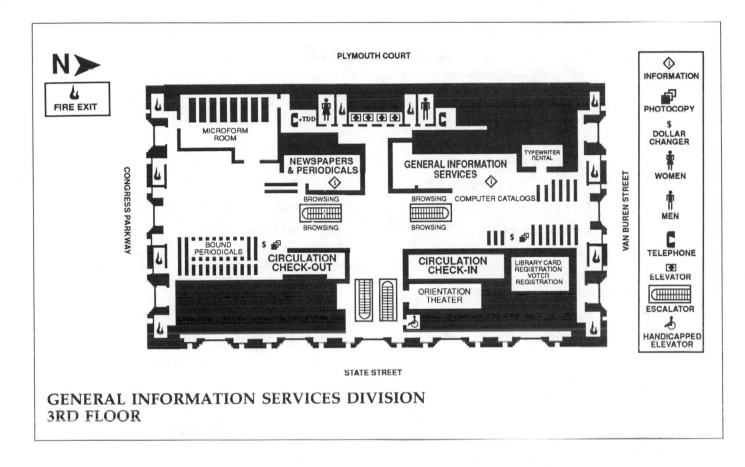

**GENERAL INFORMATION SERVICES DIVISION**
**3RD FLOOR**

1. If you walk from Circulation Check-in to General Information Services, in which direction will you be walking? _____

2. How many photocopiers are on this floor? _____

3. Can you get to the Orientation Theater if you are in a wheelchair? _____

4. Can you look up the title of a book on this floor? _____

5. If you get off an elevator on the west side, which two directions will you walk to the Voter Registration Desk? _____

6. How many fire exits are there? _____

7. Is the fiction section on this floor? _____

8. Could you find a newspaper on this floor? _____

The directory below lists the stores in the Town & Country Mall. The floor plan shows the locations of the businesses. Use the directory and the floor plan to answer the questions.

## Business Directory

| | |
|---|---|
| Allen Patton's Pets   A–5 | Eaton's   A–8 |
| Avenue Fashions   B–4 | Harrison's Men's Shop   B–3 |
| Burgers Deluxe   B–1 | Jim's Jewelry   A–2 |
| Carolyn's Boutique   A–7 | Kid's World   A–6 |
| Charles's Chop House   A–10 | Martin's Travel   A–9 |
| Chinese Cuisine   A–4 | Norge's Portraits   B–2 |
| Daisy's Donut Shop   A–1 | Vicky's Hat Rack   A–3 |

| A–5 | A–6 | A–7 | A–8 |
|---|---|---|---|

A–4
A–3
A–2
A–1

Main Floor

A–9
A–10

You Are Here

| B–1 |
|---|
| B–2 |

Mezzanine

| B–4 |
|---|
| B–3 |

1. Are the businesses in the directory listed by types of business or alphabetically? _____

2. Will you walk right or left to find Chinese Cuisine? _____

3. Is Eaton's right or left of Carolyn's Boutique? _____

4. Is Harrison's Men's Shop on the main floor or on the mezzanine? _____

5. Where will you stop if you want a donut? _____

6. Where could you get your picture taken? _____

## The telephone book

Knowing how to find information in the phone book is a useful everyday skill. There are many times when you need to use the phone book. You may need to find a name, an address, or a telephone number. The telephone book has two sections. They are the white pages and the yellow pages. In larger cities, the white pages and yellow pages are separate books.

## The white pages

Most people are familiar with the white pages of the phone book. This is where you find the telephone numbers of people you want to call. Businesses might also list their numbers in this section, but the white pages are mainly for home listings.

The white pages are easy to use if you understand how they are arranged.

### Fernandez - Filbert

| | |
|---|---|
| Fernandez, Lola 141 State St | 555-8332 |
| Fernandez, M. 4245 Burt Rd. | 555-7899 |
| Fernandez, M.L. 223 Orange Bl | 555-8254 |
| Fernandez, Martino | |
|     8610 Gladstone Av Bloomfield | 555-4149 |
| Filbert, Abbott 61 N Park Pl | 555-7083 |
| Filbert, Alvin 2109 2nd Av | 555-3321 |
| Filbert, Bertha 18 Lane Dr | 555-2578 |
| FILBERT TOOL & DIE CO | |
|     44 Main Lane | 555-8866 |
| Filbert, Stanley 621 Cherry St | 555-5461 |

1. The white page listings are arranged in alphabetical order with last names first.
2. Businesses might appear in the same alphabetical listings.
3. Each white page listing consists of a name, address, and telephone number.
4. Addresses will often be abbreviated. (For example, "N" for north, "Rd" for Road, "Pk" for Park.)
5. Headings are at the top of the white pages. They tell you the first and last names on a page.

**Reading the white pages**

Use the white page listings on the previous page to answer these questions.

1. What is the number for Lola Fernandez?_____

2. What is the number for Martino Fernandez? _____

3. What is the number for Filbert Tool & Die Co.? _____

4. What number do you call to reach Alvin Filbert on 2nd Ave.? _____

5. What number do you call to reach M. Fernandez at 4245 Burt Rd.? _____

6. What is the number for M. L. Fernandez on Orange Blvd.? _____

**ACTIVITY 6**

**Locating telephone numbers for persons with the same names**

Sometimes white-page listings are confusing. Names may be similar or even the same. Answer the questions about the telephone listings below.

### Jones - Jones

| | |
|---|---|
| Jones Della 1676 Grassylawn Drive .............555-8421 | Jones E S 2001 Main St ...............................555-6666 |
| Jones Dwight 8989 Rhine Rd .....................555-2813 | Jones Earl, MD 923 Derby Lane...................555-3245 |
| Jones E 171 Lois Lane................................555-8210 | Jones Earl 44 Pine St Ferry Pk.....................555-7110 |
| Jones E 6 S. Ohio Ave ...............................555-9828 | Jones Earl 18095 Steel St .........................555-7808 |
| Jones E 712 Colorado Blvd Farmington ........555-7241 | Jones Earlie 1409 Raleigh St.......................555-4648 |
| Jones E 7918 St. Agnes.............................555-6471 | Jones F 106 Wyoming Blvd..........................555-5523 |
| Jones E A 817 Marked Dr ...........................555-8010 | Jones F 614 Greenlawn Ave ........................555-6010 |
| Jones E C 230 Van Born Rd ........................555-3331 | Jones Fred 601 Wright Pl............................555-7041 |

1. What number do you call to reach Dwight Jones? _____

2. If you are trying to reach Dr. Earl Jones, what number do you call? _____

3. What number do you dial if you are trying to reach E. Jones at 7918 St. Agnes? _____

4. How many Earl Joneses are shown? _____

5. What is the number for the Earl Jones in Ferry Park? _____

6. What number do you dial to reach E. C. Jones on Van Born Rd? _____

**The yellow pages**

The yellow pages of your phone book list the names, addresses, and phone numbers of businesses. Doctors, lawyers, and dentists are also found in the yellow pages. But there are no residential listings. Businesses appear in both the white pages and the yellow pages, but the yellow pages give more information about the services these businesses provide.

The yellow pages are a handy reference. Look at the yellow page sample on page 267. To use the yellow pages, you need to understand how they are arranged.

1.  Businesses are listed under the service, product, or specialty they offer. Examples are RESTAURANTS, PLUMBING, AIR-CONDITIONING, AUTO SALES, and PHYSICIANS.

2.  These headings, showing the service, product, or specialty, are arranged alphabetically.

3.  Under these headings, the names of the businesses appear in alphabetical order.

4.  Each listing consists of the name, address, and telephone number, just as it does in the white pages, but these listings are under a heading. For example, Smith's Garage is not under "S" for Smith. It is under GARAGES or AUTOMOBILE SERVICE.

5.  Many of these yellow page listings also appear as advertisements. These ads give more information about a business. They may give hours, location, and directions.

## ACTIVITY 7

### Deciding when to use the yellow pages

Answer these questions about the yellow pages.

1.  If you are a shopper, what are some benefits of looking for a business in the yellow pages? (Name at least three.)

    _____

    _____

    _____

2.  John Watts owns a VCR. He needs to have it repaired. Should he look in the white pages or yellow pages for a repair shop?

    _____

3.  You want Carlos' Car Repair to give your car a tune-up. You know where the repair shop is. But you need the telephone number to call for an appointment. Would you use the yellow pages or the white pages?

    _____

    Explain your answer.

    _____

    _____

    _____

# ACTIVITY 8

## Classifying yellow-page listings

Below are yellow page headings that deal with furniture and automobiles. These headings are lettered. Stores are also listed. Decide under which heading each store belongs.

a. FURNITURE DEALERS - RETAIL
b. FURNITURE  RENTING & LEASING
c. FURNITURE REPAIRING & REFINISHING

_____ 1. Universal Refinishers

_____ 2. The Restore

_____ 3. Quality Furniture

_____ 4. Flex-A-Lease, Inc.

_____ 5. I.F.G. Furniture Rentals

_____ 6. Frank's Used Furniture Store

_____ 7. Scandinavian Furniture

_____ 8. American Furniture Rentals

_____ 9. Mitchell Upholstery

_____ 10. Imported Oriental Furniture

Now classify the car businesses listed below under the correct yellow page heading.

a. AUTOMOBILE BODY REPAIRING & PAINTING
b. AUTOMOBILE DEALERS - ANTIQUE & CLASSIC
c. AUTOMOBILE DEALERS - NEW CARS
d. AUTOMOBILE PARTS & SUPPLIES
e. AUTOMOBILE RADIOS & STEREO SYSTEMS

_____ 1. Smith's Car Parts

_____ 2. Clark Auto Parts, Inc.

_____ 3. Pierre's Classic Cars, Inc.

_____ 4. Vintage Vehicles, Inc.

_____ 5. Bob's Hubcap Specialists

_____ 6. J & G Automotive Parts

_____ 7. Dan's Body & Fender Shop

_____ 8. Dependable Auto Parts Store

_____ 9. A & E Auto Supply

_____ 10. George's Body Shop

_____ 11. Central Chevrolet

_____ 12. Autosound, Inc.

_____ 13. Glenbrook Ford, Inc.

_____ 14. Bill's Auto Painting

_____ 15. Sound Experience, Inc.

_____ 16. Chrysler-Plymouth Sales

# ACTIVITY 9

## Reading and understanding the yellow pages

Use these yellow-page listings to answer the following questions.

### Cleaners—Cont'd

**Advertisers at this heading are required by law to be licensed. (See Page A)**

**DeLUXE DRY CLEANERS PLANT**
Main Plant Bay At Weiss
2700 Bay Sag ............ **792-8779**
**FENT'S LAUNDRY CENTER**
9141 E Birch Run BrchRn.. **624-9698**
Frankenmuth Cleaners Inc
160 S Main Frkmth....... 652-2551

**GEORGE'S DRY CLEANERS**

"Serving Saginaw Since 1945"

**QUALITY WORK
ONE DAY SERVICE**

In By 10 A.M. Out By 4 P.M.
Just East Of N. Michigan On Shattuck

509 Shattuck Rd Saginaw ... **754-8543**

Giant Wash-O-Matic & Dry Clng
2320 Webber Sag .......755-5064
**GOODWILL CLEANERS**
SUDDEN SERVICE
IN BY 10 AM OUT BY 4 PM
402 N Mich Sag.......... **754-6112**
1900 Hess Sag Plant...... **753-4401**

**GUIDA DRY CLEANERS**

| PICK-UP AND DELIVERY | **GUIDA** QUALITY CLEANING |
|---|---|

*Serving Saginaw For Over 60 Years*
1 Day Service On Request
★ Alterations
★ Button Replacements
★ Zippers Repaired
★ Leather Cleaning
★ Drapery Cleaning
COMPLETE SHIRT SERVICE

**DIAL 754-9793**

700 Lapeer Saginaw

**JACOB'S CLEANING VILLAGE**
2714 Center Av Essex..... **893-6191**
**MR SUDS DRY CLEANING**

**SUEDE & LEATHER
SERVICES**

- Cleaning
- Re-Dyeing
- Re-Styling
- New Linings
- Zippers
- Mending
- Leather
- Buttons

**CALL 755-5700**

2319 Webber        Saginaw

Mr Suds Laundry & Professional Dry
Cleaners
1215 E Genesee Sag..... 754-2063
3860 Dixie Sag ......... 777-9954
O & O Fabric Care Center
1000 Columbus ByCy..... 894-2281

**PHYL'S ONE HOUR MARTINIZING**
**DRY CLEANERS**
Draperies ● Leathers
Shirt Service ● Wedding Gown
Preservation ● Repairs & Alterations

(Drive-Up Window)

3416 State Saginaw...... **792-7861**

**QUERBACH LEATHER PROCESS INC**
Insist On Professional Care For All
Your Leathers - Weekly Pick-Ups At
Your Cleaners Where Signs Displayed
M-40 North Allegan.... **616 673-8140**

**REALGOOD CLEANERS**

*"A LITTLE BETTER —
A LITTLE MORE CAREFUL"*

ASK ABOUT OUR CASH & CARRY
DISCOUNT — ALTERATIONS
& REPAIRS ● EXPERT SHIRT SERVICE
DRAPERY CLEANING SPECIALISTS
WITH PERFECT PLEAT METHOD
FOLDED & READY TO HANG

Retain Original Beauty To Your
Drapes - Loc-Tite Stretch "N" Pleat
Draperies Taken Down and Hanging
Service Available With Cleaning

**MAIN OFFICE - 793-6511**

1317 COURT — SAGINAW

**SHIELDS OFFICE - 781-0270**

7871 GRATIOT — SAGINAW

**ROTH DRY CLEANERS**
2526 Broadway ByCy    892-2573
(See Advertisement This Page)
**SALZBURG CLEANERS INC**
Dry Cleaning & Shirt Service
1906 S Erie ByCy .... **893-5561**
3417 Center Av Rd Essex... 892-9070
(See Advertisement This Page)
Spotless Cleaners
1516 S Mich Sag ....... 799-5161
(See Advertisement This Page)
State Street Dry Cleaners
4742 State Sag......... 793-7444
Steven's Dry Cleaning
3393 S Huron Rd ByCy ... 686-0911
**SUBURBAN DRY CLEANERS &
SHIRT LAUNDERERS**
- 1 Hr Service On Request
- Shirt Laundry
- Drapery & Leather Cleaning
- Storage
- Alterations & Reweaving

6853 Gratiot Saginaw..... **781-3650**

**SUDDEN SERVICE CLEANERS
& SHIRT LAUNDERERS**
1-HOUR DRY CLEANING SERVICE
2 Drive-In Windows
412 Wash By Cy ......... **893-0071**

---

1. What is the type of business found on this page? _____

2. What is the *first* alphabetical listing on this page? _____

3. What is the *last* alphabetical listing on this page? _____

4. Did any listings under the same heading come *before* this page?

_____

5. Are the businesses on this page providing products or a service? _____

Some of the listings give more than telephone numbers and addresses. These listings appear in boxes. They tell about the services and sometimes the hours of the business. They are called classified-ad listings. Refer to these ads in answering the remaining questions.

6. What place cleans wedding gowns?

_____

7. Name three places that clean leather.

_____

_____

_____

8. Which cleaner replaces buttons?

_____

9. Which cleaner will take down your drapes?

_____

## ACTIVITY 10
### Choosing the yellow pages or the white pages

Classify the items below according to where they are most likely found—yellow pages, white pages, or both.

a. WHITE PAGES
b. YELLOW PAGES
c. BOTH

——— **1.** Jones, Charles

——— **2.** Bambi Department Store

——— **3.** Acme Printing Company

——— **4.** Smith, T. J.

——— **5.** Chun King Restaurant

——— **6.** Posey, Ernest

——— **7.** Central Television Repair Shop

——— **8.** Restaurants—Italian

——— **9.** Penn, Carolyn

——— **10.** Banks

——— **11.** Robinson, Charles, M.D.

——— **12.** Poison Control Center

——— **13.** Lawson, E. J.

——— **14.** Lawson Brothers Realty

——— **15.** James, Fred

——— **16.** Interior Decorators

——— **17.** Smith's Transfer

——— **18.** Chi Mer Restaurant

——— **19.** Wilson, John T. (attorney)

——— **20.** A & B Clothing

### The area code map

The United States is divided into telephone dialing areas. Each area has an area code. This is a three-digit number. You use this number to dial long distance. For example, you want to call 555-2364 in South Carolina. But you live in Utah. You must dial 1 first and then the area code. It is 803. So you must dial 1, 803, and then 555-2364. When you do not know an area code, you can use the area code map in your telephone book. The map divides the United States into time zones. Notice that when it is 1:00 in California, it is 4:00 in Michigan.

## ACTIVITY 11
### Reading area code maps

Study the following area code map. Use this map to answer the following questions.

**1.** Give the area codes for   Arizona ——————————   Wyoming ——————————

South Dakota ——————————   Utah ——————————

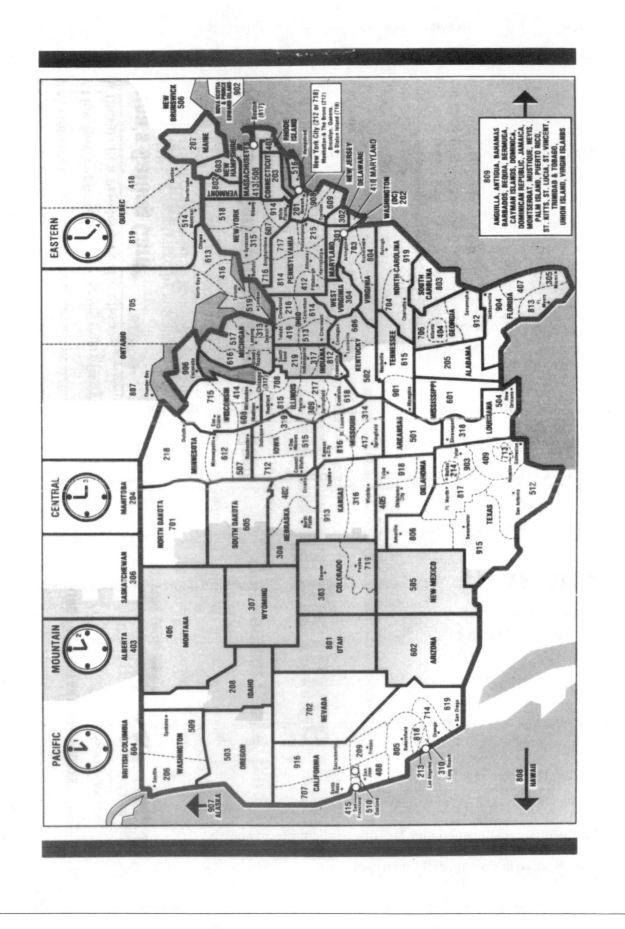

**2.** Give the area codes for Alaska ———————— Bermuda ————————————

Hawaii ———————— Puerto Rico ————————————

**3.** Give the area codes for Ontario, Canada ————————————————————

Quebec ————————————————————————

Saskatchewan ————————————————————

**4.** How many dialing areas (area codes) are in the state of Florida? ————————————

West Virginia? ————————————

Georgia? ————————————

Montana? ————————————

Texas? ————————————

**5.** What city in Texas is in the 512 area? ————————————————————

the 713 area? ————————————————————

the 214 area? ————————————————————

**6.** If you wanted to make a long distance call to Philadelphia (Phila.), Pennsylvania, from out of state, what

area code would you dial before the number? ————————————————————

**7.** If you wanted to call Atlanta, Georgia, what area code would you dial? ————————————

# ACTIVITY 12
## Reading area code maps

The area code map is divided into four time zones. They are Pacific, Mountain, Central, and Eastern. Screened areas indicated the four different geographical areas. Read each of the situations below. Decide which statement is correct. Also answer each time question.

**Situation 1**

You live in Seattle, Washington. At 9:01 A.M., you make a business call to New York City. You want to catch Jim Brown, the president of Lyons Construction, as soon as he arrives at work. The office hours are 9 to 5.

When you call, the secretary tells you:

——— **A.** Mr. Brown just left for lunch.

——— **B.** the office just opened and Mr. Brown should be in shortly.

——— **C.** the office is closing, call tomorrow.

What time is it in New York? ————————————

270

**Situation 2**

John Johnson calls his insurance company in Des Moines, Iowa. The person who answers the phone tells him that his agent, Mr. Brown, will be in at 3:00. John is calling from Maryland. When John calls back, his watch reads exactly 3:00.

But the receptionist tells him:

_____ **A.** his agent is at lunch from 12 to 1:00.

_____ **B.** call back at 4:00.

_____ **C.** call back in an hour.

What time is it in Des Moines? _____

## CHECK YOUR UNDERSTANDING OF THE TELEPHONE DIRECTORY

1. A listing for The Skillful Carpenter is under what letter in the white pages? _____

2. Under what heading in the yellow pages would you most likely find The Skillful Carpenter?

   _____

3. You want to know which bus line has a route to Phoenix. What heading do you look up in the yellow

   pages? _____

4. How do you find a plumber in the yellow pages? _____

5. You want to call your friend Jason Pierce. You look under the letter _____ in the white pages.

6. You live in Chicago, Illinois. You want to call your friend in Los Angeles, California, at 8:30 in the

   morning, California time. What is the time in Chicago when you make the call? _____

7. You are at work in New York City. You place a business call to Houston, Texas. It is 1:00 P.M. in New York. In Houston:

   _____ **a.** the workday is over    _____ **b.** it is the lunch hour    _____ **c.** the workday has not begun

8. Put the following names in alphabetical order. Names beginning with *Mac* or *Mc* are alphabetized letter by letter. So all the *Macs* come before the *Mcs*.

   McNeil _____    MacDonald _____    Miner _____    Mack _____    Major _____    McKay _____

9. What does the abbreviation Av. mean? _____

10. Why might Dr. Gilbert Brown, Dentist, have two numbers listed after his name in the white pages?

   _____

# Special reading strategies

Often information you need will require special reading skills. You may have to interpret a sign, symbol, or drawing. You may have to make comparisons using a chart or graph. You may have to read a schedule.

This chapter gives you practice in using everyday reference skills. First you will learn how to identify street and highway signs. Then you will read trail, street, and highway maps. You will practice reading bus, train, and plane schedules, and you will interpret line, bar, and circle graphs.

## Street and highway signs

### WORDS TO KNOW

**guide signs**   signs that show exits, distances, and directions, such as route numbers

**maximum speed**   the fastest speed allowed

**minimum speed**   the slowest speed allowed

**obstruction**   something that is blocking the road

**pedestrian**   a person who is walking

**regulatory signs**   signs that give information about traffic laws such as speed limits

**right-of-way**   the right to go first

**service signs**   signs that point out services such as rest stops, telephones, and gas stations

**warning signs**   signs that give warnings or cautions about possible dangers such as low bridges or sharp curves in a road

Street and highway signs carry important messages for drivers. They tell them the traffic laws. They warn of possible dangers ahead. They give distances and directions. They even direct drivers to telephones, gas stations, and rest stops.

Street and highway signs are grouped in three categories. They are REGULATORY SIGNS, WARNING SIGNS, and SERVICE AND GUIDE SIGNS.

**Regulatory signs** These signs show speed limits and other traffic regulations. Most regulatory signs are white with black letters.

Traffic in the right lane must turn right. Traffic in the left lane may go straight or turn right.

Drivers should keep to the right of an obstruction.

This sign is posted over a turning lane. Traffic from both directions uses this lane.

The fastest safe speed is 55 miles per hour. The minimum safe speed is 45 miles per hour.

These signs mark Passing and No Passing zones.

Sometimes a message on a regulatory sign is very important. This sign will be red with white letters.

This sign means come to a complete stop.

The driver *does not* have the right-of-way. Slow down and let right-of-way driver go first.

Don't drive onto any street or enter any highway with this sign.

You are driving the wrong way on a freeway, ramp, or street. You may meet another car.

A red circle with a line through it always means NO.

NO RIGHT TURN

NO TRUCKS

NO U TURN

Some regulatory signs are for pedestrians also. NO HITCHHIKING is an example. Can you think of others?

# ACTIVITY 1

Match the signs with their meanings.

## Identifying regulatory signs

A. B. C. D.

E. F. G. H.

I. J.

_____ **1.** No "U" turn.

_____ **2.** No trucks allowed.

_____ **3.** This sign means the opposite of "Go."

_____ **4.** Slow down. Be prepared to stop for drivers who have the right-of-way.

_____ **5.** Turning lane.

_____ **6.** Stay out!

_____ **7.** Maximum safe speed.

_____ **8.** You're driving in the wrong direction.

_____ **9.** Keep to the right of an obstruction.

_____ **10.** No right turn.

**Warning signs** Warning signs are yellow with black letters. They're usually diamond-shaped.

Sharp curve ahead. Take curve at 35 mph.

Crossroads or side roads ahead. Watch for other vehicles entering, leaving, or crossing highways.

A bridge or underpass ahead. Clearance is 12 feet 6 inches.

Traffic light ahead. Be prepared to stop.

Traffic island or obstruction ahead. Drive to either side.

Reminder: two-way highway

Slow down and watch for schoolchildren.

Begin slowing down. You must stop soon.

A section of the highway is slippery when wet. Driver should slow down.

Traffic may be moving into your lane. Be ready to change speed or lane.

This means pedestrian crossing. Watch out for people walking across highway.

This means bicycle crossing. Watch out for people riding bicycles.

This sign warns of a hill where driver must take special care.

The unpaved edge of the road is soft. Stay on pavement.

Almost everyone has seen these two warning signs.

This No Passing Zone sign is usually followed by a black and white regulatory sign.

Train may be crossing highway. Slow down and be prepared to stop.

## ACTIVITY 2   Match the signs with their meanings.
### Identifying warning signs

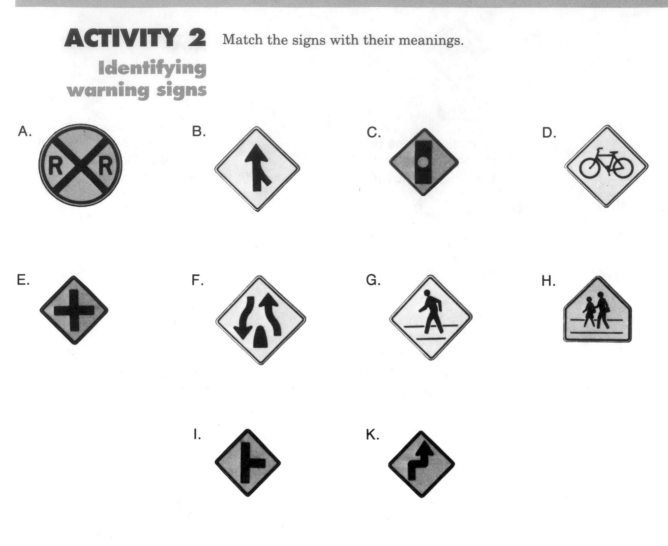

A.   B.   C.   D.

E.   F.   G.   H.

I.   K.

_____   **1.** Pedestrian crossing.

_____   **2.** Watch for bike riders.

_____   **3.** Watch out for schoolchildren.

_____   **4.** Highway ahead has two-way traffic.

_____   **5.** Watch for traffic moving into your lane.

_____   **6.** Side road ahead—watch for vehicles entering highway.

_____   **7.** Traffic light ahead. BE PREPARED TO STOP!

_____   **8.** Railroad Crossing.

_____   **9.** Curve ahead.

_____   **10.** Intersection ahead. Watch for vehicles entering, leaving, or crossing highway.

**Service and guide signs**

Service and guide signs are usually seen on major routes and interstate highways. These signs tell you what to expect ahead. Guide signs are white and green. They point out such things as exits, bike routes, and hiking trails.

They also give distances and directions:

Found in front of intersections, they show the direction to cities.

Used on main highways, these signs show distance.

Others identify routes by number, symbol, and shape. These routes are part of national, state, and local highway systems.

Interstate sign

U.S. Route markers

A State Highway sign for Michigan

Expressway Exit

On interstate highways and freeways you may see blue-and-white service signs. These signs direct you to rest rooms, telephones, restaurants, and gas stations. Sometimes you will see words and symbols. Sometimes you will see only symbols.

Rest stops

No handicap barriers

Route to nearest hospital

Location of picnic table

Signs showing state and local parks are usually brown with white letters or symbols.

## ACTIVITY 3
### Identifying street and highway signs

Label these signs as REGULATORY, WARNING, or SERVICE AND GUIDE.

_____

_____

_____

_____

_____

_____

Tell the meaning of each of the following signs.

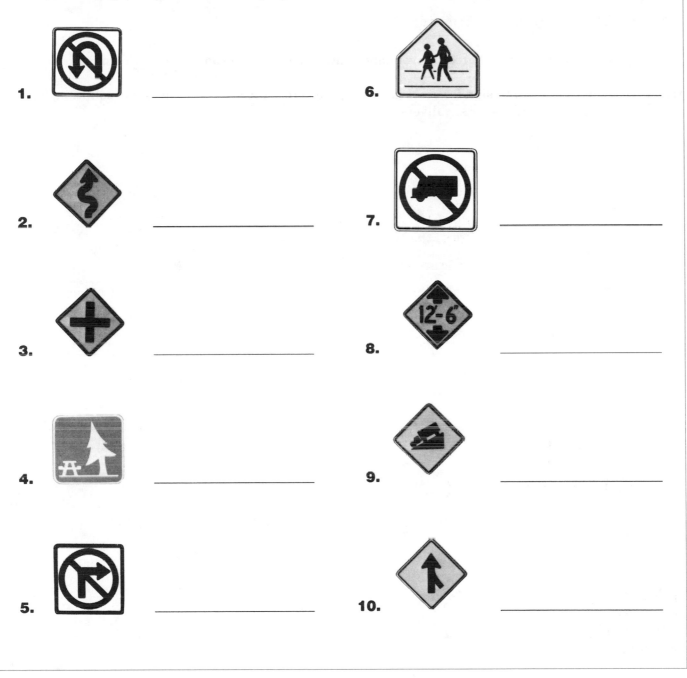

1. _____

2. _____

3. _____

4. _____

5. _____

6. _____

7. _____

8. _____

9. _____

10. _____

# SHOW WHAT YOU KNOW . . .

## About Street and Highway Signs

Working with others in a small group, invent and draw some warning signs and service signs.

**HINT:** Start with a warning sign for some hazard in your area, such as high waves, air pollution, loud music, skate boarders, or sky divers.

## Maps

**WORDS TO KNOW**

**county route**   local road maintained by a county

**divided highway**   highway that has a strip of grass or concrete between opposite lanes

**expressway**   divided highway intended for high speeds and having limited entrances and exits

**freeway**   highway with limited access and without toll charges. Both expressways and freeways usually have two or more lanes in either direction.

**grid**   system by which points are plotted on a map to help find a location

**interchange**   place where one or more highways connect. Interchanges usually connect highways intended for high speed.

**interstate highway**   limited-access federal highway crossing several states

**junction**   place where two or more roads meet

**legend**   section of a map where map symbols and signs are explained. Also called a key.

**limited-access highway**   same as expressway; sometimes called controlled-access highway

**points of interest**   public places indicated on a map that might be of special interest to travelers. Historic sites and natural features such as waterfalls or rock formations are examples of points of interest.

**state highway**   highway within a state and maintained wholly or partly by that state

**toll road**   road on which fees are charged. Fees are also charged on some bridges.

**trail**   walking or hiking path in a non-urban area. Some highways are called trails.

**turnpike**   usually refers to a toll road, but some toll-free roads are also called turnpikes

**U.S. highway**   federal road going across several states but not having controlled access

A map is a drawing that shows some part of the surface of the earth. Maps can show the whole world, a continent, a country, or a state. They can show a county, a city, a town, or a neighborhood. A city map shows streets, neighborhoods, and public buildings. Some city maps show suburbs surrounding a city. Some special maps show rapid transit or bus routes. A map of a park may show trails. Highway maps show roads, highways, and distances between cities. Many maps show natural features, such as rivers, mountains, and lakes. All maps help you find where you are. They also help you get where you're going.

Most maps are drawn so that *north* is at the top of the map. This means that *south* is at the bottom, *east* is at the right, and *west* is at the left. Occasionally, a map will show north slightly to the right or left of the top. A directional symbol on the map will tell you which way is north.

**Trail maps**  A trail map helps you find your way in a park or wilderness area. Since there are no street signs, only trail markers, you will probably need to carry a trail map when you go to a large park. Study the trail map and the legend below. Notice that each trail is marked with a different symbol.

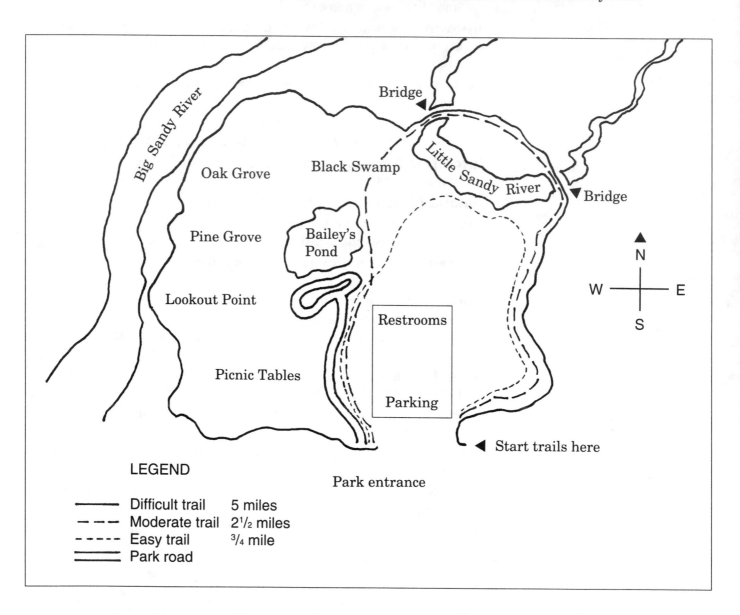

Big Sandy River

Oak Grove

Pine Grove

Lookout Point

Picnic Tables

Black Swamp

Bailey's Pond

Little Sandy River

Bridge

Bridge

Restrooms

Parking

N
W — E
S

◄ Start trails here

Park entrance

LEGEND

——— Difficult trail    5 miles
— – — Moderate trail   2½ miles
- - - - Easy trail      ¾ mile
═══ Park road

## ACTIVITY 4

**Understanding a trail map**

Use the trail map to answer the questions below.

1. How long is the difficult trail? _____

2. Which trails cross the Little Sandy River? _____

3. Which trail runs closest to Bailey's Pond? _____

4. Can you drive to Bailey's Pond? _____

5. How many trails go to Lookout Point? _____

6. If you are hiking from the second bridge to the Oak Grove, which direction are you going? _____

7. If you are at Lookout Point facing the Big Sandy River at 5 P.M., will the sun be behind you or in front of

   you? _____

8. If you are walking south at the end of the easy trail, will you turn right or left into the parking lot?

   _____

**Map legends**  A map legend explains the symbols on a map. You used a map legend when you answered the questions about the trail map. On city and highway maps, a map legend will show if you must pay a toll to drive on a road. It will show where you can get on and off a limited-access highway. It will also show a scale of miles. The map legend shown in the next activity also has other information.

# ACTIVITY 5

## Understanding a map legend

Study this legend from a Wisconsin state map and explain what the following symbols mean.

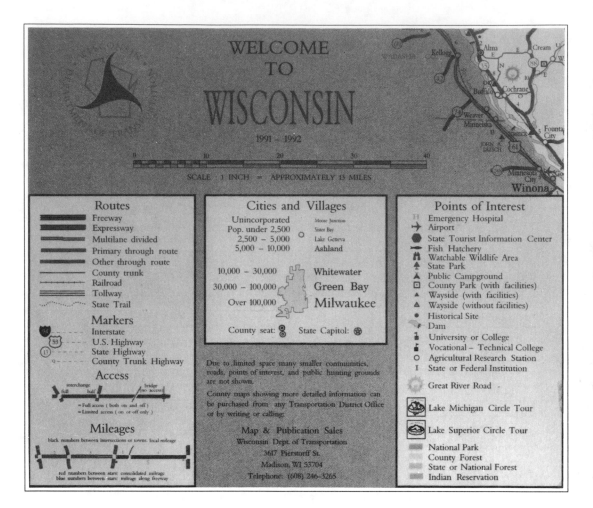

1. ⑬ _____

2. ┼─┼─┼─ _____

3. 🛡94 _____

4. ♠ _____

5. ≡ _____

6. ⬡53 _____

7. ✈ _____

8. ⊙ _____

9. •••••••• _____

10. ⬢ _____

**Street maps** Street maps show the streets in a town or city. Most maps of the downtown area of a city will show all the streets. Some maps of suburban areas show major streets only.

Most street maps show the streets that divide north addresses from south addresses and east from west addresses. For example, there may be an East Washington Street and a West Washington Street. A map will show you where east becomes west.

Streets may be called avenues, boulevards, drives, pikes, places, parkways, trails, and roads. A city may have two streets with almost the same name. For example, there may be a Springfield Road and a Springfield Avenue. There may be an Adams Street and an Adams Parkway. If you are trying to find a certain street, you must know the exact name.

If there are major highways running through a city or town, these will be shown on a city map, too. In addition, some public places may be shown.

In some cities, numbered streets run one direction and non-numbered streets run another. In other cities, streets run in all directions instead of in straight lines. Before you try to find your way, it is a good idea to study a map first.

# SHOW WHAT YOU KNOW . . .

## About Maps

Draw a map showing the route you take from home to your school. Show major streets and highways only. Include a directional symbol for your map.

Study the map of downtown Detroit. Then answer the questions that follow.

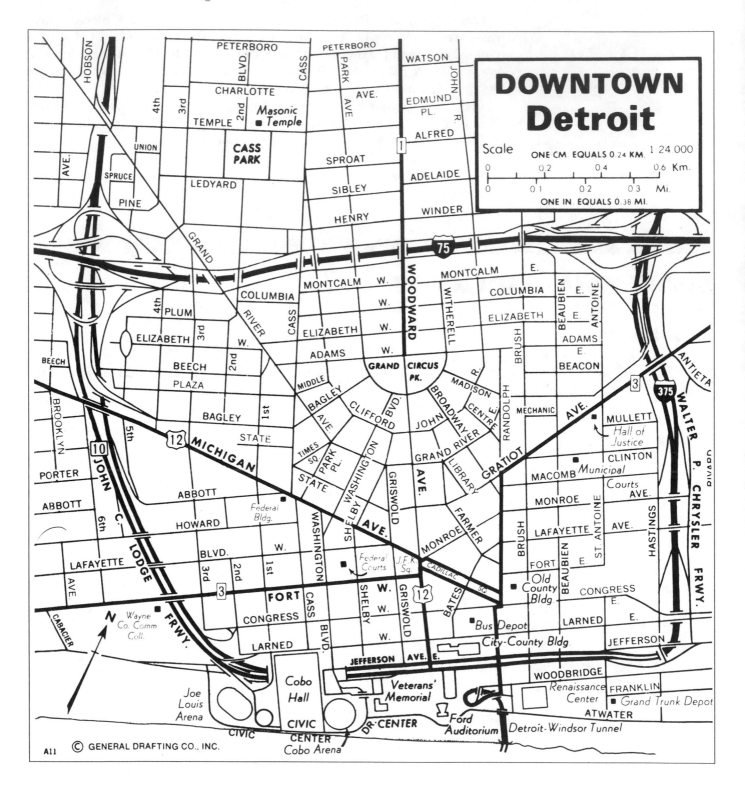

1. Find Grand Circus Park in the middle of the map. Notice that the east-west streets north of the park are named Adams, Elizabeth, Columbia, and so on. What is the dividing street between West Adams and East Adams or between West Elizabeth and East Elizabeth?

   _____

2. Locate Fort Avenue near the bottom of the map. With your finger trace the route to Woodward Avenue (Highway 12) and turn south. Travel Woodward south until you come to Larned Avenue. Turn east and go to Beaubien. Travel north on Beaubien past Macomb and to the corner of Clinton and Beaubien. What public place are you near?

   _____

3. Locate Charlotte Avenue in the upper left portion of the map. Travel east on Charlotte to Cass and turn right. Take Cass to Michigan and travel southeast until you run into Woodward. Take the first right off Woodward to Fort. Take Fort past the John C. Lodge Freeway. Name the educational institution on your left.

   _____

4. You have to meet a friend at the bus depot at the lower right corner of the map between Congress and Larned. If you are coming into the city on the John C. Lodge Freeway, can you exit at Congress?

   _____

5. Is Route 75 an interstate highway or a state highway? _____

6. Look at the scale of kilometers and miles in the upper right-hand corner. Approximately how many kilometers is it from where Route 75 crosses Woodward north to Watson?

   _____

   How many blocks is it? _____

7. Find the directional symbol in the lower left corner of the map. Which way does Michigan Avenue run?

   _____

8. Find Cass Park at the top of the map. Trace the route south on 2nd Blvd. Can you turn right onto Columbia if you are going south?

   _____

**Map grids and indexes**  A map index and a grid system help you find a place on a map. A map index lists places in alphabetical order. It also lists the *grid points*. A map with grid points usually has letters running vertically on the right side. Numbers run horizontally along the bottom.

A
B
C
D
E
F
G

1 2 3 4 5 6 7 8

If you want to find a place shown as D–3, run your finger up from 3 and over from D. The location you want should be in that area.

Indexes for cities list streets and public places. Indexes for states list counties and cities.

Here is a map index and a grid for an imaginary place.

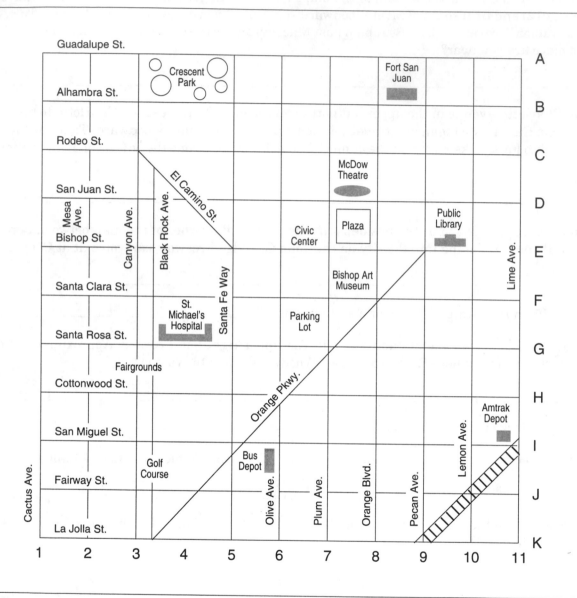

## INDEX

### Streets

| | | |
|---|---|---|
| Alhambra B1–B11 | Guadalupe A1–A11 | Pecan A9–K9 |
| Bishop E1–E11 | La Jolla K1–K11 | Plum A7–K7 |
| Black Rock D4–K4 | Lemon A10–K10 | Rodeo C1–C11 |
| Cactus A1–K1 | Lime A11–K11 | San Juan D1–D11 |
| Canyon C3–K3 | Mesa A2–K2 | San Miguel I1–I11 |
| Cottonwood H1–H11 | Olive A6–K6 | Santa Clara F1–F11 |
| El Camino A3–E5 | Orange Blvd. A8–K8 | Santa Fe Way A5–K5 |
| Fairway J1–J11 | Orange Pkwy. E9–K4 | Santa Rosa G1–G11 |

### Points of Interest

| | |
|---|---|
| Amtrak Depot I10 | McDow Theatre D7–8 |
| Bishop Art Museum E7 | Parking Lot F6–7 |
| Bus Depot I6 | Public Library E9 |
| Civic Center E6–7 | |
| Crescent Park A3–5 | |
| Fairgrounds G2–4 | |
| Fort San Juan B8–9 | |
| Golf Course I2–3 | |

## ACTIVITY 7

### Finding locations with an index and grid

Using the index and grid, answer the following questions.

1. Is Santa Rosa north or south of Bishop? _____

2. What street divides east addresses from west addresses? _____

3. How many blocks away is Plum from Santa Fe Way? _____

4. What are the grid number and letter for the corner of Alhambra Street and Canyon? _____

5. You live on West San Miguel between Mesa and Canyon. How many blocks will you have to walk to

   the Fairgrounds? _____

6. With the help of the index, find the Bishop Art Museum. Which direction is it from Crescent Park?

   _____

7. If you are driving south on El Camino, will you turn right or left to get to the library? _____

8. If you are driving south on Pecan at 7 A.M., will the sun be on your right or your left? _____

9. Orange Boulevard is closed for repairs from Guadalupe to Santa Rosa. Lemon is closed from La Jolla

   to Cottonwood. How will you get from the Amtrak Station on San Miguel to Fort San Juan?

   _____

   _____

10. Assume that you have a friend who lives at C–3. What streets intersect at this junction?

    _____

### State highway maps

Highway maps are important for travelers. Truck drivers need them, bus drivers need them, and tourists need them. State maps show many kinds of highways. Even-numbered highways run generally east and west. Odd-numbered highways run generally north and south.

## ACTIVITY 8

### Understanding a state highway map

Study the map of the southeast part of Wisconsin to answer the questions. The legend for the map is on page 286.

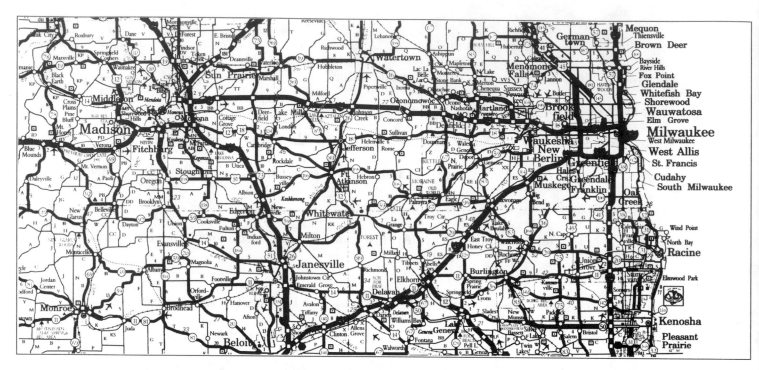

1. What highway will you take from Madison to Milwaukee if you are in a hurry? _____

2. What highway might you take from Madison to Milwaukee if you want to travel more slowly?

   _____

3. Locate two state parks in the southeast area of the map.

   Write their names here. _____

4. What is the name of the state forest west of Milwaukee? _____

5. Can you camp in this forest? _____

6. Racine and Kenosha are south of Milwaukee on Lake Michigan. Are they county seats? _____

7. Highway 90 goes from Madison southeast to Janesville. Can you get off 90 at route 26? _____

8. Find Beloit at the bottom of the map. If you take route 213 northwest out of Beloit, what is the first

   town you come to? What is the next town on route 213? _____

9. Continue on route 213. Is Evansville a bigger or smaller town than Beloit? _____

10. Is there an airport near Janesville? _____

Study this map of Baltimore, Maryland. Answer the questions about it.

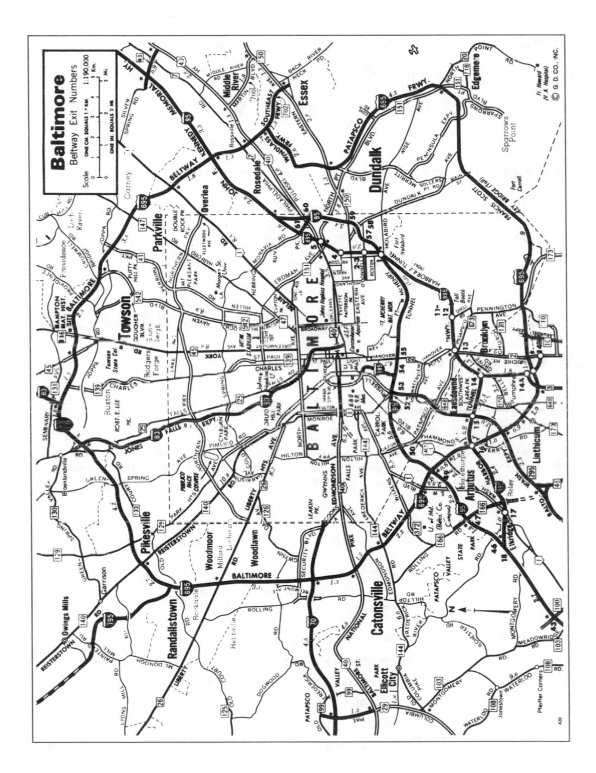

1. Which interstate route goes to the center of Baltimore? _____

2. Which highway is named after John F. Kennedy? _____

3. What are two ways to get from Dundalk to Brooklyn? _____

    _____

4. Is the Pimlico Race Course southeast or northwest of Pikesville? _____

5. What highway is also called the Baltimore Beltway? _____

6. What state park is in the southwest corner of the map? _____

    _____

7. What is the most direct route from Arbutus to downtown Baltimore? _____

    _____

8. Does this map show all the streets in Baltimore or just major routes? _____

# SHOW WHAT YOU KNOW . . .

## About Mapping a Route

Using a road atlas that has a map of the whole United States, find the state where you live. Trace the route you would take to the nation's capital. If you live in or near Washington, D.C., trace the route you would take to get to St. Louis, Missouri. If you do not own the atlas you are using, photocopy the map first for this activity.

## Timetables

### WORDS TO KNOW

**A.M.**   from midnight to noon (morning)

**arrival time**   the expected time you will get where you are going

**departure time**   the time of leaving

**originating point**   the place a trip starts

**P.M.**   from noon to midnight (afternoon and evening)

**terminating point**   the place a trip ends (last stop on bus, boat, train, or plane)

**timetable**   schedule that shows the times when planes, trains, and so on arrive and depart

What time will your train leave Charleston, West Virginia, for Washington, D.C.? Is there a morning bus to Hillside, New Jersey? Are there any evening flights from Chicago to Denver? When does the last ferry boat leave Mackinac Island?

Being able to read a schedule or timetable can come in very handy. Timetables can help you get to work on time. They can make travel and vacations easier. They can help you plan your time. They can help keep you from being in the wrong place at the wrong time. Timetables tell you when you'll get where you are going. Some timetables tell you all the stops along the way. Before you take a bus, train, boat, or plane, you should know how to read a timetable.

## Reading timetables

All timetables show the starting or originating point and the ending or terminating point.

The bus timetable below shows only two points—originating and terminating. But some timetables show all points between these locations. These points are called stops.

All timetables show departure times and arrival times.

Most timetables are read either down or across. This means that you may read across the schedule to locate your arrival time. Or you may read down the schedule to locate your arrival time. When there is only one place of departure and arrival, timetables usually read *across*.

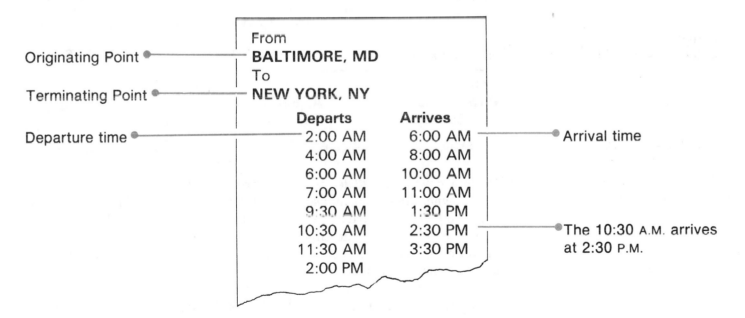

Originating Point
Terminating Point
Departure time

From
**BALTIMORE, MD**
To
**NEW YORK, NY**

| Departs | Arrives |
|---------|---------|
| 2:00 AM | 6:00 AM |
| 4:00 AM | 8:00 AM |
| 6:00 AM | 10:00 AM |
| 7:00 AM | 11:00 AM |
| 9:30 AM | 1:30 PM |
| 10:30 AM | 2:30 PM |
| 11:30 AM | 3:30 PM |
| 2:00 PM | |

Arrival time

The 10:30 A.M. arrives at 2:30 P.M.

In the sample above, the column headings help you read this timetable. First you read your departure time under "Departs." Then you read across the same line. You locate your arrival time under "Arrives." Many transportation schedules have several columns. They also show many stops. You must study these timetables to determine how you should read them.

In the next schedule there are five columns showing departures. These show buses going from Baltimore to New York. These are buses #1, #2, #3, #4, and #5. They all make the same run. This schedule reads *down*.

| From **BALTIMORE, MD** To **NEW YORK, NY** | #1 Sun | #2 | #3 | #4 | #5 |
|---|---|---|---|---|---|
| Baltimore, MD | 9:00 | 8:00 | **12:00** | **6:00** | 2:00 |
| Joppatowne, MD | – | 8:15 | **12:15** | **6:15** | 2:15 |
| Edgewood, MD | – | 8:30 | **12:30** | **6:30** | 2:30 |
| Aberdeen, MD | – | 8:45 | **12:45** | **6:45** | 2:45 |
| Havre de Grace, MD | – | 9:00 | **1:00** | **7:00** | 3:00 |
| Elkton, MD | – | 9:30 | **1:30** | **7:30** | 3:30 |
| Wilmington, DE | 10:45 | 9:45 | **1:45** | **7:45** | 3:45 |
| Newark, NJ | **1:00** | 12:00 | **4:00** | **10:00** | 6:00 |
| New York City | **1:30** | 12:30 | **4:30** | **10:30** | 6:30 |

Notes:
**P.M.—Boldface**      All trips operate daily
Sun–Sundays only      unless otherwise noted.

*Read down from Baltimore to New York*

*Bus #3 Leaves at 12:00 noon*

*Arrives at 4:30 P.M.*

Reading down, Bus #3 leaves Baltimore at 12:00 noon. It goes through Joppatowne, Edgewood, and so on until it arrives in New York City at 4:30 P.M. If you want to leave at 2:00 A.M., you locate the 2:00 A.M. bus (#5). You then read down to your destination for the arrival time. At the bottom of a schedule is a "notes" section. Abbreviations and symbols used are explained here. On many transportation timetables this section is called the "key." Look at the "notes" section of this timetable.

The "notes" section tells you that buses that run between 12 noon and midnight are shown in boldface (dark) type. The symbols A.M. and P.M. do not appear on the timetable. You must read the notes in order to get the correct time for the bus you want to take. Also notice that bus #1 runs only on Sundays. It is possible to travel from Baltimore to New York City by bus on Sunday, but you must take the 9 A.M. bus. There are no other buses that day from Baltimore to New York City.

## ACTIVITY 9

### Understanding timetables

The timetable below shows trains going from New York City to Detroit. You have to read *down* this schedule to find stops (and departure times) between these two cities.

### New York-Albany-Syracuse- Rochester-Buffalo-Niagara Falls-Detroit

| | | Train Number | | 63 | 69 | 73 | 71 | 75 | 65 | 49 | 79 |
|---|---|---|---|---|---|---|---|---|---|---|---|
| | | Train Name | | The Niagara Rainbow | The Adirondack | The Empire State Express | The Henry Hudson | The Washington Irving | The Salt City Express | The Lake Shore Limited | The DeWitt Clinton |
| | | Frequency of Operation | | Daily | Daily | Daily | Daily | Daily | Daily | Daily | Daily |
| | | Type of Service | | ☒ ⌂ | ☒ | ✓ ☒ | ☒ | ☒ | ✓ ☒ | ⇌ ✗ ⌂ | ☒ |
| Km | Mi | | | | | | | | | | |
| 0 | 0 | (Conrail) New York, NY (ET) (Grand Central Terminal) | Dp | 8 40 A | 9 15 A | 12 40 P | 2 40 P | 4 40 P | 5 40 P | 6 40 P | 8 40 P |
| 53 | 33 | Croton-Harmon, NY ⑲ | | R 9 37 A | R 10 03 A | R 1 28 P | R 3 28 P | R 5 28 P | R 6 28 P | R 7 37 P | R 9 28 P |
| 119 | 74 | Poughkeepsie, NY ⑲ (Highland) | | R 10 21 A | R 10 48 A | R 2 13 P | R 4 13 P | R 6 13 P | R 7 13 P | R 8 21 P | R 10 13 P |
| 143 | 89 | Rhinecliff, NY (Kingston) | | 10 37 A | 11 04 A | 2 29 P | 4 29 P | 6 29 P | 7 29 P | 8 37 P | 10 29 P |
| 185 | 115 | Hudson, NY | | 11 02 A | 11 27 A | 2 52 P | 4 52 P | 6 52 P | 7 52 P | 9 02 P | 10 52 P |
| 230 | 143 | Albany-Rensselaer, NY | Ar | 11 45 A | 12 05 P | 3 30 P | 5 30 P | 7 30 P | 8 30 P | 9 45 P | 11 30 P |
| 230 | 143 | | Dp | 12 05 P | | 3 40 P | | | 8 40 P | 10 00 P | |
| 245 | 152 | Colonie-Schenectady, NY | | 12 26 P | | 3 55 P | | | 8 55 P | | |
| 257 | 160 | Schenectady, NY | | ㉘ | | ㉘ | | | ㉘ | ㉘ | |
| 286 | 178 | Amsterdam, NY | | 12 54 P | | 4 20 P | | | 9 20 P | | |
| 383 | 238 | Utica, NY | | 1 55 P | | 5 17 P | | | 10 17 P | 11 52 P | |
| 406 | 252 | Rome, NY (Griffiss AFB) | | 2 11 P | | 5 31 P | | | 10 31 P | | |
| 460 | 286 | Syracuse, NY | | 2 42 P | | 6 02 P | | | 11 05 P | 12 45 A | |
| 599 | 372 | Rochester, NY | | 4 15 P | | 7 32 P | | | | 2 20 A | |
| 695 | 432 | Cheektowaga, NY ㉘ ● | | | | | | | | | |
| 705 | 438 | Buffalo, NY (Central Tml.) | | 5 32 P | | 8 40 P | | | | 3 50 A | |
| 708 | 440 | Buffalo, NY (Exchange St.) | Ar | 5 37 P | | 8 45 P | | | | | |
| 748 | 466 | Niagara Falls, NY | | 6 40 P | | 9 45 P | | | | | |
| 938 | 583 | St. Thomas, Ont. ● | | 9 28 P | | | | | | | |
| 1115 | 693 | Windsor, Ont. ● (Amtrak Sta.) | | 11 10 P | | | | | | | |
| 1120 | 696 | Detroit, MI (Amtrak Sta.) (ET) | Ar | 11 30 P | | | | | | | |

Answer these questions about the train schedule above.

1. How many trains appear on this schedule? _____

2. What is the distance between New York City and Rochester? _____

3. What is the number of the train that goes all the way from New York City to Detroit? _____

4. If you want to be in Utica by 3 P.M., which train will you take? _____

5. What time does this train leave New York City? _____

6. What time does this train arrive in Detroit? _____

7. What is the last stop for the Henry Hudson? _____

8. What time does the Adirondack get to Hudson? _____

9. What time does the Washington Irving leave New York City? _____

10. Does the Lake Shore Limited leave New York City in the morning or evening? _____

# ACTIVITY 10

## Understanding timetables

As you read *across* the airline schedule on the next page, each column gives you information on a specific flight. (The codes and abbreviations used here would be explained at the bottom of the schedule.) You learn when a flight leaves and when a flight arrives. You learn a flight's number and how often a plane flies. Continuing to read across, you will find a column for connecting cities and one showing the stops a plane makes. Use this schedule to answer the questions below.

1. Determine the departure time, the arrival time, and the number of stops for each of these Asheville flights:

FROM ASHEVILLE, N.C.

TO

| | Flight # | Departure Time | Arrival Time | # of Stops |
|---|---|---|---|---|
| Augusta, Ga. | 88/918 | _____ | _____ | _____ |
| Charleston, W. Va. | 60 | _____ | _____ | _____ |
| Columbia, S.C. | 88/918 | _____ | _____ | _____ |

2. How many flights leave Asheville each day for

    Atlanta, Ga.? _____

    Chicago, Ill.? _____

    Columbus, Ohio? _____

3. If you leave for Atlanta, Ga., at 9:52, you will be on what flight? _____

4. If you leave Asheville for Augusta, in what city will you have to make a connection? _____

5. What will be your flight number when you leave the connecting city for Columbus, Ohio? _____

6. Name at least four cities to which this airline has nonstop flights. _____

    _____

    _____

7. Flight #62 from Asheville to Fayetteville/Fort Bragg, N.C., operates daily except _____ .

8. Which flight makes the most stops? _____

Column 1–*Leave* = Time plane leaves Asheville, N.C.

Column 2–*Arrive* = Time plane arrives in desired city

Column 3–*Flight No.* = Number identifying a particular flight

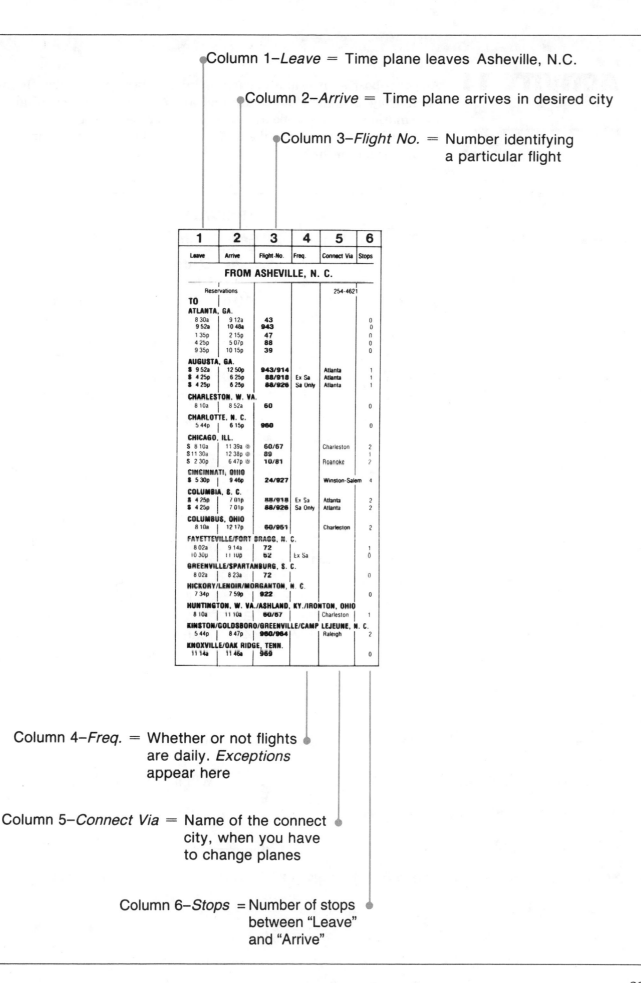

| 1 | 2 | 3 | 4 | 5 | 6 |
|---|---|---|---|---|---|
| Leave | Arrive | Flight-No. | Freq. | Connect Via | Stops |

### FROM ASHEVILLE, N. C.

| | | | | | |
|---|---|---|---|---|---|
| Reservations | | | | 254-4621 | |

**TO**

**ATLANTA, GA.**
| 8 30a | 9 12a | 43 | | | 0 |
| 9 52a | 10 48a | 943 | | | 0 |
| 1 35p | 2 15p | 47 | | | 0 |
| 4 25p | 5 07p | 88 | | | 0 |
| 9 35p | 10 15p | 39 | | | 0 |

**AUGUSTA, GA.**
| S 9 52a | 12 50p | 943/914 | | Atlanta | 1 |
| S 4 25p | 6 25p | 88/918 | Ex Sa | Atlanta | 1 |
| S 4 25p | 6 25p | 88/926 | Sa Only | Atlanta | 1 |

**CHARLESTON, W. VA.**
| 8 10a | 8 52a | 60 | | | 0 |

**CHARLOTTE, N. C.**
| 5 44p | 6 15p | 960 | | | 0 |

**CHICAGO, ILL.**
| S 8 10a | 11 39a ⓐ | 60/67 | | Charleston | 2 |
| S 11 30a | 12 38p ⓐ | 89 | | | 1 |
| S 2 30p | 6 47p ⓐ | 10/81 | | Roanoke | 2 |

**CINCINNATI, OHIO**
| S 5 30p | 9 46p | 24/927 | | Winston-Salem | 4 |

**COLUMBIA, S. C.**
| S 4 25p | 7 01p | 88/918 | Ex Sa | Atlanta | 2 |
| S 4 25p | 7 01p | 88/926 | Sa Only | Atlanta | 2 |

**COLUMBUS, OHIO**
| 8 10a | 12 17p | 60/951 | | Charleston | 2 |

**FAYETTEVILLE/FORT BRAGG, N. C.**
| 8 02a | 9 14a | 72 | | | 1 |
| 10 30p | 11 10p | 62 | Ex Sa | | 0 |

**GREENVILLE/SPARTANBURG, S. C.**
| 8 02a | 8 23a | 72 | | | 0 |

**HICKORY/LENOIR/MORGANTON, N. C.**
| 7 34p | 7 59p | 922 | | | 0 |

**HUNTINGTON, W. VA./ASHLAND, KY./IRONTON, OHIO**
| 8 10a | 11 10a | 60/67 | | Charleston | 1 |

**KINSTON/GOLDSBORO/GREENVILLE/CAMP LEJEUNE, N. C.**
| 5 44p | 8 47p | 960/964 | | Raleigh | 2 |

**KNOXVILLE/OAK RIDGE, TENN.**
| 11 14a | 11 46a | 969 | | | 0 |

Column 4–*Freq.* = Whether or not flights are daily. *Exceptions* appear here

Column 5–*Connect Via* = Name of the connect city, when you have to change planes

Column 6–*Stops* = Number of stops between "Leave" and "Arrive"

## ACTIVITY 11
### Reading an airport terminal schedule

Airports post arrival and departure information. They show flight numbers. They also show departure and arrival times for these flights. This information usually appears on a screen or board. Some airports show destinations and gate numbers. They may also show whether a plane is delayed, on time, or boarding.

### ARRIVALS

| Time | Flight # | Gate | From | Comments |
|------|----------|------|------|----------|
| 2:15 | 72 | 7 | Detroit | Arrived |
| 2:20 | 174 | 9 | Chicago | Landing |
| 2:45 | 49 | 10 | Houston | On Time |
| 2:50 | 74 | 6 | Dallas | On Time |
| 3:00 | 711 | 5 | Los Angeles | Delayed |
| 3:10 | 80 | 4 | Roanoke | On Time |
| 3:15 | 39 | 3 | Houston | On Time |
| 3:20 | 63 | 2 | Boston | On Time |

TIME 2:17

### DEPARTURES

| Time | Flight # | Gate | To | Comments |
|------|----------|------|------|----------|
| 3:10 | 71 | 33 | Cleveland | Boarding |
| 3:20 | 412 | 36 | Boston | On Time |
| 3:30 | 576 | 34 | San Francisco | On Time |
| 3:45 | 232 | 35 | Dallas/Ft. Worth | On Time |
| 4:00 | 109 | 39 | Chicago | On Time |
| 4:10 | 57 | 41 | Detroit | On Time |
| 4:15 | 74 | 32 | Memphis | Delayed |

TIME 3:06

Answer these questions about the schedules above.

1. What time is flight 80 scheduled to arrive? _____ Will it be on time? _____

2. What time is flight 711 scheduled to arrive? _____ Will it be on time? _____

3. Which flight arrives at Gate 10? _____ Gate 6? _____ Gate 3? _____

4. You have to meet a friend arriving from Chicago at 2:20. It is 2:17. Is the plane at the gate?

_____

**5.** What time is flight 74 scheduled to leave for Memphis? _____

Will it leave on time? _____

**6.** Is flight 71 to Cleveland delayed? _____

**7.** Are passengers boarding flight 71 to Cleveland? If so, what gate are they using? _____

**8.** What is the flight number of the 3:20 flight to Boston? _____

**9.** Where is flight 57 scheduled to go? _____

# ACTIVITY 12
## Understanding timetables

Some timetables must be read down one side and up the other. The names of the stops are centered. Schedule information is on both sides.

In this timetable you read down to find departure times for buses going in one direction (Ocean City, Md.) You read up the opposite side to find departure times for buses going in the opposite direction (Philadelphia, Pa.). Like all transportation timetables, this timetable shows arrival and departure times as either A.M. or P.M. In this timetable, A.M. is in lightface type, P.M. is in boldface (heavier) type. Other special information is explained at the bottom of the timetable.

Answer the questions about this interstate bus timetable.

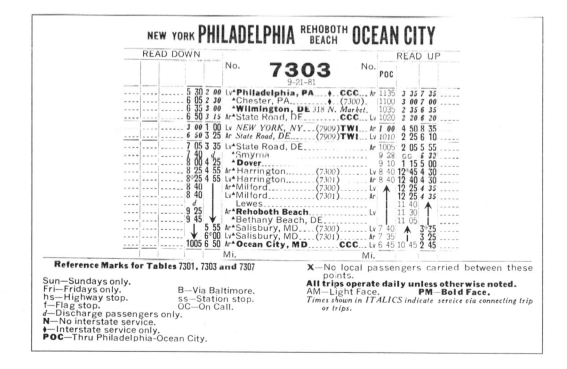

**1.** This timetable shows buses connecting what two main points? _____

**2.** If you were traveling from Chester, Pa., to Ocean City, Md., would you read *up* or *down* the schedule?

_____

3. If you were traveling from Ocean City, Md., to Chester, Pa., would you read *up* or *down* the schedule? _____

4. What time does the bus that leaves Philadelphia at 5:30 arrive in Ocean City? _____

5. What time is this bus scheduled to leave Chester, Pa.? _____

   Wilmington, Del.? _____

6. What time is this bus scheduled to arrive at Delaware (State Road stop)? _____

   Harrington, Del.? _____

   Milford, Del.? _____

7. If you left New York City at 3:00 in the afternoon, at what stop would you connect with the bus going to Ocean City? _____

8. List all the stops the 2:45 Ocean City bus makes before it gets to State Road.

   1st STOP _____

   2nd STOP _____

   3rd STOP _____

   4th STOP _____

   5th STOP _____

9. If you left New York City on the 1:00 bus, what time would you arrive at the State Road stop in Delaware? _____

10. What time does the 5:30 bus out of Philadelphia arrive at the State Road stop in Delaware?

   _____

The timetable below shows the train going from Salt Lake City to Seattle. And it shows the train from Seattle to Salt Lake City. You read down the left side of the schedule to find departure times for trains going to Seattle. These trains are traveling westward. You read up the opposite side of the schedule to find departure times for trains going to Salt Lake City. These trains are traveling eastward.

### The Pioneer

**Salt Lake City
Ogden
Boise
Portland
Seattle**

| READ DOWN | | | | | READ UP |
|---|---|---|---|---|---|
| 25 | | | Train Number | | 26 |
| Daily | | | Frequency of Operation | | Daily |
| 🛏 ☒ ▢ | | | Type of Service | | 🛏 ☒ ▢ |
| | Km | Mi | *(Union Pacific)* | | |
| 11 25 P | 0 | 0 | Dp **Salt Lake City, UT** *(Amtrak Sta.) (MT)* Ar | | 7 10 A |
| 12 20 A | 58 | 36 | Ar **Ogden, UT** Dp | | 6 10 A |
| 12 35 A | 58 | 36 | Dp Ar | | 5 55 A |
| F 1 05 A | 92 | 57 | Brigham City, UT ● | | F 5 25 A |
| 3 20 A | 276 | 170 | Ar **Pocatello, ID** Dp | | 3 10 A |
| 3 30 A | 276 | 170 | Dp Ar | | 3 00 A |
| 5 15 A | 447 | 278 | Shoshone, ID ● | | 1 10 A |
| F 6 30 A | 576 | 358 | Mountain Home, ID ● | | F 11 55 P |
| 7 30 A | 650 | 404 | **Boise, ID** | | 10 50 P |
| 8 10 A | 682 | 424 | Nampa, ID ● *(Caldwell)* | | 10 10 P |
| 8 50 A | 750 | 466 | Ontario, OR ● *(MT)* | | 9 30 P |
| 9 50 A | 890 | 553 | Baker, OR ● *(PT)* | | 6 30 P |
| 11 10 A | 975 | 606 | La Grande, OR ● | | 5 30 P |
| 1 30 P | 1094 | 680 | Pendleton, OR ● | | 3 10 P |
| 2 05 P | 1144 | 711 | Hinkle, OR ● *(Hermiston)* | | 2 35 P |
| 3 35 P | 1302 | 809 | The Dalles, OR ● | | 1 00 P |
| F 4 10 P | 1339 | 832 | Hood River, OR ● | | F 12 30 P |
| 5 50 P | 1440 | 895 | Ar **Portland, OR** Dp | | 11 10 A |
| 6 00 P | 1440 | 895 | Dp Ar | | 11 00 A |
| | | | *(Burlington Northern)* | | |
| 6 21 P | 1456 | 905 | Vancouver, WA | | 10 33 A |
| 7 00 P | 1519 | 944 | Kelso-Longview, WA | | 9 55 A |
| 7 45 P | 1588 | 987 | Centralia, WA | | 9 06 A |
| 8 05 P | 1619 | 1006 | East Olympia, WA ● | | 8 46 A |
| 8 50 P | 1675 | 1041 | Tacoma, WA | | 8 06 A |
| 9 50 P | 1740 | 1081 | Ar **Seattle, WA** *(King St. Sta.) (PT)* Dp | | 7 10 A |

**The Pioneer
Salt Lake City-Seattle**

### Services

Amfleet
Service

**Tray Meal and Beverage Service**—*Am-dinette*
**Sleeping Car Service**—Complimentary coffee and tea served on request 6.30-9.30 AM.
**Coach Service**—Reserved and unreserved seats.
**Baggage Service**—Checked baggage handled at Ogden, Pocatello, Boise, Portland and Seattle.

Answer these questions about this timetable. Read *down* the schedule.

**1.** What is the name of this train? _____

**2.** What is the number of this train when it is going from Salt Lake City to Seattle? _____

Seattle to Salt Lake City? _____

**3.** What time does this train leave Salt Lake City for Seattle? _____

**4.** What time does this train arrive in Ogden? _____

303

**5.** What time does it leave Ogden? _____

**6.** What time does this train leave La Grande, Ore.? _____ Pendleton, Ore.? _____

Portland, Ore.? _____ Vancouver, Wash.? _____

**7.** What time is the train scheduled to arrive in Seattle? _____

Answer these questions about this timetable. This time read *up* the schedule.

**1.** What time does the train leave Seattle for Salt Lake City? _____

**2.** What is the first stop after Seattle? _____

**3.** What time does the train arrive in Portland? _____

**4.** What time does it leave Portland? _____

**5.** What is the stop before Nampa, Idaho? _____

**6.** What time is this train due to arrive in Salt Lake City? _____

# SHOW WHAT YOU KNOW . . .

## About Timetables

According to the timetable on page 303, how many hours does it take the *Pioneer* to go from Salt Lake City to Seattle? How many miles is it? Figure out how many miles an hour the train travels on the average.

## Charts and graphs

**Charts**   Some information can be found and understood more quickly if it appears in a chart or graph. It is often easier to see how one set of information changes or depends on another. A chart lists information. It also helps you make comparisons.

**ANNUAL FUEL COSTS CHART**

**Dollars Per Gallon**

| ESTIMATED MPG | 1.40 | 1.30 | 1.20 | 1.10 | 1.00 | 0.90 | 0.80 |
|---|---|---|---|---|---|---|---|
| 50 | $420 | $390 | $360 | $330 | $300 | $270 | $240 |
| 49 | 428 | 398 | 367 | 337 | 304 | 275 | 245 |
| 48 | 437 | 406 | 374 | 343 | 312 | 281 | 250 |
| 47 | 447 | 415 | 383 | 351 | 320 | 288 | 256 |
| 46 | 456 | 423 | 391 | 358 | 326 | 293 | 260 |
| 45 | 466 | 433 | 400 | 366 | 333 | 300 | 266 |
| 44 | 477 | 443 | 409 | 375 | 340 | 306 | 272 |
| 43 | 489 | 454 | 419 | 384 | 350 | 315 | 280 |
| 42 | 500 | 464 | 428 | 393 | 357 | 321 | 286 |
| 41 | 512 | 476 | 439 | 403 | 366 | 329 | 293 |
| 40 | 525 | 488 | 450 | 412 | 375 | 338 | 300 |
| 39 | 538 | 499 | 461 | 422 | 384 | 346 | 307 |
| 38 | 552 | 513 | 473 | 434 | 394 | 355 | 316 |
| 37 | 567 | 526 | 486 | 446 | 405 | 364 | 324 |
| 36 | 584 | 542 | 500 | 459 | 417 | 375 | 334 |
| 35 | 601 | 558 | 515 | 472 | 429 | 386 | 343 |
| 34 | 617 | 573 | 529 | 485 | 441 | 397 | 353 |
| 33 | 636 | 591 | 545 | 500 | 454 | 409 | 364 |
| 32 | 655 | 608 | 562 | 515 | 468 | 421 | 374 |
| 31 | 678 | 630 | 581 | 533 | 484 | 436 | 388 |
| 30 | 699 | 649 | 599 | 549 | 500 | 450 | 400 |
| 29 | 724 | 673 | 621 | 569 | 518 | 466 | 414 |
| 28 | 750 | 696 | 643 | 589 | 536 | 482 | 428 |
| 27 | 777 | 722 | 666 | 610 | 555 | 500 | 444 |
| 26 | 808 | 751 | 693 | 635 | 578 | 520 | 462 |
| 25 | 840 | 780 | 720 | 660 | 600 | 540 | 480 |
| 24 | 876 | 813 | 751 | 688 | 626 | 563 | 500 |
| 23 | 914 | 848 | 783 | 718 | 652 | 587 | 522 |
| 22 | 956 | 887 | 819 | 751 | 682 | 614 | 546 |
| 21 | 1000 | 928 | 857 | 785 | 714 | 643 | 571 |
| 20 | 1050 | 975 | 900 | 825 | 750 | 675 | 600 |
| 19 | 1105 | 1026 | 947 | 868 | 789 | 710 | 631 |
| 18 | 1168 | 1084 | 1001 | 917 | 834 | 751 | 667 |
| 17 | 1235 | 1147 | 1058 | 970 | 882 | 794 | 706 |
| 16 | 1312 | 1219 | 1125 | 1031 | 938 | 844 | 750 |
| 15 | 1401 | 1301 | 1201 | 1101 | 1000 | 900 | 800 |
| 14 | 1499 | 1392 | 1285 | 1178 | 1071 | 964 | 857 |
| 13 | 1615 | 1500 | 1384 | 1269 | 1154 | 1038 | 923 |
| 12 | 1749 | 1624 | 1499 | 1374 | 1250 | 1125 | 1000 |
| 11 | 1909 | 1773 | 1636 | 1500 | 1364 | 1227 | 1091 |
| 10 | 2100 | 1950 | 1800 | 1630 | 1500 | 1350 | 1200 |
| 9 | 2333 | 2166 | 2000 | 1833 | 1666 | 1500 | 1333 |
| 8 | 2625 | 2438 | 2250 | 2062 | 1875 | 1688 | 1500 |
| 7 | 3001 | 2787 | 2572 | 2358 | 2144 | 1929 | 1715 |
| 6 | 3501 | 3251 | 3031 | 2751 | 2500 | 2250 | 2000 |
| 5 | 4200 | 3900 | 3600 | 3300 | 3000 | 2700 | 2400 |

The chart shows annual fuel costs. Different cars get different gas mileage. This chart shows the cost of gasoline for one year. It shows this based on the average number of miles a car gets per gallon of gas. The miles per gallon (MPG) are shown vertically. They are on the left side of the chart. The cost of gasoline is shown horizontally. "Dollars Per Gallon" appears across the top of the chart. Let's say your car gets about 36 miles to a gallon. You locate "36" in the vertical column labeled ESTIMATED MPG. Then you read across the top of the chart. You find what you pay for gasoline. If you pay $1.30 per gallon, your annual fuel cost is $542.

# ACTIVITY 13
## Reading a temperature chart

Below is a temperature chart. It gives the average high and low Fahrenheit temperatures for three states. They are Georgia, North Carolina, and South Carolina. Study the chart. Then answer the questions.

Note: Maximum temperatures appear above the line. Minimum temperatures appear below the line.

### Temperature Averages - Maximum/Minimum
From the records of the National Weather Service

| | JAN. | FEB. | MAR. | APR. | MAY | JUNE | JULY | AUG. | SEPT. | OCT. | NOV. | DEC. |
|---|---|---|---|---|---|---|---|---|---|---|---|---|
| **GEORGIA** | | | | | | | | | | | | |
| Atlanta | 54/36 | 57/37 | 63/41 | 72/50 | 81/59 | 87/66 | 88/69 | 88/68 | 83/63 | 74/52 | 62/40 | 53/35 |
| Augusta | 59/36 | 62/37 | 67/43 | 77/50 | 84/59 | 91/67 | 91/70 | 91/69 | 87/64 | 78/52 | 68/40 | 59/35 |
| Columbus | 59/37 | 61/38 | 67/43 | 76/51 | 85/60 | 91/68 | 92/71 | 91/70 | 87/65 | 78/53 | 67/42 | 59/36 |
| Macon | 60/38 | 63/39 | 69/45 | 78/53 | 87/61 | 93/69 | 93/71 | 92/70 | 88/65 | 79/54 | 68/43 | 60/38 |
| Savannah | 63/41 | 64/42 | 70/47 | 77/54 | 85/62 | 90/69 | 91/71 | 91/71 | 86/67 | 78/56 | 69/46 | 63/40 |
| **NORTH CAROLINA** | | | | | | | | | | | | |
| Asheville | 49/30 | 51/31 | 57/36 | 68/44 | 76/53 | 83/60 | 85/64 | 74/63 | 79/57 | 69/46 | 57/36 | 50/30 |
| Cape Hatteras | 52/40 | 54/40 | 58/44 | 66/52 | 75/61 | 82/69 | 84/72 | 84/72 | 80/68 | 71/59 | 63/50 | 55/42 |
| Charlotte | 53/33 | 56/34 | 62/39 | 72/49 | 80/58 | 88/66 | 89/69 | 88/68 | 83/62 | 74/50 | 63/39 | 53/33 |
| Raleigh | 52/31 | 54/32 | 61/38 | 72/47 | 79/56 | 86/64 | 87/68 | 88/67 | 82/60 | 73/48 | 62/38 | 52/31 |
| Winston-Salem | 50/32 | 52/32 | 59/37 | 70/47 | 79/56 | 87/65 | 88/68 | 87/67 | 81/62 | 72/49 | 60/38 | 50/32 |
| **SOUTH CAROLINA** | | | | | | | | | | | | |
| Charleston | 59/44 | 60/44 | 65/50 | 73/58 | 81/66 | 86/73 | 88/75 | 82/75 | 83/70 | 75/61 | 66/50 | 59/44 |
| Columbia | 58/36 | 61/36 | 67/42 | 76/51 | 85/60 | 92/70 | 93/71 | 92/70 | 86/65 | 77/52 | 67/41 | 58/35 |
| Florence | 58/37 | 60/37 | 67/43 | 76/51 | 84/60 | 90/68 | 91/70 | 90/70 | 85/64 | 77/53 | 67/43 | 58/36 |
| Spartanburg | 53/35 | 55/35 | 62/40 | 72/50 | 81/59 | 88/67 | 89/69 | 88/68 | 82/63 | 73/52 | 62/41 | 53/34 |

1. What is the maximum average temperature in Atlanta, Georgia, in January? _____

2. What is the minimum average temperature in Atlanta, Georgia, in January? _____

3. What is the maximum average temperature in Macon, Georgia, in July? _____

4. During which month does Columbus, Georgia, have its lowest temperature? _____

5. During which month does Raleigh, North Carolina, have its highest temperature? _____

6. Which city has the highest temperature in August—Charleston or Florence? _____

7. Which city has the lowest temperature in January? _____

8. Which city has the highest temperature in January? _____

# ACTIVITY 14

Use this chart of recreation areas to answer the questions below.

## Reading a recreation site chart

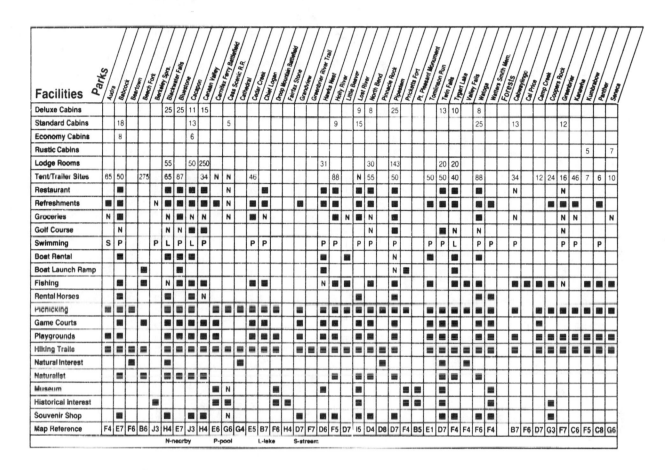

1. If you want to know which parks have a particular feature (for example, hiking trails), would you read *down* this chart or *across* ? _____

2. If you want to know which features a particular park has (for example, Bluestone), would you read *down* this chart or *across*? _____

3. Does Grandview have cabins? _____

4. List the parks with boat ramps. _____

_____

5. Which parks have lakes? _____

_____

6. How is a "nearby" facility shown on this chart? _____

**Graphs** Graphs give information, too. Look at the graph below. It shows the annual attendance at the local zoo.

**ATTENDANCE AT LOCAL ZOO**

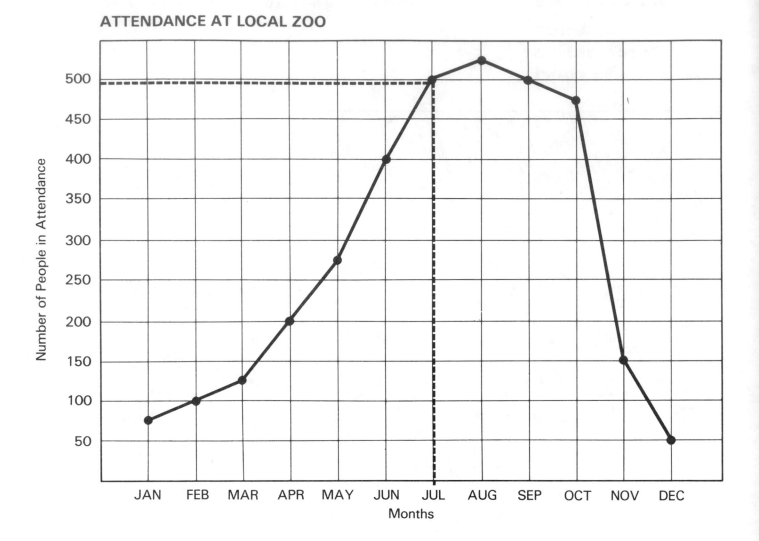

The vertical axis shows the number of people in attendance. It is divided into units of 50 through 500. The horizontal axis shows the months of the year. You plot information on the graph. You do this by locating the point where the horizontal and vertical lines meet. The horizontal point shows the month. The vertical point shows the number of people at the zoo. In July there were 500 people in attendance at the local zoo.

You form the lines on the graph by connecting the dots. Each dot represents attendance for a given month. This type of graph is a line graph.

# ACTIVITY 15

### Reading a line graph

How did the track team do with its potato chip sales? How many cases of popcorn did the cheerleaders sell? What is the best month for popcorn sales? What is the best month for potato chips? Use the information plotted on this line graph to answer the questions below.

**POPCORN & POTATO CHIP SALES:**
Cheerleading Squad and School Track Team

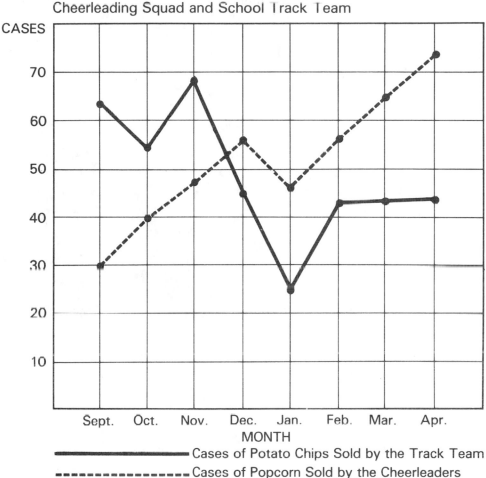

———— Cases of Potato Chips Sold by the Track Team
-------------- Cases of Popcorn Sold by the Cheerleaders

1. Which group had the highest sales in the month of September? _____

2. Which group had the highest sales in the month of January? _____

3. How many cases of popcorn did the cheerleaders sell in March? _____

4. How many cases of potato chips did the track team sell in November? _____

5. Which group had the lowest-selling month? _____

6. The sales program came to an end in April. Which group was making the most sales by the end of the

   selling program? _____

## ACTIVITY 16

### Reading a bar graph

Another type of graph is the bar graph. Here is an example of a bar graph.

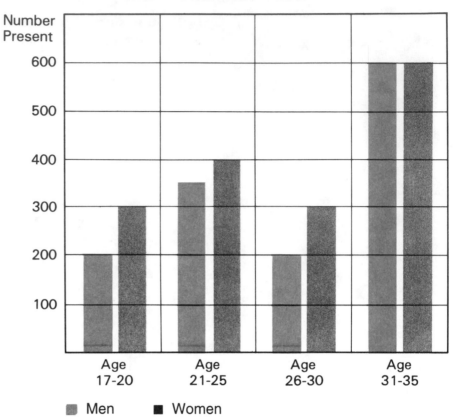

**THEATER ATTENDANCE – MAY 5**

■ Men    ■ Women

Use the graph to answer these questions.

1. How many women between 17 and 20 attended the theater on May 5? _____

2. How many men between 17 and 20? _____

3. Which age group had the highest attendance on May 5? _____

4. What was the total attendance for the 26–30 age group? _____

5. Which age group, including men and women, had more than 500 present? _____

6. Which age groups had the same overall attendance on May 5? _____

7. What was the total attendance for the 17–20 age group on May 5? _____

8. On May 5, did more men or more women attend the theater? _____

# ACTIVITY 17

### Reading a circle graph

A circle graph shows the relationship of parts to a whole. You can divide a circle into sections. Then you can compare one section with another. You can also compare one section with the whole circle. Look at the budget circle below.

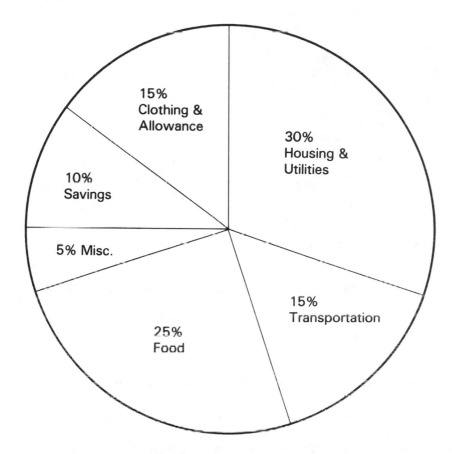

This graph shows how the Jacksons, a family of three, spend their yearly income. The questions that follow are about the Jacksons' budget circle. Choose the letter that correctly answers each question.

_____ 1. How much of the Jacksons' budget goes toward housing and utilities?
a. 10%     c. 30%
b. 20%     d. 40%

_____ 2. What percent do they save?
a. 10%     c. 30%
b. 20%     d. 5%

_____ 3. Which two sections make up a little more than half of the Jacksons' budget?
a. Savings and Food
b. Food and Transportation
c. Miscellaneous (Misc.) and Food
d. Housing & Utilities and Food

_____ 4. Which section is the smallest part of the budget?
a. Transportation
b. Miscellaneous (Misc.)
c. Food
d. Clothing & Allowances

_____ 5. If the Jacksons' budget got too tight, which of these items could they eliminate?
a. Housing & Utilities
b. Food
c. Transportation
d. Savings

Study the circle and bar graphs below.

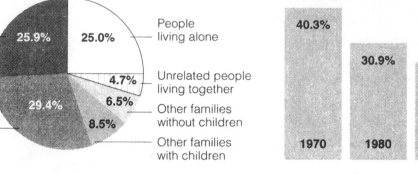

**Family Arrangements**

Percentage of all U.S. households in 1991. "Children" refer to a family's own child or children under age 18.

Married couple with children — 25.9%
25.0% — People living alone
4.7% — Unrelated people living together
6.5% — Other families without children
29.4%
Married couple without children
8.5% — Other families with children

**Shrinking Minority**

Married couples with a child or children under age 18, as a percentage of all households.

40.3% — 1970
30.9% — 1980
25.9% — 1991

Source: U.S. Census Bureau

1. Look at the circle graph. What percentage of people in the United States live alone? _____

2. Which percentage is greater—married couples with children or married couples without children?

   _____

3. Add the percentage of married couples with children to the percentage of married couples without children. Is the total number of married couples over or under 50 percent? _____

4. Look at the bar graph. What was the percentage of married couples with a child or children in 1970?

   _____

5. Was the decrease shown on the bar graph greater between 1970 and 1980 or between 1980 and 1991? _____

# SHOW WHAT YOU KNOW . . .

## About Charts and Graphs

Turn back to the temperature chart on page 306. On a sheet of graph paper make a bar graph showing the average maximum and minimum temperatures for Cape Hatteras. Use the graph on page 310 as a model. Label your graph and show a key.

HINT: Show the temperatures on a vertical axis in multiples of 5, beginning with 35° at the bottom. Show months on the horizontal axis.

# 12

# Writing Workshop

You will need effective written and oral English skills throughout your life. By now you have probably mastered oral skills. There are many reasons why people understand you when you speak. First, you are able to use gestures and facial expressions. Second, you can use your voice to stress words and phrases. Anyone can tell when you are happy or annoyed. Your tone of voice helps to carry the message. Your voice has pitch patterns, too. You raise your voice at the end of a question. You use a lower pitch when you make a statement. Finally, people give you feedback. People listening to you respond in some way to what you say. If someone doesn't understand you, he or she may frown or raise an eyebrow. A person may even ask, "What did you say?" or "What do you mean?" When speaking you can always rephrase what you have said. If you have to, you can start over. A person's response to what you say can let you know if you've said enough or too much.

Written communication is different. No one can hear your voice rise when you ask a question. No one can hear it fall when you make a statement. A reader cannot sense any pauses between thoughts. If you use a wrong word, a reader can't tell you he or she is confused. And if you make mistakes in spelling, a reader may simply conclude that you're not very smart.

You will be asked to express yourself in writing many times. There are always written assignments in school. There will be times when you will have to write on the job, too. Social workers write case reports. Secretaries write minutes of meetings. Supervisors often have to write training materials and employee evaluations. Almost everyone will have to write messages and memos. You need basic writing skills in managing your personal life, too. Both business and personal letters require writing skills. Resumes and job applications require that you write. Good writing skills are a necessary part of adult life. These skills must be mastered if you are to express yourself effectively.

In any subject you study, such as sports, cooking, or business, there are certain words you need to know. You need to know certain words when you study writing, too. The following word list is divided into two parts: Words for Parts of Speech and Words for Parts of a Sentence. Refer to these two lists as you study this chapter.

## Words for parts of speech

### WORDS TO KNOW

**adjective**   word that limits or adds to the meaning of a noun (a *large* hat, *his* chair)

**adverb**   word that modifies a verb, adjective, or another adverb (dive *deeply, very* deep dive, dive *quite* deeply)

**conjunction**   word joining two words, clauses, phrases, or sentences. Some conjunctions are *and, but, however, since, after,* and *because.*

**noun**   name of a person, place, thing, or quality. *Connie, home, car,* and *happiness* are nouns. The plural of most nouns is formed by adding *-s* or *-es.* In a sentence, a noun functions as a subject, object of a verb, or object of a preposition. *Proper nouns* are names of particular people and places and are capitalized (*Fred, Kansas City, Field Museum*).

**preposition**   word relating a noun, phrase, or clause to another word. It usually comes before a noun in a sentence (wheel *of* fortune, *in* the shower, *over* the fence).

**pronoun**   word used instead of a noun. *I, me, we, you, whose, which, mine,* and *myself* are some pronouns.

**verb**   word that expresses action or being. In the sentence "Carrie plays the guitar," *plays* is the verb.

>   **helping verb**   word used with other verbs. *Am, will, have* are some helping verbs. They are sometimes called *auxiliaries.*

>   **linking verb**   word that connects or links the subject of a sentence with another word. Linking verbs have very little meaning of their own. Some linking verbs are *is, was, became.*

## Words for parts of a sentence

**WORDS TO KNOW**

**clause**   part of a compound or compound-complex sentence. It usually has a subject and a verb. Main clauses can stand alone. Dependent or subordinate clauses cannot stand alone.

**complement**   noun or adjective that completes the meaning of a linking verb. A complement modifies the subject. In "She was kind," *kind* modifies *she.*

**direct object**   noun or pronoun that follows a verb and is related to the action of a verb. (Oscar moved the *furniture.*)

**indirect object**   noun or pronoun used with verbs of giving, telling, asking, sending, and so on. It usually comes before the direct object. (Bob gave the *child* a quarter.)

**modifier**   word that limits or makes more exact the meaning of another word. Adjectives and adverbs are two kinds of modifiers (a *cold* day, sitting *quietly*).

**object of a preposition**   word or group of words whose relation to another part of a sentence is shown by the preposition. In "She pitched the ball to the catcher," *to* is the preposition and *catcher* is the object of the preposition.

> **phrase**   group of two or more words that are related. A phrase has no subject. In "He jumped over the fence," *over the fence* is a prepositional phrase.
>
> **predicate**   the verb part of a clause or sentence with its modifiers, object, complement, and so on. A predicate tells what is said about the subject. In "The horse won," the verb *won* is the predicate. In "The horse won the race easily," *won the race easily* is the predicate.
>
> **subject**   word or group of words that perform the action of a verb. It usually stands before the verb (*Greg* disappeared; *Sara* and *Lucy* planted a garden).

## Sentence patterns

What makes your writing effective? What must you do to be sure a reader can make sense of what you say? A number of skills are needed to produce clear writing. One of these skills is using correct sentence patterns. For example, you would never write *John home went*. It is not a correct speech pattern in English. Your knowledge of the English language is probably greater than you realize. You are probably already familiar with basic sentence patterns in the English language.

**Pattern 1**

| Subject | Verb |
|---------|------|
| The boy | walked. |
| I | listened. |
| He | jumped. |

**Pattern 2**

| Subject | Verb | Direct Object |
|---------|------|---------------|
| Birds | eat | seeds. |
| The plumber | fixed | the faucet. |
| I | bought | the book. |

**Pattern 3**

| Subject | Verb | Indirect Object | Direct Object |
|---------|------|-----------------|---------------|
| You | gave | the birds | the seeds. |
| The plumber | gave | Mary | the bill. |
| I | asked | Hector | a question. |

**Pattern 4**

| Subject | Linking Verb | Complement |
|---------|--------------|------------|
| Pierre | is | French. |
| Marva | was | angry. |
| They | were | winners. |
| Natalie | is | happy. |
| We | are | busy. |

**Verbs**     A sentence is the expression of a complete thought. Except in a very few cases, a sentence has a subject and a verb.

A verb expresses action or being. It tells what is or what is done. The verbs below express some sort of action.

       **v**
Joyce smiled.

  **v**
I stopped the noise.

Some verbs are called *linking* verbs. Some typical linking verbs, forms of the verb *be,* are: *became, tastes, looks, seems, felt.* They link the subject with other words. The verbs in the sentences below are linking verbs.

   **l v**
Mark was rich.

            **l v**
Uncle Bill and Aunt Tina became worried.

Verbs can tell you whether the action occurred in the past or will happen in the future. Verbs can tell you whether the action is happening now. Sometimes *-s, -ed,* or *-ing* is added to a verb.

My dog *follows* me everywhere.
He *followed* them, too.
He is *following* you.

Sometimes another word is added to a verb. This added word is called a *helping* verb.

  **h v**                **h v**
She has run away.        I am leaving.
 **h v**                  **h v**
I will return.           He should stay.

Some verbs change their form to show when an action happens.

You will *tear* your raincoat.
I *tore* my sweater.
I have *torn* my jacket.

You will learn more of these verbs that change their form later.

## ACTIVITY 1
### Using Verbs

Add a different verb to each item to make it a sentence.

1. Sam _____ silently.

2. They _____ quickly.

3. You _____ clearly.

4. Kim _____ a delicious dinner.

5. Cal _____ an old movie.

6. Rosie _____ the piano.

7. Kezia _____ a silver ring.

8. David _____ a cartoon.

9. Laura and her sister _____ glasses of cider.

10. Margarita _____ a long letter.

## Subjects

The subject of a sentence is a word or group of words that perform the action of a verb. Often the subject is a noun or pronoun.

   **s**    **v**
Marla hates celery. (Marla performs the action of hating.)

   **s**      **s**   **v**
Lee and Adrienne won the trophies. (Lee and Adrienne performed the action of winning.)

       **s**   **v**
Four nations signed a peace treaty. (The nations performed the action of signing.)

**s**   **v**
I repaired the chair. (I performed the action of repairing.)

## ACTIVITY 2
### Using subjects

Add a different subject to each item to make it a sentence. Draw a line under the verb in each sentence.

1. _____ blew a whistle.

2. _____ swam under water.

3. _____ delivered the paper.

4. _____ scrubbed the floor.

5. _____ and _____ found ten dollars.

6. Three _____ contributed twenty-five dollars.

7. Two _____ fought over boundaries.

8. One aunt and two _____ sat on the porch.

9. Several _____ wrote letters to the paper.

10. Some _____ seldom vote.

## Direct objects and indirect objects

A sentence may have a direct object. A direct object usually follows the verb, and it is related to the action of the verb.

    **s**    **v**   **d o**
Marla hates celery.

    **s**    **v**   **d o**
James made popcorn.

    **s**    **v**    **d o**
Jennifer could see the boat plainly.

With verbs of giving, telling, asking, sending, and so on, there is often an indirect object. An indirect object names the receiver of the gift, the message, the question, and so on.

    **s**    **v**   **i o**   **d o**
Stephen gave Marysue a ring.

     **s**    **v**   **i o**     **d o**
Mr. Munoz gave the college a large donation.

    **s**    **v**   **i o**    **d o**
Beth asked Miss Quinn a question.

## ACTIVITY 3
### Using direct objects

From the list at the right, choose a direct object to complete these sentences.

1. Janet bought _____ .

2. Will wrote _____ .

3. We planted _____ .

4. Mother baked _____ .

5. Dad washed _____ .

this book

a cake

the car

a letter

that rose

a sweater

a chicken

a pear tree

319

## ACTIVITY 4
### Using indirect objects

Add a different indirect object to each item to make it a sentence. Underline the direct objects.

1. The waiter gave _____ the bill.

2. The bus driver handed _____ a transfer.

3. Fred sent _____ a present.

4. Susan passed _____ a note.

5. Lupe brought _____ a photo.

## Complements

Complements come after linking verbs and refer to the subject. Complements are nouns or adjectives.

      s      lv   c
Mother and Dad were tired.

        s   v   c
The window is cracked.

     s          v  c
The boy in the red wig is Peter.

## ACTIVITY 5
### Using complements

Add a different complement to each item to make it a sentence. Underline the linking verb.

1. We felt _____ .

2. They are _____ .

3. Carol seems _____ .

4. Bea will be _____ .

5. Michael was _____ .

320

# SHOW WHAT YOU KNOW . . .

## About Sentence Patterns

Make up four sentences and write them on the lines below. The first two should have a direct object. The third should have a direct object and an indirect object. The fourth should have a complement.

(Use a direct object.) 1. _____

_____

_____

(Use a direct object.) 2. _____

_____

_____

(Use a direct object and an indirect object.) 3. _____

_____

_____

(Use a complement. Don't forget to use a linking verb.) 4. _____

_____

_____

## Modifiers

In addition to these basic sentence parts, a sentence may have modifiers. Modifiers are words or groups of words that limit meaning or make meaning more exact.

**m**
Kim was ten minutes early. (*Ten* tells how many minutes.)

**m**
Is that white sweater mine? (*White* tells which sweater.)

**m**
Slowly he crawled across the slippery deck. (*Slowly* tells how he crawled.)

**m**
The chorus, which was directed by Miss Page, sang five songs. (The modifier tells who directed the chorus; it modifies *chorus*.)

Two common types of modifiers are *adjectives* and *adverbs*. Adjectives modify nouns. *Ten* and *white* in the sentences above are adjectives. Adverbs modify verbs, adjectives, and other adverbs. *Slowly* modifies the verb *crawled* in the sentence above.

## ACTIVITY 6
### Using modifiers

Add modifiers to the sentences below.

1. Kate read _____ books last summer.

2. She likes to read on the _____ porch.

3. Her _____ brother likes _____ stories.

4. Does that _____ book belong to him?

5. She has to run _____ to the library before it closes.

## Kinds of sentences

Sentences are classified into four types.

1. simple

2. compound

3. complex

4. compound-complex

Being able to recognize these four types can help you write better sentences.

## The simple sentence

A simple sentence has one subject and one verb:

**s**    **v**
He drove to the airport.

A simple sentence is not necessarily a short sentence. It may have one or more modifiers. Modifiers are words or groups of words that limit meaning or make meaning more exact.

_____ **modifier** _____    _____ **modifier** _____
After stopping to buy gas, he drove to the airport through dark and rainy

_____
weather.

In a simple sentence, two or more words may be the subject:

**s**    **v**
John and I drove to the airport.

A simple sentence may have two or more verbs with the same subject:

**s**  **v**
He drove to the airport and parked.

## The compound sentence

The part of a sentence having a subject and verb is called a clause. A compound sentence has two main clauses:

**s**  **v**        **s**  **v**
He drove to the airport, but he missed his plane.

Each clause in a compound sentence can stand alone and make sense. The clauses in a compound sentence are often joined by _and, or, but,_ or _yet._ Notice the simple and compound sentences in the paragraph below.

A low hill rises at the north end of the park, the result of glacier activity thousands of years ago. A trail winds through the park, and it skirts the hill. Visitors who choose to climb the hill take a narrow path, bordered on both sides by oak and aspen trees. At the top of the hill, a breeze stirs the trees, sparrows flit quietly through the branches, and golden leaves float gently to the forest floor.

## ACTIVITY 7
### Writing sentences

Write a simple sentence with one subject and two verbs. Write a compound sentence with two main clauses joined by *and*.

1. _____

_____

2. _____

_____

### The complex sentence

A complex sentence also contains two clauses, but one clause cannot stand alone and make sense. It depends on the main clause.

        **s**    **v**      **s**  **v**
Although he was tired, he drove to the airport.

In the above sentence, one clause can stand alone and make sense: He drove to the airport.

The other clause cannot stand alone and make sense by itself: Although he was tired.

Here are some other complex sentences.

    **dependent**
  — **clause** —
Unless you call, we will leave without you.

    **dependent**
  —— **clause** ——
While you were away, we fed the fish.

      **dependent**
  ——— **clause** ———
I hope that you watered the plants.

      **dependent**
  —— **clause** ——
That teacher whom I bumped into teaches English.

In the last sentence above, *whom I bumped into* is a clause that modifies *teacher*. This clause cannot stand alone. What is the other clause in the sentence?

## The compound-complex sentence

A compound-complex sentence has two or more main clauses and one or more clauses that cannot stand alone.

    **s**    **v**                   **s**    **v**
He drove to the airport, but he missed his plane

            **dependent**
———————— **clause** ————————
because he forgot his ticket.

This sentence contains two main clauses: *He drove to the airport* and *he missed his plane.* The third clause cannot stand alone: *because he forgot his ticket.* This clause does not make sense without *he missed his plane.* It is the *complex* part of a compound-complex sentence.

---

## ACTIVITY 8

### Identifying main and dependent clauses

Each item below contains a clause. Put a check before the clauses that can stand alone. Also put a period after the clauses that can stand alone.

———— **1.** Since he was leaving anyway

———— **2.** Although she passed the house twice

———— **3.** He bought a tie for his father

———— **4.** Sweden is pleasant in June

———— **5.** If you do not think about the future

———— **6.** Because she dropped an antique dish

———— **7.** In April the road flooded

———— **8.** The gates were tightly shut

———— **9.** Poverty is the parent of revolution and crime

———— **10.** Little green leaves showed through the glass

———— **11.** When the park was filled with snow

———— **12.** All the flags were flying

———— **13.** While you were away

———— **14.** So that you can become the kind of person you want to be

———— **15.** Fortunately, the fog lifted

## ACTIVITY 9

### Using main and dependent clauses

A dependent clause is shown in each item below. These clauses cannot stand alone. Add a main clause to each item to make a complex sentence. The clause you add must have a subject and a verb and be able to stand alone.

*Example:* Before we planned our vacation, *we went to a travel agent* .

1. After we hiked ten miles, _____

    _____ .

2. Because we forgot the thermos, _____

    _____ .

3. _____ because Sue sprained her ankle.

4. _____ that rain was predicted.

5. Since the tent had a hole, _____ .

---

### CHECK YOUR UNDERSTANDING OF SENTENCES

Review the definitions of the four sentence types: simple, compound, complex, and compound-complex. Identify each sentence type below. The first one is done for you. *Hint:* There are 4 simple sentences, including the first one. There are 3 complex sentences. There are 2 compound sentences and 1 compound-complex sentence.

1. We moved into our new apartment Thursday. *simple*

2. Before we moved, we sold our couch. _____

3. The carpeting and drapes in our apartment are new. _____

4. We hired a moving company, and we moved some things ourselves. _____

5. Debbie carried the goldfish, but she forgot the cat because the cat hid in a closet. _____

    _____

6. We drove back to our old apartment. _____

7. Peaches was sitting on the front step when we arrived. _____

326

8. She looked very angry. _____

9. We took her to our new address, and Tim brushed her. _____

10. Although we like our new apartment, Peaches hates it. _____

# SHOW WHAT YOU KNOW . . .

## About Sentences

Make up a complex sentence and write it on the lines below. It must have a main clause and a dependent clause.

_____

_____

_____

_____

## Improving sentences

### Revising fragments

Writers sometimes punctuate a group of words as if it were a sentence.

> For some reason, I continued to drive the car. Although it was making an odd noise.

The writer has punctuated a sentence fragment as if it were a sentence. The fragment does have a subject and a verb, but it cannot stand alone as a sentence.

The sentence can be revised in two ways.

> For some reason, I continued to drive the car, although it was making an odd noise.

*or*

> Although the car was making an odd noise, for some reason, I continued to drive it.

A phrase is a group of two or more words that are related, but a phrase is not a sentence. In the next sentence the writer has punctuated a phrase as if it were a sentence.

> Many people fail to eat nutritious foods. Like fresh fruits and vegetables.

This fragment has no subject and no verb. It should be attached to the preceding sentence.

> Many people fail to eat nutritious foods, like fresh fruits and vegetables.

Seeing a verb form often makes writers think they see a sentence.

> Running down the hill
> Helping people who are in trouble
> Dressed as Spider Man
> To run a good race

The examples above are all fragments.

# ACTIVITY 10

## Revising sentence fragments

All of the items below contain fragments. Rewrite the items correctly.

*Example:* For only pennies a year, you will receive generous benefits. Like a subscription to our newsletter.

*For only pennies a year, you will receive generous benefits, like a subscription to our newsletter.*

1. Of the boys who tried out for basketball, only three failed to make the team. Partly because they were still too short. _____

2. Unfortunately, when we were already late. We were given the wrong directions. _____

3. The telephone rang four times. While you were watching television. _____

4. We thought you would pick up the dry cleaning. Since you were going that way. _____

5. We discovered Amy was going to be out of town. After we planned her surprise party! _____

6. The last runners arrived about four o'clock. Some limping, some barely able to talk. _____

7. People fled Europe in the nineteenth century for many reasons. Such as famine and persecution. _____

8. Flea markets do not appeal to me. Especially when they are out-of-doors in rainy weather. However, some people never miss one. _____

**Run-on sentences**    Some writers make the mistake of putting two sentences together as if they were one. They use the wrong punctuation or no punctuation at all. The result is called a run-on sentence. Run-on sentences are easy to spot. If there are two main clauses, check to see if you have a word that connects them.

> **Run-on:** I opened the door the salesperson walked in.

> **Revised:** I opened the door, *and* the salesperson walked in.

If there are two main clauses, check to see that your punctuation is correct.

> **Run-on with the wrong punctuation:** I enjoy walking on the beach, it is very relaxing.

> **Revised:** I enjoy walking on the beach. It is very relaxing.

> **Run-on with the wrong punctuation:** We studied hard for the exam, however our notes were not detailed enough.

> **Revised:** We studied hard for the exam. However, our notes were not detailed enough.
>
> *or*
>
> We studied hard for the exam; however, our notes were not detailed enough.

> *Note:* In a sentence with two independent clauses, use a semicolon (not a comma) before words like *however, therefore,* and *consequently*.

Try reading your sentences aloud. If your voice drops, or you pause at the end of the first clause, you probably need to correct the sentence. Read this sentence aloud: Eight people were invited to the party, only three came. Revise the sentence.

_____

_____

_____

_____

_____

_____

# ACTIVITY 11

## Revising run-on sentences

Revise the run-on sentences below.

1. Tornadoes and flooding often follow hurricanes, they are often as destructive as hurricanes.

2. Hurricanes frequently start in the West Indies they hit a coastline with great force they eventually lose their force as they blow across land.

3. Hurricane winds revolve in a violent counterclockwise direction as a hurricane moves, winds are often clocked at well over a hundred miles an hour.

4. Hurricanes are a fact-of-life for many U.S. coastal cities, the 1992 hurricane named Andrew was the most destructive ever known up to that time.

5. Hurricanes cannot be prevented however loss of life can be diminished when people leave homes and businesses in coastal areas and travel inland.

## Verb tenses and agreement

Using verbs correctly is important to improving sentences. A verb must *agree* in number with the subject of a sentence. The subject of a sentence is often a noun or pronoun.

A *pronoun* is a word that can be replaced by a noun. Personal pronouns are classified according to person and number.

|  | Singular | Plural |
| --- | --- | --- |
| First person | I, my, me | we, our, us |
| Second person | you, your, | you, your |
| Third person | she, her, hers, he, him, his, it, its | they, them, their |

Nouns are considered to be third person.

Most people have no trouble making verbs in the present and past tense agree with pronouns.

I play ball. We played ball.

Some writers forget that in the third person singular, *-s* is added to a verb.

|  | Singular | Plural |
| --- | --- | --- |
| First person | I ask | We ask |
| Second person | You ask | You ask |
| Third person | He ask*s* | They ask |

*Be* is a special verb. It has many forms. In the present tense, *be* has three forms:

|  | Singular | Plural |
| --- | --- | --- |
| First person | I am | We are |
| Second person | You are | You are |
| Third person | He is | They are |
|  | She is |  |
|  | It is |  |

In the past tense, *be* has two forms: *was* and *were.*

|  | Singular | Plural |
| --- | --- | --- |
| First person | I was | We were |
| Second person | You were | You were |
| Third person | She was | They were |
|  | He was |  |
|  | It was |  |

# **ACTIVITY 12**
## Using verb tenses

Select the correct verb form for each of the following sentences, and write it on the blank.

1. I (am/is) going to the beach today. ———————————————

2. The team (is/be) happy about winning. ———————————————

3. Sally (like/likes) pizza. ———————————————

4. He (buy/buys) lunch in the cafeteria. ———————————————

5. She (take/takes) her lunch to school. ———————————————

6. They (calls/call) home when they are late. ———————————————

7. You (stay/stays) there until we arrive. ———————————————

8. (Was/Were) you pleased with your grade? ———————————————

9. (Were/Was) he promoted to manager? ———————————————

10. We (was/were) on the lake when it rained. ———————————————

11. It (be/is) hard to tell which sister is younger. ———————————————

12. It (look/looks) like rain. ———————————————

13. Ken (try/tries) to be a good student. ———————————————

14. She probably (wishes/wish) she had an umbrella. ———————————————

15. He (work/works) from three to eleven on Fridays. ———————————————

# SHOW WHAT YOU KNOW . . .

## About Using Verb Tenses

Write a sentence using the verb *am.*  _____

_____

_____

Write a sentence using the verb *is.*  _____

_____

_____

## Principal parts of verbs

The principal parts of a verb are the base forms, the past tense, and the past participle. Most English verbs are *regular*. They form the past tense and past participle by adding *-ed* to the base form.

### SOME REGULAR VERBS

| Base form | Past | Past participle (with *has, have,* or *had*) |
|---|---|---|
| ask | asked | asked |
| look | looked | looked |
| work | worked | worked |
| stay | stayed | stayed |

Regular verbs cause no trouble for people. However, some verbs are classified as *irregular*. Some of these verbs change their vowels. Some of them do not change at all. Irregular verbs can often cause trouble in writing. Here is a list of some irregular verbs.

### IRREGULAR VERBS

| Base Form | Past | Past Participle (with *has, have,* or *had*) |
|---|---|---|
| begin | began | begun |
| blow | blew | blown |
| break | broke | broken |
| burst | burst | burst |
| catch | caught | caught |
| choose | chose | chosen |
| come | came | come |
| do | did | done |
| draw | drew | drawn |
| drive | drove | driven |
| eat | ate | eaten |
| freeze | froze | frozen |
| give | gave | given |
| go | went | gone |
| know | knew | known |
| run | ran | run |
| see | saw | seen |
| sit | sat | sat |
| steal | stole | stolen |
| swim | swam | swum |
| take | took | taken |
| tear | tore | torn |
| throw | threw | thrown |
| write | wrote | written |

## ACTIVITY 13

**Using verb tenses**

Select the correct verb tense for each of the following sentences.

1. The rain has (began/begun) to turn to ice. _____

2. I wonder who (wrote/has wrote) the script for that movie. _____

3. Have you (seen/saw) my watch anywhere? _____

4. He (go/went) to the park about noon. _____

5. He has (went/gone) to the pool every day. _____

6. Have you (ate/eaten) dinner yet? _____

7. They (given/gave) me the wrong change. _____

8. They have (give/gave/given) you the wrong package. _____

9. She has (run/ran) the mile. _____

10. They (throwed/threw/thrown) the suitcases in the car. _____

11. The balloon (bursted/burst), and the baby cried. _____

12. I (knowed/knew/known) the answer, but I couldn't think of it. _____

13. May I read what you have (wrote/written)? _____

14. Matt (drew/drawed) a cartoon that made us laugh. _____

---

Some writers mistakenly shift **verb tenses** in a sentence or paragraph. Verb tense shows the time of an action. Usually, the tense of all verbs in a piece of writing should be the same. The paragraph below illustrates the tense shift error.

> In the morning, Beverly *takes* a subway uptown to work. Then she *went* to her job on 58th Street. She *talks* with her boss for a few minutes. Then she *goes* to her own office. There, Beverly *planned* her day's work.

Here is the paragraph with the tense shift corrected.

> In the morning, Beverly *takes* a subway uptown to work. Then she *goes* to her job on 58th Street. She *talks* with her boss for a few minutes. Then she *goes* to her own office. There, Beverly *plans* her day's work.

## ACTIVITY 14

### Correcting tense shifts

Correct the tense shifts by rewriting each sentence below. Make your tense corrections agree with the first verb in each sentence.

*Example:* When I looked in his direction, he looks the other way.

*When I looked in his direction, he looked the other way.*

1. She took a cab downtown and gets out at my apartment.

   _____

   _____

2. I told him that the store was closing, but he comes in anyway.

   _____

   _____

3. The teacher presented the basic format, and then she has the students fill in the details.

   _____

   _____

4. He gave an excellent performance as Othello; he really studies the part.

   _____

   _____

5. The director strolled onto the stage, gives us a few instructions, and then passed out the scripts.

   _____

   _____

Fill in the correct verb form in each of the sentences below.

1. **Past tense**   My Aunt Alice _____ the incident to me.
   relate

2. **Present tense**   Simon _____ blueberry yogurt.
   like

3. **Present tense**   Chester _____ us with his great jokes.
   amuse

4. **Past tense**   Sylvia _____ six people to the concert.
   take

5. **Past tense**   We _____ a blue shirt for Dad.
   choose

6. **Past tense**   Joe _____ with us to the zoo.
   go

7. **Present tense**   Mel _____ a disc jockey in Cleveland.
   be

8. **Past tense**   He _____ in Columbus last winter.
   be

9. **Present tense**   She _____ all her own clothes.
   sew

10. **Past tense**   She _____ four yards of green wool.
    buy

11. **Present tense**   I _____ bread every other Saturday.
    bake

12. **Present tense**   Do you _____ to see that movie?
    want

## Paragraphs

As you know, a sentence is the expression of a complete thought. Put simply, someone or something usually *does* something. An action occurs. An idea is expressed. Something is described. Page 316 show you some basic sentence patterns.

Sentences do not stand alone. Sentences must work together to create ideas. Paragraphs are a practical way of expressing these ideas in writing. Often your paragraphs will be developed into longer papers. Paragraphs are what hold a paper together, and topic sentences are one key to writing good paragraphs.

## Topic sentences

A topic sentence is the sentence that says what a paragraph is all about. A topic sentence can appear anywhere in a paragraph. Often it is in the first part of a paragraph. Look for the topic sentence in each of the following paragraphs.

1. Visitors to the Winterthur Museum near Wilmington, Delaware, are usually awed by the wealth of American decorative arts displayed there. The Museum has nearly 200 rooms. It contains over 70,000 objects dating from 1640 to 1840, including silver, glassware, paintings, furniture, and porcelain displayed in room settings.

2. We had a difficult time finding the old house we had driven so far to see. Although we took the correct exit off the main highway, it was getting dark, and we missed the sign that said Richmond Road. After driving for several miles, we turned around and finally found Richmond. However, we turned right instead of left and soon reached a dead end.

The first sentence in each of these paragraphs is the topic sentence. The topic sentence in the first paragraph tells that visitors are usually in awe of the great number of decorative art objects in the Winterthur Museum. The rest of the sentences help to explain why the visitors are awed.

The topic sentence in the second paragraph tells the reader that the paragraph will be about the difficult time the writer had in finding the old house.

A topic sentence can appear anywhere in a paragraph. Find the topic sentence in the paragraph below.

When we finally reached the old house, there were no lights anywhere. The headlights of our car illuminated the sagging front porch, and we could hear a loose shutter banging in the wind. In the sky, a full moon was obscured from time to time by racing clouds. The whole scene was like something out of a horror movie.

In this paragraph, the last sentence is the topic sentence. Even though the sentence summarizes the paragraph, it still tells what the paragraph is about.

A topic sentence is more effective when it gives your attitude toward a topic. Read the topic sentences below. They appear in pairs labeled A and B. Both sentences in a pair are on the same topic. Which topic sentence in each pair is more effective—A or B?

**A** I spent my summer vacation in West Virginia.

**B** My summer vacation was an unforgettable adventure spent in the hills of wild, wonderful West Virginia.

**A** My room is on the second floor of our house.

**B** My room is a tiny loft-like retreat on the second floor of our house.

**A** My family owns an old upright piano.

**B** My family's old upright piano is the center of life in my house.

In each case, Sentence B is more effective. You learn about the topic as well as the writer's attitude toward the topic. For example, in Sentence A of the first example you do not learn what a vacation in West Virginia might be like. You are not told anything about the writer's opinion. But in Sentence B you get the writer's impression of a West Virginia vacation.

TOPIC vacationing in West Virginia

WRITER'S IMPRESSION an unforgettable adventure

Now you can read for the details, the sentences that support the topic sentence. The topic sentence, *My summer vacation was an unforgettable adventure spent in the hills of wild, wonderful West Virginia,* helps the writer *limit* what he or she will write about. You know that within the hills of West Virginia the writer had an exciting summer. As the reader, you now expect to share in those adventures.

Below are examples of topics and topic sentences. Notice how the topic sentence both *limits* the topic and states the opinion of the writer.

| Topic | Topic Sentence |
| --- | --- |
| students in English 12 | Everyone in Mr. Hamilton's English 12 class is intelligent, eager to learn, and creative. |
| my friend's character | Yesterday I realized that sincerity and loyalty are a significant part of my best friend's character. |
| high school sports | Baseball and soccer are especially good sports for high school students. |

## ACTIVITY 15
### Analyzing topic sentences

Read the topic sentences below. First, find the topic. Then find the word or words that give the writer's opinion or attitude toward the topic.

*Example:* Mrs. Marlow has the respect and admiration of all the students at Carl Sandburg High School.

*Topic:* Mrs. Marlow

*Attitude:* respect and admiration

1. I will always regret the day I disobeyed my father. _____

2. My bedroom is the messiest room in our house. _____

3. Everyone attending last night's game was physically and emotionally exhausted. _____

4. Yesterday I discovered the value of real friendship. _____

## ACTIVITY 16
### Writing better topic sentences

The sentences below are topic sentences. Some of these sentences need to have their topics *limited*. Some sentences need to include the writer's attitude or opinion. Other sentences need details to make the topic clear. *Rewrite* each of these topic sentences. Improve the sentences as you rewrite them.

*Example:* I will never forget my summer vacation.

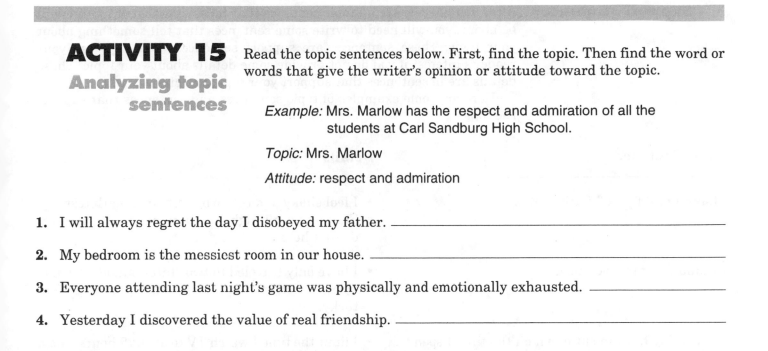
My summer vacation in Kentucky bluegrass country was the best vacation I ever had.

1. I will never forget what happened last night.

_____

2. I will write about my best friend.

_____

3. I visited my grandmother last winter.

_____

4. My parents often tell me about life in Puerto Rico.

_____

5. On the plane I noticed several people staring at me.

_____

**Support sentences**    After you have written a topic sentence that tells what the paragraph will be about, you will need to write some sentences that tell something about your topic. These sentences are support sentences. You will lose your reader's interest if you do not provide some details about your topic. These details are in sentences that support your topic sentence.

Here are some examples of topic sentences and sentences that support the topic.

| Topic Sentence | Details |
| --- | --- |
| I have a real fear of math exams. | • I feel shaky and cold when I take a math test.<br>• Staying up all night to study before a math test doesn't help. |
| I would like to travel more. | • I have only traveled to two states outside of Ohio.<br>• Once I visited relatives in Michigan and Kentucky. |
| I am trying hard to cut down on the time I spend watching television. | • I limit the time I watch TV to about 2 hours a day.<br>• I watch one program after school and two programs at night. |
| High schools spend too much money on sports while neglecting other areas. | • In many schools, funding for sports is nearly double the funding for other extracurricular activities.<br>• In our science classes, we are using ten-year-old textbooks. |

Notice how the next writer supports her topic sentence.

My life is a lot different this year than it was last year. Last year I lived in an apartment building in a large city. I took a city bus to school. There were 3000 students in my high school. This year, I'm living with my aunt and uncle on a farm. A yellow school bus picks me up every morning, and there are only about 500 students in the school.

The first sentence is the topic sentence. It tells the reader that the writer is going to compare this year with last year. The next five sentences support the topic.

**Sticking to the topic**    Support sentences should relate to the topic sentence. Sometimes writers add details that don't support the topic sentence. Below are three paragraphs. Each paragraph contains a sentence that does not support the topic. Draw a line through those sentences.

1. George Washington lived at Mount Vernon from 1754 until he died in 1799. Martha Washington died in 1802. He expanded the original 2,126 acres into 8,000 acres with five farms which were maintained chiefly by slave labor. (His will provided for the freeing of the slaves, however.) Originally, the main crop grown on the farms was tobacco, but because tobacco depleted the soil, he gradually planted wheat and other grains.

2. My cousin David's surprise birthday party on December 24 turned out to be a surprise for everyone. The party was scheduled to be held in our apartment. We live at 1253 Linden Street. By 6:30, when David had not arrived, we decided to have dinner without him and save the birthday cake for his arrival. Just as we were sitting down, we heard a knock on the door. When I opened the door, I saw someone dressed in a Santa Claus outfit carrying a bag of presents for everyone. Santa Claus turned out to be David.

3. Many people in history, some famous, some not so famous, have given their names to words common in our vocabulary today. The cardigan sweater was named for the 7th Earl of Cardigan. Cardigan sweaters are still worn today. The mackintosh, a waterproof raincoat, was named for its inventor Charles Macintosh, and the sandwich was named for the 4th Earl of Sandwich. The poinsettia was named for Joel Poinsett, once the American ambassador to Mexico, and the begonia for Michel Bégon, a French botanist. The unit of electrical power, called a watt, was named after James Watt, a Scottish inventor. The next time you check a thermometer, you might want to remember that the Fahrenheit and Celsius scales are named for Gabriel Fahrenheit, a German physicist, and Anders Celsius, a Swedish astronomer. These are just a few of the common words derived from proper names.

# ACTIVITY 17

## Writing support sentences

Write at least two *support sentences* for one of the topic sentences below.

**Topic Sentence**

**Support Sentences**

My vacation in Florida was a real disaster.

_____

_____

_____

_____

_____

Inflation hurts all Americans, regardless of age, race, or income.

_____

_____

_____

_____

_____

My birthday is an exciting day for me.

_____

_____

_____

_____

_____

# ACTIVITY 18

**Evaluating writing**

Read the following paragraph. Then answer the questions.

Sugar is bad for your health. When first eaten, it leaves you with a feeling of "quick energy." Very soon, however, the sugar level in your body goes down, leaving you feeling more tired than before. In addition, sugar is a leading cause of tooth decay, resulting in discomfort and expense for millions of people. Then, too, sugar is high in calories. When used in large amounts, it can lead to a weight problem. As you can see, too much sugar in your diet can affect your health.

1. What is the topic sentence in this paragraph? _____

_____

2. What is the topic of this paragraph? _____

_____

3. Does the writer stick to this topic? Explain. _____

_____

4. Are there at least three support sentences in this paragraph? _____

5. What words in the closing sentence go back to the topic and attitude expressed in the topic sentence?

_____

## Writing conclusions

A good paragraph needs a closing sentence. A closing sentence tells the reader that you have expressed your ideas. It is the logical last statement. It is your conclusion. The conclusion should maintain the tone you have set and the point you have made.

In a one-paragraph paper you may be able to close effectively with just one sentence. In a longer paper, you may need two or three sentences to bring your writing to a close. You may even need an entire paragraph for the conclusion.

Here are some ideas to keep in mind when you write a closing sentence.

1. Bring the topic sentence to the reader's mind again. However, you don't have to use the same words you used in the topic sentence.
2. Use transition words to help you conclude your thoughts: *consequently, therefore, then, in the same way.*
3. *Don't* contradict the point you have already made.
4. *Don't* start a new topic.
5. *Don't* apologize for what you didn't know or say.
6. *Don't* say that you are finished with statements like these:
   - And that's all I have to say on the subject.
   - And I hope you understand what I mean.
   - That's the end of my paragraph.
   - I hope you enjoyed this paper.
   - And so my closing sentence is . . . .
7. Be brief and clear.

## ACTIVITY 19
### Choosing a closing sentence

Below are three topic sentences. Opposite each sentence are three closing sentences. Which closing sentence fits the topic sentence best?

1. Mrs. Marlow has the respect and admiration of all the students at Carl Sandburg High School.

   a. Good teachers are hard to find.
   b. Mrs. Marlow has taught many students.
   c. Mrs. Marlow's hard work and fairness have earned the respect of all.

   Explain. _____

   _____

2. Our society must realize that drunk driving is a problem that must be solved.

   a. Drunk drivers are a menace to other people.
   b. As I have shown you in the above paragraph, this is a serious problem.
   c. Therefore, efforts to stop people from driving after drinking must be increased.

   Explain. _____

   _____

3. More students are dropping out of high school each year.

   a. However, many students are realizing the value of a high school diploma.
   b. Teachers should make school more enjoyable.
   c. Students must be forced to stay in high school until they graduate.

   Explain. _____

   _____

### Punctuation

Revising and editing your writing requires that you check over your punctuation and correct mistakes. This section contains some things to watch for.

**End marks for sentences**  A sentence must have a punctuation mark at the end. Most sentences end with a *period*. Questions should always end with a *question mark*. Use an *exclamation mark* after a sentence that shows strong feeling.

*Examples:*

Statement:  She went home.

Question:   Did she go home?

Exclamation:  Go home right now!

**Commas in sentences**

1. The two clauses of a compound sentence are separated by a comma. Remember that each clause in a compound sentence can stand alone and still make sense.

   *Examples:*

   She went home, and she carried all her books with her.

   John is a good student, and he is also a fine athlete.

2. In a complex sentence a comma separates clauses *when the dependent clause comes first*. Remember, a dependent clause cannot stand alone and still make sense:

   Because I feel tired, I'm going to lie down.

   When Tanya is ready, we'll go to a movie.

   If a dependent clause comes after the independent clause, you *do not* need a comma:

   I'm going to lie down because I'm tired.

   We'll go to a movie when Tanya is ready.

3. A compound-complex sentence should be punctuated as follows:

   Because I'm tired, I will lie down, but I won't fall asleep.

   - The first comma separates the independent and dependent clauses when the dependent clause comes first.

   - The second comma separates two independent clauses joined by *but*.

   She bought a book at the book store, and she bought some flowers while she was in the flower shop.

   - The comma separates two independent clauses joined by *and*.

   - No comma is necessary after the word *flowers* because the dependent clause comes at the end of the sentence.

**Other uses of commas**

1. Use commas to separate items in a series. Do not use a comma after the last item.

   *Examples*:

   Jim, David, Lisa, and Angela went to the movies.

   You should take books, paper, pencils, and an assignment notebook to every class.

2. Use a comma between the day of the week and the date. Use a comma between the date and the year.

   *Examples*:

   Pearl Harbor was attacked on Sunday, December 7, 1941.

   I was born on June 9, 1975.

3. Use a comma after introductory words like *well, yes,* and *no.*

   *Examples*:

   No, I don't want to go to the game.

   Well, you really tried hard on the test.

4. Use a comma around words that interrupt a sentence.

   *Examples*:

   The story, however, is true.

   Their trip, consequently, had to be delayed.

---

## ACTIVITY 20

### Using end marks and commas

Rewrite the following sentences. Use end marks and commas correctly in each sentence.

1. Jane please come home with us

   _____

2. Do you like playing soccer

   _____

3. Watch out

   _____

4. I bought hamburgers potato chips and soft drinks

   _____

**5.** Joe likes football but he dislikes baseball

_____

**6.** Although sports programs for girls are new in some schools the teams have done well

_____

**7.** Because it was raining the game was canceled

_____

**8.** No I don't like jogging

_____

**9.** Tina likes her new job but the hours are too long

_____

**10.** "M*A*S*H" was on TV for eleven years and the reruns will be on for a few more years

_____

## Capitalization

Using capital letters correctly is important in your writing. Here are the basic rules for capital letters.

**1.** Use a capital letter to begin each sentence.

_Examples:_
Here are your shoes.
Today is my birthday.

**2.** Always capitalize the pronoun "I."

_Examples:_
Dad and I like to take long walks.
He and I went to a movie.

**3.** Use capitals for the names of specific persons, places, or things.

_Examples:_

| | |
|---|---|
| New York City | Nichols Middle School |
| Chevrolet | France |
| Jon Walters | Civic Center |
| Kansas | Michigan Avenue |

4. Capitalize the first and last words and all important words in titles.

*Examples:*

| | |
|---|---|
| Book | *The Outsiders* |
| Magazine | *Road and Track* |
| Record Album | *Concert in Central Park* |
| Song | "Take the A Train" |
| Movie | *Fantasia* |
| TV Show | "Jeopardy" |

5. Capitalize the names of religions, nationalities, and races.

*Examples:*

They belong to the Protestant, Catholic, or Jewish faiths.

Last night we had Mexican food.

Who are the real Native Americans?

6. Capitalize the name of a family relationship when it is used with a person's name. Do not capitalize the name of a family relationship when it is not used with a person's name.

*Examples:*

I want you to meet my Aunt Bessie.

My aunt is coming next week.

7. Capitalize the names of companies and organizations.

*Examples:*

Woolworth's

American Legion

Parkside Chess Club

# ACTIVITY 21
## Using capital letters

Copy each of the following sentences. Put capital letters where they belong.

1. I really enjoyed the book, *all creatures great and small.*

_____

2. my aunt ruth took me to a french restaurant with my cousins.

_____

3. Is austin a large city?

_____

**4.** I always enjoy our family picnic at greenland national park.

_____

**5.** Alex has a job at bob's big burger on elm street.

_____

**Spelling** When you speak, no one knows if you are saying "it's" or "its" for _it is_. But "it's" and "its" have two different meanings. If you write the wrong word, the reader may get confused or think you are not very smart. The words listed here are words people misspell or misuse the most often. These words either sound alike or have almost the same spelling. Study these words and their meanings. Then complete Activity 22.

> **accept**   to take something that is offered
>    I accept your gift.
>
> **except**   not including, leaving out
>    Everyone was invited except me.
>
> **already**   by that time, previously
>    We had already seen the show.
>
> **all ready**   everyone ready, all prepared
>    When you are all ready, we will go.
>
> **altogether**   completely, entirely
>    You are altogether correct.
>
> **all together**   everyone together in the same place
>    We were all together for the celebration.
>
> **alright**   a wrong spelling of _all right_
>
> **all right**   correct form
>    Is going to a movie all right with you?
>
> **capital**   a chief city; money; an upper-case letter
>    Washington, D.C., is the capital of the United States.
>    Put your capital in the bank.
>    Use a capital letter.
>
> **capitol**   a building where a law-making body meets
>    We visited the Capitol in Washington, D.C.
>
> **council**   a group that makes decisions
>    She is a member of the city council.
>
> **counsel**   advise, to give advice
>    I need someone to counsel me.
>
> **desert**   dry land; to leave or abandon
>    He rode across the desert.
>    Do not desert me.
>
> **dessert**   final course of a meal
>    I enjoyed the fancy dessert.

**its**  possessive
The cat licked its paws.

**it's**  contraction of *it is*
It's very cold today.

**lead**  to go in front (present tense)
You should lead us.

**led**  to go in front (past tense)
He led the parade.

**lead**  a heavy metal
The box is made of lead.

**loose**  free, not tight
The belt feels loose.

**lose**  to misplace
Did you lose your keys?

**peace**  absence of war
We all want world peace.

**piece**  part of something
I'd like a piece of cake.

**passed**  to go by
I passed Joe's house.

**past**  time gone by
I like to think about past vacations.

**principal**  head of a school; most important
She is our principal.
The principal reason for mistakes is carelessness.

**principle**  rule, belief
The principle of solar energy is clear.

**stationary**  standing in one position
The train is stationary.

**stationery**  writing paper
Buy some stationery at the store.

**there**  in that place
Put the book over there.

**their**  belonging to them
It is their car.

**they're**  contraction of *they are*
They're ready to leave.

**to**  preposition
Give the books to me.

**too**  also
You may go, too.

**two**  number
He has two brothers.

**who's** contraction of *who is* or *who has*
Who's your friend? Who's lost a dollar?

**whose** possessive
Whose jacket is this?

**your** possessive
Is that your coat?

**you're** contraction of *you are*
You're very busy today.

## ACTIVITY 22    Select the right word for each sentence.

### Selecting the right word

1. My friend was able to _____ me.
(council/counsel)

2. The _____ of our school is also an experienced teacher.
(principal/principle)

3. We had chocolate cake for _____ .
(desert/dessert)

4. I am so glad I _____ the exam.
(past/passed)

5. I hope I don't _____ my gloves.
(lose/loose)

6. We took the books _____ the library.
(to/too)

7. _____ got the money?
(Who's/Whose)

8. The evening star is almost _____ .
(stationery/stationary)

9. The business failed because there was not enough _____ .
(capital/capitol)

10. _____ certain to rain the day of the school parade.
(Its/It's)

**11.** I hope he will _____ your first offer.

(except/accept)

**12.** I am not _____ pleased with Paul's behavior.

(altogether/all together)

**13.** I hope it is _____ for me to be here.

(alright/all right)

**14.** _____ always on time for work.

(Their/They're)

**15.** Please put the box over _____ .

(their/there)

**16.** Please pass me a _____ of pie.

(peace/piece)

**17.** He _____ the marching band.

(lead/led)

**18.** I have _____ seen that movie.

(all ready/already)

**19.** I hope you can learn to drive _____ .

(too/to)

**20.** Please let me know if _____ not going.

(your/you're)

## Everyday writing

In addition to the writing you do in class, you may want or need to do other types of everyday writing. You may write an editorial for the school paper, a letter to a newspaper or magazine, the minutes of a meeting, a memo, or instructions for someone. All of these types of writing require correct sentences, clear paragraphs, and proper capitalization and punctuation.

Some types of everyday writing do not require paragraphs with topic sentences. Instructions, some memos, or the minutes of a meeting may not need topic sentences in paragraphs. Newspaper editorials and letters to magazines or newspapers may require that paragraphs have topic sentences, however.

## Letters to the editor

In Chapter 6 you learned the correct format for letter writing. When writing a letter to a newspaper or magazine, it is important to follow this format. Some newspapers and magazines provide the form of address on the letters page for those who wish to write. Below is a sample letter to a newspaper. Does it have a topic sentence?

```
                                    4165 W. Vista
                                    Anytown, Arkansas 71800
                                    September 5, 19—

Editor
Morningside News
1149 N. Delaware St.
Morningside, Arkansas 71900

Dear Editor:

    I wish to applaud the efforts of the
city Streets and Sanitation Department for
its excellent and timely work at cleaning
the streets after the Labor Day Parade. In
approximately two hours after the end of the
parade, the streets were totally free of
paper and other debris. As a taxpayer, I feel
that in this instance my dollars were well
spent.

                        Sincerely yours,

                        John Stoner

                        John Stoner
```

Notice that the letter writer comes right to the point. He tells why he is writing in his topic sentence. His second sentence supports his reason for writing by telling what he saw. His concluding sentence sums up his feelings.

Here is a letter to the editor of a school newspaper. In this letter, the writer mentions a problem and makes a specific proposal. (The street address is not included because the letter writer dropped the letter in a box outside the newspaper office.)

129 E. Hubbard
Anyplace, Alabama 35000
October 4, 19—

Editor
Fair Ridge Observer

Dear Editor:

The appearance of the school grounds around Fair Ridge School is an indication that students do not care about their surroundings. Last week, a maintenance team of three people collected four large plastic bags of trash. Most of the trash consisted of soft-drink cans. In addition, the maintenance crew found styrofoam cups, plastic pens, three soggy paperbacks, a half-eaten sandwich, and a pair of socks! Since Fair Ridge students have mistaken the school grounds for the city dump, I suggest that we have a student clean-up day once a month. Maybe if students had to clean up their own trash, they wouldn't litter!

Sincerely yours,

Wanda Davis

Wanda Davis

# ACTIVITY 23

## Writing a letter to the editor

On a separate sheet of paper, write a letter to your school newspaper on one of the following topics, or on a topic of your own choosing. Make your letter brief. Include a topic sentence. Remember to back up your opinion with facts if possible. Finish your letter by suggesting some course of action.

noise in the school cafeteria

computers in the classroom

school dress code

school uniforms

## Instructions

There may be times when you will have to write instructions. You may have to leave instructions for someone at home, or you may have to tell someone how to do something or what to do on the job. Even though you may give instructions orally, it is always a good idea to have them written down. Then someone can refer to your instructions if you are not present. Instructions may need an introductory sentence instead of a topic sentence.

Below are two sets of instructions. The first set is written by a manager to her secretary. The second set is written by a manager to his new employee. Study the two sets of instructions to see which one seems clearer to you.

---

A. Alice,

Please see that the following things are completed before you leave. Call Max about the missing chairs (I forgot to tell you that there are six missing from the con. rm.) Make a res. for me on a flight to Springfield. I'll need a room too. Thanks. (Before you do any of this, call Acme copier!)

Mary

---

B. Jerry,

Please do the following things before you leave this evening. 1. Fill the salt and pepper shakers. 2. Empty the trash bins. 3. Mop the floor. 4. Lock the Erie Street door. If you have any questions, you may call me at home at 555-6830. Thanks for your help.

Ben

---

Which set of instructions is more likely to be followed without a mistake? What questions would you have if you received the first set of instructions? What questions would you have if you received the second set of instructions?

## ACTIVITY 24
### Writing instructions

On the lines below, write a set of instructions for one of the following people or group of people.

- a babysitter who is to arrive at 5 p.m. to stay with your two children, ages 2 and 5

- a newly hired dental receptionist who works in your office from 8 to 4

- a newly hired school bus driver in a rural area who must arrive at school by 8 a.m. and 3 p.m.

- a new school-crossing guard who works mornings and afternoons

- new members of a cheerleading squad

- new manager of a football or basketball team of which you are coach

_____

_____

_____

_____

_____

_____

_____

_____

_____

_____

_____

_____

_____

_____

_____

**Memos**  Memos are used mainly to communicate information within a company or an organization. Memos may be written to one person or to five hundred people. They may be one paragraph or several pages. They are usually written on paper provided by the company or organization. Below is an example of a memo written to announce a meeting.

---

HILLTOP NURSERY

DATE:  7/19/1994
TO:  All employees
FROM:  Jason Williamson
SUBJECT:  Meeting

There will be a short meeting in my office Wednesday at 8:30 a.m. to discuss repairs to the greenhouse damaged in last night's storm.

---

Notice that the memo writer gives day, time, and place of the meeting and tells what the meeting will be about. Some memo writers are not so brief. They may use unnecessary sentences or phrases that waste paper and the reader's time. They may leave out important information. In the memo below, the sentences or phrases with a line drawn through them should be omitted.

---

ACE MANUFACTURING, INC.

DATE:  November 13, 19—
TO:  All employees
FROM:  Jack Kempel, President
SUBJECT:  Parking

~~It has come to my attention that~~ people are parking in spaces reserved for staff officers. ~~Owing to this state of affairs,~~ beginning today, a large sticker will be placed across the windshield of all offenders' cars ~~in an effort to prevent this from happening again. In the event that this is not sufficient,~~ offenders who persist in parking in reserved places will have their cars towed to the back of Lot C.

---

## ACTIVITY 25

### Editing a memo

Draw a line through the words or phrases that could be omitted from the memo below.

BRADLEY OFFICE SUPPLY, INC.

DATE:   December 4, 19—
TO:   All employees
FROM:   S. Lewis, VP, Building and Grounds
SUBJECT:   Security

For security reasons and to prevent unauthorized people from entering and leaving the building, the Adams and Franklin doors will be locked at 5 p.m. in the evening every day, seven days a week. Employees and vendors may enter and exit only at the Maple Street entrance after 5 p.m. Before 5 p.m., any entrance may be used. We are sorry for any inconvenience this may cause, but we are doing it for security reasons.

## ACTIVITY 26

### Rewriting a memo

The following memo omits some important information. Read the memo and see if you can answer the questions.

WEST SIDE COMMUNITY ORGANIZATION

DATE:   October 2, 19—
TO:   Members, WSCO
FROM:   Manual Estevez
SUBJECT:   Annual fish fry

Plans for the WSCO annual fish fry are almost complete, thanks to the work of many volunteers. If you would like to help set up tables and chairs, cook, or serve on the day of the big event, please call. Volunteers should be at Mason Park by 3 p.m. Remember, we need your help!

1. What phone number is a volunteer supposed to call?

2. Where is Mason Park?

3. On what day is the fish fry?

On the following lines, rewrite the memo, adding the missing information.

_____

_____

_____

_____

_____

_____

_____

_____

_____

When writing a memo, 1. decide on the purpose(s) of the memo and stick to the point. 2. Omit unnecessary words or phrases. 3. Be sure to include all necessary information.

## ACTIVITY 27
### Writing a memo

Assume that you are the coach for an athletic team. Write a memo to the team for posting on a bulletin board in the athletic department. The memo may be about practice, tryouts, uniforms, or any other information you might want to communicate.

_____

_____

_____

_____

_____

_____

_____

_____

Correct the errors in the memo below. Look for fragments, run-ons, faulty subject-verb agreement, and tense shifts. Draw a line through any unnecessary words or phrases. Correct all errors in punctuation, capitalization, and spelling. You should be able to make 15 corrections.

---

Mill Street Art Fair

DATE:   May 2,  19—
TO:   Mill Street Art Fair Committees
FROM:   Julie Sanderson, chairperson
SUBJECT:   Complaints

   Your chairperson met with members of the Mill Street Community Organization last week to discuss complaints about the Mill Street Art Fair in prevous years. Most of the complaints were about excessive noise, illegal parking, and inadequate clean-up at the end of the weekend on Sunday night. I feel that most complaints was justified. And that we have to be better mill Street nieghbors.

   I beleive that we can solve the noise and clean-up problems, but I'm not certain how to deal with illegal parking. By closing the fair at 6 p.m. in the evening and asking for more volunteers to help clean up. We might also ban street musicions entirely, preventing illegal parking may require more creative solutions.

   Please plan to meet at my home, 22 E. Mill Street, on May 9 at 7 to discuss these complaints.

---

### Organization

- Does your paragraph have a topic sentence?

- Did you write support sentences to make your paragraph complete?

- Do you have a closing sentence?

- Are your sentences arranged in a logical order?

### Sense

- Have you used correct sentence patterns?

- Do any of your sentences sound awkward? Do they need to be rewritten?

- Did you make the correct word choices? Check your dictionary if you are not certain of the word you should use.

- Have you checked for fragments and run-ons?

- Have you checked spelling?

- Have you accidentally left out a necessary word? You can use a caret (∧) to insert a missing word.

- Did you avoid any shifting of tenses?

### Grammar, Usage, & Punctuation

- Did you use the correct part of speech?

- Do all subjects and verbs agree in number? In the present tense, plural subjects take plural verbs. But watch for the third person singular. Third person singular subjects need -s added to the verb.

- Do you have all the necessary punctuation marks?

- Do all sentences begin with a capital letter?

- Do all sentences have an end punctuation mark?

- Have you shown all -d and -ed endings on past tense verbs?

- Have you used all *irregular* verbs correctly?

# NTC LANGUAGE ARTS BOOKS

**Business Communication**
Handbook for Business Writing, *Baugh, Fryar, & Thomas*
Meetings: Rules & Procedures, *Pohl*

**Dictionaries**
British/American Language Dictionary, *Moss*
NTC's Classical Dictionary, *Room*
NTC's Dictionary of Changes in Meaning, *Room*
NTC's Dictionary of Debate, *Hanson*
NTC's Dictionary of Literary Terms, *Morner & Rausch*
NTC's Dictionary of Shakespeare, *Clark*
NTC's Dictionary of Theatre and Drama Terms, *Mobley*
NTC's Dictionary of Word Origins, *Room*
NTC's Spell It Right Dictionary, *Downing*
Robin Hyman's Dictionary of Quotations

**Essential Skills**
Building Real Life English Skills, *Starkey & Penn*
Developing Creative & Critical Thinking, *Boostrom*
English Survival Series, *Maggs*
Essential Life Skills, *Starkey & Penn*
Essentials of English Grammar, *Baugh*
Essentials of Reading and Writing English Series
Grammar for Use, *Hall*
Grammar Step-by-Step, *Pratt*
Guide to Better English Spelling, *Furness*
How to Be a Rapid Reader, *Redway*
How to Improve Your Study Skills, *Coman & Heavers*
How to Improve Your Test-Taking Skills, *Boone*
How to Write Term Papers and Reports, *Baugh*
NTC Skill Builders
NTC Vocabulary Builders
Reading by Doing, *Simmons & Palmer*
303 Dumb Spelling Mistakes, *Downing*
TIME: We the People, *ed. Schinke-Llano*
Vocabulary by Doing, *Beckert*

**Genre Literature**
Coming of Age, *Emra*
The Detective Story, *Schwartz*
The Short Story & You, *Simmons & Stern*
Sports in Literature, *Emra*
You and Science Fiction, *Hollister*

**Journalism**
Getting Started in Journalism, *Harkrider*
Journalism Today, *Ferguson & Patten*
Publishing the Literary Magazine, *Klaiman*
UPI Stylebook, *United Press International*

**Language, Literature, and Composition**
African American Literature, *Worley & Perry*
An Anthology for Young Writers, *Meredith*
The Art of Composition, *Meredith*
Of Bunsen Burners, Bones, and Belles Lettres: Classic Essays
    Accross The Curriculum, *Lester*
Creative Writing, *Mueller & Reynolds*
Creative Writing Portfolio, *Purves, et al.*
Daughters of The Revolution: Classic Essays by Women, *Lester*
Diverse Identities: Classic Multicultural Essays, *Lester*
Everyday Creative Writing, *Smith & Greenberg*

Handbook for Practical Letter Writing, *Baugh*
How to Write Term Papers and Reports, *Baugh*
In a New Land, *Grossman & Schur*
Literature by Doing, *Tchudi & Yesner*
Lively Writing, *Schrank*
Look, Think & Write, *Leavitt & Sohn*
NTC Shakespeare Series
NTC's Anthology of Nonfiction, *Gordon & Kuehner*
Plato's Heir: Classic Essays, *Lester*
Poetry by Doing, *Osborn*
West African Folktales, *Gale*
World Literature, *Rosenberg*
Write to the Point! *Morgan*
The Writer's Handbook, *Karls & Szymanski*
Writer's Mind: Crafting Fiction, *Cohen*
Writing by Doing, *Sohn & Enger*
Writing in Action, *Meredith*

**Media Communication**
Getting Started in Mass Media, *Beckert*
Photography in Focus, *Jacobs & Kokrda*
Television Production Today, *Bielak*
Understanding Mass Media, *Jawitz*
Understanding the Film, *Bone & Johnson*

**Mythology**
The Ancient World, *Sawyer & Townsend*
Mythology and You, *Rosenberg & Baker*
Welcome to Ancient Greece, *Millard*
Welcome to Ancient Rome, *Millard*
World Mythology, *Rosenberg*

**Speech**
Activities for Effective Communication, *LiSacchi*
The Basics of Speech, *Galvin, Cooper, & Gordon*
Contemporary Speech, *HopKins & Whitaker*
Creative Speaking, *Frank*
Dynamics of Speech, *Myers & Herndon*
Getting Started in Oral Interpretation, *Naegelin & Krikac*
Getting Started in Public Speaking, *Carlin & Payne*
Getting Started in Speech Communication, *Lenning*
Listening by Doing, *Galvin*
Literature Alive, *Gamble & Gamble*
Person to Person, *Galvin & Book*
Public Speaking Today, *Carlin & Payne*
Speaking by Doing, *Quattrini*
Speech: Exploring Communication, *O'Connor*

**Theatre**
Acting & Directing, *Grandstaff*
The Book of Cuttings for Acting & Directing, *Cassady*
The Book of Monologues for Aspiring Actors, *Cassady*
The Book of Scenes for Acting Practice, *Cassady*
The Book of Scenes for Aspiring Actors, *Cassady*
Directing For The Stage, *Frerer*
The Dynamics of Acting, *Snyder & Drumsta*
Getting Started in Theatre, *Pinnell*
An Introduction to Modern One-Act Plays, *Cassady*
An Introduction to Theatre and Drama, *Cassady & Cassady*
Play Production Today, *Mobley*
Stagecraft, *Beck*

For a current catalog and information about our complete line of
language arts books, write:
National Textbook Company
a division of *NTC Publishing Group*
4255 West Touhy Avenue
Lincolnwood (Chicago), Illinois 60646–1975 U.S.A.